SAUDI ARABIA IN TR ...ION

Insights on Social, Political, Economic and Religious Change

Making sense of Saudi Arabia is today crucially important. The kingdom's western provinces contain the heart of Islam, its two holiest mosques in Mecca and Medina, and it is the United States' closest Arab ally and the largest producer of oil in the world. However, the country is undergoing rapid change: its aged leadership is ceding power to a new generation, and its society, which is dominated by young people, is restive. Saudi Arabia has long remained closed to foreign scholars, with a select few academics allowed into the kingdom over the past decade. This book presents the fruits of their research as well as those of the most prominent Saudi academics in the field.

The fifteen chapters in this volume focus on different sectors of Saudi society and examine how the changes of the last few decades have affected each. Many of the authors have conducted archival and fieldwork research in Saudi Arabia, benefiting from the recent opening of the country to foreign researchers. As such, the chapters reflect new insights from the field and provide the most up-to-date research on the country's social, cultural, economic and political dynamics.

Bernard Haykel is a professor of Near Eastern Studies at Princeton University where he teaches and researches the history and politics of Islam and the Arabian Peninsula. He has published *Revival and Reform in Islam* (Cambridge, 2003) and various articles on Islamic law, Salafism and al-Qaeda, among other subjects.

Thomas Hegghammer is senior research Fellow at the Norwegian Defence Research Establishment in Oslo. His book *Jihad in Saudi Arabia* (Cambridge, 2010) won the silver medal of the Arthur Ross Book Award from the Council of Foreign Relations. He also co-authored *Al-Qaida in Its Own Words* (2008) and *The Meccan Rebellion* (2011).

Stéphane Lacroix is associate professor of political science at Sciences Po, Paris, and research Fellow at the Centre d'Etudes et de Recherches Internationales. He is the author of *Awakening Islam: The Politics of Religious Dissent in Contemporary Saudi Arabia* (2011) named "Book of the Year 2011" on Foreign Policy's Middle East Channel. He also co-authored *Al-Qaida in Its Own Words* (2008) and *The Meccan Rebellion* (2011).

Saudi Arabia in Transition

INSIGHTS ON SOCIAL, POLITICAL, ECONOMIC AND RELIGIOUS CHANGE

Edited by
BERNARD HAYKEL
Near Eastern Studies, Princeton University

THOMAS HEGGHAMMER
Norwegian Defence Research Establishment

STÉPHANE LACROIX
Sciences Po, Paris

CAMBRIDGE
UNIVERSITY PRESS

CAMBRIDGE
UNIVERSITY PRESS

University Printing House, Cambridge CB2 8BS, United Kingdom

One Liberty Plaza, 20th Floor, New York, NY 10006, USA

477 Williamstown Road, Port Melbourne, VIC 3207, Australia

314-321, 3rd Floor, Plot 3, Splendor Forum, Jasola District Centre, New Delhi - 110025, India

79 Anson Road, #06-04/06, Singapore 079906

Cambridge University Press is part of the University of Cambridge.

It furthers the University's mission by disseminating knowledge in the pursuit of
education, learning and research at the highest international levels of excellence.

www.cambridge.org
Information on this title: www.cambridge.org/9780521185097

© Cambridge University Press 2015

First published 2015

A catalogue record for this publication is available from the British Library

Library of Congress Cataloging in Publication data
Saudi Arabia in transition : insights on social, political, economic and religious change /
[edited by] Bernard Haykel (Near Eastern Studies, Princeton University), Thomas
Hegghammer (Norwegian Defence Research Establishment), Stéphane Lacroix (Sciences Po,
Paris, France).
    pages cm
Includes bibliographical references and index.
ISBN 978-1-107-00629-4 (hardback) – ISBN 978-0-521-18509-7 (paperback)
1. Saudi Arabia – Social conditions.   2. Social change – Saudi Arabia.   3. Saudi Arabia –
Politics and government – 1982–   4. Saudi Arabia – Economic conditions.   5. Saudi Arabia –
Religion.   6. Islam – Social aspects – Saudi Arabia.   I. Haykel, Bernard, 1968–
II. Hegghammer, Thomas.   III. Lacroix, Stéphane, 1978–
HN663.A8S28   2014
306.09538–dc23   2014020955

ISBN 978-1-107-00629-4 Hardback
ISBN 978-0-521-18509-7 Paperback

Contents

Acknowledgments

This volume is the result of two successive conferences held in Menton, France, and in Princeton, New Jersey, on the history and politics of Saudi Arabia. The editors would like to thank the Institute for the Transregional Study of the Contemporary Middle East, North Africa, and Central Asia at Princeton University as well as the Kuwait Program at Sciences-Po in Paris for jointly funding these conferences. The Kuwait Program at Sciences-Po is a partnership between the Kuwait Foundation for the Advancement of Sciences and Sciences-Po. Professor Gilles Kepel of Sciences-Po was particularly instrumental in providing support and guidance for this project, and we would like to extend a special thanks to him. We would also like to express our gratitude to the Department of Near Eastern Studies at Princeton University for providing funding to cover the cost of the index.

Introduction

Bernard Haykel, Thomas Hegghammer, and Stéphane Lacroix

March 11, 2011, was declared on Facebook a "Day of Rage" in Saudi Arabia, in imitation of the various popular uprisings that were taking place throughout the Arab world in the spring of that year. By this time two Arab dictators had fallen in Tunisia and Egypt and unrest was spreading to Bahrain, Libya, and Yemen. Several online petitions also were urging political reform, and some Shiite demonstrations were taking place in the Eastern Province. Many predicted that Saudi Arabia was not immune to revolution and that the regime would succumb to the same forces that had effected change elsewhere. However, no mass protests or mobilizations occurred, and over the following months the Saudi government was able to contain and ward off any significant opposition.

This is not the first time that observers had wrongly predicted the demise of the Al Saud, the royal family that has ruled all or parts of the country since the eighteenth century. In the 1960s, Arab nationalism under the leadership of President Nasser of Egypt was expected to sweep the royals away. Later in 1979, with the Iranian revolution and the uprisings in Mecca and those of the Shiites in the Eastern Province, the Saudis were again given a short lease on life. In the early 1990s, an indigenous Islamist movement called the Sahwa was again challenging the regime. And in the early 2000s al-Qaeda in the Arabian Peninsula stoked fears of instability through a series of violent attacks and muscular propaganda. In each of these cases, the Saudi regime weathered the storm through a complex set of policies and tactics that today are being deployed again.

Why have so many observers been wrong in their assessment of the politics of Saudi Arabia? One reason is that Saudi Arabia is a particularly opaque society because its politics are not institutionalized but highly personal in nature. Another is the set of stereotypes that has impeded nuanced analysis, for example, that the kingdom is constituted of a combustible mixture of religious zealots, rebellious Bedouins, and rich oil sheikhs. In one common portrait,

Saudi Arabia is the West's petrol station while also being a factory of "Wahhabi terrorists."[1] But the main reason is that Saudi Arabia has been understudied and, until relatively recently, was not open for fieldwork to outside scholars.

This book offers a number of studies by scholars who have an intimate understanding of Saudi Arabia, many of whom have conducted extensive fieldwork on the ground. Their chapters look carefully at key constituent elements of Saudi society: women, Islamic scholars and activists, economic actors, tribes, royals, and technocrats among others. They provide a nuanced reading of the grammar of Saudi political and social life, allowing also for a better understanding of the country's present situation and future prospects.

Making sense of Saudi Arabia is today crucially important. The kingdom's western provinces contain the heart of Islam, its two holiest mosques in Mecca and Medina. Saudi Arabia has 25 percent of the world's proven oil reserves and is the unquestioned leader of OPEC. It is also one of the dominant countries in the Arab world and the self-declared leader of Sunni Islam. In addition, Saud Arabia has been an important site for Islamist ideology and activism, both locally and internationally. Last but not least, Saudi Arabia is arguably the United States' closest Arab ally and a pillar in the American security architecture of the region.

Saudi Arabia faces several major challenges in the near future. First, a series of successions in rule is going to take place very soon because the king and his designated successor are in their eighties and therefore quite literally octogenarians. Second, a major youth bulge in the population is about to enter the labor market, and the country must produce several million new jobs in the coming decade if social tensions are not to explode into the open. Third is managing the new expectations for popular participation, transparency, and accountability in governance that have been raised by the recent uprisings in the Arab world. Fourth, Saudi Arabia faces external challenges in the form of a nuclear Iran, a turbulent Bahrain, a potentially failed state in Yemen, the festering Israeli-Palestinian conflict, and uncertainty in both Iraq and Egypt.

As the chapters of this book will show, Saudi Arabia has significant resources, both material and symbolic, to confront these challenges. A beneficiary of massive oil revenues, the kingdom has in the last decade amassed over half a trillion U.S. dollars in cash assets. It produces on average around 10 million barrels of oil per day and is expected to do so for many years to come. This wealth has long allowed the state to dominate the economy and to create public sector jobs so that a majority of Saudis work for the government. It has

---

[1] Cf. Dore Gold, *Hatred's Kingdom: How Saudi Arabia Supports the New Global Terrorism* (Washington, DC: Regnery Publishing, 2003).

also permitted Saudi Arabia to make enormous investments in infrastructure development and education, changing both the physical and social landscape of the country. Most recently, during the "Arab Spring" of 2011, oil wealth allowed the government to allocate $130 billion in domestic subsidies (salary increases, housing, and other benefits) to stem the unrest of the kind that swept Ben Ali and Mubarak out of power. The financial resources at the state's disposal also enable it to co-opt dissenters and neutralize potential opposition forces.

Another key material resource is the country's coercive apparatus. There are multiple military and security services, including the regular armed forces, the National Guard, the police, and the notorious *mabahith* (domestic intelligence). These have been used to control and contain opposition elements and were effective in repelling al-Qaeda in the Arabian Peninsula's armed threat in the early and mid-2000s. Moreover, the fight against al-Qaeda made Saudi security services even more powerful, because they benefited from Western intelligence expertise and massive hardware investments. Most recently, the security services have been out in force to quell Shiite protests in the east and to prevent popular demonstrations elsewhere, notably on the so-called Day of Rage on March 11.

A third material resource is the media and the communications infrastructure. Members of the royal family control two of the three international pan-Arab daily newspapers: *al-Sharq al-awsat* and *al-Hayat*. They also have significant influence over online sites such as Elaph.com as well as the Al-Arabiyya satellite television network. In addition, some of the most watched religious television channels are sponsored by the kingdom, such as Iqra' and al-Majd. Domestically, the government has effective editorial control over all print and television news media. Equally important is the government's ownership of the physical telecommunications infrastructure, such as the centralized internet node, known as the King Abdulaziz City for Science and Technology. The government's control of the telecommunications infrastructure proved to be a vital asset in its fight against al-Qaeda in 2003–4. In the days before March 11, 2011, the Saudi media outlets inundated the public with articles and editorials discrediting the call for revolt and emphasizing the need for loyalty. And when no uprising took place on that day, the media celebrated this as a victory for Saudi Arabia and a defeat for the kingdom's enemies. Finally, even when the government or the royal family are not owners of the media asset, they still might enjoy a degree of influence as appeared to have been the case in Al-Jazeera's timid coverage of the unrest in Bahrain and the Eastern Province.

At least as important as the material resources of the Saudi state are the symbolic ones. The most obvious is religion. Saudi Arabia unabashedly bases its legitimacy on Islamic norms. Despite having a basic law, it claims that the Qur'an is its constitution. Since the mid-twentieth century the government developed a vast institutionalized religious sector, which includes missionary, educational, and legal activities. The state employs a large religious bureaucracy, which spans a range of functions from the great mufti and eminent jurists down to the local religious enforcers (*mutawwi'a*) and school teachers. This religious sector is headed by the Committee of Senior Scholars, one of whose functions is to issue fatwas, including those that support the government and its policies. For example, prior to the so-called Day of Rage on March 11, this council issued an edict that declared street demonstrations to be un-Islamic and therefore forbidden in the kingdom.

The state has also grounded its legitimacy on more secular bases, namely, that it is the purveyor of the country's modernization and development. Its infrastructural and industrialization projects are branded as milestones on the path to inexorable progress. More recently, King Abdallah has advanced the idea that for Saudi Arabia to thrive it must develop the human capital of its citizens. Following up on this he has founded a new university, the King Abdallah University of Science and Technology (KAUST), which is held up as a flagship of technological and social advancement. King Abdallah's commitment to this vision was such that he dismissed a senior religious scholar who had objected to its coeducational curriculum.

A third symbolic resource is the myth of the Saudi nation. Here the state promotes a discourse of exceptionalism in which Saudi Arabia is a blessed land, an island of stability and a harmonious family. In this paternalistic myth, the king is cast as the father of the nation and the royal family is the custodian of its well-being. In return the citizenry owe them obedience and gratitude. More recently the Saudi government has also promoted a distinctive Saudi nationalism through the media as well as educational and cultural institutions and practices. In the late 1990s it founded a national museum in Riyadh and introduced the subject of "national education" (*al-tarbiya al-wataniyya*) into the school curriculum. It also encouraged all media outlets to use nationalist language, especially during the campaign against al-Qaeda from 2003 onwards. This increased emphasis on indigenous culture may have played a role in the recent upsurge of interest in tribal culture and identity.

Although these resources are significant they also have important limitations. Oil prices, for example, fluctuate, and a sustained low price might constrain the government's ability to satisfy the country's fiscal needs and to co-opt forces of opposition. And even with relatively high prices, the uneven allocation of resources is a potential source of political tension. As for the coercive apparatus of the state, the use of excessive force always carries the risk of backfiring. Moreover, the Arab Spring appears to have introduced new norms of state conduct toward its citizens, somewhat constraining the coercive options available to the government. A related development is the increased transparency resulting from the rise of new media and communication technologies such as Facebook, Twitter, and smartphone cameras. The government's media control has been eroding slowly since the late 1990s, first with the arrival of Al-Jazeera and the Internet, and more recently with the emergence of online citizen journalism (blogs, Facebook pages, YouTube videos).

Symbolic resources also have limitations. The state's monopoly on Islam is contested by a plethora of actors, including the Islamists of the Sahwa movement and the jihadis. In this contest, the state's position has been vitiated by the death, around the turn of the millennium, of the most charismatic figures of the official religious establishment (e.g., Shaykhs ʿAbd al-ʿAziz Ibn Baz and Muhammad Ibn ʿUthaymin). They have been replaced by less respected scholars, such as the current mufti ʿAbd al-ʿAziz Al al-Shaykh, whose legitimacy in the religious field rests on his being a descendant of Muhammad ibn ʿAbd al-Wahhab more than on his own scholarly achievements. This weak position has given him no choice but to act as a servile ally of the monarchy, thus undermining the credibility of the establishment that he represents and heads.

As for the discourse on progress and development, its efficacy is contingent on the ability of the state to deliver the promised goods and services. This in turn is dependent on the financial resources of the state and their effective deployment and administration. Corruption and mismanagement can jeopardize delivery and frustrate expectations, leading to potential dissent. For instance, the repeated destruction caused by the floods in Jeddah in 2009 and 2011 has fueled public anger against the government. Last, the nationalist project of the state faces certain challenges that are rooted in the country's regional, tribal, and sectarian diversity. To be sure, all nations are constructs, but in the Saudi case the nationalism is arguably shallow because it is a recent development, one that is centered on the royal family and superimposed on a society with particularly deep cleavages. Moreover, like other nationalist projects, the Saudi one faces the challenge of centrifugal forces of globalization.

The future of the country is shaped not only by the government's policies and resources, but also by deeper changes occurring in society more broadly. And despite its reputation for being conservative and static, Saudi Arabia is in fact a dynamic and rapidly evolving society. The youth bulge it faces has not only economic effects, but also deep social and cultural consequences. Many of these young people have preferences, expectations, and communication habits that differ from those of their parents. At least 100,000 young Saudis are currently studying abroad, most of them on full scholarships from the Saudi government. As for women, who started being educated only in the early 1960s, they now represent more than half of all university students in the kingdom. The obstacles they face in finding employment and restrictions on their mobility, since they are not allowed to drive, are bound to generate increasingly vociferous demands for more rights. Acknowledging this, the government has taken small but symbolically important steps such as the appointment of a woman, Nora al-Fayiz, as Deputy Minister of Education for girls.

Yet another important set of changes are those associated with rapid urbanization (today above 85 percent). Families are increasingly nuclear, and individuals are more atomized. This has led to the disruption of traditional social structures and identities. In this respect, new social solidarities are being created, some based on the reinvention of traditional elements such as tribal genealogies, others on alternative forms of socialization linked to contemporary urban lifestyles. A café and street culture are, for instance, developing quickly in Riyadh and Jeddah. More extreme practices such as *tafhit* (car drifting) have also started to attract young urban Saudis.

The pace of those developments in the last few decades means that today's young Saudis live in a wholly different world from that of their parents. Depending on how the regime handles the situation, they can represent either a formidable challenge or a key asset for the future of the country.

COMPLEXITY AND CHANGE IN SAUDI ARABIA

This volume presents a collection of chapters that focus on different sectors of Saudi society and examine how the changes of the last few decades have affected each sector. Many of the authors have conducted archival and field-work research in Saudi Arabia, benefiting from the relative opening of the country to foreign researchers since 2000. As such, its chapters reflect new insights from the field and provide the most up-to-date research on the country's social and political dynamics.

A first set of contributions deals with domestic politics. Greg Gause questions widespread assumptions about what he calls the "rentier exceptionalism" of Saudi Arabia. Most of the literature on rentier states assumes a negative relationship between oil prices and political mobilization; that is, when prices are high, political opposition will be low, and vice versa. This assumption, however, does not appear to hold in Saudi Arabia, where the most intense political mobilization occurred in times of high (1979–80) or rising (1990–4; 2001–5) oil prices, not in times of economic difficulty. In the kingdom's case, Gause argues, mobilization has tended to be triggered by regional and international crises rather than domestic economic downturns.

In the following chapter, Toby Jones asks whether Saudi Arabia is best understood as an Islamic state or a technostate. Jones considers the role of science, technology, nature, and expertise in the making of modern Saudi Arabia. While noting that religion continues to play an important role in the kingdom's political history, the chapter suggests that Saudi political authority as well as Saudi authoritarianism have other, more modern, origins.

The religious sector is explored in more depth by Nabil Mouline, whose chapter examines Saudi official Islam through an analysis of the Committee of Senior Scholars (*hay'at kibar al-'ulama'*). After examining the historical relationship between the political and religious spheres in the kingdom, Mouline puts into context the Saudi state's desire, in the 1960s and 1970s, to "bureaucratize the ulama" and establish official religious institutions, the most important of which being the Committee of Senior Scholars. Mouline describes the different religious, social, and political functions fulfilled by the committee, and argues that it has great powers but remains entirely dependent on the royal family.

The second set of chapters looks at the issue of oil. Giacomo Luciani examines the extent to which Saudi Arabia controls the price of oil. He argues that, contrary to common assumptions, Saudi Arabia is a price taker, not a price maker. The kingdom individually and OPEC collectively have only limited tools at their disposal to influence the price of oil. What is worse, their influence is significant only if world oil stocks are low, meaning that the market is in fragile equilibrium. He further argues that to stabilize significantly oil prices, it is necessary for Saudi Arabia and some of the other leading oil exporters to take a much more active role in global oil trading, shifting from their current position of price takers to the position of price makers.

Moving from the economics to the politics of oil, Bernard Haykel's chapter analyzes how oil has been invoked and discussed by various actors, official and dissident, in the highly contested politics of Saudi Arabia. The focus is various political and social actors, including in the final section al-Qaeda's ideological and strategic analysis of the unparalleled hydrocarbon reserves in Arabia. Two points are highlighted: (1) the continuities between al-Qaeda's discourse on oil and the means of its exploitation and older non-Islamist Saudi views and critiques on the same topic from at least the 1950s; and (2) the evolution of al-Qaeda's views on this matter and its increasing advocacy of the use of ever more violent means to damage the global economy through attacks on Saudi oil facilities. One conclusion of the chapter is to argue that oil should be understood as one of the principal leitmotifs of Saudi political thought, contestation, and engagement.

Who gets what from the kingdom's oil income is further explored in Steffen Hertog's chapter on the political economy of Saudi regions. Hertog starts with the observation that Saudis maintain an elaborate mythology about how different regions of the kingdom have lost or gained in the course of Saudi Arabia's unification and the state's subsequent expansion. He then subjects the different claims to empirical scrutiny, adducing and analyzing available data about administrative, infrastructure, public service, public employment, and economic development since the early 1960s. The analysis shows that, contrary to widespread assumptions, the Hijaz has been doing relatively well on most accounts, although not as well as Najd, while the south has remained a thoroughly marginal player despite its substantial population.

A third set of chapters looks more specifically at the Islamic discourse and at how – and by whom – it is used in the kingdom. David Commins describes how the name "Salafism" was gradually adopted to designate what historians have usually called "Wahhabism." Going back to the late nineteenth century, he disentangles the different factors that interacted in this evolution, namely, the fact that Wahhabis developed contacts with proclaimed "Salafi" modernists of neighboring countries, and the Saudi desire to integrate into the wider Muslim world.

In his chapter, Stéphane Lacroix sheds light on another, more controversial actor in the Saudi religious sphere. He examines the Sahwa (from *al-Sahwa al-Islamiyya*, the Islamic Awakening), the mainstream Islamist movement that has developed in Saudi Arabia since the 1960s by taking inspiration from both Wahhabism and the Muslim Brotherhood. He shows that the Sahwa constitutes the better-organized nonstate group in Saudi Arabia, and the only one capable of effectively challenging the government. However, because of the "incestuous" relationship it maintains with the Saudi state, it has – with one important exception – not been able to generate any genuine and sustainable opposition to the royal family.

Saud al-Sarhan also addresses Saudi Islamism, focusing on a crucial phase of the intellectual history of the movement, namely, the debates that took place between the so-called Salafi-Jihadi thinkers Hamud al-Shu'aybi, Nasir al-Fahd, and Ali al-Khudayr and their opponents in the religious sphere between 1997 and 2003. Al-Sarhan's chapter explains the origin, nature, and significance of those debates, which, the author argues, illustrate the weakening of official religious authority in Saudi Arabia at the turn of the millennium.

Also writing on the more radical Islamist fringe, Thomas Hegghammer explains the difference between Abdallah Azzam's "classical jihadism" and

Usama bin Ladin's "global jihadism," which advocate restricted and unre-stricted private warfare for the defense of Muslim lands, respectively. Although existing literature on jihadism has distinguished between local and global jihad, the dual nature of transnational violent Islamic activism has been over-looked. Yet it is especially relevant in Saudi Arabia because the two doctrines generated two semidistinct militant communities, the relationship between which is crucial to understanding the evolution of jihadism in the kingdom. Most Saudi militants were classical, not global, jihadists. This helps explain why so many Saudis fought in Afghanistan, Bosnia, Chechnya, and Iraq while al-Qaeda never thrived in the kingdom.

A last set of chapters addresses sociocultural change. Abdulaziz al-Fahad looks at the fate of Saudi Arabia's Bedouins through a study of the life and works of a Bedouin poet named Bandar ibn Surur, who was active during the period of intense modernization that spans from the 1950s to the 1980s. Al-Fahad shows how the Bedouins lost their political and social status relative to the sedentary population, thus detailing one of the most dramatic transfor-mations undergone by Saudi society in the twentieth century. By stressing the profoundly anti-Bedouin ethos of the Saudi state, he challenges the classic "orientalist" perception of the Al Saud's rule. In a second chapter Abdu-laziz al-Fahad investigates the phenomenon of producing family and tribal genealogies that has caught the interest of many contemporary Saudis. He locates this in a reaction to some of the manifestations of modern prosperity, urbanization, and an all-powerful state that has successfully undermined most traditional institutions and forms of solidarity. The genealogical reaction is therefore a practical attempt by families to organize their affairs so as to create a buffer between the state and the individual, and also produces a modicum of stability in an otherwise chaotic and anonymous urban landscape. In short, the production of genealogy performs important social functions, as it has done for many centuries past in Arabia, but in the contemporary context it has been repurposed for present-day needs.

Madawi al-Rasheed's contribution deals with the situation of Saudi women. Al-Rasheed's main contention is that, contrary to the common view, women's exclusion in Saudi society is a political, rather than simply a social or religious, fact. The subordination of women, she argues, is intimately linked to the project of the state and to the fabrication of its own legitimacy narrative, in which women occupy a central position. Since 9/11, however, the state has been oscillating between contradictory narratives – the state as both protector and emancipator of women. Yet, the ultimate objective remains the same: to achieve control and surveillance practiced under the guise of protecting the moral order.

Looking at another understudied component of Saudi society, Amélie Le Renard examines recent changes in the women's sphere. She shows how the growing number of shopping malls in Riyadh over the past decade or so has transformed not only the city's landscape but also its female inhabitants' lifestyles. In a strictly segregated city, malls have been used by women as public spaces, which has contributed to the redefinition of Saudi Arabia's conservative social norms.

Saudi Arabia is on the cusp of a dramatic change and transformation, not least because its aging leadership is bound to give way soon to a younger generation of princes. Social change is also palpable because of a number of factors: a large number of young people with unsated expectations, a revolution in information sharing and delivery with the pervasive use of social media, the return of so many thousands of students from study abroad, and the Arab Spring uprisings and the policies that the state has pursued to quell its effects both domestically and abroad. Some will argue that the fate of the political system is intimately linked to the price and quantity of oil produced. The rule of thumb is that as long as the price is high (roughly over $100 per barrel) and revenues are steady, the country will remain relatively stable. The government will simply buy social peace and people's consent. But as these chapters will show you, Saudi Arabia's reality is more complex and dynamic, and its past and present, let alone its future, cannot be explained by any single factor such as the price of oil.

PART 1

Politics

2

Oil and Political Mobilization in Saudi Arabia

F. Gregory Gause III

Although Saudi Arabia is not a hotbed of political activism, it is still possible to discern periods when Saudis are more engaged in political activity than in other periods. Those periods of greater political mobilization do not coincide with downturns in oil prices. This is counterintuitive, as oil wealth is the motor of the Saudi economy. Given the enormous role of oil in the economy and the government's implicit claim to citizens' loyalty based upon its ability to provide them a comfortable lifestyle, it would seem logical that Saudis would be most likely to mobilize against the government when oil prices fall. Moreover, periods of lower oil prices should weaken the Saudi regime, which relies almost exclusively upon oil revenues to fund its government. Thus both incentives to mobilize should be higher and the ability of the government to control the population reduced during periods of low oil prices. However, political mobilization has occurred in Saudi Arabia during times of relatively high oil revenues. This chapter will suggest a number of reasons for this anomalous result, including a fiscal system that has allowed the Saudi government to tap private sector funds during periods of budget stringency and an ability by its own actions to affect the price of oil and thus the size of its treasury. Because of these factors, Saudi Arabia has been able to avoid the regime crisis that falling oil prices have frequently caused in other oil states. It will also explore the dynamics of political mobilization in Saudi Arabia, suggesting that regional crises more than domestic economic swings motivate Saudis to act politically.

The chapter begins with a brief discussion of a number of efforts in the theoretical literature to conceptualize the relationship between great oil wealth and both political mobilization and state (or regime) capabilities. I argue that Saudi Arabia is not a good fit for any of these theories. I go on to discuss periods of political mobilization, arguing that it is regional political crises, not domestic economic downturns, that lead to political mobilization in Saudi Arabia. In the following section, I argue that the Saudi government has been able to ward off fiscal crises during periods of oil price decline not only because of its wealth, but also because of its banking system and its ability to affect the world oil market through its own decisions. Finally, I consider why Saudi Arabia has been able to avoid political crises during oil price downturns, looking at both the Saudi state's ability to avoid fiscal crises and the drivers of political mobilization in the country.

OIL, STATE CRISIS, AND POLITICAL MOBILIZATION

Early work on the rentier state speculated that oil wealth depoliticizes citizens, making it easier for authoritarians to maintain their regimes. The old saw from the American Revolution, "no taxation without representation," is in this view turned around: "no representation without taxation."[1] However, the political upheavals experienced by oil states like Iran, Algeria, Venezuela, Nigeria, and Indonesia since the late 1970s calls into question this contention about depoliticization. Although Saudi Arabia has not experienced upheaval on the level of those states, it has seen variations in the levels of political mobilization of its citizens since the oil revolution of the early 1970s. Those variations indicate that even Saudis, who enjoy a much greater per capita windfall from oil than Iranians or Indonesians or Nigerians (but not that much more than Venezuelans), are not uniformly depoliticized by oil rents.

Research on the oil-politics nexus in the 1990s proposed a state-, rather than a society-, centered set of explanations for how oil relates to authoritarian outcomes and how it can also explain crises in the regimes of oil-producing states. One strand of this research focused on state capacity, taking a central insight of the state-building literature – that the development of taxing power was the key driver to building strong states – and turning it on its head. Since oil states have no need to tax their citizens, they build large but "flabby" states, characterized by huge bureaucracies that serve the purpose of giving citizens jobs, and thus redistributing income, but that play little role in actually monitoring and governing society. Thus, this argument runs, when a crisis hits, the oil state is unable to extract revenue from, monitor, or control its

---

[1] This argument is made in a direct way by Giacomo Luciani, "Allocation vs. Production States: A Theoretical Framework," in *The Arab State*, ed. Luciani (Berkeley: University of California Press, 1990), 77: "The fact is that there is 'no representation without taxation' and there are no exceptions to this version of the rule." See also Hazem Beblawi, "The Rentier State in the Arab World," in the same volume, 89: "With virtually no taxes, citizens are far less demanding in terms of political participation." This type of argument is made in a more sophisticated way by Jill Crystal, *Oil and Politics in the Gulf: Rulers and Merchants in Kuwait and Qatar* (Cambridge: Cambridge University Press, 1990).

society.[2] The problem with this argument is that it is hard to call the Saudi state "flabby." It certainly does have a huge bureaucracy, many of whose parts are more redistribution than governing agencies.[3] However, it has developed an administrative and judicial system that controls its territory (as opposed to its neighbor Yemen, for example) and a coercive apparatus that contains and puts down dissent. The agencies of internal security in Saudi Arabia are not usually described as "flabby." Certain islands of competence like Saudi Aramco and the Saudi Arabian Monetary Agency exceed international administrative standards. The Saudi state's role in constraining and directing the economy is substantial. The dependence of its citizens on the state for the provision of services and subsidies is extensive. The Saudi state might not have a robust extractive capacity, but it certainly governs Saudi Arabia. It is hard to escape its numerous tentacles.[4]

Another strand of the 1990s research focuses not simply on society or the state, but rather on how oil links the two and how fluctuations in oil revenues can affect political mobilization and regime security. In her 1997 book on Venezuela, Terry Karl makes the larger argument that during periods of high oil prices, regimes in oil states build support through distributive policies. When prices fall, these distributive policies cannot be sustained, and then the regime faces a crisis without a strong core base of support upon which to rely.[5] Karl's findings can help us explain the problems numerous oil regimes (e.g., Venezuela, Indonesia, Algeria) have faced during oil price downturns of the mid-1980s and the late 1990s. There is also an appealingly direct logic to this argument – regimes built on oil wealth should face serious problems when the oil money declines, and they are no longer able to service their patronage networks. By the same token, declines in oil prices should lead to political mobilization in the polity, because the bonds of loyalty to the regime are defined by patronage. So a serious fall in oil prices both weakens the regime and mobilizes the population.

---

[2] For an early version of this see Hussein Mahdavi, "The Patterns and Problems of Economic Development in Rentier States: The Case of Iran," in *Studies in the Economic History of the Middle East*, ed. M. A. Cook (London: Oxford University Press, 1970). Kiren Chaudhry develops it fully in *The Price of Wealth: Economies and Institutions in the Middle East* (Ithaca, NY: Cornell University Press, 1997).

[3] Steffen Hertog, *Princes, Brokers and Bureaucrats: Oil and the State in Saudi Arabia* (Ithaca, NY: Cornell University Press, 2010).

[4] Chaudhry argues that the Saudi state was actually more capable in the pre–oil period, but her argument is convincingly refuted by Robert Vitalis in his review of Chaudhry's book, *International Journal of Middle East Studies* 31, no. 4 (1999): 659–61.

[5] Terry Karl, *The Paradox of Plenty: Oil Booms and Petro-States* (Berkeley: University of California Press, 1997).

Saudi Arabia, however, does not fit this argument either. The Saudis had difficult choices to make during the two major oil price downturns of the post-1973 era, but the regime was not shaken. It survived both of these downturns, in part because it had resources that other oil states could not call upon during times of fiscal crisis. But the regime's ability to ride out these dips in the world oil market was also a factor of the lack of political mobilization in Saudi Arabia during these periods. The Saudis did not have to face a mobilized population demanding political change during economic downturns. On the contrary, the Saudi case is a double outlier from this perspective, in that serious political mobilization occurred not when the regime was facing an economic downturn, but rather when oil prices were relatively high – in 1979–80, in 1991–6, and in 2001–6.

POLITICAL MOBILIZATION AND OIL PRICES IN SAUDI ARABIA

By the logic of set out by Terry Karl and others, Saudi Arabia should have seen its most intense periods of political mobilization during or just after serious oil price declines, in the mid-to-late 1980s and in the late 1990s. In those periods Saudi GDP and per capita income were falling. Although the government was able to avoid a serious fiscal crisis, by means that will be discussed below, the Saudi economy stagnated during these periods of oil price declines, and the general standard of living for the average Saudi suffered as a result.[6] Yet these periods did not witness overt political mobilization. Saudis were more politically active during periods when oil prices were high or relatively moderate and steady: the late 1970s, the early 1990s, and the early 2000s. In each case, the spur to political mobilization was regional political crisis, not domestic economic downturn.

Charting periods of more or less intense Saudi political mobilization is a subjective matter. We do not have reliable public opinion polls to indicate levels of popular discontent or regular elections for which we can compare voter turnout levels and voter choices. But we can use a number of indicators to gauge levels of political mobilization: political violence, demonstrations, and the generation of public petitions to the rulers.[7] Even during the periods of greater political mobilization I identify, in comparison to other countries Saudi

---

[6] Shireen Hunter, "The Gulf Economic Crisis and Its Social and Political Consequences," *Middle East Journal* 40, no. 4 (1986): 593–613.

[7] I limit these categories to domestic manifestations. Thousands of Saudis fought in Afghanistan and elsewhere in the 1980s, which could be taken as an indicator of political mobilization, but their focus was outside the country.

Arabia might seem politically quiescent. But in testing the effects of oil price fluctuations on political sentiments and behavior, the relevant comparison is across time within individual countries. If the baseline level of political mobilization in an oil country is high, the rentier literature would predict that it should be even higher during oil price downturns. Likewise, in a country with a low baseline of political activity like Saudi Arabia, we are less concerned with absolute levels of political activity, which might be consistently low by global standards, than with comparative levels during periods of oil price troughs and oil price peaks.

The periodization of political mobilization I suggest here is, unfortunately, not based upon a data set of indicators of political mobilization that spans the entire post–oil period since 1973. Although the evidence of mobilization in those periods is strong, I cannot point to average number of petitions generated or incidents of violence for each year, to establish quantitatively the difference between those periods I identify as characterized by higher levels of political mobilization and other periods. However, the periodization I suggest is consistent with the secondary literature on Saudi Arabia[8] and with accounts by Saudis themselves generated through interviews over the course of twenty years of field work in the country.

Since the oil revolution of the early 1970s, Saudi Arabia has experienced three periods of comparatively intense political mobilization. The first was in 1979–80, which saw a series of political demonstrations and disturbances among the Shia population of the Eastern Province, and, during November 1979, the takeover of the Grand Mosque in Mecca by Juhayman al-Utaybi and his followers. The latter event, as consequential as it was for the subsequent course of Saudi politics, was occasioned by neither domestic economic trends nor by regional crises, but by the advent of a round-numbered year in the Muslim calendar.[9] Al-Utaybi's group was millenarian, claiming that al-Utaybi's brother-in-law was the Mahdi and that they were ushering in a new era in Muslim history. They certainly put forward a political critique of the Al Saud regime, but the impetus for their political mobilization seems to have been

---

[8] See, for example, Mamoun Fandy, *Saudi Arabia and the Politics of Dissent* (New York: Palgrave, 2001); Joshua Teitelbaum, *Holier than Thou: Saudi Arabia's Islamic Opposition* (Washington, DC: Washington Institute for Near East Policy, 2000); Abdulaziz Sager, "Political Opposition in Saudi Arabia," in *Saudi Arabia in the Balance*, ed. Paul Aarts and Gerd Nonneman (London: Hurst, 2005); Madawi Al-Rasheed, *Contesting the Saudi State: Islamic Voices from a New Generation* (Cambridge: Cambridge University Press, 2007); and Robert Lacey, *Inside the Kingdom* (New York: Viking, 2009).

[9] Yaroslav Trofimov, *The Siege of Mecca* (New York: Random House, 2007).

neither the specifics of the Saudi economy nor the regional crisis occasioned by the Iranian Revolution. It was the advent of the hijri year 1400.[10]

The same cannot be said for the Shia unrest in the Eastern Province. Although there were numerous reasons for Saudi Shia to be unhappy with the government, there had been little political activism manifested in the Saudi oil patch since the labor and Arab nationalist agitations of the 1950s.[11] Buoyed by the success of the Iranian Revolution and the broadcasts from Tehran calling for similar uprisings throughout the region, Saudi Shia activists defied the authorities and organized public commemorations of Ashura in November 1979. Clashes with Saudi security forces led to casualties, and the mourning period for those who died led to new demonstrations in early 1980. The Saudi state finally pacified the area through a combination of harsh security measures and, subsequently, more spending in the region.[12]

The Saudi Shia undoubtedly had economic and social grievances against the government, but that agenda had existed for decades. It is hard to make the argument that immediate economic circumstances spurred the 1979–80 protests. Although Saudi Shia were not sharing in the oil bonanza of the 1970s equally, they certainly benefited from the general increase in Saudi economic activity and wealth. It is hard to escape the conclusion that the spur to their mobilization in this period was the demonstration effect of the Iranian Revolution. The fact that Saudi Shia demonstrators carried pictures of Ayatollah Khomeini and their leaders adopted the rhetoric of the Islamic Republic strengthens this conclusion.

The second period of greater political mobilization occurred during and after the Gulf War of 1990–1. The regional crisis, the deployment of hundreds of thousands of American and coalition forces to Saudi Arabia, and the intense international media focus on Saudi Arabia led to a spurt of overt political activity unparalleled since the labor and Arab nationalist activism of the 1950s. Salafi critics of the regime who would later be recognized as the founders of the *sahwa* (Awakening) movement were emboldened to directly criticize the

---

[10] Joseph Kechichian, "Islamic Revivalism and Change in Saudi Arabia: Juhayman al-'Utaybi's 'Letters' to the Saudi People," *The Muslim World* 80, no. 1 (1980): 1–16. The letters themselves can be found in Rifa't Sayyid Ahmad, *rasa'il juhayman al-'utaybi* (Cairo: Maktabat Madbuli, 1988). On the background and consequences of his movement, see Thomas Hegghammer and Stéphane Lacroix, "Rejectionist Islamism in Saudi Arabia: The Story of Juhayman al-'Utaybi Revisited," *International Journal of Middle East Studies* 39, no. 1 (2007): 103–22.

[11] Robert Vitalis, *America's Kingdom: Mythmaking on the Saudi Oil Frontier* (Stanford, CA: Stanford University Press, 2007), especially chs. 5–7.

[12] Toby Jones, "Rebellion on the Saudi Periphery: Modernity, Marginalization and the Shia Uprising of 1979," *International Journal of Middle East Studies* 38, no. 2 (2006): 212–33.

Al Saud rulers even as the crisis was ongoing.[13] A group of more liberal Saudi women engaged in a highly public challenge in November 1990 to the informal ban on women driving cars, in front of the international media, evoking a harsh backlash from the religious establishment and the Salafi movement and leading the regime to codify the prohibition on women driving.[14] The departure of almost all of the foreign forces and the end of the media spotlight did not end this period of political mobilization. It continued through a series of semipublic petitions in 1991–2 addressed to King Fahd calling for substantial changes in Saudi political life.

Even before the end of the crisis, a group of forty-three prominent Saudis identified as "liberals" and/or "secularists" addressed the king with a series of requests for political, judicial, and administrative reform. They took the king's revival in a November 1990 interview of an earlier promise to create a consultative council as an opening to advocate other constitutional reforms as well: the promulgation of a constitution, the revival of municipal councils, the establishment of provincial-level councils, and permission to form professional syndicates on the model of the existing regional chambers of commerce. They called for limits to the religious establishment's control of the judicial system, for greater media freedoms, and for complete citizen equality. This "liberal" petition elicited a counterpetition signed by more than four hundred Saudis identified as "Islamists," including Shaykh Abd al-Aziz bin Baz, the kingdom's Grand Mufti, and a number of his colleagues among the senior ulama. While echoing some of the themes of the "liberal" petition, including support for the establishment of a consultative council, the petition emphasized the central role of the religious establishment in any government reform. It advocated the creation of a commission to examine all state regulations in light of the Shari`a, with the power to veto legislation, and called for the unification of the judicial system under the authority of religious courts. The "Islamist" petition, unlike its "liberal" counterpart, delved into criticisms of Saudi economic policy as well, calling for an end to corruption, the reduction of taxes and fees for government services, the end of banking based on interest, and lifting what the signers called the ban on Islamic banks. A third petition, from prominent Saudi Shia, also supported the idea of a consultative council and called for an end to discrimination against Shia in state institutions.[15]

---

[13] Mamoun Fandy, "The Hawali Tapes," *New York Times*, November 24, 1990, 21.

[14] Eleanor Abdella Doumato, "Women and the Stability of Saudi Arabia," *Middle East Report*, no. 171 (July/August 1991), 34–7.

[15] F. Gregory Gause, III, *Oil Monarchies: Domestic and Security Challenges in the Arab Gulf States* (New York: Council on Foreign Relations Press, 1994), 94–8. I obtained copies of the first two petitions during research in Saudi Arabia immediately following the Gulf War.

The post–Gulf War ferment did not end with these rather mild (though in the Saudi context unusual) calls for political change. In 1992 a much more critical forty-six-page "Memorandum of Advice" was sent to the rulers by a group of about one hundred Salafi Islamist activists. It was unprecedented in the bluntness of its tone, the public nature of its dissemination, and its detailed critique of a range of Saudi policies. It complained that the ulama were being marginalized in the policy process and that there was a "lack of seriousness" in implementing Shari`a. The memorandum called for specific changes in Saudi economic policy, including the elimination of all manifestations of interest in the Saudi banking and financial systems (including a prohibition on Saudi funds being held in interest-bearing certificates in international financial institutions) and an end to "overproduction of oil," because production cuts would lead to higher prices. The signers' critique of Saudi foreign policy was even more pointed, questioning the huge amounts of money spent on defense when, in a crisis, the government called upon foreign forces for protection. They called for an end to Saudi support for "un-Islamic" regimes in Syria, Algeria, and Egypt, the formation of a 500,000-man national army, and a reversal of the close Saudi relations with the United States.[16]

The "Memorandum of Advice" was a distillation of the platform of an inchoate but important political movement emerging from the extensive Saudi religious establishment. This movement, termed the "Awakening" (al-sahwa), was committed to the Salafi-Wahhabi principles of official Islam in Saudi Arabia, but rejected the principle of deference to the Al Saud political authorities that dominated the behavior of the Wahhabi ulama through the history of the kingdom. "Awakening" leaders Safar al-Hawali and Salman al-Awda stepped up their public criticisms of the government, eventually leading to their arrest and home confinement for most of the rest of the decade. Salafi activists established the "Committee for the Defense of Legitimate Rights" in 1993 (in Arabic the name could also be rendered as "Shari`a rights") and, when suppressed at home, set up shop in London where they used fax machines and access to Western media to publicize their critique of the regime.[17] At this time Usama bin Laden also broke publicly with the Saudi regime, echoing the Sahwa critique that the Al Saud had abandoned their own religious principles

---

See also Joshua Teitelbaum, *Holier than Thou*, ch. 3; and Gwenn Okruhlik, "Rentier Wealth, Unruly Law and the Rise of Opposition: The Political Economy of Oil States," *Comparative Politics* 31, no. 3 (1999): 295–315.

[16] Gause, *Oil Monarchies*, 35–7. Quotes from author's translation of a copy obtained in Saudi Arabia.

[17] Fandy, *Saudi Arabia and the Politics of Dissent*, chs. 2–5; and Teitelbaum, *Holier than Thou*, chs. 3–4.

in their politics.[18] The Sahwa ferment was not limited to words. In 1994 the Saudi security services arrested 157 people, including al-Hawali and al-Awda, who had participated in a demonstration in Burayda, a city north of Riyadh.[19] Incidents of violence followed. In August 1995 a Salafi activist was executed for attacking a police officer. Three months later, in November 1995, an office of the American training mission to the Saudi Arabian National Guard in Riyadh was bombed, killing five Americans and injuring scores. Saudi authorities executed four men for that attack in May 1996. In public statements before their execution, they referred to bin Laden and other Salafi activists as their inspiration.[20]

There is no denying that economic issues played a role in the political ferment that accompanied and followed the Gulf War. The economic downturn of the mid-1980s raised questions among the Salafi Islamists who would become the leaders of the Sahwa movement about the regime's policies.[21] The petitions discussed above criticized government corruption and called for more economic equity. But it is noteworthy that the economic downturn began years before the public emergence of the Sahwa movement as a political force challenging, if not opposing, the regime. It was the shock of the Gulf War crisis that led the inchoate stirrings of opposition to coalesce into a public movement. It is also noteworthy that, although economic demands are not absent from the petitions, they tend to be either general (anticorruption, pro-equality) or related to Islamist principles (the condemnation of interest in the Saudi banking and financial system). Only the Shia petition of late 1991 specifically calls for job creation policies and the end to discrimination against Shia in educational institutions and government employment. The other petitions emphasized political and legal grievances more than economic ones.

The third period of more intense political mobilization in Saudi Arabia came in the wake of the 9/11 attacks on the United States and the Iraq War. Much as the case in the previous period, this period was preceded by a period of economic difficulty caused by falling oil prices in the late 1990s, but once again it was a political crisis that mobilized political activity in the kingdom.

---

[18] Fandy, *Saudi Arabia and the Politics of Dissent*, ch. 6. On bin Laden's career at this point, see Lawrence Wright, *The Looming Tower: Al-Qaeda and the Road to 9/11* (New York: Knopf, 2006), ch. 7.

[19] *al-Hayat*, September 27, 1994, 1, 4. Anonymous Western diplomatic sources put the number of arrests during this period between four and five hundred: "Hundreds Arrested in Riyadh," Associated Press (online), September 19, 1994.

[20] Edward Cody, "Saudi Islamic Radicals Target U.S., Royal Family," *Washington Post*, August 15, 1996, 1.

[21] Stéphane Lacroix, *Awakening Islam: A History of Islamism in Saudi Arabia* (Cambridge, MA: Harvard University Press, 2010).

The intense international focus on Saudi Arabia in the wake of 9/11, in light of the fact that both Usama bin Laden and fifteen of the nineteen hijackers were Saudis, created pressure on the Al Saud for political reform. Taking advantage of the international spotlight, in January 2003 a coalition of moderate Islamists (some associated with the small Muslim Brotherhood current in the kingdom) and liberals addressed a petition entitled "A Vision for the Present and Future of the Country" to Crown Prince Abdallah. The petition called for an elected consultative council with real legislative powers, directly elected provincial assemblies, stronger guarantees of freedom of expression and political organization, and a larger role for women in public life. It also indirectly criticized the religious establishment's central role in policing public discourse, advocating a wide-ranging national dialogue based on mutual respect and tolerance.[22]

This petition was followed during 2003 by a number of others addressed to the Crown Prince. In April more than four hundred Shia notables in the Eastern Province reiterated the calls from the 1991 petition for an end to sectarian discrimination.[23] In September over three hundred Saudis, many involved in the January "Vision" petition, presented a sharper call for political reform in a petition entitled "In Defense of the Nation," directly connecting the political violence in the country to the lack of political participation and the monopoly held by "those who are fundamentally unable to engage in dialogue with others" (a not-so-veiled reference to those in the official and opposition Salafi trends who opposed more secular trends) over national discourse.[24] Finally, in December yet another, more detailed petition from the same political trend, signed by 106 Saudis, entitled "Constitutional Reform First," called for the conversion of the Saudi political system into a constitutional monarchy with greater freedom of expression and political organization and elected institutions. It repeated the September petition's contention that a lack of political participation encouraged domestic violence, but added that the country's religious education system also encouraged extremism.[25]

This bout of "petition fever" was originally encouraged by Crown Prince Abdallah, who publicly received the organizers of both the January "Vision"

---

[22] *al-Quds al-'Arabi* (London), January 30, 2003, 13; Stéphane Lacroix, "Between Islamists and Liberals: Saudi Arabia's New 'Islamo-Liberal' Reformists," *Middle East Journal* 58, no. 3 (2004): 345–65.

[23] *Middle East Economic Survey*, June 2, 2003. The original Arabic was published in the Lebanese newspaper *al-Safir*, May 22, 2003.

[24] This petition was published on the Arabic internet site Elaph on September 28, 2003, with the names of the signatories: www.elaph.com. I obtained a copy from one of the organizers of the petition.

[25] This petition was referenced in a BBC broadcast on December 23, 2003, http://news.bbc.co.uk/2/hi/middle_east/3344655.stm. I obtained a copy of the petition from one of the organizers.

petition and the April Shia petition.[26] He organized a series of "national dialogue" meetings in 2003 and 2004 that included notable Saudis from across the ideological spectrum, and in October 2003 he announced that elections would be held for municipal councils. (They were eventually held in 2005.) However, the regime also signaled the limits of its tolerance for calls for political reform, arresting four of the organizers of the "Constitutional Reform First" petition in March 2004.[27]

As more moderate political reformers were mobilizing through petitions, the Salafi jihadist opponents of the regime were also mobilizing, through violence, to attack it. In May 2003 al-Qaeda in the Arabian Peninsula (AQAP) attacked three housing compounds in Riyadh, killing twenty and wounding dozens. This began a violent campaign that lasted through 2005, before Saudi security forces were able to get the upper hand, although episodic violence continues to the present. AQAP began organizing in Saudi Arabia before the 9/11 attacks, in 1999, but could only mobilize for their sustained campaign against the regime after the attacks.[28] The AQAP campaign was the most sustained domestic challenge to the Saudi regime since the Arab nationalist challenge of the 1950s and 1960s and the most violent since the Ikhwan uprising of the late 1920s. The campaign against AQAP led to hundreds of deaths, including more than one hundred Saudi security forces killed. The rebels struck targets as important and diverse as the Ministry of the Interior in Riyadh, the American consulate in Jidda, and luxury compounds for foreign workers in the Eastern Province. A failed attack on the oil installations at Abqaiq in the Eastern Province, had it been successful, could have crippled the kingdom's export capacity temporarily.[29]

Neither the petition fever nor the armed campaign that followed the 9/11 attacks seems to be related to economic issues. Some of the petitions did mention the need to end corruption and protect the public treasury, but the overwhelming concentration was on political and ideological, not economic,

---

[26] Abdallah told the January petition organizers that the regime was considering a number of the suggested reforms. *al-Sharq al-Awsat*, January 31, 2003, 4. Three of the organizers of the Shia petition issued a press release after their meeting with Abdallah, which was distributed via e-mail, from which I obtained a copy.

[27] "Saudi Arabia Detains Reformers," *Washington Post*, March 17, 2004, A17.

[28] Thomas Hegghammer, "Islamist Violence and Regime Stability in Saudi Arabia," *International Affairs* 84, no. 4 (2008), 708.

[29] On AQAP, see along with the Hegghammer article cited in the previous note Madawi Al-Rasheed, *Contesting the Saudi State*, ch. 4; Roel Meijer, "The 'Cycle of Contention' and the Limits of Terrorism in Saudi Arabia," in Aarts and Nonneman, *Saudi Arabia in the Balance*; and Bruce Riedel and Bilal Y. Saab, "Al Qaeda's Third Front: Saudi Arabia," *Washington Quarterly* 31, no. 2 (2008): 33–46.

issues. AQAP never put forward an economic agenda nor can its activities be traced to socioeconomic causes.[30] Rather, its agenda was directed against the foreign, particularly American, presence in Saudi Arabia and the Saudi regime that encouraged it. Its campaign seems to have been sparked by the American invasion of Iraq more than anything in the Saudi domestic political economy. It is hard to avoid the conclusion that this third period of notable political mobilization in Saudi Arabia was the product of political crisis, not an economic downturn caused by oil price fluctuations.

SAUDI ARABIA, REGIME RESILIENCE, AND OIL PRICE DECLINES

The Saudi regime was fortunate that periods of political mobilization did not coincide with oil price downturns. However, the regime was not simply lucky in this regard; it was able to make its own luck in avoiding the kinds of fiscal crisis that could have weakened the regime and invited greater political mobilization during periods of economic stagnation. How has the Saudi regime, dependent almost completely upon oil revenues to fund its operations, been able to do this? The short answer is that the Saudis had two advantages not shared by most other oil producers: (1) the government had revenue cushions that allowed it to sustain higher levels of deficit spending during low oil revenue periods, thus shielding their population from the full effect of oil recessions; and (2) Saudi Arabia is the only oil producer that can, by its own actions, affect the price of oil.

The Saudi ability to fund sustained budget deficits during oil price downturns is a major reason why it has not faced the kind of regime crises experienced by other oil producers. But the sources of that ability have changed over time. During the oil price declines of the early and mid-1980s, Saudi Arabia drew down the reserves it built up over the boom years of 1974–82 to sustain government spending. Although Saudi government revenues fell from a high of SAR 368 billion in 1981 to SAR 76 billion in 1986, current expenditures fell by a much smaller amount, from SAR 114 billion in 1981 to SAR 99 billion, in the same years. In 1987 the Saudi government spent more in terms of current expenditures than it had in 1981, despite the fact that oil prices had declined by more than 50 percent between the two years, running a budget deficit that year that exceeded 25 percent of GDP. Budget deficits were higher than 10 percent of GDP from 1984 to 1992.[31] The Saudi regime was able to lessen the

---

[30] "It is difficult to link the violence of 1979, 1995 or 2003 with particular economic conjunctions, regime crackdowns or social crises." Hegghammer, "Islamist Violence," 702.

[31] Kingdom of Saudi Arabia, Saudi Arabian Monetary Agency, *Annual Report*, no. 43, 1428 (2007), Statistical Appendix, Section 5, Table 2, 293 http://www.sama.gov.sa/sites/SAMAEN/ReportsStatistics/ReportsStatisticsLib/5600_R_Annual_En_43_2007_11_25.pdf.

burden of the oil price recession of the mid-1980s on its population because it had money in the bank and was not afraid to spend it. Other major oil states, having larger populations and smaller oil production profiles, were not able (or willing) to save during the boom years. They could not sustain the streak of budget deficits run by the Saudis without experiencing fiscal crisis.

The Saudi regime was not forced during the oil price downturn of the 1980s to resort to the fiscal or political expedients that other oil states adopted to deal with their fiscal and economic crises. Riyadh did not have to go to international financial institutions for loans, and thus did not have to adopt the kinds of economic policies demanded by those institutions in exchange for such loans: reductions in government spending and consumer subsidies, currency devaluation, and tax reform. It was not forced to consider political reform and democratization moves, to which other regimes facing such unpopular changes in economic policy have resorted in an effort to reduce discontent. It even backed away from its one modest proposal to increase nonoil government revenues – an income tax on foreign workers.[32] Saudi reserves were so substantial that not only could they cushion the blow of the price downturn of the 1980s for their citizens, but they could also help fund the Iraqi war effort against Iran to the tune of over \$25 billion and spend much more than that to sustain the regime and fund the coalition war effort during the Gulf War of 1990–1.[33] The explanation for Saudi regime stability during the oil price decline of the 1980s is relatively simple – they spent down their reserves, thus shielding their population to a great extent from the consequences of the oil market crash.

When oil prices declined in the late 1990s, however, the Saudis could not follow this course of action. They had already spent down their reserves. Although getting an exact figure for Saudi Arabia's official cash in hand is difficult, it appears that by 1993 the Saudis had less than \$30 billion in the bank, and perhaps less than \$10 billion.[34] The smallest budget deficit run

---

[32] Chaudhry, *The Price of Wealth*, ch. 7; and Kiren Aziz Chaudhry, "The Price of Wealth: Business and State in Labor Remittance and Oil Economies," *International Organization* 43, no. 1 (1989): 101–45.

[33] Figure cited by King Fahd in a speech during the Gulf War of 1990–1. *al-Sharq al-Awsat* (London), January 17, 1991, 4. The IMF estimated the direct costs of the Gulf War to Saudi Arabia at \$55 billion. Gause, *Oil Monarchies*, 148.

[34] *Middle East Economic Survey*, January 25, 1993, B3, put usable Saudi government reserves at \$7.1 billion at the end of October 2002, although other analysts put the figure much higher, closer to \$20 billion. The *New York Times* (August 22, 1993, 1, 12, and August 23, 1993, 1, A6) quoted an unnamed Saudi official as estimating the country's liquid reserves at \$7 billion. Saudi Finance Minister Muhammad Aba al-Khayl responded that the country had a \$20 billion hard currency fund to support the Saudi riyal and that Saudi banks held hard currency reserves in excess of \$15 billion. *New York Times*, August 26, 1993, A18.

by the Saudi government between 1993 and 1999 was more than $4 billion (1997), and deficits ran as high as $12.9 billion (1998).[35] The Saudis could not cover their deficits from cash on hand. In fact, in 1998, as hedge funds were speculating against the Saudi riyal, Riyadh was forced to go to the United Arab Emirates for a currency swap, exchanging nearly $5 billion in riyals for U.S. dollars held by the Emirati government, to scare off the hedge fund wolves.[36] The relevant conclusion from this event is that, in 1998, the Saudi government did not have the cash available even to support its own currency.

Saudi rulers recognized that they were in a tough spot. At the December 1998 GCC summit, then Crown Prince Abdallah publicly declared that "the age of abundance is over.... We must all get used to a new lifestyle that does not rely entirely on the state."[37] They took a number of small steps at this time to increase revenues from citizens and foreign residents, including reducing farm subsidies, increasing fees for government services, and raising the price of subsidized consumer products like gasoline. There were rumors that political reforms were in the offing, as have occurred in other rentier states during periods of lower oil prices, including a persistent story that some form of elections would be introduced to fill some of the seats in the Consultative Council.

However, the Saudis did not follow through on these rumored political changes. Although private sector investment was encouraged to a greater degree than in previous decades, the basic "rentier bargain" between state and citizens was not substantially altered. The Saudi regime could avoid these difficult decisions for two reasons. First, it had access to a source of revenue that many oil states do not – its own banking system. Second, unlike any other oil state, Saudi Arabia can affect the price of oil by its own decisions. Riyadh took the politically easier path of borrowing domestically and using oil diplomacy to ride out the oil downturn of the late 1990s, without making fundamental political or economic changes.

There is a paradox behind the Saudi government's ability to tap its own private sector for loans. Saudi Arabia places no impediments upon capital transfers by its citizens. Should they want to, Saudis can hold all of their assets outside the country. Because they are confident that they can move their money if they have to, however, many Saudis actually keep substantial

---

[35] See note 31.
[36] Robin Allen, "Oil Price Crash Forces Saudis to Seek $ 5 Billion Bail-Out," *Financial Times*, December 4, 1998, 4.
[37] Stuart Wallace, "Saudi Arabia Tackles Reality as Boom Ends with a Bang," Agence France-Presse, December 13, 1998.

amounts of money in the domestic banking system.[38] That is money that the Saudi state can tap, through the sale of government bonds, to cover its deficits, and that is what the government did in the 1990s. Some of the borrowing that occurred in the 1990s came from Saudi government agencies, like the General Organization for Social Insurance (GOSI). GOSI, like the American Social Security Administration, collects payroll deductions to fund pensions and had an excess of liquidity in the 1990s. The government borrowed from it, much as the U.S. government "borrows" from the Social Security Trust. The Saudi government also sold government debt to Saudi banks to help cover the deficit. By 2000 Saudi Arabia's government debt was about $133 billion, more than 100 percent of GDP.[39] The relevant political fact about this debt is that it was almost entirely domestic. The Saudis did not go to international institutions or private international banks to cover their deficit. By keeping their debt local, they were not subject to the economic reforms frequently demanded by international lending agencies nor were they subject to the crises that can result when private international banks decide that their debtor is no longer credit worthy.

The second avenue by which the Saudis dealt with their fiscal problems in the late 1990s was to take the lead in the international oil market to try to push prices higher. In March 1998 the Saudis led an effort to achieve an informal agreement with Venezuela and Mexico (not an OPEC member) to cut production. The Saudis agreed to reduce their output by 300,000 barrels per day (b/d) for proportional cuts from the two Latin American producers. OPEC as an organization and non-OPEC producers Norway and Oman signed on to this framework, leading to cuts of 1.5 million b/d during the course of 1998. However, Iran refused to join the framework, and oil prices continued to fall. In March 1999, after intensive engagement with Tehran, Moscow, and other OPEC and non-OPEC producers, the Saudis were able to broker a further production cut of 2 million b/d. These deeper cuts, combined with the relatively quick Asian demand rebound from the Asian financial crisis, led to price increases through the remainder of 1999 and into 2000.[40] Despite these production cuts, Saudi government revenue increased by 75 percent from 1999 to 2000, yielding a surplus in the government budget for the first time since 1982. Although Riyadh ran small deficits in 2001 and 2002,

---

[38] On the Saudi banking system, see Chaudhry, *The Price of Wealth*, 277–85.

[39] "Saudi Arabia 2000 Economic Trends," U.S. Embassy, Riyadh, April 2000; *al-Hayat*, October 1, 1999, 11.

[40] F. Gregory Gause III, "Saudi Arabia over a Barrel," *Foreign Affairs* 79, no. 3 (May/June 2000): 80–94.

from 2003 to 2006 it enjoyed substantial government surpluses, building up its reserves.

Saudi Arabia weathered the two oil price downturns of the past thirty years without substantially changing its political or its economic system, something that the theoretical literature on oil states would not expect. It did so in the first instance because it had enough money in the bank to cover its deficits – not a particularly interesting theoretical finding. But the Saudi ability to ride out the second, albeit shorter and less severe, price downturn, turned not on having lots of money, but being able to access lots of money in ways that other oil states could not – through its own domestic banking system and by taking the lead in efforts to change the price of oil. In these interesting ways, Saudi Arabia is a rentier exception.

WHY IS SAUDI ARABIA AN OIL STATE EXCEPTION?

Saudi Arabia is an exception to the rentier model, both in terms of the regime's ability to avoid the fiscal and political consequences of oil price drops and in terms of the issues that spark political mobilization. The reasons behind the Saudi state's ability to avoid rentier fiscal crisis during periods of oil price decline is clear: its reserves, its ability to tap private domestic wealth through the banking system, and its unique role of being able to affect global oil prices by its own decisions. Discerning the roots of that exceptionalism in terms of political mobilization requires further research, but I can put forward a few plausible hypotheses.

Some of the earliest literature on the rentier state speculated that politics in such states would revolve around symbolic more than material issues, since the state's control over so much of the national wealth and its ability to spread that wealth to the citizenry would take economic issues off the political agenda.[41] We know that this extreme statement of the argument has not been borne out by the experience of oil states. Economic issues do arise, even in the richest rentier states. Saudi Arabia, unlike Kuwait and the UAE, is not super-rich. In terms of per capita wealth, it is a middle-income country with some real regional and class disparities of wealth. The central role of the state in economic life in Saudi Arabia can help us explain the concentration in the petitions of both the early 1990s and the early 2000s on the rule of law – constraining the state through law is a guarantee (one hopes) of more fairness

---

[41] Jacques Delacroix, "The Distributive State in the World System," *Studies in Comparative International Development* 15, no. 3 (1980):w 3–21.

and less corruption in the distribution of resources.[42] However, this insight, in a less categorical form, might help us understand why economic crisis did not lead to immediate political mobilization in Saudi Arabia. But it cannot explain why political mobilization occurred around foreign crises more than domestic events.

A more fruitful approach to explaining the pattern of political mobilization in Saudi Arabia might focus on identity and class issues. Given that there is a very low level of national feeling in Saudi Arabia, and comparatively little state effort to create such a feeling, it might not be that unusual that regional issues rather than domestic economic issues spark political mobilization. To the extent that the Saudi state promotes an Islamic rather than a national basis of political legitimacy, this could encourage citizens to identify with the broader Muslim world as intensely as their own state and thus be as likely to mobilize on regional issues as on domestic issues.[43] In terms of class, the absence of an indigenous proletariat can also help to explain the lack of political mobilization around domestic economic issues.[44] Labor movements have been key actors in other contexts in generating political opposition based upon domestic economic and distributive issues. The absence of a citizen labor class in Saudi Arabia since the 1960s certainly removes one actor that could have potentially focused opposition on domestic economic issues, although it must be noted that in the 1950s Saudi labor seemed to be mobilized as much by Arab nationalist regional appeals as by labor conditions at Aramco.

Finally, it is important to consider the role of the state itself in channeling and constraining manifestations of political mobilization. Many analysts have noted that the most powerful opposition movements in contemporary Saudi Arabia emerge from the Islamic institutions created by the state and call the regime to account on the Islamic terms it itself uses to justify its rule. This is a perceptive insight about the ideological nature of opposition in the kingdom, but it cannot help us to understand when that inchoate opposition will mobilize publicly. In two of the three periods of more intense mobilization, during and immediately after the Gulf War and after the 9/11 attacks, the Saudi state actually permitted a greater degree of political freedom for its citizens than it normally does. In each case, the intense international political and media concentration on the country led the rulers to permit, or to tolerate, a more

---

[42] Okruhlik, "Rentier Wealth, Unruly Law and the Rise of Opposition."

[43] This is a variant of the argument made in a much more cogent and detailed way by Thomas Hegghammer, "Islamist Violence," to explain the mobilization of Saudis into transnational jihadist movements.

[44] This has been highlighted by a number of analysts of rentier state politics. For one very good example, see Crystal, *Oil and Politics in the Gulf.*

open domestic debate. In the first case, with the country under a propaganda assault by Saddam Hussein, the Al Saud encouraged manifestations of national loyalty that they previously would have either eschewed or discouraged, and this opening helped to create the climate for the petition fever of 1991–2. The political reforms announced in 1992 gave another indication that the rulers might be easing up on political activity. In the second case, the crown prince himself encouraged the mobilization by publicly receiving petitions and organizing his national dialogue movement. In both cases, the regime eventually closed down these brief periods of greater political freedom through clear signals of the limits of its tolerance, including the arrests of activists. Although this explanation does not apply to the first period of mobilization, where activists were driven by their own deadline (the Juhayman al-'Utaybi movement) or by a regional event (the Shia and the Iranian Revolution), it can help explain the political mobilizations of the Gulf War and 9/11–Iraq War periods.

3

The Dogma of Development

Technopolitics and Power in Saudi Arabia

Toby C. Jones

In late September 2009 Saudi Arabia celebrated the grand opening of the King Abdullah University of Science and Technology (KAUST) near Jeddah overlooking the Red Sea. KAUST's founders harbored great ambition for the new institution, declaring that they hoped to see it become "a globally renowned graduate research university that makes significant contributions to scientific and technological advancement, and will play a crucial role in the development of Saudi Arabia and the world."[1] In a tribute to Islam's rich scientific history, King Abdullah, for whom the university is named, declared it a new "house of wisdom," a reference to the center of research founded in ninth-century Baghdad. The original House of Wisdom was the site of considerable scientific and intellectual achievement, where for more than three centuries Muslim thinkers made seminal contributions to the study of mathematics, astronomy, and medicine. Mongol invaders razed the center in the thirteenth century. Their destruction did not undo the foundational work carried out there or undermine the achievement of its contributors.[2] In encouraging and supporting the construction of a new "house of wisdom," Abdullah announced that the "University shall be a beacon for peace, hope, and reconciliation and shall serve the people of the Kingdom and benefit all the peoples of the world in keeping with the teachings of the Holy Quran, which explains that God created mankind in order for us to come to know

---

[1] See the university's mission statement at http://www.kaust.edu.sa/about/vision_mission.html# mission.

[2] For more on Islamic science see Ahmad Dallal, *Islam, Science, and the Challenge of History* (New Haven, CT: Yale University Press, 2010); George Saliba, *A History of Arabic Astronomy: Planetary Theories during the Golden Age of Islam* (New York: NYU Press, 1995); George Saliba, *Islamic Science and the Making of the European Renaissance* (Cambridge, MA: MIT Press, 2007); and Toby E. Huff, *The Rise of Early Modern Science: Islam, China, and the West* (New York: Cambridge University Press, 2003).

each other. It is my desire that this new University become one of the world's great institutions of research; that it educate and train future generations of scientists, engineers and technologists; and that it foster, on the basis of merit and excellence, collaboration and cooperation with other great research universities and the private sector."[3]

The opening of KAUST marked an important moment in Abdullah's tenure as king. Widely considered to be a reformer, and even as something of a liberal social innovator, the university was received as a powerful signal of his commitment to opening the kingdom politically, socially, and culturally – not just a university that aimed to compete with other leading global scientific institutions. Although the university's grandiose aspiration to rival the MITs of the world was meant to evoke enthusiasm, perhaps its most important aim was to transform the kingdom itself. Indeed, KAUST has also rightly been understood as an earnest effort on the part of the country's most important figure to create an institutional foundation for future economic and professional development in the kingdom. Although it has long possessed fantastic oil reserves and the great wealth that such abundance has bestowed, Saudi Arabia has rarely put its wealth to use in developing a more sophisticated or sustainable economy.[4] The country remains entirely dependent on oil and oil revenues. It has limited industry, lacks a technical elite, and has consistently failed to successfully promote economic diversity. KAUST's construction was meant, in part, to remedy this and to build the infrastructure for a future economic and technical transformation.

KAUST's construction also came in stark contrast to the kinds of commitments the kingdom has made to university learning in the recent past. Moreover, it seemed to herald an important transformation in how the country's rulers have thought about the role of both science *and* religion in Saudi society and politics. Since the early 1980s, when in response to conservative pressures the kingdom charted a more religious political course, the country's rulers have played down science and technology and emphasized the central importance of Islam and Wahhabism in particular. This appears to be at an end. Although Abdullah carefully framed the building of KAUST in terms of Islam's legacy of the pursuit of knowledge and scientific learning, the university's construction and the king's personal investment in it sent a clear message that the stranglehold enjoyed by Islamists over learning and society in the last three decades was no longer unquestioned. The university's mere

---

3 For the king's message, see: http://www.kaust.edu.sa/about/kingsmessage.html.
4 See Steffen Hertog, *Princes, Brokers, and Bureaucrats: Oil and the State in Saudi Arabia* (Ithaca, NY: Cornell University Press, 2010).

existence is no small evidence of this. In contrast to the vast majority of the king-dom's other universities, most of which are devoted to a religious curriculum, KAUST appeared innovative for its commitment to scientific and technolog-ical achievement.[5] The university was also considered a radical social space, particularly because of its open policy allowing men and women to mix in classrooms and other university facilities. Abdullah came under criticism for challenging the strict beliefs regarding gender separation held by some.

Not only did Abdullah hold his ground in the face of criticism, he also sent a clear message that KAUST and his vision for both it and for Saudi society were indelibly tied to his personal political authority. His legitimacy and the considerable regard that the vast majority of Saudis hold for him was meant to translate directly into the legitimacy of the university built with his image in mind. Almost immediately, KAUST and all that it was intended to be – both scientific and representative of a more open variety of Islam – was understood to be not just a reflection of, but also a material manifestation of, the king's power. Scientific progress and technical achievement were meant to take hold as key parts of a new narrative about what it meant to be Saudi and how to think about Saudi Arabia's future. But although it is true that Abdullah's embrace of science marked an important transformation in the context of the kingdom's recent history, particularly the era after 1979, science, technology, and politics have long been connected in Saudi Arabia. Since the middle of the twentieth century, when the kingdom first began building the mechanisms of gover-nance, Saudi and foreign experts played key roles in establishing, constructing, and consolidating a centralized state as well as the authority of the ruling Al Saud. Science and technology were instrumental to controlling the country's natural resources (water as well as oil), space, and society. Over the course of the century, political authority was often exhibited via development projects and an emphasis on technological works such as dams and irrigation and drainage networks. As is the case with the interconnection between Abdul-lah's personal authority and KAUST's legitimacy, scientific and technological projects have historically been deeply tied to the legitimacy of the royal family, emblematic of its power, and meant to embody the family's authority. Science and technology have also possessed ideological and symbolic significance over time. Development and progress, mediated by the state, have consistently been

---

[5] KAUST was preceded by the creation of the College of Petroleum and Minerals in Dhahran in 1963, which was elevated to university status in 1975. In 1986 it was renamed the King Fahd University of Petroleum and Minerals (KFUPM). KFUPM's strength has been in engineering, and until recently it offered technical training unavailable elsewhere in the kingdom. But its mission was always more limited than KAUST's and has been geared toward training experts to serve the country's oil industry.

pointed to as part of a larger social and political contract that has bound ruler and ruled.[6] This chapter outlines this history by pointing out some of the ways that politics, science, and society were connected in the twentieth century.

One of the main aims of this short chapter is to encourage readers to reconsider claims that Saudi Arabia is somehow exceptional. The most enduring feature of most studies of Saudi society and culture is the dominance of a central assumption that argues that Saudi Arabia's rulers and its society are essentially "traditional" and that each has historically been and continues to be culturally and socially determined by a timeless Islam. Studies that purport to examine Saudi Arabia's social and cultural history tend to look uncritically at the importance of religion, and even take the official state narrative that the Al Saud are the guardians of the faith and that Saudi society is essentially "conservative" as an article of faith.[7] Greg Gause has noted critically that a "conventional wisdom" exists in the field of Saudi studies that assumes the existence of an unchanging traditional influence on Saudi Arabia, especially its political order, in which religion, tribe, and family exert the most profound influences.[8] Although unintended, the focus on Islam has had the effect of narrowing the ways we think about politics and power in Saudi Arabia.[9] It has also had the effect of establishing a widely held belief that the kingdom is exceptional. Islam, although important, was one part of a broad set of political relations that shaped the kingdom's modern history. Along with religion, science, technology, and technopolitics were also important to the making

6 See Toby Craig Jones, *Desert Kingdom: How Oil and Water Forged Modern Saudi Arabia* (Cambridge, MA: Harvard University Press, 2010). Material in this chapter is adapted from this book.
7 See in particular David E. Long, *The Kingdom of Saudi Arabia* (Gainesville, FL: University Press of Florida, 1997); Alexei Vassiliev, *The History of Saudi Arabia* (London: Saqi Press, 1998); and Rachel Bronson, *Thicker than Oil: America's Uneasy Partnership with Saudi Arabia* (New York: Oxford University Press, 2006).
8 F. Gregory Gause, *Oil Monarchies: Domestic and Security Challenges in the Arab Gulf States* (New York: Council on Foreign Relations, 1994), 25.
9 Religion, of course, was fundamental to the rise of the Al Saud. From the origins of the nascent state, Saudi leaders and their advocates claimed for themselves the mantle of Islamic stewardship. In part, the family achieved this by drawing on their partnership with a community of religious scholars (commonly known as Wahhabis) from central Arabia to legitimize their political power. Appropriating Islam served several purposes. It provided the ideological substance and appeal that helped facilitate military conquest and the securing of the realm. It was also partly through religion that the Al Saud sought meaning and justification for their rule. The Al Saud were quick to anoint themselves as the guardians of the faith in addition to the holy cities of Mecca and Medina. Even though religion played an important role in shaping the modern Saudi Arabian state, interest in it has obscured as many of the complexities of the kingdom's twentieth-century experience as it has revealed. The best work to date on this is David Commins, *The Wahhabi Mission and Saudi Arabia* (New York: I. B. Tauris, 2006).

of Saudi power. By directing attention at these factors, the veneer of Saudi exceptionalism can partially be stripped away. We are left with a history of politics and power that suggest the kingdom was more similar than dissimilar to developing states elsewhere in the twentieth century.[10]

Science and technology have been important parts of Saudi political calculus from the beginning of the twentieth century. Efforts to subdue Bedouins, to build an imperial army (known as the *ikhwan*), and then to use it to establish Saudi suzerainty across most of the Arabian Peninsula in the first three decades of the century depended initially on the control of water and the remaking of nomads into settled agriculturalists. Even though the *ikhwan* ultimately rejected settled agricultural life, it is telling that the first generation of Saudi rulers pursued their expansionist political agenda by blending Islamic proselytism with environmental and social engineering. Other efforts followed, including decisions to court American experts, before the age of oil, to explore for water and mineral resources. Karl Twitchell, a mining engineer turned geologist, who played an important role in the kingdom's discovery of oil, was also influential in other less visible, but equally important, ways. He carried out the country's first survey of its water and agricultural resources. He also carried out extensive surveys of Asir, mapping out roads and suggesting agricultural projects. These were not merely the efforts of a benevolent philanthropist. Rather Twitchell was a rent seeker who happened to be serving a still vulnerable but ambitious imperial power, doing the work necessary to shore up a remote, contested, and coveted corner of Arabia on the behalf of the central authorities. Other experts followed, all lending their scientific and technical expertise to the consolidation of centralized power.

Saudi Arabia's technopolitical history intensified in the second half of the twentieth century. The successors to the kingdom's founder, Abd al-Aziz ibn Saud, began in earnest the slow process of shifting the politics of governance away from manipulating tribes and micromanaging personal networks to constructing the institutions and bureaucracies that eventually constituted the administrative heart of the state. Although King Abd al-Aziz had employed scientists and engineers to bolster his own authority in the first half of the twentieth century, after his death technology and the development of large technological systems became a principal means by which and the framework through which Saudi leaders and officials built the state. Although the process was uneven, subject to various factors, development remained a major political, economic, and social program until the late 1970s. Developing Saudi

---

[10] On technopolitics see Gabrielle Hecht, *The Radiance of France: Nuclear Power and National Identity after World War II* (Cambridge, MA: MIT Press, 1998), 15.

Arabia was a major component of a deliberate strategy in which state leaders sought to use technology and science to establish their political authority. State officials and high-ranking members of the royal family came to see technology and technical management as instrumental in solving environmental, agricultural, and economic as well as broader social and political challenges. In particular, it was the building of dams, irrigation and drainage projects, and agricultural loan programs as well as the design and implementation of sedentarization schemes that led to the creation of both the physical *and* administrative networks that connected Saudi Arabian subjects around the Arabian Peninsula to a centralized political network.[11] Enabled by growing oil revenues, Saudi leaders turned to technology and the building of technological systems to cast the net of Saudi authority over large swaths of territory.[12]

The realization of a strong state and a technopolitical order, which refers to the interconnection of state offices, technologies, and the people who administrated them, was a product of a historical process. The projection of centralized power, or perhaps more accurately early on the attempt to centralize power, and the construction of technological systems occurred simultaneously in time and space. Saudi officials and especially members of the ruling elite understood that their authority was linked to nature and set out to master it through science and technology, even if their original intent was not the creation of a political system that came to be defined by technological systems. Although the state used technology to project the power of the Al Saud into society, the modern Saudi state was *also* the product of these practices.[13] The designing and building of infrastructure and development projects, and the bureaucracies that supported them, allowed the state to come to better know the communities over which it ruled and to attempt to reshape them and their natural environments. Political authority, authoritarian governance, and stability were all outcomes of these efforts.

One area in which science, development, state power, and control over the environment converged was in agriculture. Agricultural development projects, from the building of dams to irrigation networks to settlement projects, became increasingly important beginning in the 1960s. Although Saudi Arabia is particularly water poor – it has no natural lakes or rivers – agriculture remained an important part of economic and social lives for hundreds of thousands of

---

[11] See James Scott, *Seeing like a State: How Certain Schemes to Improve the Human Condition Have Failed* (New Haven, CT: Yale University Press, 1998).

[12] Thomas P. Hughes, *Networks of Power: Electrification in Western Society, 1888–1930* (Baltimore: Johns Hopkins University Press, 1983).

[13] Timothy Mitchell, *Rule of Experts: Egypt, Techno-politics, Modernity* (Berkeley: University of California Press, 2002), 74–6.

Saudi citizens through the early 1970s. And although agriculture declined in importance overall in the Saudi economy after the rapid rise of oil revenues in the 1950s, it remained a fixture of the state's imagination and development efforts, an area in which it continuously sought to expand its capacity, as a way to redistribute oil wealth, and an arena to build up its institutional power vis-à-vis society.

There was a clear logic to the focus on agriculture. Controlling agriculture, or at least becoming a major factor in the lives of the country's settled, semisettled, and nomadic pastoralists, was tantamount to controlling space, territory, and markets as well as the bodies of individual cultivators. Building up the state's ability to manage, "aid," and regulate agricultural activity was also bound up with its desire to enroll citizens into the administrative embrace of the emerging state. Through the distribution of patronage, financial and technical assistance, development work, and expertise, large parts of the country's society, which might have otherwise remained outside the scope of state authority, were brought into contact with state institutions and the authority of a central government. Other, perhaps more practical, aims were at work as well. Given the paucity of arable land and agricultural productivity, the kingdom grew increasingly dependent on food imports. Beginning in the 1960s state officials and the kingdom's leaders began to speak publicly about the need for food sovereignty, using its immense wealth to wean the country from foreign dependence.

To stimulate productivity, and as a means of reaching into the lives of as many of the kingdom's subjects as possible, the country launched an ambitious project to expand agriculture nationally in 1964 with the founding of the Saudi Agricultural Bank. The bank's activities over several years, including at the height of the oil boom in the mid-1970s, make clear the state's commitment to expanding the country's agricultural base. Both Saudi and foreign experts worked together in charting a plan to expand agriculture. Initial surveys of existing resources showed that the vast majority of those who worked their own land did so on plots of land that were too small to generate the kind of yield that would help grow the kingdom's overall productive capacity. Since the 1950s agricultural production had become mostly subsistence oriented, and dependence on foreign food compounded the challenge of expansion. As imports flooded into the country, the agricultural market became a tight niche for smaller cultivators to break into.

The Agricultural Bank sought to relieve pressure on middle-sized and smaller farmers, providing capital to entice farmers to stay at home and help develop both cultivation and the agricultural base. At its founding in 1964, the bank enjoyed a modest capital investment of just under SAR 11,000,000

(Saudi riyals).[14] In its first year of operation, the bank distributed SAR 4.5 million in loans.[15] Both of those numbers rose considerably over the next decade. The bank's capital increased to SAR 30,000,000 in 1967–8[16], and after five full years in operation to SAR 50,000,000, a 400 percent increase.[17] In 1974–5, ten years after the Bank's founding and one year after the influx of revenues that followed the oil boom, it enjoyed SAR 150,000,000 in capital.[18] Over the first five-year period of its operation, the Bank loaned a total SAR 52,486,218 to more than 13,102 borrowers.[19] The overwhelming majority of the loans went to small farmers, with the average loan running between SAR 1,000 and 3,000. The 1967–8 annual report remarked that the objectives of the loans were to finance the purchase of irrigation and pumping equipment, with more than 58 percent of loans going to that purpose.[20] But by 1968 the loan program had achieved mixed results. Although it had loaned out millions of riyals, it had not alleviated pressure on farmers working on medium or small scales. In the hope that it might boost security and entice landless agricultural workers back to farming their own land, the king issued a royal decree on September 28, 1968, distributing uncultivated land in plots up to 10 hectares to any citizen who promised to farm it.[21]

It appears that the new land distribution program failed to significantly expand the area under cultivation. Not surprisingly, the 1974–5 loan data dwarfed the earlier totals with SAR 145,505,437. But it is not clear from the data whether smaller cultivators were actually being served by the loan program by the mid-1970s. The Ministry of Agriculture and Water announced in 1975 that it had only recently established a program "for the expansion of agriculture by intensive means." According to a ministry report published

---

[14] *Al-bank al-zirā'ī al-sa'ūdī: al-taqrīr al-sanawī*, hereafter known as the Saudi Agricultural Bank (SAB), 1964–5, 21.

[15] SAB, 1964–5, 17.

[16] SAB, 1967–8, 6.

[17] SAB, 1968–9, 6.

[18] SAB, 1974–5, 5.

[19] SAB, 1968–9, 22. The geographic distribution of loans raises questions about the bank's activities and why certain areas had a higher rate of borrowing than others that are difficult to answer. From the beginning, the central office in Riyadh awarded the highest number of loans at 83 percent. That rate dropped to 27.5 percent five years later, although it was still the highest. Jeddah and Burayda lent 23.2 percent and 22.3 percent, respectively, in 1968–9, approximating the rates from the central office and up from 4.7 percent and 1.8 percent from five years earlier. But the rates in the Hofuf branch in the Eastern Province remained mysteriously low in the first five years of the bank's operation. In 1964–9 the Hofuf branch lent 7.2 percent of the total loans given. The number actually declined to 6.9 per cent in 1967–8 before increasing to 8.5 percent in 1968–9. SAB, 1968–9, 11–12.

[20] SAB, 1968–9, 14.

[21] SAB, 1968–9, 6.

in 1975, "this programme includes the introduction and development of farm machinery through the principles of farm self-help."[22] Given the 1968 decision to distribute land as a mechanism to promote agricultural expansion, the need to explore other means to achieve the same goal in 1975 suggests that the government was struggling to meet its stated goals of expanding the agricultural market.

The results of the Ministry of Agriculture and Water's and the Saudi Agricultural Bank's efforts to contribute to and diversify the productive base of the national economy were more mixed. Economic growth was seen in the 1960s and early 1970s, even in agriculture.[23] Although agriculture's share of total GDP decreased during the decade of the 1960s, the sector did grow, albeit in limited fashion. Farming contributed around 10 percent of GDP in 1962–3 but fell to around 6 percent in 1970. It declined even further as a total contributor to GDP in 1975 to around 1 percent.[24] Considering that oil revenues grew so spectacularly in the same period, this decline is not surprising. In spite of growth, additional indications show that economic growth did not stimulate an expansion in the number of cultivators, nor did it serve the interest of smaller ones. The total area under cultivation only expanded from 200,000–300,000 hectares in the 1960s to 385,000–525,000 hectares in 1975. The Ministry of Agriculture and Water reported in 1975 that the small expansion represented a fraction of the country's potential, claiming that there were potentially 4,500,000 hectares of arable land, of which 600,000 were good for cultivation and around 3,500,000 were potentially good.[25] Even more revealing, over this same time period, agriculture's share of per capita GNP failed to rise in relation to other sectors. From 1964–5 to 1974–5 the country's

---

[22] Kingdom of Saudi Arabia, Ministry of Agriculture and Water, *Seven Green Spikes, 1965–1972: Water and Agricultural Developments* (Riyadh, 1974), 21.

[23] Alexei Vassiliev, *The History of Saudi Arabia* (London: Saqi Press, 1998), 409. Vassiliev claims that "Gross Domestic Product expanded from SR 8.6 billion in 1962 to SR 21.3 billion in 1973 at a rate of around 1.6 percent per annum, but most of this was a result of rising oil revenues" (409). The Saudi Ministry of Information notes that "The total value added by agriculture in 1974/75 was estimated at $SR1.4 billion or 8.6 per cent of private non-oil GDP, reflecting a growth rate of about 3.6 per cent over the last five years. With a very large and growing gap between food consumption and local production, the planners have devoted special attention to easing restraints and increasing productivity" (Kingdom of Saudi, Ministry of Information, *Saudi Arabia and Its Place in the World* [Lausanne: Three Continents, 1979], 6). The Saudi Ministry of Planning gave slightly different figures in the second Saudi Five Year Development Plan, saying that GDP rose from SR 3.185 billion in 1969 to SR 23.98 billion in 1974 (Kingdom of Saudi Arabia, Ministry of Planning, *Second Development Plan*, 1975–9 [Riyadh], 38).

[24] Mohammed Hussein al-Fiar, "Faisal Settlement Project, Haradh, Saudi Arabia: A Study of Nomad Attitudes toward Sedentarization" (Ph.D. diss., Michigan State University, 1977), 84.

[25] Ministry of Agriculture and Water, *Seven Green Spikes*, 15.

overall per capita income rose from $460 to $1,300, but the rates for cultivators rose only from $85 to $105.[26] Also, by the 1970s Saudi Arabia continued to rely on imports for around 55 percent of domestic agricultural consumption, indicating that not only had the kingdom fallen short in alleviating pressure on smaller farmers, but it also had yet to achieve its goals with respect to diversifying and strengthening the national economy.

In spite of its limited success, the operation and impressive expansion of the Agricultural Bank itself was consistent with the emphasis on building technocratic institutions as a way to strengthen central oversight. Over ten years the bank expanded from five to ten branches and from fourteen to forty-one offices, offering services in every major city in the kingdom.[27] Its personnel increased from 95 employees to 714.[28] In addition to growing in size and placing technically educated personnel in decision-making positions, agricultural institutions also increasingly emphasized and incorporated the principles of scientific planning and development thinking. In 1969 the Ministry of Agriculture and Water brought in the Menlo Park–based Stanford Research Institute (SRI) to train and help shape the ministry's short- and long-term thinking regarding not only the development of agriculture, but also the operations and strategies of the ministry itself.[29] In March 1964, King Faisal charged the Ministry of Agriculture and Water with the responsibility of "developing the land and water resources of the country and thereby increase[ing] agricultural production."[30]

The king and the ministry both claimed that the purpose of these efforts was to serve the people and to improve the living conditions of the struggling farmers, including the Bedouins. But the program also had an underlying political logic, most notably the need for the central powers to become more involved along the margins of the kingdom, lending a spatial reasoning to the government's domestic geopolitical strategy. As was the case earlier in the

---

[26] Vassiliev, *The History of Saudi Arabia*, p. 420.

[27] SAB, 1974–5, 10.

[28] SAB, 1964–5, 20; SAB 1974–5, 8.

[29] From 1969 to 1971 SRI, which was officially part of Stanford University until the mid-1970s, also undertook work on specific agricultural sectors. The Saudi-based field teams authored five reports (SRI Project ECH 8680, Menlo Park, CA, various dates) on how to improve livestock production among the Bedouin as well as how to improve the production and marketing of agricultural commodities. See "Selected Commodity Situations in Saudi Arabia, with Views on Policy Alternatives," "A Synthesis of Policies to Attain the Goals of the Agriculture Sector Plan of the Ministry of Agriculture and Water," 'A Program for the Improved Marketing of Agricultural Commodities in Saudi Arabia," and "Improvement of Livestock Production by Bedouin Nomads on Semidesert Rangelands of Saudi Arabia."

[30] Ministry of Agriculture and Water, *Seven Green Spikes*, 12.

century, command of nature and natural resources provided a context and a pretext for moving forward with the greater incorporation of the provinces into the orbit of central authority. Indeed, efforts to stimulate agriculture and, in particular, to enroll Saudi subjects who depended on the land for their livelihoods proved a key arena of state-building activity.

In addition to building up its administrative and technical powers, the kingdom's leaders also increasingly made the case for a symbolic component to their efforts. In 1962 Faisal had outlined something of his vision in a ten-point program that he claimed would serve as the new political-economic blueprint for national development. In the plan he promised a "sustained endeavor to develop the country's resources and economy, in particular roads, water resources, heavy and light industry, and self-sufficient agriculture."[31] Faisal's political rhetoric and strategy was orchestrated partly for public consumption. It represented a response to the growing social discontent that had first emerged in the 1950s and that continued to find expression in the early 1960s. That Faisal determined a public declaration of his intent was necessary was remarkable.[32] Never before had the kingdom's rulers felt publicly accountable to the people and communities over whom it ruled, at least not to those who held no positions of power or influence. The ten-point program proved only the first such public statement, reflecting a new political reality in Saudi Arabia in which the government would have to respond to public pressure, at least appearing to be interested in ameliorating grievances and justifying its authority. Just as important, the ten-point program made clear to both the public and the rest of the royal family the "development"-focused political strategy that would be at the heart domestic policy for at least two decades.

After the mid-1960s development became much more than the pursuit of technological projects or the construction of big infrastructure. It also became a narrative that detailed the significance of the government's role in bringing about material, scientific, and technological progress. Development, then, was also ideological and was cast as part of what it meant to be a citizen in Saudi Arabia. Development discourse took shape in various forms including in the print media as well as glossy publications that various ministries published in the late 1960s and 1970s. From the perspective of the rulers, although development

---

[31] Vassiliev, *The History of Saudi Arabia*, 365.

[32] According to Vassiliev, in a major speech delivered in al-Taif on September 6, 1963, Faisal listed the projects that were to be given priority: development of a telephone network, roads and airports; settling of the Bedouin; a reduction in water charges; the construction of a metallurgical works, an oil processing plant in Jidda and a paper and pulp mill; prospecting for and exploitation of other mineral resources; opening a college of petroleum and minerals; and a reduction in electricity prices (*The History of Saudi Arabia*, 366).

continued to be mostly about strengthening their power, development discourse was an effort to mask this. The narrative sought to deemphasize the actual processes of state building, the centralization of power, and the subordination of citizens to the Saudi authority.

In 1964 the Saudi Agricultural Bank honored the new monarch for coming to understand the importance of becoming modern, citing that "it is in the context of the complete renaissance (*al-nahda al-shāmala*) that brings civilization to life in the kingdom thanks to the stewardship of the wise leader, his highness King Faisal, whose government focused on paving the way for development of the agricultural sector in all its aspects, which ensures that it will develop and flourish."[33] Madawi al-Rasheed has written that Faisal cultivated "a vision that Saudi Arabia can import technological expertise and modernize economically while remaining faithful to authentic Islam" and that he adopted a "discourse of modernization within an Islamic framework."[34] Even after Faisal's death, this pattern continued. Saudi Arabia's *Second Development Plan*, for the period 1975–9, noted that its first goal was to "maintain and preserve the religious and moral values of Islam." With this made clear, the plan put equal emphasis on economic growth, reducing dependence on oil, developing human resources, promoting social stability, and developing the physical infrastructure.[35]

Agriculture and the environment more generally were important areas in which the state expanded the meaning of development. Agricultural loans, water subsidies, and other forms of development work were framed as part of a paternalistic order in which the government was responsible for caring for those in its charge. The kingdom's leaders also thought of it as a contractual relationship. The state also engaged in the production of a narrative that publicized government-led efforts, marketing the kingdom and its development program to the citizens. The government's narrative made clear that the kingdom's leaders expected something in return, most importantly that those over whom they ruled would accept development work in exchange for the consolidation of political power in the hands of the ruling elite. Published materials did not demand loyalty and political quiescence outright. Instead, the state placed the burden of responsibility on those who benefited from its generosity to take advantage of the opportunity, help themselves, and strengthen the nation and especially the national economy.

On February 9, 1965, King Faisal delivered a speech in Dammam, the administrative capital of the Eastern Province of Saudi Arabia, entitled "The

---

[33] SAB, 1964, 7.
[34] Al-Rasheed, *A History of Saudi Arabia*, 121–6.
[35] Ministry of Information, *Second Development Plan*, 4.

Duties Incumbent upon Us," in which he outlined the emerging development discourse. The king spoke about the various achievements that he, as "representative of the state [*dawla*]," claimed had been undertaken in the service of "our religion, our *umma* and our nation."[36] Although he noted that "all our hopes have not been realized" he used his address to discuss recent accomplishments and his vision for future progress. In his comments on agriculture, Faisal acknowledged the need for a strong farming foundation for the kingdom to feed itself. But the king also argued that the government expected farmer-citizens to act responsibly and work earnestly toward the goal of improving not only their lives, but the nation's as well. Unnerved by the growing expectation among many that government handouts would continue forever, the king stated that no longer would the government support those who abused state support. He threatened that there "may come a time when the government is unable to pay subsidies" to agriculturalists struggling to make their way.[37] The threat was most likely empty. That he made it at all make is nevertheless instructive. Saudi officials rarely appealed directly to Saudi citizens to bear some responsibility for the direction of future development. Faisal left little doubt that productivity was to become a measure of service to the state and the community.

Development came with multiple layers of expectation. Although citizens came to expect ongoing levels of government support, subsidy, and largesse, the state responded by articulating expectations in return. In this respect development fell something short of an ideological program, but it did serve as a package of meanings in which the central authorities hoped both to assert their authority and to encourage citizens to buy in. It is notable that at the heart of the compact was an understanding that development and Islam went hand in hand. They were seen not as contradictory or exclusive, but as mutually reinforcing, connected as part of a broader national project and set of meanings that made the kingdom, its people, and especially its rulers special. Rather than displacing Islam, development discourse integrated modernity and religion. In the first major academic study of Saudi development by a Saudi citizen written in the late 1970s, Fouad al-Farsy (Minister of Information from 1995 and Minister of Culture and Information between 2003 and 2005) summed it up nicely on the cover of his book *Saudi Arabia: A Case Study in Development*. He wrote that "Saudi Arabia, the only nation to use the

---

[36] King Faisal Ibn Abd al-Aziz, "The Duties Incumbent upon Us," in *Da'wat al-haqq: al-majmu'a al-kāmila li-khitābāt wa aqwāl wa ahadīth sāhib al-jalala al-malik Faisal bin 'Abd al-'Aziz*, al-Juz' al-Thani (Riyadh: Dar al-Faisal al-Thaqāfiyya), 1.

[37] King Faisal Ibn Abd al-Aziz, "The Duties Incumbent upon Us," 5.

Holy Qu'ran as a State Constitution, is adjusting well to the conditions of the twentieth century while sustaining its distinctive Islamic identity. This demonstrates, therefore, that neither is Islam an obstacle in the way of progress, nor is secularism a pre-requisite for development."[38] Saudi celebrations of managing the modern/tradition divide were informed by their buying into and claiming to follow the basic assumptions of modernization theory, which also put forward the argument that the traditional had to be overcome to become modern. The Saudi variant, which valued Islam as traditional for ideological and political reasons, was modified and, from the perspective of Saudi proponents, improved. Because the kingdom's leaders also cited their religious stewardship as justification for political power, they could not reject the traditional altogether. Instead, they argued that they had achieved a special compromise, one that successfully balanced what others argued were incompatible conditions. The narrative has served to divert attention from the political objectives that it served. Timothy Niblock observed that "the explanation of developments in terms of a contest between traditionalism and modernism is frequently made use of within the context of Saudi Arabian politics to justify and validate courses of action whose principal motivation may lie elsewhere."[39]

At the level of state and national strategy, Saudi Arabian development was modeled on the basic principles of modernization theory held to be true in the West.[40] This was partly the result of close ties between foreign experts and Saudi decision makers. American and European engineers and scientists cooperated closely with their Saudi counterparts, shaping the way Saudi officials came to view development and the utility of modernization theory. The consequences of this interaction proved profound for the shaping of the Saudi state. Development and modernization not only served as modes of technical and political action, but assumed normative power as well. Although science and technology did not displace Islam as the kingdom's ideological centerpiece, they did come to possess a dogmatic importance of their own. The overlap of the work of foreign engineering and technical organizations and the training and emergence of a Saudi technocratic class after midcentury

[38] Fouad al-Farsy, *Saudi Arabia: A Case Study in Development* (New York: Kegan Paul International, 1978).

[39] Timothy Niblock, "Social Structure and the Development of the Saudi Arabian Political System," in Niblock, ed., *Social and Economic Development in the Arab Gulf* (New York: St. Martin's Press, 1980), 75.

[40] For more on modernization theory's history in the United States, see Nils Gilman, *Mandarins of the Future: Modernization Theory in Cold War America* (Baltimore: Johns Hopkins University Press, 2007); and David C. Engerman, Nils Gilman, and Mark H. Haefele, eds., *Staging Growth: Modernization, Development and the Global Cold War* (Amherst: University of Massachusetts Press, 2003).

also helped in the construction of technical expertise as one of the bases that helped augment state authority. Expertise became a marker that distinguished the state and state officials from regular citizens. This was true in the state bureaucracy, where midlevel officials determined the distribution of agricultural loans and the uses that they could be put to, participated in the design of development projects, and influenced their operation. It was also true at the heights of power. Successive Saudi monarchs came to characterize themselves as the state's "chief modernizers." The claims by almost every king after Abd al-Aziz to being the nation's chief modernizer was part of a political strategy to deflect threats to authority and to specifically usurp the political credibility of those who claimed the need for the sharing of political power in the interest of becoming modern. The identification of Saudi kings as the principal forces for technological change was part of their broader political strategy.

Symbolically, linking kings with modernity and development also underscored the connection between technical expertise and political authority. Saudi rulers came to be seen not only as the stewards of Islam but also as the engines of progress. By extension, Saudi as well as foreign engineers and technocrats served as extensions of the authority of the king. Expertise was not just an alternative expression or manifestation of political authority. Rather, it was a particularly important variety of political authority, one that assumed significance because it was connected to the actual operation of the physical systems that engineers and scientists designed and built in Saudi communities. As the state initiated massive technological works, it reshaped not only nature and society, but more importantly the relationship between the two, and, the state's relationship to both. Saudi Arabian citizens, even though some resisted or responded in unpredictable ways to the construction of technical networks, still had little choice but to deal with the new material and administrative realities wrought by them. As a result they became reliant not only on the rules, regulations, and authority of government officials and agencies, but also on their expertise and knowledge about how systems operated. Technology and expertise, then, also generated networks of dependency that connected citizens to the state, further reinforcing not only the government's authority but also the belief that it was distinct.

Although the central government and those who drove both domestic and foreign policy attempted to define and control the discourse about Saudi modernity and development, they proved unable to fully do so. State-led attempts to construct ideas of the nation as well as the meanings of technology, development, and modernity did shape the scope and the general character of discussions about the nation, but they did not contain them. After all, the government alone possessed the funds and means to match developmentalist rhetoric with practice and in particular with the building of large technological systems. Talk of progress and especially the promotion of the idea that the state sought to serve society and at least partly the interests of citizens provided a platform and a framework for them to respond to it. After midcentury, it also raised their expectations. Subsequently, at least in some communities, development and modernity took on multiple and contested meanings as citizens attempted to make sense of their citizenship. As has been the case with developing states elsewhere, expectations in Saudi Arabia were often hard to meet, which led to frustration about the failure of modernity and even the generation of confrontational political tendencies. Residents in the kingdom responded in various ways, including acceptance and resistance. Perhaps the most spectacular example of resistance came in the Eastern Province in 1979, when tens of thousands of the region's frustrated Shiites broke out in rebellion. Although their frustration had much to do with their second-class status and the pains of religious discrimination, it also had much to do with their having been neglected by the development rush. Saudi Arabians understood early on the political consequences, some intended and some unintended, of the introduction and construction of new technologies. These understandings helped energize the disparate responses, including generating political dissent that specifically targeted the failures and dislocations of Saudi Arabia's national development program.

Much of the support, particularly the emphasis on development discourse, receded from the foreground after the late 1970s. Pressure from religious radicals and conservatives, culminating in the siege of the Mecca Mosque in 1979, compelled Saudi Arabia's leaders to emphasize their religious bona fides and to at least reduce their efforts to cultivate an image of themselves as modernizers. Technopolitics and the importance of pursuing modernity did not disappear, but the state's emphasis was redirected toward Islam. In the following three decades, science and technology have taken back seats in public discourse and imagination. Although the state has provided material support for infrastructure and important technical projects, the pace of development work slowed considerably. This was partly the result of a drop in oil prices after the bust of the mid-1980s. But it was also a reflection of a new political reality in the kingdom, in which religious forces strong-armed the state to rethink its development strategy.

Thirty years later, with the construction of KAUST and King Abdullah's strong, albeit cautious, insistence that science and technology will once again factor politically and symbolically in Saudi Arabia, it is more than a little noteworthy that the kingdom is both looking forward and turning back the clock. Like Faisal before him, Abdullah has determined that not only are science, technology, and development areas in which the country's longer term interests might be better served, but that they are also powerful political tools that may allow the state to reestablish its authority at the expense of more austere religious powers.

4

Enforcing and Reinforcing the State's Islam

The Functioning of the Committee of Senior Scholars

Nabil Mouline

The historical alliance that was established between Muhammad b. 'Abd al-Wahhab (d. 1792) and Muhammad b. Su'ud (d. 1765) and gave birth to the Saudi state was accompanied by a "division of labor" between the political authority and the religious authority. Ibn 'Abd al-Wahhab, his descendants, and his disciples inherited the socio-religious domain, while Ibn Su'ud and his successors would monopolize the political domain. This theoretically laid the ground for the existence of two distinct spheres, apparently autonomous. Yet this was only apparent, for during the entirety of Saudi-Wahhabi history, these spheres have overlapped, each vying for "control" over the other.

During the second half of the eighteenth century, the charismatic figure of Ibn Abd al-Wahhab, the founder of the Hanbali-Wahhabi movement, dominated the politico-religious domain of central Arabia and its periphery. However, this pattern was reversed during the nineteenth century with the advent of the second Saudi state, as a consequence of the state's fiscal monopoly, claim to legitimate violence, and active religious policy.[1] This desire to seize power, exerted by the political sphere over the religious sphere, was accelerated after the final consolidation of the Saudi state under King 'Abd al-'Aziz (1902–53) in 1932 and with the influx of oil revenues.

Henceforth, the political power would attempt to "unify" all authority around a central pole, breaking the historical balance of the Saudi

---

[1] The adoption of the religious title of *imam* by the Emir Faysal b. Turki (1834–8 and 1843–65), which had until then only been held by Ibn 'Abd al-Wahhab, demonstrates this well. See Nabil Mouline, *Les Clercs de l'islam: Autorité religieuse et pouvoir politique en Arabie Saoudite (18ᵉ-21ᵉ S.)* (Paris: PUF, 2011), 111–17. An Arabic translation of this book is available under the title *'Ulama' al-islam: Binyat wa tarikh al-mu'assasa al-diniyya fī al-Su'udiyya bayna al-qarnayn 18 wa 21* (Beirut: Arab Network for Research and Publishing, 2011). This has been published in English as *The Clerics of Islam: Religious Authority and Political Power in Saudi Arabia* (New Haven, CT: Yale University Press, 2014).

sociopolitical structure. This attempt provoked the unprecedented "opposition" – although it remained symbolic as we shall see – of the ulama of the Hanbali-Wahhabi establishment during the 1950s and 1960s. This said, the same ulama never ceased to provide support to the political power, legitimizing and even sanctifying its actions. This first symbolic friction between the guardians of the legitimizing discourse and the political power has pushed the latter to strive for the definite subjugation of the former, to avoid the emergence of an opposition in the medium run. Nevertheless, this "monopolistic" enterprise allowed the religious establishment to take advantage of state resources to modernize its structures and improve its control over the "market of salvation."

In this chapter we will examine how the Saudi political authority attempted to control the Hanbali-Wahhabi ulama by setting up certain political-religious institutions inspired by the Egyptian model. The most notable of these institutions is the Committee of Senior Scholars (*Hay'at kibar al-'ulama'*) created in 1971. Less than a half century after its creation, the Committee of Senior Scholars has imposed itself as the second major legislative body in the country, next to the Council of Ministers, and the principal legitimizing power behind political actions. The importance of this pivotal institution for the Saudi political authority prompted the latter to try to control its access[2] and direct its actions to avoid any trouble.

The objective of this chapter is to analyze the structure and working mechanisms of the Committee of Senior Scholars, by putting it into historical perspective. This will allow us to gauge the extent to which the political authority controls this decision-making body.

A BRIEF HISTORICAL BACKGROUND

The death of King 'Abd al-'Aziz in 1953 was followed by a period of instability, which corresponded to the reign of King Su'ud (1953–64). During this transitional period, the kingdom encountered great difficulties due to the archaic nature of its political and administrative structures, the incapacity of the king to manage the affairs of the state, and the struggle for power between different factions within the royal family (the two most important factions were respectively led by King Su'ud and his heir apparent Faysal).[3]

---

[2] On this question see Nabil Mouline, "Les oulémas du palais: le parcours des membres du Comité des grands oulémas," *Archives de sciences sociales des religions* 149 (2010): 229–53.

[3] Alexander Bligh, *From Prince to King: Royal Succession in the House of Saud in the Twentieth Century* (New York, 1984); Nabil Mouline, "Pouvoir et transition générationnelle en Arabie Saoudite," *Critique internationale* 46 (2010): 125–46.

At the international level, the rivalry with Egypt for regional hegemony, which started during the second half of the 1920s, was getting more and more intense with the rise to power of Jamal 'Abd al-Nasser.[4] Egyptian influence on Saudi Arabia became apparent at the internal level with the emergence of several socialist and pan-Arabist movements that called for constitutional reforms and even for regime change. Those reformist and modernist ideas even attracted members of the royal family, some of whom established the Movement of Free Princes at the beginning of the 1960s.[5]

The extent of Egypt's influence pushed the king to repress the socialist movements by relying on religious and conservative elements, before allying himself, later, with the Movement of Free Princes so as to better stand up to his brother Faysal and his allies. The presence of these "leftist atheists" could only upset the members of the religious establishment and a significant portion of the royal family.[6]

The ulama, who feared for their future and autonomy, leaned toward Faysal's faction. Led by the Grand Mufti Muhammad b. Ibrahim Al al-Shaykh (d. 1969), the ulama addressed, in 1962, a letter of admonition to King Su'ud, calling for the right to veto all decrees or decisions approved by the Council of Ministers. This right of veto would allow the ulama to check whether royal decisions conformed to the Islamic law.[7] In the domain of international affairs, the ulama promulgated a fatwa forbidding the king to attend the nonaligned conference in Belgrade in 1961, justifying this with the fact that Yugoslavia, the country hosting the conference, was an "atheist" communist country.[8] Consequently, the king declined to participate in the conference so as not to offend these opinion leaders who could easily harm his image, using their countless societal connections, and so as not to encourage them to join the camp of his brother and rival, Faysal.

The ulama continued their "incursion" into the political domain, reserved traditionally for the royal family, by actively participating in the struggle for power between Su'ud and Faysal. Haunted by the idea of *fitna*, or great discord, which could destroy the Saudi state and de facto put an end to the hegemony of the Hanbali-Wahhabi discourse in the Saudi social sphere, the religious leaders finally decided to ally themselves with the family faction led by the princes Faysal and Fahd, who they hoped would take control of the situation.

---

4 Ghassan Salamé, *al-Siyasa al-kharijiyya li-l-mamlaka al-'arabiyya al-Su'udiyya mundhu 1945* (Beirut: Ma'had al-inma' al-'arabi, 1980), 617–40.
5 David Holden and Richard Johns, *La maison Saoud* (Paris: Ramsay, 1982), 195–276.
6 Gerald de Gaury, Faisal, *King of Saudi Arabia* (London: A. Baker, 1966), 91–2.
7 Alexei Vassiliev, *The History of Saudi Arabia* (London: Saqi Books, 2000), 359–60.
8 *Middle East Record* (Jerusalem: Israel Universities Press, 1961), 2:427.

On March 29, 1964, the country's main ulama issued a fatwa ordering King Su'ud to transfer full power to his brother Faysal. Seven months later, on October 2, 1964, sixty-five ulama gathered at the residence of the Grand Mufti before meeting with the leading princes who were attending a council meeting. The twenty most prominent ulama issued another fatwa dethroning King Su'ud and installing, de jure, Faysal as king (1964–75).[9]

Contrary to appearances, this intrusion of the ulama into the political affairs of the country was not voluntary. Prince Faysal and his supporters directed them to discredit the policies of King Su'ud and to provide religious legitimacy for the deposition. The fatwas of the ulama would consecrate only the declarations, written and oral, of the proponents of Prince Faysal. This temporary intrusion was therefore engineered by Faysal, who continued, once on the throne, to call upon the ulama in cases of need. Thus the apparent connivance between the ulama and the royal family could not conceal the fact that the royal family had been trying, since the beginning of the 1940s, to control the Hanbali-Wahhabi establishment and especially to amputate a certain number of its prerogatives, most notably in the legislative, judicial, and educational fields.

Since 1953, Faysal, as crown prince, prime minister, and subsequently as king, had been leading a battle on two fronts: on the one hand, an internal battle to preserve and reinforce the power of the royal family, and, on the other hand, an external battle against Egypt for hegemony in the region. At the internal level, Faysal initiated a program of budgetary austerity, projects to improve the infrastructures of the state, and policies aiming at the development of the educational system and the institutionalization of the legal system. At the regional level, he launched a policy of "Islamic Solidarity" that opposed socialist and pan-Arabist ideologies by creating the Muslim World League and the Organization of the Islamic Conference.[10]

Although the ulama looked favorably upon these initiatives toward "Islamic Solidarity," which would allow them to spread their influence to the whole of the Sunni world,[11] King Faysal's domestic policies were far less agreeable to them. Faisal's domineering policy, which required the adoption of positive

[9] *Umm al-Qura*, no. 2045, 1–2 ; Amin Sa'id, *Faysal al-'azim* (Beirut: Dar al-Katib al-'Arabi, 1965), 64–5 and 87–8; Amin Sa'id, *Tarikh al-dawla al-su'udiyya* (Beirut: Dar al-Katib al-'Arabi, 1965), 3:301–9.

[10] Gilles Kepel, *Jihad: Expansion et déclin de l'islamisme* (Paris: Gallimard, 2003), 89–92; 'Abd al-'Aziz al-Suwayyigh, *al-Islam fi al-siyasa al-kharijiyya al-su'udiyya* (Riyadh: Institute of Diplomatic Studies, 1992), 83–93.

[11] Muhammad b. Ibrahim Al al-Shaykh, *Fatawa wa rasa'il* (Mecca: Matba'at al-hukuma, 1978), no. 4539–6.

laws, went against the principles and interests of the ulama. Indeed, other than the fact that they believed that the adoption and application of positive law was contrary to religious precepts and constituted a grave sin, if not an act of impiety, they were aware that this "innovation" would facilitate the emergence of a legal system and judicial power parallel to their own and completely out of their control. The end of the monopoly of the Hanbali-Wahhabi establishment in the legal and judicial domains threatened not only to diminish their influence but to end their autonomy altogether.

This situation prompted the ulama to gather around Grand Mufti Muhammad b. Ibrahim Al al-Shaykh, beginning in 1955. Until his death in 1969, the Grand Mufti constantly opposed the royal decisions to create "civil" judicial institutes and to issue codes inspired by positive laws.

From 1956 onward, the Grand Mufti contested the legality of the creation of courts and chambers of commerce in charge of preparing the cases for and deciding on litigation in the financial and commercial domains.[12] He affirmed that only Islamic tribunals are competent to handle litigation, owing to the "transcendental and eternal" superiority of Islamic law over human law. Relying on these human institutions would be, according to him, nothing but a "path toward impiety, injustice, and immorality"[13] synonymous with "blasphemy deserving religious excommunication."[14] Ibn Ibrahim continued his "crusade" against positive laws by circulating in 1960 an epistle entitled "On the Application of Positive Laws" (*Tahkim al-qawanin al-wad'iyya*) in which he condemned, once more, the adoption of such laws, while excommunicating all those who sought to use them, with the exception of he "who, led by his desires and vices, adopts positive laws concerning a particular case, while recognizing that the divine law is the truth and that he has done evil and deviated from the straight path. He is not excommunicated, but he has nevertheless committed a sin graver than the major sins (*al-kaba'ir*), such as adultery, consumption of alcohol, stealing, false testimony, etc." There is no doubt that this last passage refers to the Saudi government, whose actions the Grand Mufti tries to justify while still maintaining some form of pressure.[15]

Muhammad b. Ibrahim inundated the king, the influential princes, and the high-ranking civil servants with letters reminding them that Islamic tribunals

---

[12] Ibid., nos. 4037 and 4039. The chambers of commerce have many other functions such as organizing private sector interests, providing business support services, and validating documents. Their dispute tribunals consist of a small unit within a larger structure.

[13] Ibid., no. 4033.

[14] Ibid., no. 4038.

[15] We must not forget that, even while criticizing this political aspect of the Saudi government, the grand mufti never stopped supporting and defending it. Ibid., no. 3868.

are capable of presiding over all litigation, including civil, criminal, administrative, and commercial. Hence, the new "civil" judicial institutions and their codes were pointless.[16] In addition, he refused to confirm the decisions taken by those bodies whenever he could, claiming that their rulings were not grounded in Islamic law.[17] In addition, Ibn Ibrahim mobilized the whole of the Hanbali-Wahhabi establishment by inciting the ulama to use all the resources at their disposal (preaching, teaching, publishing, etc.) to defend Islamic law and its application and to attack positive laws and their application.[18]

With great tenacity, Muhammad b. Ibrahim continued his fight, condemning, one by one, the civil service code, the labor law, and the Committee for the Resolution of Litigation,[19] without ever succeeding in swaying the government.[20] Rather than giving up, however, he finally decided to change his strategy. Instead of vainly calling on the government to suppress these institutions, Muhammad b. Ibrahim adapted to the situation by trying to control these new institutions through the appointment of ulama and Hanbali-Wahhabi dignitaries as the heads of these bodies, while marginalizing judges with a modern educational background.[21] From then on, this became the central strategy of the Hanbali-Wahhabi establishment as a whole, allowing it to take over a number of institutions.

The positions of Muhammad b. Ibrahim show that the Hanbali-Wahhabi establishment during the 1950s and 1960s was above all seeking to maintain a certain balance and to prevent its political partner from removing its legal and judicial prerogatives. Far from opposing the government, the ulama defended, on the one hand, what was, to them, a religiously just cause, and, on the other hand, protected their own status, corporate privileges, and even existence.

The rulers could not be indifferent to the clerics, given their unity and the energetic way in which they defended their interests. Although symbolic and without real impact, the criticisms of the clerical body of the government's policies were undoubtedly considered by the royal family as a precedent that

---

[16] Ibid., nos. 4037, 4039, 4040, and 4048 ; Muhammad b. Qasim, *al-Durar al-saniyya fi al-ajwiba al-najdiyya* (Riyadh, 2004), 16:204–19.

[17] Ibid., nos. 4049–53.

[18] Ibid., nos. 4035 and 4041.

[19] Ibid., nos. 4042, 4043, 4045, 4046, 4047, and 4048. 'Abd Allah b. Humayd, principal disciple of Ibn Ibrahim and judge of the province of Hijaz, wrote a violent diatribe against the labor law. See Ibn Qasim, *al-Durar al-saniyya*, 16:233–313.

[20] It is interesting to note that, regardless of his condemnation of the civil service code, the grand mufti did not hesitate to use it to further the interests of the religious scholars who held public functions. See Ibn Ibrahim, *Fatawa wa rasa'il*, nos. 421 and 1194.

[21] Ibid., no. 4044.

could have serious consequences in the future.[22] In addition to this purely con-
junctural factor, there is another, structural one. Any process of state building
requires the emergence of a central authority that implements a homogenizing policy in all areas. Since the (re-)unification of the kingdom in 1932,
the monarchy engaged in this dynamic, which was accelerated in the 1950s
and 1960s. However, this orientation was impeded by the will of the Hanbali-
Wahhabi establishment, which sought to preserve its autonomy and privileges
in accordance with the tradition of the division of labor between religious
and political authorities. Like most Arab countries at the time, more or less
inspired by Egypt,[23] the Saudi monarchy seriously considered controlling the
clerics to be able to act freely in the institutional domain and to better deploy
their religious authority for its own purposes.[24]

In the religious domain, it seems that the fundamental objective of the
monarchy was to end the monopoly of the Grand Mufti and destroy the vertical structure of the establishment he led. The desire to create a Department of
Justice, a Supreme Judicial Council, a public prosecutor, and a central authority issuing fatwas and the reform of the Committee for Promoting Good and
Preventing Evil from 1962 did not simply aim at "the improvement of public
service." These institutions were meant to fragment the legal-religious space.
The aim was to impose a form of collegiality within the religious establishment, that is to say, to create a horizontal structure, like the organization of the
royal family itself. Some prominent members of the ruling family, including
Prince Faysal, did not appreciate the "opinionated" religious authority that
could, were it to be controlled by ambitious hands, become a menace to the
political authority.

The bureaucratization of the legal and religious fields would not be completed until 1971, however. Two reasons explain this lag. First, from 1962 to
1964, Faysal was helped by the ulama in his struggle for power, as we noted
above. Furthermore, during the labor riots, which lasted from 1962 to 1966,
and the troubles that followed the creation of the first television station in
Saudi Arabia in 1965, the ulama firmly supported the royal authority. The
second reason is linked to the person of Muhammad b. Ibrahim, Grand Mufti

---

[22] The jihadists and the Saudi Islamic opposition used these fatwas and the writings of Muhammad b. Ibrahim to delegitimize and even excommunicate the Saudi state. See, for example,
Abu Muhammad al-Maqdisi, *al-Kawashif al-jaliyya fi kufr al-dawla al-su'udiyya*, available on
www.almaqdese.net, and Muhammad al-Mas'ari, *al-Adilla al-qat'iyya 'ala 'adam shar'iyyat
al-dawla al-su'udiyya* (London, 1997), available on http://www.alhramain.com.

[23] Malika Zeghal, *Les gardiens de l'islam, les oulémas d'Al Azhar dans l'Égypte contemporaine*
(Paris: Presses de Sciences-Po, 1996), 91–130.

[24] *Umm al-qura*, 1944 (Nov. 9, 1962), 1–6.

and maternal uncle of King Faysal, who was, if not as important, at least very respected and did all he could to oppose the bureaucratization policies of the government.

On his side, Muhammad b. Ibrahim put in place a certain number of institutions to reinforce the position of the religious establishment and to keep the political power at bay. From the 1950s onward, he founded institutes of religious sciences (*al-ma'ahid al-'ilmiyya*), which were inspired by a similar Egyptian model. These were religious high schools designed to groom students in accordance with the most orthodox precepts of Hanbali-Wahhabism, at least in theory.[25] To allow the graduates of these institutes to continue their studies, he created the Faculty of Islamic Studies and the Faculty of Arabic Language in 1954, both important kernels of the Islamic University of Riyadh (Jami'at al-imam Muhammad b. Su'ud al-islamiyya).[26] After one year, the mufti put in place the House of the fatwa "House Fatwa" (*dar al-ifta'*), a body in charge of issuing legal opinions, designating the imams of the mosques of the kingdom, managing the Saudi Library, censoring imported works to ensure they were "orthodox," and fulfilling the role of legal courts, among other functions.[27] Twelve years later, Ibn Ibrahim completed this program by founding the Higher Institute of the Judiciary (*al-Ma'had al-'ali lil-qada'*).[28]

Based on the scanty information available, it seems that Muhammad b. Ibrahim was attempting to prevent at all costs the intervention of the political authority in the religious space. And recognizing that none of his sons or disciples had the charisma necessary to replace him at the head of the religious establishment, at least in the short term, he undertook to establish a collective leadership to stay ahead of King Faysal and his entourage. Only months before his death, Ibn Ibrahim finished designing the Senior Council of Scholars (Majlis kibar al-'ulama'), whose budget had been approved by the government.[29] This shows that, until the last moments of his life, he felt a great sense of responsibility for the future of the clerical establishment he led.

The work of Muhammad b. Ibrahim is unprecedented in the history of Hanbali-Wahhabism. It was indeed the first attempt to institutionalize what until them had been personal and informal. In sum, the Grand Mufti also aspired to create a modern religious institution. His death in 1969 marked the end of an era in Hanbali-Wahhabism. King Faysal gave final shape to the once pyramidal organization of the religious elite by dispersing all the functions

---

[25] *Al-Da'wa*, no. 659 (1978), 7.
[26] Jami'at al-imam Muhammad b. Su'ud, *al-Kitab sanawi li-'am 1394*, 43, 65.
[27] *Umm al-qura*, no. 1565 (May 13, 1955), 2.
[28] *Umm al-qura*, no. 2079 (June 16, 1965), 1, 4; *Risalat al-ma'ahid al-'ilmiyya*, no. 7, 1391–2, 56–9.
[29] *Al-Kitāb al-ihsa'i al-sanawī 1970*, table 10/4.

previously held by the Grand Mufti: the Ministry of Justice, the Ministry of Islamic Affairs, the Supreme Judicial Council, and the Committee of Senior Scholars were all created in 1971. Finally, the function of Grand Mufti was suppressed and would be reestablished only in 1993.

This enterprise did not seek to bureaucratize the clerics, as was the case in other Arab countries, or to marginalize and weaken them, but only to fragment the religious authority to better control this intellectual instrument par excellence of political domination and use it at will if necessary. We should not forget that in fact since the emergence of the Saudi state the religious leaders were part of its political and administrative apparatus.[30] The monarchy had therefore no need to bureaucratize them, contrary to the claims made by other scholars.[31] Furthermore, the transition from a centralized monocephalic institution to a fragmented and headless organization was made possible through the charisma of King Faysal. The success of his policy of Islamic solidarity and demonstrations of piety, coupled with the fact that he was a descendent, from his mother's side, of Muhammad b. 'Abd al-Wahhab, bestowed upon him, in the eyes of the population, great religious legitimacy. The explosion of oil prices in 1973 came to top it all.

Yet, instead of weakening the ulama, this period of marginalization allowed them to make their entry finally into "modernity" by gaining impressive infrastructure (colleges, universities, high schools, NGOs, etc.) and to open up to other religious institutions. Indeed, they initiated the interreligious dialogue with the Vatican,[32] used the organizational experience of the Muslim Brothers installed in Saudi Arabia to build modern religious institutions,[33] and initiated contact with the University of al-Azhar in Egypt.[34] In other words, the clerical body adapted very quickly to this new situation by adopting a strategy that, just as before, allowed it not only to protect its interests by significantly

---

[30] Ibn Bishr, *'Unwan al-majd fi tarikh Najd* (Riyadh: Darat al-malik 'Abd al-'Aziz, 1982), I:174.

[31] Ayman al-Yassini, *Religion and State in the Kingdom of Saudi Arabia* (Boulder: Westview Press, 1985), 67–79; Joseph Kechichian, "The Role of the Ulama in the Politics of an Islamic State: The Case of Saudi Arabia," *International Journal of Middle East Studies*, no. 1 (1986): 53–71.

[32] There were between 1972 and 1974, five meetings between the ulama of the Hanbali-Wahhabi establishment and representatives of the Christian world and the Vatican. After a first interreligious meeting in Riyadh on March 22, 1972, the ulama took a tour of Europe, which included Paris on October 23, 1974, the Vatican on the October 25, Geneva on October 30, and Strasbourg on November 4.

[33] Gilles Kepel, *Fitna: Guerre au cœur de l'Islam* (Paris: Gallimard, 2004), 208–12; Stéphane Lacroix, "Les champs de la discorde: Une sociologie politique de l'islamisme en Arabie Saoudite," Doctoral Dissertation of the Institute of Political Studies, Paris, 2007, 187–218.

[34] A significant number of Hanbali-Wahhabi ulama obtained their doctoral degrees from al-Azhar.

strengthening its social base and organizational frameworks, but also to impose itself, when the opportunity arose, as a reliable and durable partner for the political authority. Indeed, the sudden death of King Faysal in 1975, the messianic uprising in Mecca in 1979 – which will be discussed later – the Islamic revolution in Iran and the Shiite insurgency in the province of al-Ahsa, also in 1979, the decline in oil prices from 1982 onward, and the "immoral" behavior of several influential members of the ruling family, to mention only the most significant events, affected the religious legitimacy of the House of Saud while undermining its legitimating discourse, centered on economic development, for many years to come. A return to old structures of power and authority turned out to be necessary. Thus the tacit alliance between the Al Saud and the ulama was reactivated in 1979.

Thereafter, the Committee of Senior Scholars, and the institutions that depended on it, directly served the Saudi dynasty, as much in the religious domain (by propagating Hanbali-Wahhabism) with the goal of spreading the prestige of Saudi Arabia to the whole Muslim world and even beyond, as in the political domain (by defending the social and political positions of the regime). The functions of the committee, however, remained unclear and included several gray zones. De jure, only a few elements describe these functions. We will take into account its de facto tasks as uncovered during our fieldwork.

THE STRUCTURES OF THE COMMITTEE OF SENIOR SCHOLARS

Although a rival of Egypt, Saudi Arabia always considered its neighbor as a model to be emulated. A large part of the Saudi institutions and laws imitated those of Egypt. This is because of the significant head start that Egypt had in terms of institutionalization, the prestige that came with this, and also the fact that several of the advisors of the Saudi dynasty were Egyptians. In terms of faith, al-Azhar was a model for the organization of religion throughout the Arab east. The Saudi Committee of Senior Scholars was consequently inspired by its older sibling, the Egyptian Committee of Senior Scholars, itself created in 1911.

The Egyptian Committee counted thirty ulama, belonging to the four Sunni legal schools. This committee was meant to teach the religious sciences and the Arabic language, to set the syllabi for religious education in schools, and to monitor teaching. It also had the liberty to promulgate its own fatwas and to censor any works deemed to violate Islamic norms. The members of the committee met once each month, or more often during exceptional circumstances. The presence of at least half of the committee's members was

required for the meeting to be deemed official. The decisions were taken
by majority vote. Clear conditions were laid out in writing describing the
procedure and guidelines for membership in the Egyptian committee: The
candidate must be at least forty-five years of age; he must have obtained at
al-Azhar the degree of '*alimiyya* – the equivalent of a doctoral degree; he must
have been a teacher, judge, or high-ranking civil servant in religious affairs; he
must respond to the moral criteria set by the committee; he must be elected
by the members of the committee by obtaining more than sixteen votes; he
must have written a work of reference in religious matters, history, or Arabic
literature; and he must have at least fifteen years of experience in the religious
domain.[35] The new members were therefore elected by incumbent members,
before being appointed by royal decree (the palace intervenes, it should be
pointed out, neither in the choice of new members nor in their eventual
dismissal). The Grand Shaykh, who is also a member of the committee, was
similarly elected by his colleagues.[36]

The practical role of the Egyptian committee was in fact rather small,
and its members were concerned only with the technical aspects of religious
education, religious rituals, and religious ethics. The committee very rarely
intervened in public affairs, be they social or political. It was, in the end,
really nothing more than one of many bodies of scholars within al-Azhar. The
Egyptian Committee of Senior Scholars, called Hay'at kibar al-'ulama', did
change its name twice: The first time it was called Jama'at kibar al-'ulama',
and then, after the reform of 1961, it took the name of Majma' al-buhuth
al-islamiyya.[37]

King Faysal chose, for the committee that he created in 1971, to use the name
the Egyptian committee had used during the monarchy and by doing so was
able to distance himself from his rival Nasser. Royal order A/137, dated August
28, 1971, led to the creation a supreme religious body in Saudi Arabia called
the Committee of Senior Scholars (*Hay'at kibar al-'ulama'*) whose seventeen
members[38] are to be specialists of Islamic law.[39] This institution is meant to

---

35 Mujahid Tawfiq al-Jundi, "Hay'at kibar al-'ulama', safahatun matwiyya min tarikh al-Azhar,"
    al-Azhar 11 (1983): 1621–33.
36 'Abd al-Muta'al al-Sa'idi, "Ra'yun fi al-shart al-rabi' fi 'udw Hay'at kibar al-'ulama'," *al-Risala*,
    1945, no. 635, 2–3.
37 'Abd al-'Azim al-Mat'ani, "Majma' al-buhuth al-islamiyya wa al-mahamm al-manuta
    bihi," *Majallat al-da'wa*, 1977, no. 13, 36–7 and al-Lajna al-'ulya li-l-ihtifal bil-'id al-alfi li-
    l-Azhar, *Majma' al-buhuth al-islamiyya: tarikhuhu wa tatawwuruhu*, Cairo: al-Azhar al-sharif,
    1983.
38 The royal order A/88 of May 29, 2001, stipulated that the number of members in the committee
    could not be inferior to 12 and not exceed 22.
39 *Umm al-Qura*, no. 2387, Sept. 3, 1971.

decide whether any given question asked by the king, or such and such point raised by the government, is in accordance with the Shari'a.[40]

The committee is composed of three bodies: the Council of the Committee of Senior Scholars (*Majlis hay'at kibar al-'ulama'*), the General Presidency of Religious Research, Preaching, and Guidance (*al-Ri'asa al-'amma li-idarat al-buhuth al-'ilmiyya wa al-da'wa wa al-irshad*) and, the Permanent Commission for Research [in religious matters] and the Issuing of Legal Rulings (*al-Lajna al-da'ima li-l-buhuth wa al-ifta'*). These three structures that form the committee have domains of competence that are distinct but nevertheless complementary. The council is active at the macrosocial level; the General Presidency takes care of macrosocial, microsocial, administrative, and international questions and is, so to say, the linchpin of the Committee of Senior Scholars. The Permanent Commission deals exclusively with individual behavior. Thus, the Saudi Committee of Senior Scholars disposes of more subbodies than its Egyptian counterpart (three as compared to one) but is composed of fewer members (between seventeen and twenty-one while the Egyptian Committee counted thirty). Finally, the Saudi committee enjoys more prerogatives than the Egyptian. The two, therefore, have little in common except for the name and a structure for collegiality. We will now attempt to describe the more specific structures, mechanisms, and prerogatives of the Saudi committee.

The Permanent Commission for Research [in religious matters] and the issuing of legal rulings acts exclusively at the microsocial level. Its members issue fatwas that deal with personal affairs. The questions discussed by the Permanent Commission are directly sent to the ulama by the population at large or are received by mail, telephone, or through the internet. The ulama answer all the questions: immediately in the case of questions asked face-to-face or by telephone, or without much delay in other cases. The most recurrent questions and those that preoccupy the population the most are discussed during weekly meetings that generally take place on Tuesdays and Thursdays.

The four to seven members (currently there are six)[41] who constitute the Permanent Commission are chosen from among the members of the committee.[42] The fatwas that are the most recurrent are collected and

---

[40] Since 1971, membership of the committee is open to ulama from the four Sunni Schools. However, the Hanbali-Wahhabi ulama dominate this institution for historical, sociological, and dogmatic reasons. See Nabil Mouline, *Les Clercs de de l'islam*, 223–58.

[41] The six current members of the Commission are Sālih al-Fawzān, 'Abd Allāh al-Mutlaq, 'Abd al-'Azīz āl al-Shaykh, Ahmad Sīr al-Mubāraki, Muhammad āl al-Shaykh, and 'Abd al-Karīm al-Khudayr.

[42] We should remark that the scholar 'Abd Allah b. Jibrin (d. 2009) was a member of the *ifta'* as a civil servant of al-Ri'asa al-'amma without ever being a member of the Committee of the Grand Scholars.

published at the end of the year. About twenty volumes and a CD-ROM
are available currently, and the whole is available for download on the internet on an important number of Arab-Islamic websites. Each deliberation for a
fatwa demands the presence of at least three members of the commission, and
the vote is decided by an absolute majority. In the case of a tie, the vote of the
president prevails. On the other days of the week, at least two ulama ensure
a daily presence to respond directly to the questions of the population.[43] The
ulama of the Permanent Commission are, as its name indicates, permanently
available and easy to reach.

The position of president rotated among the members from 1971 to 1975;
in 1975 a permanent president was designated, 'Abd al-'Aziz b. Baz (d. 1999).
Finally, since 1993,[44] it has been the Mufti of the Kingdom himself who has
served as president of the commission. It is noteworthy that the Permanent
Commission does not have the right to respond to questions regarding a field
other than the microsocial (i.e., questions on daily life). If it were to receive
such a question, it must prepare a memorandum of research on the matter and
send it to the Council of the Committee of Senior Scholars. Nevertheless, the
members of the commission[45] can on rare occasions sidestep this limitation
and provide an opinion on a macrosocial question of political importance.
For example, during the attack by Israel on Gaza in December 2008 the
commission published, on the internet, a condemnation of this war and called
for support for the people of Palestine.[46] It seems that the ulama took this
path and overlooked the normal process, which obliges them to submit all
macrosocial questions for approval by the Royal Cabinet (as we shall see), so
as to respond to popular expectations and without giving the government a
choice in the matter.

The General Presidency of Scholarly Research [in religious matters],
Preaching and Guidance, is the cornerstone of the committee. The purpose
of this body is to propagate the official ideology, to consolidate the prestige of
the kingdom, and to manage the administration of the Committee of Senior
Scholars. The General Presidency takes care of the "promotion, defense, and
propagation of Islam," but only a particular interpretation of Islam, that which
adheres to the Hanbali-Wahhabi doctrine, in the kingdom and abroad.

---

[43] To aid them, the members of the committee have at their disposal a cabinet director, a
secretary, and a researcher who is a graduate of theology.

[44] The post of Grand Mufti had been vacant since the death of Muhammad b. Ibrahim in 1969.

[45] The members of the Permanent Commission are also members of the Council of the Committee of Senior Scholars.

[46] http://www.alifta.com/bayan.aspx; http://www.alriyadh.com/2009/01/01/article399204.html.

The General Presidency also ensures the "coordination" between all the associations and organizations of preaching in Saudi Arabia. The goal of this "coordination" is in effect to control the statements of the preachers, which are often quite divisive. The General Presidency has given itself the mission of protecting and preserving Islamic thought, including of course the Hanbali-Wahhabi doctrine, by editing and publishing books on theology, jurisprudence, and preaching.[47] Most of these books are sold at low prices or are handed out for free at the exits of mosques, schools, and universities and are now available for free online. During the pilgrimage season, the General Presidency takes over the instruction and orientation of the pilgrims and visitors of the two sacred sites and takes advantage of these great gatherings to "proselytize," although this has become more and more discrete since 2001.

Within the kingdom, the General Presidency offers its support to students of the religious "sciences" by providing a number of scholarships and by giving free access to the libraries of the kingdom. To promote their world view, the senior ulama have been publishing, since 1975, a quarterly review – the *Review of Islamic Research* (*Majallat al-buhuth al-islamiyya*) – and have had a website since October 2007. Finally, the General Presidency controls the edition and printing of the Qur'an and has the power to censor books entering from abroad.

However, the situation changed in 1993 when a Ministry of Islamic Affairs, Preaching and Guidance was established. It inherited most of the prerogatives of the General Presidency. The latter, which henceforth bore the name of General Presidency of Religious Research and Issuing of Legal Rulings (*al-Ri'asa al-'amma li-l-buhuth al-'ilmiyya wa al-ifta'*), was to focus exclusively on managing the ideological authority of the Committee of Senior Scholars. The General Presidency thus remains in charge of the management of the *Journal of Islamic Research*, the website, the publication of the fatwas of the Permanent Committee, research, and the fatwas of the Council Committee of Senior Scholars, as well as the publication of theological and legal works (mostly classic Hanbali-Wahhabi books and those by members of the committee). That said, its main mission is the management of the large number of religious scholars and their relations with believers. Indeed, these scholars are responsible for answering thousands of socio-religious questions (those that members of the Permanent Committee are not able to answer), which arrive daily at the headquarters of the Presidency (referred to as *Dar al-Ifta'*), and prepare research papers on various topics at the request of the Grand Mufti

---

[47] The books most published by the General Presidency are those of Ibn Taymiyya, Ibn Qayyim al-Jawziyya, Ibn 'Abd al-Wahhab and his descendants, and those of the members of the Committee of Senior Scholars.

or members of the Committee of Senior Scholars. Since 1993, the General Presidency has been headed by the Grand Mufti, attended by a number of technocrats, including a vice-president who is the real head of the administrative apparatus.[48]

One should not see the creation of the Ministry of Islamic Affairs in 1993 as a lessening of the role of the religious establishment. This development was part and parcel of the process of institutionalization, rationalization, and optimization of the operations of the Hanbali-Wahhabi establishment so that it could address more effectively socio-political changes that were occurring in Saudi Arabia and in the world in the early 1990s. If the fall of the Berlin Wall offered Hanbali-Wahhabism tremendous opportunities for expansion, the Gulf War led to Islamist unrest, which forced the religious establishment, supported by the political authorities, to reorganize its structure for more effective control. The separation of the management of social and religious organizations (mosques, associations, printing and translation of the Qur'an, preaching, etc.) along with the human resources (imams and muezzins mosques, preachers, translators, administrators, etc.) from the ideological work properly allowed the official religious establishment to strengthen its position to sustain its social and religious privileges. In addition, the Ministry of Islamic Affairs has been directed since its creation by prominent members of the religious establishment: 'Abd Allah al-Turki (b. 1940), a member of the Committee of Senior Scholars and a very active scholar, and Salih Al al-Shaykh (b. 1958), the grandson of Muhammad b. Ibrahim.

The Council of the Committee of Senior Scholars acts at the macro-social level. The seventeen to twenty-one members of the council generally meet twice a year: once in Riyadh and once in Taif. They can also meet, in exceptional cases, wherever and whenever they choose, at the request of the president of the council after consulting the Royal Cabinet. Finally, they may also meet at the request of the Council of Ministers, presided over by the king or the crown prince. The position of president of the council rotated until 1993 among the five eldest members. Since then, the Mufti of the Kingdom has presided over the sessions of the council. A session cannot, in theory, be held except in the presence of at least two-thirds of the council's members.

The council generally deals with the social and political questions. The social issues that the council looks into can range from penal laws (drug and alcohol trafficking, capital punishment, etc.)[49] to civil law (marriage, divorce, inheritance, contracts, etc.). The council of the committee can also

[48] 'Abd 'Aziz b. Baz led this institution between 1975 and 1993.
[49] *Majallat al-Tadamun al-islami*, October 1988, 77–89.

respond to diverse and varied questions coming from, for example, the medical field (clinical death, abortion, pilgrimage, etc.)[50] or the economic field (bank interest, stock investments, etc.).[51] It goes without saying that they also accept opportunities to respond to questions relating to dogma and religious ritual.

THE GRAMMAR OF THE LEGITIMIZING MACHINE

As for the answers to political questions, their goal is to legitimize and defend the government's positions and, occasionally, to attack foreign governments and leaders of enemy states or rivals of the Saudi government. The Council of the Committee, for example, supported the unpopular decision of the Saudi government to call upon the help of American forces during the Gulf War. The council excommunicated and boycotted Ayatollah Khomeini and Saddam Hussein, branding them as "enemies of Islam." The Council of the Committee condemned the actions of the Saudi Islamist opposition at the beginning of the 1990s and then did the same for the operations of al-Qaeda in Saudi Arabia, denouncing its members as heretics. Finally, fatwas have been issued condemning suicide attacks and forbidding young Saudis to go fight in Iraq during the American occupation.

The Permanent Commission can entertain questions from individuals or from entities such as the Council of Ministers or even from universities. In 2005, for example, the Permanent Commission received a question from Prince Khalid Al Faysal on the matter of forced marriage.[52] The question, being of national importance and from a governor of a province, was immediately transferred to the Council of the Committee of Senior Scholars. All questions, even the ones transferred to the council, must be accompanied by a memorandum of research drafted by one of the members of the Permanent Commission (this research is often accomplished by a theology graduate working alongside the members of the commission). The Permanent Commission establishes its agenda after examining the entire roster of questions received. The agenda, once it arrives at the Royal Cabinet, is submitted to the veto of the king, who can decide to modify it. In other terms, all that precedes the royal decision amounts to proposal and suggestions, not final decisions.

It is evident from the above that this agenda is of considerable importance for the king since in the final analysis only questions authorized by the Royal Cabinet, which is presided over by the king, are addressed by the Committee

---

[50] *Majallat al-buhuth al-islamiyya,* 2000, no. 58, 379–380.
[51] *Majallat al-da'wa,* 2005, no. 1972, 28–30.
[52] *Al-Sharq al-awsat,* no. 9633.

of Senior Scholars. This control of the Royal Cabinet demonstrates the importance of the Committee of Senior Scholars, whose decisions provide legitimacy
for the power of the royal family.

In exceptional cases (essentially in cases of grave events that threaten the
stability of the country and the regime itself), the Committee of Senior Scholars is invited to organize an extraordinary session, and the agenda is imposed
directly by the Royal Cabinet. The idea behind this, as indicated, is to legitimize a specific decision or policy, to discredit an enemy of the regime in the
eyes of the public, or to condemn an event considered to be dangerous. The
capture of the Great Mosque in Mecca by the messianic group of Juhayman
al-'Utaybi in 1979,[53] the riots of the Iranian pilgrims in 1986, and the Iraqi
invasion of Kuwait in 1990 are the principal events for which the government
has solicited a fatwa from the scholars.

The secretary general of the Committee of Senior Scholars, who is not a
member of the committee, is a civil servant named directly by the Council of
Ministers to simplify the connection between the committee and the palace.[54]
This secretary general must, however, have done his share of religious studies. His work consists of making sure that the memoranda of research on the
questions to be addressed by the council are ready a month before the beginning of the session in which they are discussed. The secretary general must
also deliver this research, accompanied by the agenda, to the members of the
committee at least fifteen days before the start of the session. He plays the role
of the intermediary and is the eyes and ears of the government within this
politico-religious body.

Depending on the importance of the questions and their context, the ulama
can call on the expertise of specialists who are not themselves members of the
committee but who are able to explain technicalities regarding issues of science
or security, for example.[55] Concerning medical questions, they may call on
teams of doctors to organize seminars and write reports. To explain a point
or clear up a misunderstanding, the ulama can also have access to classified
documents, notably reports of the security services. Finally, for the less sensitive
files, the ulama are content to read the memoranda of research prepared by
the Permanent Commission and/or to look into decisions taken on the subject
by other Islamic decision-making bodies of the Muslim world, most notably
al-Azhar and the Council of Islamic Jurisprudence whose headquarters are in
Mecca.

---

[53] *Al-Da'wa*, no. 731, 1400, 8–9.
[54] Since its creation in 1971, the committee has known four secretary generals: Muhammad b.
'Awda, 'Abd al-'Aziz al-Falih, 'Abd al-'Aziz 'Abd al-Mun'im, and Fahd al-Majid.
[55] *Al-Da'wa*, no. 623, 1397, 6.

Following this phase of expertise gathering, the council engages in debate. Most of the ulama insist on the fact that the debates should be free and transparent when it comes to religious and social questions. Yet, when it comes to political questions, especially those relating to the legitimacy or the stability of the political authority, the answers become more evasive. This leads us to suppose that the ulama legitimize automatically, without discussion, the positions maintained by the government, even if this might hurt their own credibility – the support for the call on American forces in 1990 is the best illustration of this. Having said this, we should not interpret this support as a feudal loyalty toward the government, but rather as a form of association and alliance. In fact, we observe here political co-optation in its purest form. Thanks to government's support, the religious establishment maintains great influence over several domains in the social, judicial, and religious arenas. Thus, the scholars consider themselves to be part of the regime. This is due, in part, to the mentality of the Hanbali-Wahhabi ulama and also to their pragmatism. The ulama know that if the current regime, which supports them was to disappear, their status and privileges would probably be gravely altered.

Returning to our explanation of the council's processes and deliberations, after the debate the council votes. The vote, taken by show of hands, is decided by absolute majority. In the event of a tie, it is, in theory, the vote of the president that tips the balance. In practice, however, the vote is recast. In matters pertaining to social, judicial, and legal questions, the ulama have the right to vote yes or no. However, when it comes to political questions, which are debated during extraordinary sessions, they cannot express their objection other than to remain absent from the session, which can, of course, lead to their expulsion from the committee. However, there is no instance of such a punitive measure being taken.[56]

The royal decree of 1971, which is the only document that describes the workings of the committee, does not elaborate on the modalities of deliberation. It was thus only through interviews that we were able to construct and describe these modalities. One can distinguish two types of deliberations: the first being a declaration (*bayan*). The *bayan* is nothing more than a fatwa pertaining to a political question. Solicited by the political authority, the *bayan* defends the government's decisions and sanctifies its actions.[57]

---

[56] For an analysis of the claims of some observers about the refusal of several members of the Committee of Senior Scholars to sign a fatwa condemning the letter of admonishment addressed to King Fahd by Islamists in 1992, see Nabil Mouline, *Les Clercs de de l'islam*, 314–15.

[57] After the deliberations, a member of the Council of Senior Scholars proposes a first draft of the text and circulates it among the other members, each correcting it and passing it on. The final version must satisfy the majority. If, however, there is still dissatisfaction, individual scholars can add remarks at the end of the transmitted text (*tahaffuz* or *wijhat nazar*).

Second, there are the fatwas[58] that are issued about social, religious, judicial, or legislative questions. The fatwa can be of value only if it is approved by the Council of Ministers. That is to say, these legal opinions will go unheeded if the coercive force of the state does not enforce them. For example, in 2006 King 'Abd Allah asked the committee for a fatwa allowing for the building construction to enlarge a section (*mas'a*) of the Great Mosque in Mecca, so as to be able to welcome more pilgrims. After a study of the problem in a meticulous manner, the committee deemed that the enlargement was illegal on the basis of the scriptural sources.[59] Outraged by their answer, the king decided to solicit the opinion of other ulama in the Muslim world, who gave their approval for this project.[60]

CONCLUSION

The centrality of religious discourse as a social and legitimizing tool of the Saudi state has given the political authority a strong interest in controlling the agents of this discourse. This logic of supervision and instrumentalization of the religious authority has led to the bureaucratization of the ulama by creating a certain number of decision-making bodies of which the most important is the Committee of Senior Scholars. The grand prerogatives it disposes in the religious, social, and political domains explain why the political authority controls the points of access (formal and informal) to this body (a topic of a future study), its budget, and its agenda. This control over prerogatives of the committee is intended to prevent it from ever becoming a rival power or a locus of insubordination, especially during periods of transition or political crisis. That is to say, the objective of the political authority is less to control the religious discourse itself than it is to control the religious initiative. The proof of this is the almost absolute independence of the Committee of Senior Scholars and its different suborgans in the domain of religious salvation, which falls eminently within the framework and prerogatives of the Hanbali-Wahhabi school. The external control of the political domain does not really bother the ulama, who identify themselves openly as the "ulama of the political authority" (*'ulama' al-sultan*).[61] Cooperation with and obedience

---

[58] In certain cases, it is called *qarar* (legal decision) to give it a legal force.

[59] *Fatwa* no. 227, 22 Safar 1427.

[60] See http://www.aawsat.com/details.asp?section=1&article=468485&issueno=10742; http://www.aawsat.com/details.asp?section=1&article=469695&issueno=10753.

[61] 'Abd al-'Aziz Al al-Shaykh, *Kulluna 'ulama' sultan*, http://www.sohari.com/nawader_v/fatawe/almufti.html.

to the prince (*waliyy al-amr*) are fundamental to Hanbali doctrine since without the coercive force of the state the law cannot be applied. Furthermore, the spiritual and temporal interests of the Hanbali-Wahhabi establishment are intrinsically linked to those of the regime to the point that, if the latter were to fall, the domination of Hanbali-Wahhabi doctrine in the Saudi territories – which are in Islamic terms religiously diverse – would almost certainly be vitiated if not wholly undermined.

PART 2

Oil

5

From Price Taker to Price Maker? Saudi Arabia and the World Oil Market[1]

Giacomo Luciani

OIL PRICE VOLATILITY – OLD AND NEW

Commodity prices are notoriously volatile, and oil is no exception. The structural volatility of commodity prices is a key reason why the economic development literature has concluded that specialization in commodity exports is not a valid recipe for development. The negative effect of volatility is linked to the fact that prices, and consequently revenues, may become unpredictable, foiling the possibility of rational investment and fiscal policies. Such long-term volatility – qualitatively different from short-term volatility, which occurs in a predictable pattern – constitutes a clear dilemma for commodity producers and users alike.

In the case of oil, price volatility was extreme in the early stages of the industry (at the end of the nineteenth century), until the market power of the leading players (initially, the Standard Oil Company in the United States; then the "Seven Sisters," controlling, through interlocking interests in upstream consortia, the bulk of global oil reserves), succeeded in maintaining "market discipline" for an extended period of time (about 1900 to 1970). "Market discipline" prevented cheap Middle East oil from rushing to the market in excessively large volumes, which would have brought prices down to levels at which oil produced elsewhere in the world would have been driven out of the market. Instead, prices were kept sufficiently low and stable to progressively displace other primary fuels, and the share of oil expanded rapidly.

[1] An earlier version of this chapter was presented in November 2009 in Princeton at the conference on Saudi Arabia jointly organized by Princeton University's Institute for the Transregional Study of the Contemporary Middle East, North Africa and Central Asia and Sciences-Po Paris's Chaire Moyen Orient-Méditerranée with the support of the European Commission. The present version incorporates comments received at the conference as well as from several friends, including some active in the oil trading business.

The market power of the Seven Sisters was gradually eroded, until the tables were turned in 1973, and the power to determine "posted prices" shifted to OPEC. This led to a sudden rapid increase of prices over a relatively short period of time. More importantly, OPEC never succeeded in agreeing on a "long-term strategy" for prices, which would have offered a new paradigm for price predictability. Instead, prices were pushed up by a succession of political emergencies in 1973–80 (the Yom Kippur War, the Iranian Revolution, the onset of the Iraq-Iran War), and the organization simply attempted to consolidate the higher price level, with little attention paid to its sustainability in the longer term.

At that time Saudi Arabia dissented from the rest of OPEC and for a time sold its oil at a discount to the OPEC-supported posted price, but this was not a very successful experience (it simply created an advantage for the companies that were granted access to Saudi crude).

OPEC started enforcing quotas to defend the high level of prices at the same time as non-OPEC production was rapidly increasing. By 1985 the production of Saudi Arabia, which had exceeded 11 million barrels per day in 1981, was down to less than 4 million barrels per day. At that point the kingdom abandoned the posted price system, causing a sharp downward correction in prices. After a short episode based on netback pricing, the reference pricing regime was inaugurated, which is in force to this day.

The reference price system is therefore at least to some extent the consequence of the failure on the part of OPEC – and Saudi Arabia specifically within OPEC – to validly play the role of price maker. This negative historical experience still weighs heavily on the kingdom's reluctance to play a more active role in the formation of global oil prices.

An additional consequence of the flawed pricing policy adopted by OPEC in the late 1970s and early 1980s was that the market for the Brent pricing benchmark developed rapidly, alongside the older market for WTI, providing an enhanced platform for reference pricing.

Reference pricing means that the price for the main OPEC crude oils, which are not freely available for trading, is indexed to the price of freely traded crude oils – which are primarily Brent and WTI – with a relatively small differential set by the producer. The differential changes over time, but the oscillations in the underlying price of the reference crude are by far more important.

Why are major crude oils not available for trading? The standard answer is that that there is only one seller, and therefore no competition can exist. This is literally true if the national oil company of the producing country controls all production; in countries in which international oil companies operate and have access to equity oil, they might sell their oil at prices that differ from those practiced by the national oil company. However, this "competition" is likely to be limited and, perhaps more importantly, unlikely to be made public.

A further aspect is that major crude oils are sold to the final user (refiner) "spot," that is, at the moment when the cargo is loaded on a ship or even delivered to the receiving terminal: This makes reselling a cargo rather difficult and discourages the emergence of a secondary market, that is, a market on which crude oil is sold not by the original producer, but by a party that bought it from the original producer. Cargos can be sold on while underway, and in some cases crude oil can be sold to other buyers (nearby refineries, entrepôt trade) once it is delivered, but such transactions are bound to be irregular and will not generate a transparent and credible price signal.

That said, it is important to underline at the outset that a market for the major crude oils does not exist not because it is impossible to set one up, but because the producers do not wish their crude oils to be traded. Between 1973 and 1985 the producers attempted to impose a price – but having failed to do so, they shifted to the opposite extreme of almost entirely renouncing their exercising an influence on prices. The intermediate solution consisting of setting up a market in which producers would have a strong influence, yet falling short of total control, has not been attempted.

Once the decision was made to opt for reference pricing, a major boost was given to the existing markets, which became vehicles for hedging not just the crude oils that were traded on them, but also crude oils whose price was indexed to that of the traded crude oils. In other words, the markets for Brent and WTI became a valid platform for hedging the price of the vast majority of global oil production, which is not traded.

This development was instrumental in the success of future contracts and the birth of derivatives. Since the late 1980s, investors' interest in this market has progressively increased, attracting growing liquidity. Whether the inflow of liquidity per se is a cause of greater price instability is an issue that is hotly debated and will not be resolved any time soon.[2]

Neither is there clear consensus on whether volatility has been increasing over time. Volatility refers to the scope of oscillations of a variable around its

---

[2] The so-called flow of funds hypothesis, whose original proponent was, I believe, Ed Morse, has not been supported by the empirical evidence analyzed in the "Interim Report on Crude Oil" published by the U.S. Interagency Task Force on Commodity Markets in July 2008. The report confirms that there has been a huge inflow of liquidity and increase in open interest, but denies that this has been the cause of the 2008 price spike. In contrast, Roger Diwan conclusively argues that the financialization of the oil market does influence the price of crude oil: Roger Diwan "The Financialization of the Oil Market and the Increasing Impact of Financial Institutions in the Pricing of Crude Oil," Rahmania Cultural Foundation Occasional Paper, no. 2, (Al-Ghat, Saudi Arabia, 2011).

mean or trend for a given period of time – it is indeed normally defined as the standard deviation from the trend line (ordinary least squares line). Empirical measures of volatility will greatly differ depending on the length of time over which it is measured. In our analysis what matters is not so much short-term volatility (intraday, interday, or even weekly or monthly) as oscillations over longer periods.

These oscillations may follow a pattern such that it becomes very difficult to define a stable mean or trend around which the oscillations take place. The negative impact of volatility arises from the fact that we are unable to define an underlining average level of prices, or trend over time. The average level of prices changes significantly depending on the period under consideration. This is seen clearly if moving averages of prices over extended periods of time are calculated: The 10-year moving average of oil prices is far from being flat and still shows very wide swings (figure 5.1). Moving averages are not a very sophisticated way to predict prices, but when we hear company managers arguing "today prices are x, but only three years ago the were y, so we cannot be confident . . . " they are implicitly using moving averages.

Trend lines, even when computed over 20-year periods, have dramatically different slopes depending on the time interval included in the calculation. This is shown in figure 5.2, where the trend for the period 1976–95 (in dark grey) is strongly negative, and becomes even more so for the period 1980–99 (in light grey). However, the trend for 1985–2004 (in dotted line) is positive, and even more so for the period 1989–2008 (in grey). Computing trend lines over shorter periods would strengthen the impression of instability. Statistically, our ability to model or project prices into the future is essentially nil.

It is through the resulting unpredictability of prices that long-term volatility negatively affects the industry. If we had intense volatility around a well-understood trend line, the latter could serve to shape our expectations of future prices. But the amplitude of recent price swings over months and years has been such that no reliable rule for predicting future prices is available.

The rigidity of both demand and supply in response to prices is probably the most important underlying cause of the volatility. If neither demand nor supply reacts to price changes, the adjustment mechanism that governs prices is inhibited. Prices can grow to very high levels and little effect will be seen in terms of diminishing demand or increasing supply. Conversely, prices can precipitate to very low levels, and very little effect will be visible in terms of increasing demand or decreasing supply.

The inflow of liquidity, the increasing role played by the futures market (paper barrels) over the spot (wet barrels), and the proliferation of derivatives – all contribute to worsen the situation, amplifying price oscillations. In fact,

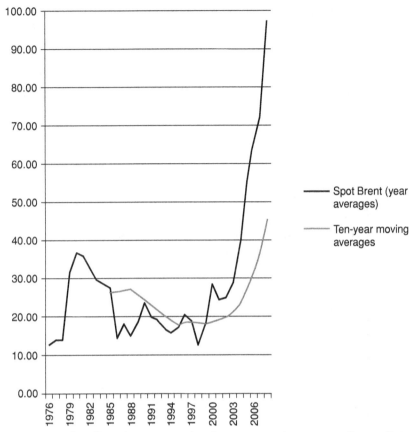

FIGURE 5.1. Spot Brent (year averages) and ten-year moving averages. *Source:* Data from BP Statistical Review of World Energy 2009.

investors are attracted by instability, because their return on investment will be potentially much greater: thus the structural, underlying instability that is the inevitable consequence of rigid demand and supply becomes amplified and attracts ever more financial investment.

One can hardly find justification[3] in supply or demand disequilibrium for the increase of prices from about $50 per barrel at the beginning of 2007 to triple this level in July 2008, followed by a collapse to less than $40 in December of the same year: There was no major shift in either of the two sides of the physical

---

[3] Not everybody would agree with this statement. The reader might remember that during the spring of 2008, as prices were climbing and climbing, the U.S. government was putting pressure on Saudi Arabia to increase production, while the Saudi Minister of Petroleum was arguing that the market was well supplied and all demand was satisfied. So: Truth is elusive.

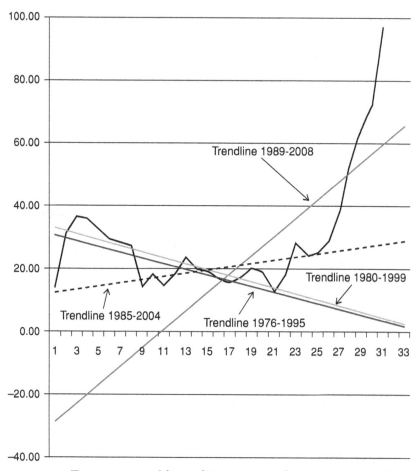

FIGURE 5.2. Twenty-year trend lines of Brent spot yearly averages. *Source:* Data from BP Statistical Review of World Energy 2009.

market. Rather, the long upward run was fueled by the expectation that prices would continue to increase indefinitely, or, in Paul Horsnell's words, by the market's search for an elusive upper limit.[4] When finally the market turned around it was not because this upper limit had been hit, but because the crisis in an entirely different market – U.S. mortgages – eventually led to precipitous disintermediation and hit the global economy and aggregate demand.

[4] Paul Horsnell "The Dynamics of Oil Price Determination" *Oxford Energy Forum* no. 71 (Nov. 2007): 13–15.

THE COST OF LONG-TERM PRICE VOLATILITY

Believers in the efficiency of markets argue that volatility is not a problem – because there is a flourishing futures market that allows efficient hedging. In fact, the main function of the futures market is precisely to allow parties that have a structural exposure to price risk (because they are structural sellers or buyers of oil-related products) to manage their risk and "sell" it, in part or in full, to other parties that are keen to underwrite such risk (parties that have a "risk appetite"). In this vision, the futures paper barrels market is a tool to provide insurance against unavoidable risk.

The other side of the coin – which cannot be separated from the desire of some to reduce their risk – is the speculation or betting on the part of parties that are in the market to take up risk. In this sense, the beneficial role of the market is indissoluble from the speculation: If there were no speculators, parties exposed to structural risk could not mitigate their position.[5]

However, the net outcome of the process, as was said, is to amplify the underlying volatility of the market. *Through successive, ever wider oscillations, the market only increases the risk that it is supposed to mitigate.* In other words, the market allows some parties to mitigate their risk – at a cost – but at the same time increases the overall risk in the industry.

It is important to note that it is difficult for a party to be a pure risk seller, without simultaneously acquiring other risk. Participating in the market in a purely defensive position may have equally disastrous consequences if the wrong line of defense is chosen. Consequently, whoever enters the market is eventually drawn into shifting positions in the attempt of maximizing his profit or minimizing his losses: There is no point in limiting oneself to an inferior trading strategy and ignore the direction of the market. Companies have gone bankrupt because of wrong hedges. Therefore, companies tend to belong to either one or the other of two very separate groups: Those that are not active on the market at all and do not attempt to mitigate their structural risk, and those that are active traders and seek to maximize their trading profit.

The downside of long-term volatility is also clear. In essence, the impossibility of predicting future prices on the basis of demand and supply trends frustrates rational investment decisions. In an industry in which investment costs are the major component of total costs, and investment projects have long gestation periods, how can a corporation decide whether a project is likely to generate sufficient return? In theory, hedging is possible even for very distant

---

[5] Robert Mabro has expressed this with the statement that the futures market is at one and the same time a tool for insurance and a betting casino: The two functions cannot be separated.

maturities; however, liquidity becomes rapidly thinner and only small deals may be envisaged.

Faced with the unpredictability of prices, the aggregate reaction of real investors is to adopt a prudent attitude and only undertake such projects that have very strong rationale and are essentially guaranteed to return very good profit. But the fact that investment will be slowed and capacity increases delayed until demand for them is clearly apparent will lead to an industry that is more fragile overall, with reduced capacity to react to extraordinary or unforeseen circumstances. As external shocks are an unavoidable fact of life, this also means that the physical market will itself be more likely to become unbalanced, further feeding into price instability.

Much of the concern over security of oil supplies that is so prominent in the political discourse of all major importing countries, including the Chinas and Indias of this world, is purely a reflection of insufficient investment and lack of flexibility in the supply chain to cope with unforeseen circumstances. Only a somewhat redundant supply system can be flexible and reliable – but corporations or oil-producing countries must be able to calculate the return on marginal investment as exactly as possible, otherwise they will simply wait.

A POLITICAL CONSENSUS ON PRICES?

The experience of the oil price yo-yo of 2007–9 was sufficiently traumatic to lead to the emergence of a degree of political consensus on the need to dampen volatility and agree on a price that may be acceptable to all sides. Expressions of concern were voiced not only by the major OPEC exporters, but also by leaders of the major industrialized countries, notably Prime Minister Brown, President Sarkozy,[6] and President Obama. It has been said that a consensus may be emerging to the extent that a "fair" price might be in the region of $65–80 per barrel.

On the basis of this impression, the proposal has been put forward to establish an international committee that would decide on prices[7] or a price band,[8]

---

[6] Gordon Brown and Nicholas Sarkozy, "Oil Prices Need Government Supervision," *Wall Street Journal*, July 8, 2009.

[7] Robert Mabro has proposed the creation of an independent commission backed by significant research capability and an international convention that would be expected to set a reference price for oil once a month. ENI has proposed the creation of a global energy agency "which might possess the tools to implement concrete initiatives as needed to stabilize the price of oil" (my translation of Scaroni's original speech, available in Italian from http://www.eni.com/ en_IT/attachments/media/speeches-interviews/italian-version-speech-scaroni-G8-energia-25-maggio-2009.pdf).

[8] In particular, Bassam Fattouh and Christopher Allsopp "The Price Band and Oil Price Dynamics," *Oxford Energy Comment* (July 2009).

similarly to what happens with interest rates (at the national level, though). But how would such a consensus be implemented and enforced? How could producers and major consumers agree on sharing the burden of implementation (which presumably would require active market intervention)?[9]

The emergence of this fledging consensus is important, yet for all awareness of interdependence the bottom line remains that in a sale the interests of the seller always are opposed to that of the buyer. We have ample experience of the fact that high oil prices worry importers more than exporters and low prices the opposite. It is only the experience of violent fluctuations in a short span of time that has crafted the consensus: The same would rapidly evaporate if prices tended to more gently evolve monotonously in one direction, be it upward or downward.

Dialogue and the awareness of interdependence certainly are useful and should be pursued, yet no attempt at dampening price fluctuations will be credible unless it is based on clear and effective market institutions. If market institutions remain prone to generating fluctuations, it will be difficult to resist them. The alternative cannot be a rule that is based on non-market institutions, because in the end what is a fair price today is unlikely to remain so forever: Prices must be allowed to adapt to changing market conditions. Here lies the challenge: Devising a set of institutions (exchanges, regulators, storage facilities, trading rules) that are sufficiently responsive to changing market circumstances, and at the same time do not generate wide fluctuations but smoother, progressive price changes more in line with the fundamental equilibrium of demand and supply.

OPEC'S STUNTED WEAPONS

It is often not fully realized how very limited OPEC's opportunities to influence prices are in a reference pricing regime. The situation might be different if OPEC countries actively traded themselves, selling or buying paper barrels whenever they see prices going in a direction that they do not approve of – however, it would be in many ways paradoxical that major producers should attempt to influence prices by trading paper Brent or WTI, when they could more easily do so by trading in their own oil.[10]

---

9 The experience of currency markets and other commodity markets in which attempts were made to enforce price bands or minimum prices shows that at some point the market will "test" the credibility of these price limits. In the absence of credible intervention mechanisms, the band will become irrelevant. OPEC's band in the earlier part of this decade finally had little meaning at all, as prices could move outside the band and there was no tool to enforce it.

10 Some major producers, notably Mexico, have actively hedged their production, in some cases successfully so—but their purpose has been guaranteeing a minimum level of prices rather

Short of actively trading, OPEC countries can influence the market only through a signaling strategy that aims at influencing "market sentiment." The key tool of this signaling strategy – besides statements and declarations by the various oil ministers and in some cases higher political authorities – is the management of OPEC quotas. However, experience shows that the reaction of "market sentiment" is not always what OPEC would like it to be.

When quotas are reduced in an attempt to shore up prices, the market may deem that the cuts are not sufficient, or it might speculate that compliance on the part of OPEC members will be low – in other words, that some countries will produce in excess of quotas. It is only when compliance is seen to be high and smaller quotas actually provoke a decline in commercial stocks that the market may finally be convinced that demand is in excess of supply and prices should be higher. Even so, restrictions to production will inevitably mean that a higher share of producers' capacity will remain unused, and this is generally interpreted as a bearish sign, especially for future prices.

OPEC has – paradoxically – still more limited influence when prices are on an upward trend. In this case, OPEC countries will obviously announce an increase in quotas, but again the market is unlikely to take such decision at face value. Several countries may not be able to increase their production to the point of filling their new quotas, and available unused capacity will appear to be dangerously low.

Specifically, the erosion of Saudi unused capacity weakens the influence of the kingdom and strengthens that of the hawks within OPEC. The market then fears that global oil production may fall short of global demand and becomes convinced that prices must inevitably rise in the future. This is the state in which the market was for most of the period 2004–8, and is again today.

When the market expects that prices in the distant future may be higher than in the close future, it will move to contango, which is the condition opposite to backwardation, that is, when prices for the front month are lower than prices for subsequent months. In a contango, it pays to accumulate and hold physical stocks: Filling the tanks will further increase global aggregate demand, encouraging bullish sentiment.

---

than influencing prices. In 2008 Mexico hedged its oil production at $70 per barrel, and reportedly gained $5 billion out of this trade when prices collapsed in the latter part of the year. At the end of 2009 Mexico again invested $1 billion to buy a put option for its entire expected 2010 production at $57 per barrel. This means that if prices fall below that level Mexico will be able to exercise the option and sell at $57 per barrel. However, if prices stay above the strike level Mexico will lose the money it has invested in buying the option. Mexico's behavior may be described as buying insurance, but the same trade represents a pure bet on the part of the banks selling the option.

It is very difficult to envisage OPEC taking drastic action to quench an upward price rally. After all, OPEC countries are sellers and draw an immediate benefit from higher prices. Even Saudi Arabia will be reluctant to open the taps in full, because their bargaining position is very weak if their production capacity is fully used.

Paradoxically, the kingdom is more likely to open taps when prices are weak whenever it feels the need to reestablish production discipline, and it has done so in 1985 and again in 1999. But when prices are rising and the world is anxious because of potential political disturbances, the kingdom generally aims at maintaining a reserve that will be used only if conditions further worsen. In practice, this reserve is almost never used: It was used in 1980–1, when Iraq attacked Iran, and again in 1990–1, when Iraq invaded Kuwait – in short, in conditions of open warfare.

We conclude that OPEC may not have sufficiently credible tools to manage the market in case it was decided to implement a price band – even assuming that they might agree on a target band that would please all. It is only if the reference price system is effectively abandoned, and some of the key producing countries establish a well-designed market for their own crude oil, that the influence of the Brent and WTI futures markets will be downsized, and a reasonable chance to achieve more stable, yet market-responsive prices may emerge.

SAUDI ARABIA: FROM PRICE TAKER TO PRICE MAKER

What is required is for Saudi Arabia to shift from the position of price taker to the position of price maker. By this I do not mean that prices should be unilaterally set by Saudi Arabia, but the kingdom should have the greatest influence in the process. The kingdom should sit in the driver's seat in this market – which is where it belongs, as the largest global oil exporter and owner of the largest share of global proven reserves.

Saudi Arabia may not be alone in this role – in fact, it should preferably not be alone. But no other producer can credibly play the role of price maker unless Saudi Arabia supports and delegates this role (e.g., choosing another Gulf crude as the benchmark)[11] – but why should the kingdom do so? It seems much more logical that Saudi Arabia itself takes the

---

[11] This may happen if, for example, Saudi Arabia decided to price its sales to Asia on the basis of the Dubai Mercantile Exchange's Oman contract, rather than the Dubai Platts assessment, as is done today. The latter is the outcome of very thin physical trading, and in practice ends up mirroring Brent almost perfectly.

initiative in shaping a new global oil market, although it should seek allies and other countries' support in doing so. Being the price maker does not mean stamping out the market and deciding prices unilaterally. The new market must be designed in such a way that the kingdom has strong, yet not sole, influence on the price discovery process.

It is a commonly repeated fallacy that a market in Saudi Arabian oil cannot exist because there is only one seller. This is certainly not true, as there exist numerous markets in which there is only one seller, and sales are conducted by auction. The parallel that interests me most is the market for government bonds, through which the interest rate is eventually set. There is indeed a strong parallel and affinity between oil and money – a point to which we shall return toward the end of this chapter. Government bonds are, by definition, sold only by the government, and the Treasury does so through an auction; once sold, bonds can be traded in the secondary market.

A market for Saudi oil may be established by conducting regular auctions of Saudi crude oil. Auctions must per force take place sometime in advance of delivery, so *an auction-based market is necessarily a physical forward market*.[12] This means that a secondary market is possible between the time the auction is conducted and the time delivery takes place: How long this time should be is one of the key parameters of designing a well-functioning market.

The longer the time that is allowed between the auction and the actual delivery of lots sold through it, the more important is the price discovery function that the secondary market will play. In the government bonds market, the secondary market has a very extended life (equal to the maturity of the bonds); it then plays a very important role and generates signals that feedback into the primary auction. Monetary authorities intervene in the secondary market through open market operations to influence the interest rate, and create or destroy money through purchases or sales of government bonds.

Because of the crucial importance of the secondary market, it is appropriate to start our discussion with its design; we will discuss the preferred organization of the auctions, so as to best serve trading in the secondary market.

Allowing a Secondary Market

The first step that the kingdom should take is to create conditions allowing for a secondary market in its own crude oils. Such a market can be established

---

[12] This would be similar to the Brent market, which is composed of a spot market (dated Brent), a physical forward market (21-day Brent), and a futures market. However, some key parameters of the structure I propose would differ, I believe substantially; this is discussed in note 15.

in the kingdom or elsewhere provided that destination restrictions are lifted. Today Saudi oil is sold at different prices depending on whether it is directed to the Far East, to the Mediterranean, to Northwest Europe, or to North America. Obviously, a secondary market could not possibly be segmented by destination, and this differentiation would have to be abandoned. Furthermore, the regular lifters of Saudi oil should be allowed to sell the oil they lift on to third parties, at prices that might differ from what they paid to Saudi Aramco.[13] This would be tantamount to appointing regular lifters as marketing agents – the kingdom would have control of the price at which it sells to them, but no control of the price at which they might sell on to other parties.

If these conditions were respected, a market could be established that might be based on standardized contracts (rather than contracts for variable quantities, as in the spot market) and an exchange (rather than bilaterally and over-the-counter) that is in desirable conditions of transparency and liquidity.[14]

It is crucially important that the physically deliverable contracts on this market be of standard size, preferably sufficiently small to facilitate trading. Trading should take place through an exchange, and OTC transactions should be discouraged. The exchange is best organized by an entity independent from the primary seller (Saudi Aramco). In fact, if Saudi Arabia is not alone in accepting to play the role of price maker, we may think of a Gulf Oil Exchange that will trade several physically deliverable contracts simultaneously, allowing for market-determined discovery of the best quality differentials, and potentially even blending strategies on the part of the final buyer. This would be very similar to a currencies market.

If the individual contract is relatively small, you will need many contracts to fill a ship when the moment comes to take delivery. Small contracts facilitate

---

[13] In the summary of the discussion at the OIES October 2009 conference cited earlier it is related: "One of the participants argued that allowing some of the crudes with large underlying physical supply to be re-traded in the market would create a very liquid and transparent market, and would cause the imperfect WTI benchmark to wither away. However, such an argument did not receive wide support" (OEF no. 79, 5). I tend to share this participant's opinion; however, as is explained in this chapter, I believe the matter is much more complicated than simply allowing secondary trading.

[14] This is how the Oman crude contract on the DME works. When the contract starts trading, the sellers are either term lifters, who know that they will receive crude from Oman to deliver on their sales, or shorters (speculators who sell something they do not have). There is only secondary trading, no primary sales from Oman to "start the game." At the end of the game, when contracts reach maturity, crude oil is delivered to net buyers (holders of long open positions), and Oman prices the oil on the basis of the DME contract price. In theory, it may happen that more oil is sold than Oman is able to deliver; however, current trading volumes are very far from that. In a sense, Oman "delegates" the task of discovering the price of its oil entirely to traders and term lifters, and has no influence on price discovery. Traders obviously are in it because they make a profit: This is their compensation for the "service" they render to Oman—finding the price that will balance demand and supply.

the task of accommodating ships of different sizes, but it is possible that at the time of delivery a buyer will be left with a difference between the number of contracts he has bought and the size of the ship he has at hand. Hence, the smooth functioning of this market certainly is enhanced if abundant storage is made available, providing the alternative of holding in storage rather than loading. Providing for abundant storage facilities is an important component of designing a well-functioning crude market.

The smooth functioning of this system would also gain if the maturity of contracts – that is, the time when physical delivery must be taken by the buyer – is referred to a week rather than a full month. A week provides sufficient flexibility for the scheduling of loading slots for incoming ships, while a full month may create conflicts (if all lifters prefer early or late delivery). Weekly contracts also would allow for easier combination of contracts with different maturities (shorter time in storage) and smoother adjustment of prices. Obviously, this requires primary sales also to be conducted weekly.

The time gap between primary sale and maturity will determine how long the contract will be available for trading on the exchange. For secondary trading to generate a valid price signal, it is necessary that this gap be sufficiently long. Also, if the objective is to compete with the existing Brent and WTI futures markets, it is preferable for the proposed contract to extend sufficiently into the future – although admittedly this is not strictly necessary, as a future market may develop also on the basis of a short-lived physical forward contract. Hence the question of the desirable life duration of the contract is one that may require further research and discussion: Our working hypothesis here for illustrative purposes is that the contract will extend over three months, that is, that the weekly primary auctions are conducted for oil to be delivered twelve weeks later.[15]

As mentioned, the Gulf Oil Exchange would also launch a future contract that might be traded for many more months ahead. If several physically delivered Gulf crude contracts are traded simultaneously on the exchange, the futures contract is likely to be pegged either to one specific crude oil stream or to an index of several crude oil streams. This future contract would be automatically converted in one of the physically delivered contracts (or a basket of

---

[15] The secondary market I propose is similar to the physical forward Brent market, but some key differences need to be stressed: First, I propose a market based on small contracts traded on an exchange, while the Brent physical forward is based on large contracts and trading takes place bilaterally; second, I propose contracts for a specific week, while Brent has contracts for a month; finally, I propose contracts that are in existence for three months (12 weeks) as opposed to contracts that are traded just one month. The merits/demerits of all these details certainly deserve further analysis and discussion.

the same in proportion to the composition of the index) immediately after the primary auction is concluded: It would, therefore, be a form of betting on the outcome of the auction.

Launching an Auction-Based Primary Market

The methodology chosen for the conduct of the auction is of crucial importance. Reluctance to use auctions for price discovery is intuitively connected to the perception that the outcome of an auction is very unpredictable: It is feared that by resorting to auctions the producing countries would be exposed to even greater uncertainty than under the existing reference pricing system. This, however, need not be the case at all. A more technical discussion of the way in which the auction should be conducted is proposed in the Appendix. Here I shall give a more discursive explanation.

The auction should be for standard parcels, such as 1,000 barrels. Bidders should be invited to submit several bids indicating the number of parcels (contracts) they would be willing to purchase at various prices. So, for example, a first bidder may offer to buy 100 contracts at $70 per barrel, a further 100 at $65 per barrel, and a further 100 at $60 per barrel. This means, that if the auction is adjudicated at $60 this bidder will acquire a total of 300 contracts; if the auction is adjudicated at $65 he will buy 200 contracts; and if the auction is adjudicated at $70 he will buy only 100 contracts.[16] As bids are received from several bidders, they can be aggregated to form a demand curve, which will indicate how many contracts may be sold at each price.

The task of receiving bids might be left to an independent authority, which will then construct the demand curve through aggregation of individual bids. The seller is notified of the demand curve and then simultaneously decides on the volume to be sold and the price at which the auction is adjudicated.

It is important that the seller does not commit to selling a fixed number of contracts in advance of the auction. If the seller commits to a definite sales volume, he will have to accept the price that clears that volume – which might not be the price that he prefers. Furthermore, if the seller is committed to a fixed volume, bidders might collude to lower the price. Therefore, it is important to maintain some uncertainty on the volume that will be sold

---

[16] This is a fairly standard way to conduct an auction and already occurs in the Brent market in the Platts window. It also occurs in auctions of government bonds, in IPOs of equity of companies going public, and so on.

through each auction. In this way, the seller maintains a degree of control on the price: if confronted with bids that he believes are too low, it can reduce the volume sold through the auction, and vice versa. The volume sold through the auction will give an immediate signal of the seller's price target and his willingness to adjust volume to achieve the same.

Indeed, it is possible to take this to an extreme and manage the volume sold through the auction so as to maintain the price at a fixed level: This would be equivalent to a return to posted prices – not a desirable solution. The suggested auction methodology allows market trends to emerge, and at the same time allows the seller to dampen price movements through variations in volumes sold.

It is also advisable that, in order to preserve the required uncertainty about the seller's supply, the auction shall not be the only method of sale, but it should be paired with term sales to established customers at prices, which will be referenced (indexed) to the prices established through the auction (more on this later).

The proportion of the total export volume that is sold through the auction will depend on the interest among bidders. In theory, the more interest there is for the auction, the better are the results for the seller. The seller should, therefore, adopt incentives to encourage even term customers to participate in the auction, and progressively increase the proportion of total exports that are directly allocated through the auction.

To better visualize the potential outcome of an auction system, we should keep in mind its recurrent nature (e.g., one auction per week) and the mutual influence of auctions for different crude oils from different producers conducted at different times during the week. A repetition of numerous smaller auctions would provide the market with almost continuous information with respect to market conditions; bids and prices would much more directly and immediately be influenced by fundamentals.

Concretely, we should visualize a Gulf Oil Exchange established in, for example, Bahrain and offering a trading platform for all major Gulf crude oils. Thus the exchange might conduct an auction for – again as a way of example – Arabian Light on Sundays, Abu Dhabi Murban on Mondays, Kuwait Export Crude on Tuesdays, Arabian Heavy on Wednesdays, and Basrah Light on Thursdays. The standard parcel should be the same for all to facilitate swap trading and market determination of quality differentials.

In this scenario, and if auctions are conducted twelve weeks forward, the exchange would be trading (via auctions and the secondary market) sixty contracts at any moment in time (five crude oil times twelve maturities), allowing for considerable flexibility and influence of fundamentals on price discovery. Liquidity on each contract is likely to be relatively limited (a majority of the trades would take place among actual lifters rather than "investors"), but an index might be constructed on the basis of the sixty contracts that may serve as the basis for a futures contract (as is common for equities), which may well be expected to attract considerable interest.

TIMING THE SHIFT FROM REFERENCE TO DIRECT PRICING

Whenever Saudi Arabia – alone or in association with other major producers – decides to shift to direct pricing through auctions and a secondary market, some time will elapse before the focus of global oil trading shifts from the existing benchmarks and their related paper markets to the new market. This time needs not be very long – in fact I expect that it would be quite short – but a transition phase is inevitable and is a delicate passage.

Ideally, a shift to direct trading should be implemented at a time when prices for the existing benchmarks are rising and possibly exceeding the wishes of the kingdom. Prices initially set through the auctions may be somewhat lower than those prevailing on the existing paper markets, because buyers entering bids for the auction will enjoy the alternative of buying paper barrels on the existing markets: although contracts sold through the auction will have the advantage of being eventually deliverable in physical oil, this may not justify bids at a premium with respect to the three months forward future Brent or WTI.

At the beginning of 2010, Saudi Aramco abandoned WTI as the reference for its sales into the United States, and adopted instead the Argus Sour Crude Index (ASCI). This decision is a very clear indication of the dissatisfaction with WTI as a valid reference and may lead to prices that will significantly diverge from WTI. Kuwait and Iraq have announced that they will follow the example of Saudi Arabia. Press reports have speculated that Saudi Aramco may soon also abandon the reference to Oman/Dubai Platts assessment for sales to the Far East and adopt instead the DME Oman contract. The implications of all these changes are very difficult to predict, and we shall have to wait and see how the market responds.

That said, all such actual or potential changes affect the definition of the reference but keep the reference pricing regime in place. There have been several such adjustments to the reference in the past, in the face of declining availability of the original reference crude oils, but these are simply plugs to prevent a badly leaking boat from sinking.

What this means is that a new regime must be studied and readied to be put in place at the right time. This, as mentioned, is likely to be a time when prices are relatively stable or rising, because the immediate impact of shifting to the proposed new system may be a slight weakening of prices in conjunction with the initial auctions.

However, as soon as trading in the secondary market begins, and if volumes for term sales are somewhat reduced, prices on the Gulf Oil Exchange will firm up, and mutual influence will arise between price signals originating in this market and price signals originating on the old paper markets. Lifters that are interested more in physical Gulf crude oils rather than in Brent or WTI or ASCI will obviously start hedging on the new secondary markets rather than using the old contracts.

Once the shift has occurred, there is no reason why the regime proposed here should generate prices that are systematically lower than those generated by the old paper markets. Volatility would be reduced through the producers' control of prices and volumes at the auctions – although secondary trading would then generate price signals that the producers do not control.[17]

Producers should normally abstain from intervening in the secondary market, because if they intervened frequently market participants would simply try and guess the producers' price preferences. However, interventions in the secondary market should be expected in cases of extreme trading conditions or political crises. Once again, this would not be dissimilar from the preferred behavior of central banks in money or currency markets, where interventions are not ruled out, but are rare and unpredictable.

Launching the new market mechanism should obviously be preceded by careful preparation and extensive consultations, including among major producers and with major oil-importing countries. There is every benefit to be derived from establishing as wide a consensus as possible on the desirability of a market based on much more credible physical volumes. However, the kingdom should make firm its intention to establish a new regime clear from the beginning and identify the key components of the proposed alternative

---

[17] It may be objected that the degree of control afforded to the producers by their handling of the primary auctions is small relative to the influence of trading on the secondary market, which eventually may lead to the birth of many complex layers (futures, swaps, derivatives OTC, etc.). I don't think it is possible to reach a definite conclusion on this short of experimenting the system in practice. I tend to believe, however, that primary trading would be very influential, especially if refiners and large volume product buyers were encouraged to buy directly at the auctions—for example, through the requirement that products prices changes be announced twelve weeks in advance of being implemented, as discussed in this chapter.

(the primary auctions, the secondary market, the end to reference pricing) to prevent the very numerous interests that are vested in the current system from succeeding in boycotting the initiative through a well-coordinated barrage of objections.

ESTABLISHING DEMAND SECURITY

As already explained, it is essential that producers do not ex ante commit to selling a predetermined volume through the auctions. This means that the volume to be sold through the auctions will remain uncertain, and should be seen to be variable, to keep the market guessing. In other words, the proposed mechanism may to some extent aggravate the lack of demand security that the producers frequently complain about.

The issue of demand security may in parallel be addressed through the modification of existing "evergreen" lifting arrangements with regular customers – which, however, do not constitute a firm obligation either on the part of the seller or on the part of the buyer – into proper long-term take or pay contracts, modeled on the experience of the gas industry.

It may be paradoxical to propose this, because take or pay contracts are not very popular with the governments of importing countries wishing to see gas markets develop in a more competitive direction – but in fact they are a perfectly rational solution for producers wishing to guarantee themselves at least a minimum level of sales and utilization of capacity, especially at times when they are called to engage in large-scale projects to increase their capacity.

The kingdom should take note of the desire of major importers – especially the large Asian emerging countries – to have access to guaranteed supplies of crude oil, and should offer a guarantee to supply in exchange for a guarantee to lift. Recent arrangements with China and India point in this direction, and may be very useful as a tool to stabilize the market and address the feeling of insecurity of both buyer and seller. The price for volumes sold through take or pay contracts would be tied to that "discovered" in the secondary market.

The combination of developing domestic refining (and exporting petroleum and/or petrochemical products) and entering into long-term take or pay supply contracts will leave a flexible smaller margin to be sold through the auctions. How important each segment should be, only experience can tell; as was said, we would expect volumes sold through the auctions to increase gradually, yet remain the smaller part of total sales. If the kingdom succeeded in selling 10 percent of its current production through auctions, the market would be based on a wider physical base than it has ever been before.

HOW MAJOR IMPORTERS MAY HELP

The transition to a redesigned global oil market has better chances of succeeding if importers also participate in the effort. The key for achieving this collaboration would be to leverage the almost universal dissatisfaction with the market as it exists, to muster sufficient goodwill for cooperation. In this context, while leadership must be taken by the producing countries – to which the major task of price making inevitably belongs – the importing countries must also act in support of the proposed new market structures. Realistically, this should not require a continuing agreement on the desirable level of prices, nor active market intervention on the part of the governments of importing countries; and it should not entail a financial burden on their budgets.

Within these limitations, however, important steps might be taken by the importing countries that would contribute to limiting oil price volatility.

Regulating Price Changes at the Retail Level

A first initiative that should be considered is limiting the freedom of marketing companies to change their retail prices. This may come under the form of either imposing upper limits to the extent of price changes in a given period of time or, and I believe preferably, as an obligation to give significant advance notice of any intended change in retail prices.[18]

The current system of total freedom in retail price determination notoriously translates into extraordinary promptness in increasing product prices to the final consumer when crude oil prices are on the increase, while movements in the opposite direction are much slower. The ease with which refiners and marketers can transfer crude oil price increases to the final customer contributes to the absence of demand resistance to such increases. Indeed, refiners and marketers frequently appear to welcome crude oil price increases – an impression supported by the consideration that many are also crude oil producers and stand to gain from the increase.

Instead, marketers should be asked to announce intended price changes at least three months in advance of being allowed to implement the same. This is a step that would be entirely feasible also in the absence of initiatives

---

[18] Oil products are heavily taxed in many industrial countries. The discussion in this paragraph assumes no changes in this taxation policy, simply introducing administrative limitations to the speed of price changes on the part of sellers (wholesalers/retailers). Indeed, it would be possible to use management of the excise taxes on oil products as a tool to stabilize prices to the final consumer. This is, however, not the concern of this chapter, which focuses on reducing long-term volatility of crude oil prices.

on the part of the producers and would simply force refiners and marketers to hedge their crude purchases on the future market to lock their prices.

The obligation to announce price changes with considerable advance notice would introduce price stability as a competitive tool between companies. In other words, the market would tend to reward those companies that are better capable of resisting price increases through hedging or other tools.

If, in parallel, the major oil producers also resort to auctions for physical sales three months forward, as proposed, a link would be established between the primary sales and price changes on the final retail market. The secondary market would then deal with short-term disequilibria and may be characterized by oscillations that might not display any strong trend. Refiners would have a strong incentive to acquire their crude supplies directly at the primary auctions.

Encouraging NOCs' Integration Downstream

A second potential line of action on the part of the major importers might be to encourage the downstream integration of the major producers' national oil companies (NOCs). To the extent that the NOCs become more vertically integrated, and own their own refineries and marketing outlets, their ability to compete at the retail level and resist undesirable price changes would be enhanced.

More direct control of their market outlets on the part of the producers will enhance both security of demand and security of supply – because producers will always supply their own refineries and these refineries will not purchase crude from other sources if there is too much crude oil around.

Better vertical integration of the major producers may shift some of the burden for adjusting production from OPEC to non-OPEC. Non-OPEC countries are simply volume maximizers with no commitment to price stability and through their actions make the task of OPEC countries for price stability more difficult. The current attitude of Russian producers, which are maximizing exports at a time when OPEC is attempting to carefully manage supplies, is a case in point.

Increasing Global Oil Stocks

A third potential approach would be to create conditions for a substantial increase of global storage capacity. This is an important component in ENI's proposed approach to reducing price volatility, and one that obviously deserves support.

Currently the major importing countries maintain strategic stocks under the IEA or EU or national schemes: These are expected to be entirely separate from commercial stocks and not to be used for market intervention, that is, to offset unwelcome movements in prices. At the same time the common definition of supply security also includes an element of price stability, meaning that it is not entirely clear whether strategic stocks may or may not be used to counteract price volatility: In practice, they have not been used.

To address volatility, it is not necessary to increase strategic stocks; what is needed is to invest in increased storage capacity, which might be made available to producers or traders at convenient cost conditions, or for free. The Saudi Minister of Petroleum has announced a deal along these lines with Japan, whereby Saudi Aramco will store oil in Japan in facilities freely made available by the Japanese.

The rationale for providing such storage capacity would be that oil that is stored might be used as strategic stock in case of an emergency. In other words, an appropriate agency of the importing countries (or each importing country individually, as Japan is doing) would invest in storage facilities and offer storage services: the stored oil would remain the property of whoever uses the service, but the importing countries might appropriate the oil under predetermined price conditions in case of an emergency threatening their security of supply. (This may not be spelled out clearly in the Saudi-Japanese case, but is at least implied by the deal.) Storage facilities might be established in the territory of the importers but also in third countries or possibly even in the producing countries if significant logistical differentiation is thereby possible (e.g., on the west coast of Saudi Arabia, which does not have the same risk profile as the east coast, where the fields are located).

The provision of storage services may be accompanied by the creation of a credit facility whereby parties depositing crude oil may then use this as collateral for loans. The stored oil would obviously be valued at a price lower than the going market price, which in turn may come to represent the minimum price "guaranteed" by the importing countries. Such guarantee would disappear only if the storage capacity came to be fully utilized, and excess oil still is present on the market. Obviously no amount of storage capacity will be enough to stabilize prices completely and maintain prices at unrealistic levels, but a substantial increase in available storage would certainly contribute to creating conditions facilitating the responsiveness of prices to fundamentals.

At present, the market is unduly influenced by storage data from the central United States. This is due also to the extraordinary reticence and/or inefficiency of the EU in promptly communicating data on volumes of crude oil in storage. The creation of a network of storage facility administered by an autonomous agency along the lines described above would greatly enhance our information on fundamentals and promote efficient market responses.

SAUDI ARABIA'S COMING OF AGE IN A MULTIPOLAR WORLD

The reasons why the kingdom might be reluctant to embark on the proposed transformation of the international oil market are not difficult to guess. Inevitably, performing the role of price maker would require making crucial decisions for the correct management of the market, decisions about price and volumes of oil to be offered at the primary auctions, and many other decisions related to the regulation of the market, additions to capacity, diversification into refining, and marketing. This would be quite a tall order for the kingdom's technocracy, although in the opinion of this writer one that the country's technical intelligentsia would be perfectly able to perform. But it is not to be denied that the potential for criticism, from internal as well as international sources, would be very substantial. In other words, the kingdom would very much acquire a visible profile on the global stage, while its traditional preference has been for maintaining a rather low profile.

In recent years, the kingdom's leadership has demonstrated growing readiness to engage in major foreign policy initiatives and has not shunned controversy. The world is rapidly evolving toward multipolarity, and emerging actors must correspondingly be ready to assume increasing responsibilities in policy making. The transition from the G8 to the G20 is symptomatic of the transformation. In the context of the G20 the emerging economic powers will inevitably be asked and expected to contribute their share.

The status of Saudi Arabia as one of the emerging world economic powers is linked to its position as the key provider of oil to the world and, to a lesser extent, a surplus country with continuing large oil revenues. The role of the kingdom must be related to the management of the international oil market. Its standing and influence in the G20 will be linked to the effectiveness with which the kingdom will manage the international oil market and contribute to global economic stability and growth.

This historical responsibility cannot be delegated to an imperfect, unregulated market based on some rapidly disappearing streams of crude oil. The collapse of the international oil market as it exists today is just a matter of time: The more we wait to put in place an alternative, the more we shall have to endure price shocks and diplomatic conflict. Creating an alternative is not an easy task, but is nevertheless one that must be undertaken urgently. It will necessarily be part and parcel of the coming of age of Saudi Arabia in the emerging multipolar world order.

APPENDIX

The essence of a well-designed auction is in the details.[19] What could be the best way to organize an auction for crude oil? The answer is relatively simple:

1. The auction would certainly be organized as a descending bid auction, in which the highest price, at which all the volume of oil is sold that is available for sale, would be accepted
2. The auction would be a multi-unit one, where the available volume of oil would be sold in parcels (each parcel equal to one physically delivered contract), not as a single indivisible unit
3. The auction should preferably be conducted through sealed bids, or book building through an exchange or independent intermediary (our proposed Gulf Oil Exchange)
4. Finally, the auction should be of the uniform-price type – that is, all accepted bids would pay the same price, which is the lowest accepted bid, even if all other bidders, except the lowest accepted, bid a higher price. The alternative is to allow for price discrimination, that is, have each bidder actually pay the price that he has bid: This alternative is more efficient in theory, as it foils the danger of collusion, but may lead to confusion because of simultaneous trading at several different prices.

An auction designed in this way is vulnerable to implicit collusion,[20] but this problem can be solved[21] if the seller does not commit to selling a given volume of oil in advance of the auction. The total volume sold must be defined only ex post, once the seller has received all the bids, and can on this basis construct a demand curve for his oil on a given date. He will then choose the combination of volume sold and price accepted that most suits his marketing strategy, and the purpose of the auction will in essence be to determine to whom the oil should go.

It is also clear that recurrent multiple-unit sealed-bid auctions of a uniform good with uncertainty in the seller's supply may, at the limit, translate into a

---

[19] Paul Klemperer "What Really Matters in Auction Design," CEPR Discussion Paper no. 2581, Oct. 2000.

[20] Ibid., 3.

[21] Klemperer, "Auction Theory: A Guide to the Literature," CEPR Discussion Paper no. 2163, June 1999.

fixed (albeit strictly speaking not "posted") price and variable volumes sold. This case is represented in the figure shown here.

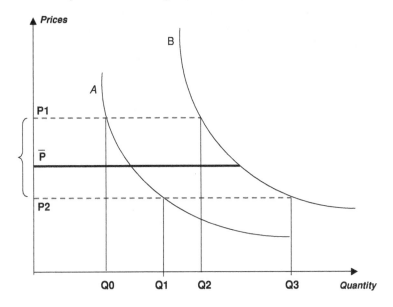

In this figure we have two different demand curves, each representing the result of one auction. The seller is free to select any combination of price and quantity along the line. In practice, the seller wishes to maintain the price within the band P1P2 and will thus determine the volume to be sold in the first auction, represented by A, in the interval Q0Q1; in the following auction, represented by B, to maintain the price within the band the adjudicated volume will need to be between Q2 and Q3. In practice, it is unlikely that we might witness such significant demand shifts, and the seller will need to implement much smaller changes in quantities sold and/or prices accepted. The limit case is one in which the price is kept fixed at **P**, represented by the bold black line, and only quantities are adjusted. This would be equivalent to imposing a fixed price: Even if it is not publicly announced, the market will soon find out.

This extreme case would of course defeat the purpose of the auction, by preventing the price discovery function of it. Yet it is clear that the possible alternative of reverting to "posted" prices, as is sometimes proposed, would have exactly this meaning and impact: Establish full producers' control over prices, and give up control over volumes.

In this respect, an auction simply is a strategy that allows for greater flexibility in trading, and acquiring greater information, than straight posted prices.

It is also clear where the major weakness of the posted prices alternative lies: It prevents the seller from acquiring information over market conditions. To gain this information, the seller *must* allow for a trading mechanism and some uncertainty, as in an auction, otherwise buyers simply will keep the information to themselves.

6

National Cohesion and the Political Economy of Regions in Post–World War II Saudi Arabia

Steffen Hertog

This chapter discusses the role of the kingdom's main regions in structuring and defining a socioeconomic pecking order that, despite increasing national integration, has lost little of its poignancy – an order that has led to strong rivalries and ill will on a quotidian level but that, at the end of the day, seems to allow the regime to keep the kingdom together through divide and rule strategies.

After a brief discussion of the infrastructural power of the Saudi state, the chapter will measure regional inequality over time through a number of proxy variables, showing that there is a rather clear socioeconomic hierarchy of regions within the kingdom. This fragments society materially. But as even the most disadvantaged groups remain strongly dependent on the state – and indeed tend to be the worst organized – it does not undermine the cohesion of the system, but rather creates an internal hierarchy that is very difficult to effectively challenge.

The subsequent pages specifically analyze regional inequality in private business over time, showing again that there has been a discernible shift of resources in favor of the more privileged central provinces. It also elucidates, however, the rather large degree of integration among top business elites across regions as evidenced by the mixed composition of boards of directors of various large enterprises. Saudi Arabia's national economy today is tightly integrated, and regional markets have lost much of their material importance, even if regionalism on a sociocultural level is still strong among many businesspeople.

In these sections I will show that different from popular perceptions, the Western province has defended its material stakes relatively well in the course of the Saudi system's material expansion, while the south has been the main loser in the process and remains marginalized and voiceless until today.

Although I will briefly propose some hypotheses to explain the historical patterns of inequality, the core empirical aim of the chapter is descriptive.

Much more research on the ground would be required to trace elite structures and the history of political integration in different regions to truly explain their diverging fates. This chapter will hopefully serve as a point of reference for such future work.

The data used here mostly come from Arabic language official documents since the 1950s – which are, if anything, likely to underreport regional inequalities. Comparisons over time can be difficult as full time series are lacking for many variables, and statistics can be inconsistent across different years and institutions. Some important subregional communities – such as the Shiites of the Eastern Province – cannot be discussed in this chapter, because we lack sufficient community-level data on public services and employment. Regionally differentiated figures on crucial categories, such as household income, are lacking altogether. Yet the numbers available all broadly point toward the same conclusions, as do many more figures not presented here for space constraints.

THE SAUDI STATE'S INFRASTRUCTURAL POWER

The Saudi state is different from both typical developed and developing countries in a number of ways that are important for understanding its structural power over society: Although it commands resources equal to those of many developed countries, these resources are not extracted from an economically developed and differentiated local society, but are generated externally. Conversely, although its patterns of rule are patrimonial and personalized as in many authoritarian developing countries, the regime's resources are far larger than in most of the developing world. These features together give the regime an almost unique degree of power over society and lead to a very high degree of material dependence of the average Saudi on the state's formally and informally disbursed resources.

The reach of the state is reflected in its vast infrastructure and expansive service provision to the Saudi population. The highly centralized Saudi state touches its subjects' daily lives on many levels and very deeply, and supplies more services relative to those provided from within business and society than most other states in the world.

It is important to remember that this has not always been the case. In fact, the Saudi state's infrastructural power was very weak up to the 1960s. It was only during the 1970s, in the course of the first oil boom, that the state managed to expand its service provision and patronage to the vast majority of Saudi nationals. With its budget expanding fivefold from the first to the second five-year development plan from 1970 to 1975, this happened at an unprecedented pace. Not coincidentally, this was also a time when organized opposition in Saudi Arabia had virtually disappeared, as most Saudis were drawn into the orbit of the state apparatus and young, motivated nationals enjoyed a level of social mobility that has never again been reached – often as clients of individuals in the royal family.

Even without personalized patronage, the average Saudi's dependence on the state multiplied, as the bureaucracy managed to roll out subsidized services at a high pace: The length of paved roads quadrupled from 1970 to 1984, electricity generation capacity increased twentyfold, and water desalination capacity eightyfold.[1]

The number of primary school students more than doubled from the early 1970s to the early 1980s, that of intermediary school students quadrupled, while that of secondary school pupils multiplied sixfold. By the 1990s, full enrollment was reached, in a society where illiteracy had been estimated at 95 percent only four decades earlier – all thanks to state-provided free education.[2] Saudi schoolchildren became subject to a unified and centralized educational system in a social context that remained relatively closed to the outside world.

These statistics not only indicate a rapidly improving quality of life. They are also tokens of how quickly a national bureaucracy, tightly controlled by the central government in Riyadh, managed to reach out into even remote villages of Saudi Arabia and to make Saudi nationals of various stripes structurally dependent on, and oriented toward, the state. Regional administration became increasingly standardized, and the average Saudi quickly found him- or herself dealing with the bureaucracy on many levels of daily life.

Rates of sedentarization increased rapidly, and where there previously was very little presence of the bureaucracy outside of the major urban centers, the state soon was almost everywhere, employing nationals, providing them with subsidized goods, and – not necessarily by design – destroying traditional local economies. Traditional local leaders such as tribal shaykhs were often either sidelined or co-opted through, among other things, handing them administrative jobs.[3] This does not mean that the state had perfect control over what everybody was doing or the capacity to monitor people tightly, but it had created systems of support and material dependence that strongly decreased the organizational and economic autonomy of local actors – whose fortunes now often were decided in the ministerial offices of remote Riyadh.

Despite an organic growth of private economic activity in the kingdom since the 1970s, today's Saudi state still plays a disproportionate role in daily life of most nationals. A couple of indicators will serve to illustrate this. First of

[1] Ministry of Planning, *Achievements of the Development Plans*, various issues, Riyadh.
[2] *Statistical Yearbook*, various issues, Riyadh.
[3] Ali Mashhor Al-Seflan, "The Essence of Tribal Leaders' Participation, Responsibilities, and Decisions in Some Local Government Activities in Saudi Arabia" (Ph.D. diss., Claremont Graduate School, 1980).

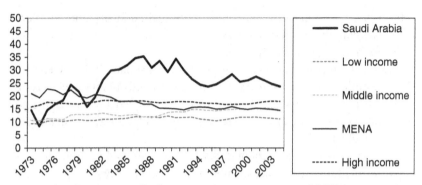

FIGURE 6.1. Government final consumption as percentage of GDP in comparison with other groups of countries. *Source:* World Bank Development Indicators.

all, the sheer size of the state as economic player relative to nonstate entities remains crushing.

The share of government final consumption in GDP in Saudi Arabia has historically been higher than among most other countries of the world, whether rich or poor, indicating a dominant role of the state apparatus in national economic life. This is although the measure in fact severely understates the role of the government, as it excludes the oil sector, which is largely or wholly state-controlled and acts as important employer and contracting agency. Much of economic activity therefore depends on the state, directly or indirectly. In the Middle East region, it is only in the small GCC states that relative dependence on the state is even higher.

A survey of specific sectors reveal the same picture: Health and education are overwhelmingly state-provided, as are subsidized utilities, transport, and infrastructure. While it is true that modern industrialized states have at times provided similarly expansive services to their citizens, they have done so at higher prices and, more important, provided them to societies that have enjoyed much larger resources of their own. In Saudi Arabia, the provision is much more lopsided, as the expanding state encountered a poor, fragmented, and underdeveloped society. This made it easy for the regime not only to take over national education, but also to dominate national media, allowing rather tight control over nationally unified information in what for many decades remained a relatively inward-looking society.

The most important measure of state dominance in Saudi society is probably the state's disproportionate role as employer: The official payroll in Saudi Arabia has increased every year since 1970, despite economic recessions in the 1980s and 1990s. In 2008 it officially counted almost 900,000 employees,

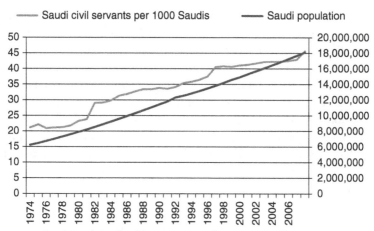

FIGURE 6.2. Number of public sector employees in Saudi Arabia since 1970

while privately employed Saudis were estimated at only about 830,000 according to Ministry of Labor figures. This means that more Saudis work in the bureaucracy than in the private sector, a phenomenon today only known in a couple of very rich oil states and the remaining few communist countries of this world. The share of public employees in the overall population moreover has been increasing for four decades despite rapid demographic growth.

What is more, the official figures on state employment from the Ministry of Civil Service seem to understate the phenomenon significantly, possibly by a factor of two or more. Several forms of state employment – most prominently in the security and religious sectors – go largely unrecorded by the ministry. A recent independent report has given a figure for actual Saudi government employment of 1.8 million individuals. The Ministry of Interior alone is reported to employ up to 500,000 individuals.[4] This would mean that for every Saudi in private employment, about two work for the government.

According to the estimates of the International Labour Office, public sector employment accounts for an average of 6 percent among total developing country employment, and even in the statist Middle East and North Africa region, the average is about 15 percent. The Saudi figure is at least three times as large. State employment serves as a huge, nationwide patronage machinery that can be used to bestow and take away favors, a machinery toward which most individuals and interest groups orient themselves in the absence of comparably large resources in society.

[4] John Sfakianakis, *Giving a Boost*, Saudi British Bank Notes, Feb. 7, 2008.

Even if many Saudis might be unhappy with their bureaucracy, it is a powerful structural factor of national integration, a stable and deeply ensconced fact
of Saudi life. Thanks to a domineering state, Saudis who used to live separate
lives in largely local contexts now think and talk of the same national institutions and policies when thinking about their sustenance and material interests.

To be sure, the Saudi state is rather fragmented in itself, as different parts
of it are dominated by patronage networks of different senior princes. Despite
all internal squabbles, however, the presence of the royal family is a unifying
rather than a dividing factor that guarantees the basic coherence of the system
thanks to the presence of hundreds of princes in the state apparatus who share
a common survival interest.

REGIONAL INEQUALITY: EVIDENCE

Given the enormous reach of the Saudi state, inequality in resource allocation
can have momentous consequences for society, which has been fundamentally
reshuffled through the oil boom. The terms on which the state has reached
out into different parts of Saudi society have indeed been unequal on many
levels. The dimension that is the most easily measurable, and in many ways
the most politicized, is the regional one.

It is also the one about which the most persistent myths are perpetuated.
Perceived regional inequalities have given rise to much resentment of the
dominance of the Al Saud and the Najd, the central province from which they
hail. Apart from the Shiites in the Eastern Province – a special social category
not only in regional terms – the most vocal complaints have arguably come
from sections of the elite in the Hijaz, Saudi Arabia's western region. The
general narrative is that historically the Hijaz has been more economically,
administratively and culturally sophisticated, but has been marginalized by
Najdi elites in the course of the state-building process. Recent years have even
seen some talk about a revived Hijazi separatism in the face of oppression and
discrimination by central Arabian elites.

The following pages will weigh the discourse of discrimination and pro-
Najdi favoritism against the available hard data about socioeconomic development of Saudi Arabia's different regions. Our results will call into question the
received wisdom of Hijazi marginalization, rather demonstrating that the real
losers of national unification by and large live in the south of the kingdom, a
large but politically less visible and vocal region.

There is good historical evidence that the central province has always been
favored in the course of Saudi state building. Even in the pre–oil age, resources
extracted from the western and eastern regions were redistributed toward
central province towns and tribes who in turn contributed to the state-building

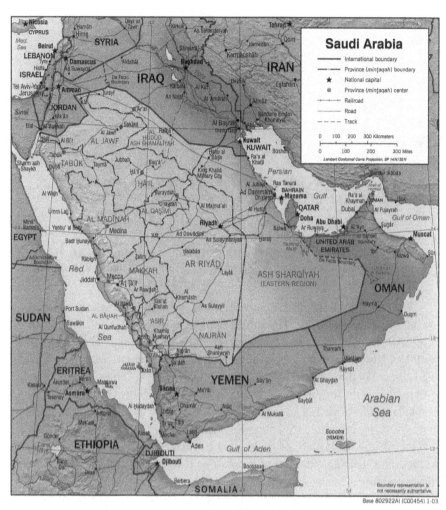

FIGURE 6.3. Map of Saudi Arabia

enterprise through their military contributions.[5] With larger-scale oil income entering the picture from the 1940s on, favoritism did not require resource extraction from the periphery anymore and started to occur on a bigger scale.

It was not, however, the more developed west that was the main victim of unequal distribution policies. Instead, peripheral regions in the populous south suffered from far worse neglect. In the first national budget from the mid-1940s, money was approved for the western province (Hijaz) and the central region (Najd), but none was earmarked for any other region.[6]

[5] Alexei Vasiliev, *The History of Saudi Arabia* (Saqi, 2000), 122f.
[6] Tariq Hassan Koshak, "The Saudi Budgetary Process: an Exploratory Case Study" (Ph.D. diss., Leeds Business School, 2001), 81.

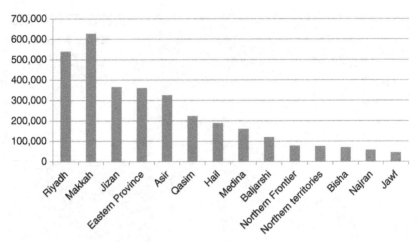

FIGURE 6.4. Population estimates in Saudi Arabia according to 1963 survey. *Source:* "Mecca" here includes Jeddah, which constitutes the bulk of the count.

A regional pecking order is also visible in early statistics on social security and pensions payments: Total disbursement to Riyadh in 1962 amounted to SAR 3.65 million, almost half of the national total of SAR 7.5 million, although Riyadh according to a 1963 population estimate contained only about 16 percent of the national population (see figure here). The western port city of Jeddah, at the time at least as big as Riyadh, received only 1 million.[7] Several smaller towns in central Saudi Arabia, and the Qasim subregion in particular, received disproportionate shares of social security payments (including Al-Rass, Shaqra, Buraydah, or Al-Majmah). These are places from which an important share of senior administrators in the Saudi state have historically been recruited.

The main disadvantaged regions were not the oil-rich east (Dammam/Khobar/Al-Hasa) or the traditionally more developed Hijaz (Mecca/Jeddah/Medina), however, but it was most of all the south: Jizan as the most strongly populated region outside of the main west–east axis received pension payments only one-tenth as large as the ones in Riyadh.[8]

Statistics about municipal budgets in the 1960s reveal a similar picture, although one more favorable to the main urban centers in the west and east: They profit from comparably large allocations than the center. Jizan again has

---

[7] *Taqrir ᶜan wizarat al-ᶜamal wa-sh-shu'un al-ijtimaᶜiyya* 1383 (Report about the Ministry of Labour and Social Affairs, 1963/64), Institute of Public Administration documentation center, Riyadh, folder 181.

[8] Cf. *Sixth Statistical Yearbook*, table 4–11.

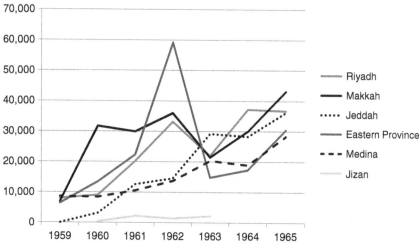

FIGURE 6.5. Municipal budgets up to 1965 (thousands SAR)

a much smaller allocation, although it was at the time still a comparable in population to the Eastern Province.

The oldest available statistics on state-provided real estate loans show a similar pattern. Although the main regions of the kingdom – western, central, and eastern – do rather well together with a couple of smaller northern regions, the south has been badly neglected.

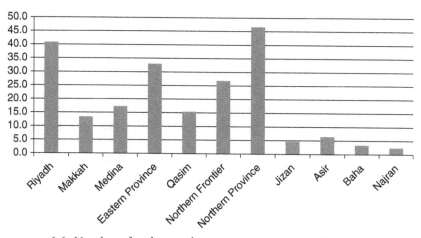

FIGURE 6.6. Number of real estate loans given per 1,000 residents by the Real Estate Development Fund by 1978.[9]

---

[9] Based on REDF figures in *Middle East Economic Digest*, Jan. 27, 1978, 31.

The fragmentary data on public employment in the early phase of Saudi state building lead us to similar conclusions. The bureaucratic build-up favored the urban classes in general: Of 252 middle managers sampled in a mid-1970s survey, only three had a nomadic background, 95 were from small villages, and the dominant rest from towns.[10] More important, employment at least on higher levels of the bureaucracy early on evinced a clear bias in favor of the Najd, that is, of central Arabia. Already in the pre–oil age, many important positions in other provinces were taken by Najdis, such as regional governorships or the presidency and the vice-presidency of the Consultative Council, although the latter was a western province body. Most southern governors and mayors also were from Najd. In the Eastern Province, government in the 1960s was dominated by Hijazis and Najdis, not locals.[11] Even the Sunni elites of the Eastern Province, such as the clans of Hofuf (a town that grew far below its potential), were marginalized.

From the 1960s on, Najids caught up with more urbane Hijazis from the western province in getting degrees abroad and quickly worked their way up the bureaucratic ranks. There was even an informal network of young Najdi nationalists – called "Fatat Najd" – that promoted the interests of this new stratum.[12] It was far from a real political organization, however, and many of the adherents were subsequently adopted by prince and later king Fahd to build his own patronage networks in the state apparatus.

At the beginning of the 1960s, Hijazis still dominated much of the bureaucratic class in the kingdom, because of their region's longer history of administration and economic development. Even among military officers, they constituted a majority – although this changed after a coup attempt in 1969 that involved Hijazi networks.

The shift in favor of Najdi bureaucratic employment happened rapidly during the 1960s, however, and earlier than some historians would have it: Already in a late 1960s sample of 271 high-level bureaucrats, 61 percent came from Najd, and most of the rest from the western province.[13] The Hijaz remained important, but quickly became the junior partner in the process of regime-building.

Najdi dominance was further deepened after the killing of King Faisal in 1975, who had built up and relied on strong Hijazi clienteles during his time

---

[10]   Mohammed Abdullah Madi, "Development Administration and the Attitudes of Middle Management in Saudi Arabia (Ph.D. diss., Southern Illinois University, 1975), 62f.

[11]   Jidda to State, The Shi'a Community of the Eastern Province, June 9, 1969, U.S. National Archives and Records Administration, College Park/Maryland, Record Group 59, 250, 5–7, box 2472, folder POL 13 SAUD (1/1/67) .

[12]   Interviews with former senior civil servants in Riyadh, 2003–8.

[13]   Ibrahim Al-Awaji, "Bureaucracy and Society in Saudi Arabia" (Ph.D. diss., University of Virginia, 1971), 169–76.

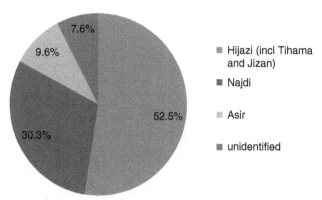

FIGURE 6.7. Background of Saudi military officers in 1965 (sample with 238 cases).[14]

as viceroy in the region from the 1920s on, while his successors, Fahd in particular, relied more strongly on Najdi links.

According to statistics compiled by Nabil Mouline, Najdis have historically dominated the Council of Ministers (set up in 1953), the Council of Senior Ulama (created in 1971), and the Majlis Al-Shura (set up in 1992). Seventy-two, 73, and 57 percent of the total membership of these three bodies, respectively, have hailed from Najd. The figures for the southern regions are 1, 6, and 7 percent. The remaining 20 to 30 percent of governing elites are mostly from the Hijaz (with the exception of the Ulama Council, where only 9 percent Hijazis have been present). The breakdown for ministers of state and senior bureaucrats is similar.[15]

At no time, then, was the Hijaz completely sidelined, as some Hijazi local patriots would make us believe. In the cabinet, for example, Saudi kings perpetuated a regional key that would reserve a minimum number of ministries for non-Najdis. The important Ministry of Petroleum was headed by Hijazi ministers until 1995, and the Ministry of Commerce and Industry has recently returned to Hijazi hands under Abdallah Alireza. The Al Saud's strategy was never to completely marginalize the Hijaz, but rather to co-opt it in a junior, but nonetheless important, position. In this sense, it has been structurally integrated into the national system.

The south has been more marginalized in terms of cabinet positions, but even Jizan, Asir, and Najran have provided a couple of deputy ministers and senior advisors to princes and are part of national patronage structures.

---

[14] Jidda to State, "The Saudi Army Officer's Role in National Affairs," Nov. 27, 1965, U.S. National Archives and Records Administration, College Park, MD, Record Group 59, 250, 5–7, box 1675, folder DEF 6 SAUD 64–66.

[15] Nabil Mouline, "Les oulémas du palais. Parcours des membres du Comité des grands Oulémas," *Archives des sciences sociales des religions*, no. 149, 229–53.

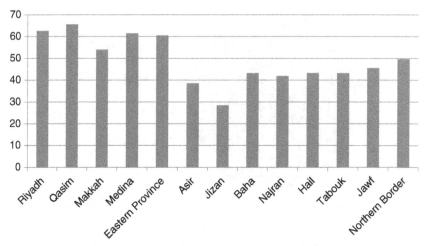

FIGURE 6.8. Saudi Regional Development Index.[17]

Core technocratic portfolios such as finance or oil, however, have been off-limits to them. The only current minister of southern extraction, Minister of State Saud bin Saeed Al Mathami, is in charge of the rather inconsequential portfolio of "Majlis Ash Shura Affairs." His family is reported to have allied with King Abdulaziz early on during his conquest of the Arabian Peninsula. The one region that has been very much marginalized in terms of senior-level employment are the Shiite communities within the Eastern Province and the Ismailis in the south.[16]

A measure for regional development in Saudi Arabia recently developed by the World Bank indicates that the hierarchy of regions in the kingdom is essentially the same today as it was four decades ago when the state first engaged in development expenditure on a large scale. The measure includes, among other criteria, the number of teachers, electricity connections, hospital beds, telephone lines, industrial establishments, industrial employees, and expenditure on municipal infrastructure per capita. While the central regions lead, the western and eastern provinces follow closely. The real laggards are southern regions, most of all Jizan. It is probably no coincidence that Qasim, the Najdi region from which the most senior administrators have been recruited, enjoys the highest ranking.

[16] For a useful discussion of the Eastern Province see Toby Craig Jones, "Rebellion on the Saudi Periphery," *IJMES* 38, no. 2: 213–33.
[17] Prajapati Trivedi, "Results-Based National Strategies," presentation to the General Secretariat for Development Planning, Qatar, Oct. 2008; http://www.gsdp.gov.qa/portal/page/portal/GSDP_Vision_Root/GSDP_EN/GSDP_News/GSDP%20News%20Files/English_Dr%20Prajapati%20Trivedi_World%20Bank_QNV%20Seminar_Pane.pdf.

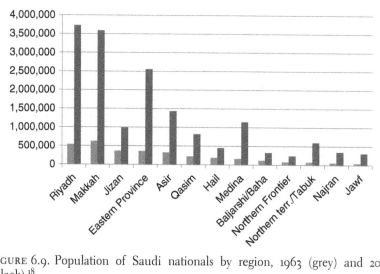

FIGURE 6.9. Population of Saudi nationals by region, 1963 (grey) and 2004 (black).[18]

To some extent, differences between regions are likely to be differences between urban and rural development, as some regions – notably Riyadh, the Eastern Province, and Mecca – are more urbanized and large cities have benefited by far the most from the kingdom's oil-financed development drive. Urban–rural disparities within governorates are probably as big as any inter-governorate differences. Yet, comparably rural regions still look fairly different: The very sparsely populated north, for example, is by and large better off than the south (we already saw above that it also has received many more real estate loans per capita). Qasim, moreover, the population of which is fairly dispersed, scores very well.

Regionally differentiated levels of development are also reflected in population movement since the 1960s.

While the population has grown sevenfold in Riyadh, it increased less than three times in Jizan. Poor as it has always been, Jizan is unlikely to have had a much lower fertility rate. Instead the main cause of slower growth probably was internal migration to the economic growth axis of Jeddah–Riyadh–Eastern Province, where nowadays one meets many Saudis with southern surnames.

---

[18] The sources are the 1963 population survey and the 2004 census. Care has been taken to make sure territorial designations in the two sources were commensurable; in some cases subregions had to be added up.

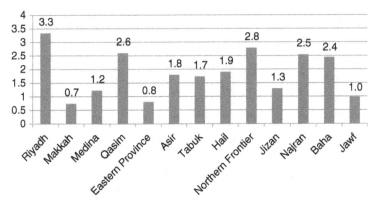

FIGURE 6.10. Civil service entrants per 1,000 nationals, by region (2007). *Source:* Ministry of Civil Service, SAMA.

One important driver of such migration has been government employment, of which the central region has historically been providing the largest share.[19] The figures shown here on the number of civil service entrants in 2007 confirm that Riyadh continues to have the highest intake while the western and Eastern provinces lag far behind even peripheral regions. The latter might be seeing a recruitment drive as result of King Abdullah's new regional development policy (to be discussed shortly). One notes, however, that within the peripheral group, Jizan (in addition to Jawf) is once again a laggard.

With government as the dominant employer, public job creation can be crucial for the economic fate of regions. The graph here shows the share of public employment in total Saudi employment in 2007, demonstrating that among the big urban conglomerations Riyadh enjoys the largest public employment ratio. The peripheral regions, in which private business tends to be weak, profit significantly from state employment, but to quite different degrees. Again, the north seems to be somewhat better off than the south, especially Jizan.

The division between urban and peripheral regions is also reflected in public and private sector wage data; in this case, it seems to dominate all other distinctions.

[19] Over longer stretches of time, Riyadh has had more than our times as many entrants than any other city; Ministry of Civil Service, *Al-khidma al-madaniyya bi-l-arqam 2005* (*The Civil Service in Figures 2005*), 69.

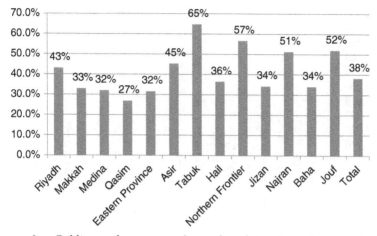

FIGURE 6.11. Public employment as share of total Saudi employment (2007). *Source:* Labour Force Survey, Central Department of Statistics.

Looking back on five decades of government development policy, we can conclude that although the regime seems to have privileged the central region in terms of direct handouts and government employment, it tried to roll out public services on a larger scale in the three main urban centers of the country in a concerted effort at integrating the national infrastructure. The southern periphery suffered from relative neglect on both accounts. Nonetheless, all

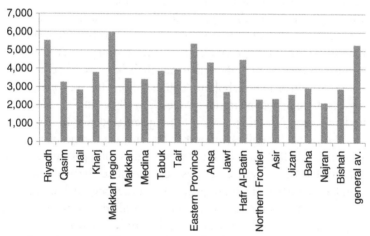

FIGURE 6.12. Average public sector wage for Saudis in 2007. *Source:* General Organization for Social Insurance.

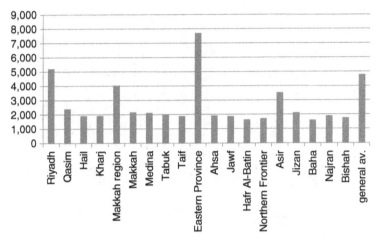

FIGURE 6.13. Average private sector wage for Saudis in 2007. *Source:* General
Organization for Social Insurance

regions of the kingdom have become part of a highly centralized system of
distribution as reflected in high dependence on state employment and other
public services.

King Abdallah has recently embarked on a new campaign of regional development, aided by greatly increased oil receipts since 2003. He has shown a
particular interest in issues of poverty, which in the Saudi context is to an
important extent a problem of regional equity, and the first national poverty
strategy is currently in the making. He has framed these efforts rather explicitly
in terms of granting equal rights to everyone and has made a point of touring
neglected regions. Recent infrastructural spending, road-building efforts, and
the announcement of new provincial universities are all part of this campaign,
as are the new "economic cities" that Abdallah has – rather consciously –
been promoting in all regions but the central one, and the "national dialogue"
sessions that have happened in various locations all over the kingdom.

The king's pronouncements seem to be given credence by a majority of
Saudis, also as he himself is somewhat peripheral to some of the central
province networks that have dominated the state in the past under his half-
brothers. It is too early, however, to measure the results of the new development
drive, and even the best of intentions are likely to get bogged down in bureaucratic red tape and particularistic agendas of local administrators. A certain
disenchantment with Abdallah's inclusive rhetoric was palpable already at the
peak of the recent boom.

For the time being, however, regional disquiet about uneven development
has not led to any significant secessionist or antigovernment ferment. Instead,

most dissident elites from deprived regions want to leverage Abdallah's inclusive and paternal rhetoric to claim their full share of the national project. As citizenship in Saudi Arabia has less to do with political rights than with material entitlements to be received from the state, this constitutes an essential component of full citizenship.

Equal treatment by the state is a staple demand in political petitions that the king has received from regional delegations in recent years, and it is perhaps the core component of regional political agendas as far as they exist. They thereby underline shared citizenship in the Saudi system rather than demand dissociation from it.[20] Because of the crushingly large role of the central state in Saudi nationals' life, this appears a rational strategy, not least as such political projects probably stand a better chance under Abdallah than under any other Saudi king. In any case, there is little by way of autonomous political organization in most of the Saudi regions, especially in the disadvantaged South, that could fundamentally challenge the existing system.

In the south the absence of a powerful historical narrative of regional identity seems to have prevented political mobilization over regional inequality, despite the very raw deal the region has gotten in the course of state building. The one community in the south that is reasonably mobilized, the Ismailis of Najran, are socioculturally very distinct from the Najdis; one might hence expect to them to lose out particularly badly in the distribution game. Instead, their region gets average scores on many indicators of development, or at least scores better than most southern neighboring regions. This might show that it is not cultural affinity to the Najd, but a common identity, articulated through tribal and sectarian cohesion, which allows a region to claim its share in the national pie. Other parts of the south follow the Hanbalo-Wahhabi creed of the Al Saud regime much more diligently than most of the Hijaz or the Eastern Province, and different from Shiites and urban Hijazis are often of tribal stock like the majority of Najids. No other bit of Saudi Arabia would appear socioculturally closer to the central region. Yet they appear worse organized and hence are effectively marginalized.

REGIONAL INEQUALITY: REGIONAL SHIFTS AND NATIONAL INTEGRATION OF BUSINESS

The following section will engage in more depth with an aspect of regional hierarchy around which a particularly elaborate mythology has grown: the

---

[20] For Shiite demands along these lines, see, for example, Laurence Louër, *Transnational Shia Politics* (New York: Hurst, 2008).

shifting fortunes of different regions' business sectors. When it comes to business, the image of a marginalized Hijaz, and of continuing separate regional
business classes, is particularly strong – at least in the some of the academic
literature.[21]

As in the case of public services and infrastructure in general, the business
elites of central Arabia have indeed profited more from the state than those of
other regions. But by no means has the Hijaz been sidelined: Its share of the
system as junior partner of the Saudi regime has remained substantial. Once
again, the south has been the biggest loser of the national economic integration process, as it has produced few big names in business. More generally,
although important sociocultural differences remain between the business
elites of different Saudi regions, their actual activities nowadays are in fact
quite closely integrated, as they have been organized around a dominant state.

In the Saudi context, there is no ideal measure for measuring the size
of regional business, as we lack reliable data on turnover and there is no
systematic taxation. We therefore have to rely on a proxy measures. In the
following, a number of diachronic comparisons will serve to show how central
region businesses have gradually acquired a dominant position.

The easiest way to measure the size of business activity in Saudi Arabia
is simply by counting the number of commercial registrations. The table
here does exactly that, showing the share of commercial registrations in the
national total broken down by region in 1967 and 2007 in comparison. The
most important finding is that Riyadh has increased its share from barely a
fifth to almost a third of total business activity, mostly at the expense of the
western region. Population movement toward Riyadh, which itself is partially
explained by pro-Riyadh government policy, explains some of this. However,
even accounting for demographic growth, all other things being equal Riyadh's
share in total national businesses should still only be about 26 percent in 2007,
while the share of the Mecca region, whose population has also grown above
the national average, should be almost 40 percent. Instead, Mecca's economic
activity has shrunk to 25.6 percent, and Riyadh's has mushroomed to 30.7
percent.

The southern regions, by contrast, have not lost out in relative terms –
considering the population decline in most of the south, they have even
gained a bit relative to other regions. But in both absolute and per capita terms,
business activity remains much weaker than either in the central regions or in
the west or east, as the table and bar graph show. The relative gains are worth
little, as the south has started from such a low baseline.

[21] Kiren Chaudhry, *The Price of Wealth* (Ithaca, NY: Cornell University Press, 1997).

TABLE 6.1. *Share of private establishments in national total by region,*
1967 and 2007

	1967		2007	
		Sums		
Riyadh	19.18%		Riyadh	30.68%
Unayzah	2.71%	3.80%	Qasim (incl. Unayzah and Buraydah)	4.66%
Buraydah	1.08%			
Mecca	15.73%	34.68%	Mecca (incl. Jeddah)	25.55%
Jeddah	18.96%			
Medina	6.79%		Medina	5.36%
Dammam	4.95%	14.18%	Eastern Province	16.89%
Al-Khobar	2.49%		(incl. Dammam,	
Hofuf	4.93%		Al-Khobar, Hofuf,	
Qatif	1.82%		Qatif)	
Najran	1.43%		Najran	1.50%
Jizan	1.41%		Jazan	1.40%

Some fragmentary data indicate that the shift in favor of the central regions already started before 1967. The table here shows how many of the commercial establishments in different cities had been set up before 1960. The share is particularly small in Riyadh and the Qasimi towns Unayzah and Buraydah, indicating that these places got an extraordinary boost in the 1960–7 period, which is when state expenditure embarked on a long-term growth path.

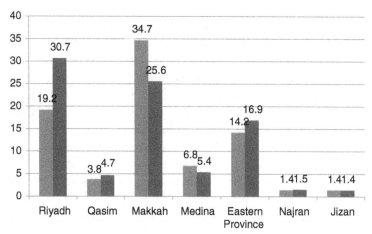

FIGURE 6.14. Share of private establishments in national total by region in percentage, 1967 (grey) and 2007 (black).

TABLE 6.2. *Commercial establishments in 1967*

	Total	Set up before 1960	Ratio
Riyadh	8,367	1,478	17.66%
Unayzah	1,184	229	19.34%
Buraydah	472	97	20.55%
Mecca	6,860	2,269	33.08%
Jeddah	8,269	2,370	28.66%
Medina	2,962	972	32.82%
Dammam	2,158	489	22.66%
Al-Khobar	1,085	367	33.82%
Hofuf	2,149	887	41.28%
Qateef	793	188	23.71%
Abha	424	125	29.48%
Najran	625	93	14.88%
Jizan	614	189	30.78%

Source: 1967 Establishment Survey

In 1967, construction was one of only a few categories in which Riyadh had more companies than Jeddah (148 as compared to 111). This is further evidence that state activity was the main driver of business growth in the central region, as contractors at the time mostly served government construction demand.[22]

Relative to the size of the population, business activity in the south, Jizan in particular, remains very weak even today – further underlining these regions' continuing dependence on government largess, which is not always forthcoming.

Patterns over time are rather similar when one looks at the number of workers in private establishments: The number of workers in Riyadh has increased significantly above proportionality, while the western provinces have lost out. In the south, the number of workers has grown quickly, but from a very low baseline of little formal economic activity in the 1960s.[23]

There has been a discernible shift from the western to the central regions also in the area of industry, which has been heavily reliant on state-provided infrastructure and cheap inputs. Whereas in 1970 the western region of Saudi Arabia hosted many more industrial establishments than the central region, the position had reversed in 2007, as many more industries were active in the

---

[22] *1967 Establishment Survey*, Institute of Public Administration Documentation Center, Riyadh, table 4.

[23] The divergence is even stronger regarding licenses for importing foreign labor, which are reported in official Ministry of Labour documentation.

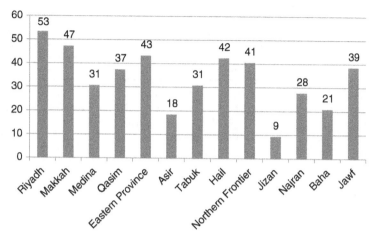

FIGURE 6.15. Commercial registrations per 1,000 Saudi residents, 2007.

central regions (the higher levels of financing for east and west are mostly explained by the presence of public or foreign-owned heavy industry at coastal industrial cities).[24] Southern and northern regions have made relative gains starting from an extremely low baseline. In absolute terms, these gains are so small, however, that the periphery has by and large been left out of the national industrialization drive – a fact that King Abdallah has only recently tried to change with the initiation of the (possibly ill-fated) Jizan Economic City.

Manufacturing in particular is a business activity that would not have come into being without extensive state support in terms of infrastructure, cheap input, and soft loans. We show in the figure some historical data on the latter broken down by region.

The dominance of the east–west axis is crushing and in line with the supply infrastructure for industrial feedstock that has been built from the 1970s on. The dominance of the Eastern Province is due to the local availability of oil and gas inputs and the presence Jubail Industrial City, while most of the funds registered in Medina governorate have gone into Yanbu Industrial City. Interestingly, the total funds made available in both west and east are larger than those accrued in Riyadh. It remains to be seen whether King Abdallah's new economic cities can change anything about the absence of industries in the north and south.

---

[24] The high level of financing for Medina is mostly explained with the location of Yanbu industrial city in the Medina governorate, which is located at the sea for logistical reasons. The same is true with the Eastern Province and Jubail Industrial City as well as other oil- and gas-related industries related to national oil company Aramco, whose facilities are located in the east.

TABLE 6.3. *Workers in private establishment as share of national total*

	1967		2005	
	Sums			
Riyadh	21.33%		Riyadh	30.68%
Unayzah	1.77%	2.34%	Qasim (incl. Unayzah and	4.95%
Buraydah	0.58%		Buraydah)	
Mecca	11.48%	39.13%	Mecca	24.58%
Jeddah	27.65%			
Medina	5.16%		Medina	4.63%
Dammam	6.61%	15.84%	Eastern Province (incl.	21.14%
Al-Khobar	4.38%		Dammam, Al-Khobar,	
Hofuf	3.82%		Hofuf, Qatif)	
Qatif	1.04%			
Najran	0.91%		Najran	1.36%
Jizan	1.22%		Jazan	1.43%

Source: 1967 Establishment Survey and 2005 Statistical Yearbook

More generally, however, Riyadh is now the business capital of Saudi Arabia, and the Hijaz has lost out in relative terms. In the early 2000s, Riyadh hosted 38 percent of the top one thousand Saudi companies, while 37 percent were located in the Eastern Province and only 24 percent in the west.

TABLE 6.4. *Industrial establishments in 1970 and 2007: Absolute numbers*

	1970				2007		
	Number	Paid-up capital (thousands SAR)	Employment		Number	Financing (million SAR)	Employment
Central Province	85	96,843	2,574	Riyadh	1,515	54,467.55	164,011
				Qasim	150	5,498.522	10,811
Western Province	149	221,560	5,666	Mecca	1,063	53,254.69	118,869
				Medina	151	53,836.82	19,196
Eastern Province	55	443,290	4,304	Eastern Region	904	161,009	110,291
Other	5	87	61	Asir	96	2,570.032	5,149
				Tabuk	34	1,700.33	3,127
				Hail	31	337.866	1,271
				Northern Frontiers	9	42.56	243
				Jazan	37	1,569.576	1792
				Najran	20	156.833	568
				Al-Baha	15	84.97	439
				Jouf	23	233.6	912

Source: Ramon Knauerhase, *The Saudi Arabian Economy* (Praeger, 1977), 143, and *Statistical Yearbook* 2007.

TABLE 6.5. *Industrial establishments in 1970 and 2007: Percentage shares in national total*

1970				2007		
	Number	Paid-up capital	Employment		Number	Financing	Employment
Central Province	28.91%	12.71%	20.42%	Riyadh	37.43%	16.27%	37.56%
				Qasim	3.71%	1.64%	2.48%
Western Province	50.68%	29.08%	44.95%	Mecca	26.26%	15.91%	27.22%
				Medina	3.73%	16.08%	4.40%
Eastern Province	18.71%	58.19%	34.15%	Eastern Province	22.33%	48.10%	25.26%
Other	1.70%	0.01%	0.48%	Asir	2.37%	0.77%	1.18%
				Tabuk	0.84%	0.51%	0.72%
				Hail	0.77%	0.10%	0.29%
				Northern Frontiers	0.22%	0.01%	0.06%
				Jazan	0.91%	0.47%	0.41%
				Najran	0.49%	0.05%	0.13%
				Al-Baha	0.37%	0.03%	0.10%
				Jouf	0.57%	0.07%	0.21%

But again, only a measly 1 percent were based in the south.[25] In specific sectors such as state-supported agricultural production, the central provinces, and Qasim in particular, have benefited from particularly blatant favoritism, despite the south's much better natural potential for agriculture.[26] Even today, Jizan receives a much smaller share of agricultural loans from the state-run Saudi Arabian Agricultural Bank (SAAB) than would be warranted by its large national workforce in agriculture.[27]

Regional disparities in business development as measured by numbers of establishments or workers employed appear even worse than those in the provision of public services. Redistribution of state resources through the private sector seems to have been the most unequal part of the Saudi state-building process – for there is little doubt that most of the original Saudi business fortunes were made with and through the state and connections with networks

[25] World Bank, "Administrative Barriers to Investment in the Kingdom of Saudi Arabia" (study for SAGIA, Riyadh, 2002), 70. The south until recently also did not have an industrial city; Ibid., 73.
[26] See Chaudhry, *The Price of Wealth*, for a detailed discussion of agriculture in the 1980s and 1990s.
[27] SAAB annual reports, Central Department of Statistics Labour Force Surveys, various. Historical data are reported in early Statistical Yearbooks and confirm the anti-southern bias.

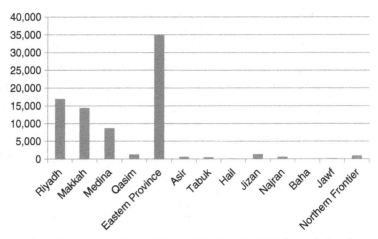

FIGURE 6.16. Cumulative loans disbursed by the Saudi Industrial Development Fund from 1974 to 2009 (million SAR). *Source:* SIDF.

in the state apparatus. Some of the divergence might be explained through different levels of entrepreneurialism and pre–oil business traditions of different regions. But given the top-down nature of much of the rent distribution process, the agency of major players within regime and bureaucracy must have played an important role. Business favoritism has been most directly visible in the field of agricultural support policies, which created a new class of agricultural entrepreneurs in the northern Najd, where there was no tradition of large-scale agriculture to speak of, while leaving established agricultural regions in the South to fend for themselves.

It might not be coincidental that the one direct consumer support mechanism that is closest to discretionary business subsidies – that of real estate financing – has also been the most unequal according to our data.

The fact that central Arabia has been favored by development policies often is often conflated with two other, faulty hypotheses: that the Hijaz has been economically sidelined, and that the Saudi economy remains regionalized, dominated by specific provincial networks. The first is not true since Hijazi business by most measures remains the second most important regional grouping in Saudi Arabia, whose leaders have access to the most senior princes and who sit on the boards of many leading national companies. In absolute terms, Hijazi business has flourished over the decades. Relative to northern and southern elites, and to the indigenous business groups of the Eastern Province, Hijazi business leaders remain in a very comfortable position. Hijazi notables often cling to the myth that they saw eye to eye with King Abdulaziz in the pre–oil era, while in fact their indigenous political institutions were gradually sidelined through Najdi administrators early on in the late 1920s and 1930s.

The second assumption, of regionalized markets, was true up to the early 1980s but is much less true today. The Saudi national market is well integrated thanks to a highly developed infrastructure and rather strong competition between companies from different regions, which became salient especially after the budget crunch of the mid-1980s, when business suddenly had to cater to private demand to survive. Although some trading and contracting, specifically on a smaller scale, is still regionalized, most larger companies today operate nationally.

It is true that the regional business communities in Saudi Arabia have their own local cultures and sometimes speak of each other in derogatory terms behind closed doors. This has led some observers to reify regional elites as closed and static categories. This is a fundamental misunderstanding. In fact, the historical links between business elites of various regions are strong, and different regional clusters in Saudi business are far from watertight categories. Historical outmigration of merchants and enterprising workers from Najd has led to the presence of Najdi-rooted businesspeople in both East and West, and these have often taken on some of the cultural accoutrements of the local elites. It is hence difficult to tell where leading western province families such as Juffali or Sulaiman really belong, as their origins are Najdi. The same is true about families active in the Eastern Province such as Gosaibi, Zamil, and Ulayan (and the same incidentally is true about many business and notable families in the rest of the GCC too, who often have central Arabian origins). The Hijaz itself has historically been a migrant melting pot and has a mixed and composite identity.

It is true that the smaller northern and southern business elites have been more systematically excluded from national development, but by the same token, they have always been politically marginal and had few organizational structures to draw on. More fundamentally, all traditional economic structures in the kingdom's regions apart from trade and pilgrimage business suffered very heavily after the onset of oil production and large-scale importation of industrialized goods. Therefore, the decks have been reshuffled for everyone in Saudi business, and most business leaders owe much of their fortune to the state and the ruling family, two structurally unifying factors.

The hub-and-spoke patronage system around the Al Saud has undermined the autonomy of pre–oil economic networks in the kingdom's different regions – and long ago marginalized those economic elites who were not willing to be co-opted by the ruling family. It has also created strata of newcomers in business with (originally) indistinct or foreign background who were patronized by the Al Saud. This boomtime social mobility has further contributed to the creation of a new kind of nationally integrated business elite that is deeply tied up with the Al Saud system.

The national integration of Saudi business elites is reflected in the board membership of leading Saudi companies: The Saudi Industrial Investment Group, for example, the largest private industrial enterprise in the kingdom, has leading western (Bin Zagr, Juffali), central (Al-Rajhi, Zamil), and Eastern (Gosaibi) province business families represented on its board.[28] In fact, several of the families mentioned straddle different regions themselves. The boards of other large industrial ventures are similarly mixed. It is true that ownership of large Saudi banks is somewhat less spread across regions, but nonetheless all banks compete on the national level and have least one representative from a second region.

Demands of business toward government tend to be rather similar in each region, focusing on protection against foreign competition and reduction of red tape. The regionalism of Saudi business at least in the elite is more of a cultural veneer than an actual political strategy. The economic dissociation of different regions is not thinkable due to close links of cooperation, cross-ownership, and dependence on the same markets and sources of income, including the government.

Hijazi business has indeed lost its national preeminence, but they are still doing better under the Al Saud than they could under any other conceivable dispensation. They are part of a national notability that is defined through its attachment to the Al Saud family and the state that they run. On the ground, the Saudi system leaves little scope for effective particularism. Lower-level particularism in the business elites does exist in the form of specific networks of mutual help and lower-scale patronage – be they regional or tribal – but all of these operate in the shadow of the larger-scale, centralized patronage of the ruling family, functioning in a tightly integrated national market. Unless there is a fundamental shift in political circumstances, it is unlikely that the existing networks of Hijazi separatists would enjoy broader backing in the region's merchant community.

---

[28] See http://www.siig.com.sa/english/page.php?i=members.

CONCLUSION: REGIONAL IDENTITY, REGIONAL ORGANIZATION, AND RESOURCE DISTRIBUTION

This chapter has documented the drastically differing socioeconomic fate of Saudi Arabia's different regions in some detail. A thorough historical explanation of why these differences have emerged is beyond the scope of this research. I will, however, conclude by outlining the hypothesis that, at first glance, seems to fit the observed patterns the best: Regional differences seem best explained by the relative coherence of regional identity narratives and the capacity of regional elites to organize on this basis.[29]

This would explain best why Hijazi elites, culturally very different from those of the central region, managed to sustain their privileged position as junior partners in the Saudi regime, and why the south failed to capitalize on the oil boom despite its cultural affinities to the center. It would also explain why the one southern region that is very different from the Najd – Najran – seems to have suffered relatively less socioeconomic discrimination than other parts of the south. Finally, it might account for the silent demise of some of the old Eastern Province merchant and notable elites, who have had less of a distinct regional (as opposed to town-based) identity to draw on.

Drawing on a strong regional identity and tight elite networks, Hijazi elites have entered the Saudi realm as the result of collective bargaining and were accorded their own state institutions early on – even if the latter were often partly colonized by Najdis. The south, by contrast, appears more fragmented and lacks a regional narrative. In the course of Saudi state building, southern elites seem to have been conquered or co-opted on a more individual basis.

Historical memory of elite alliances and tributary relationships runs deep in Saudi Arabia and still strongly influences the status of particular families. Parts of the Hijazi elite continue to enjoy access to important royal brokers such as the governor of Mecca, Khaled bin Faysal – linkages that go back to the presence of his father, the later King Faysal, as vice regent in the Hijaz. Southern elites never had access to players of that status and were instead for a long time governed by members of Al Saud vassal clans like the Al-Sudairi family.

Other explanations of regional divergence seem to be unable to account for the economic geography mapped out in this chapter: Relatively higher pre–oil levels of economic development might have helped the Hijaz to continue

---

[29] I would like to thank Stéphane Lacroix for useful discussions that have helped me to formulate this argument.

growing, but they failed to do so in the case of old Eastern Province elites. In any case, given that post–oil development was almost completely state-dominated, resources could easily be channeled into less developed regions – as has indeed happened in the case of Qasim.

Similarly, sociocultural affinities between the Najdi conquerors and their new vassals systematically fail to explain the lot of different regions: In fact, with the exception of the marginalized Eastern Province Shiites, a distinct but well-organized identity seems to rather have helped regional elites in the bargaining with the austere but pragmatic new overlords.

7

Oil in Saudi Arabian Culture and Politics

From Tribal Poets to Al-Qaeda's Ideologues

Bernard Haykel

In the study of Saudi Arabia many scholars discuss and analyze the economic, social, and political effects of oil, but they say curiously little about the place of oil in Saudi political debates and discourse. Lying at the core of the dramatic transformation that the country has witnessed since the mid-twentieth century, oil has not been analyzed in the ways the commodity itself is invoked and used by the state to garner legitimacy nor as a topic in contesting the regime by its various critics and opponents. Yet it features prominently in cultural and political debates. Most studies treat oil from the perspective of the political economy, namely, in which ways it structures governance and political life, and more specifically how revenues accruing from its production allow the state to buy social peace through co-optation of dissent and the creation of a generous system of entitlements. What often ensues from such approaches is a discussion of the so-called resource curse that plagues rentier states and whether the price of oil is sufficiently high to enable the state to persist in its entitlement policies or whether a political crisis is in the offing because the price is too low and therefore the entitlements are unsustainable. In other words, the question of the survival and longevity of the Saudi regime is often the central question, and this is invariably tied to the projected reserves and price of oil.[1]

This chapter will focus on various instances in which oil is invoked in Saudi culture and politics and will culminate with a close examination of al-Qaeda's views on oil in its ideological attacks on the legitimacy of the Saudi state

---

[1] See Thomas Lippman, *Saudi Arabia on the Edge: The Uncertain Future of an American Ally* (Lincoln, NE: Potomac Books, 2012), and Karen Elliot House, *On Saudi Arabia: Its People, Past, Religion, Fault Lines and Future* (New York: Knopf, 2012), and Hugh Eakin, "Will Saudi Arabia Ever Change?" in *The New York Review of Books*, Jan. 10, 2013.

and the world order more generally. It will present al-Qaeda's views on the question of oil, namely, its value, its "real" price and how it should be marketed, and finally whether or not the resource itself and its installations should be targeted and destroyed as part of a campaign that it labels economic jihad. Such installations have been attacked repeatedly in the 2000s, and this led one of al-Qaeda's Saudi ideologues to produce a lengthy treatise in 2004 justifying these acts in Islamic legal terms. One of the arguments of this study is that oil should be understood as important leitmotiv in the politics of Saudi Arabia and that it stands for much more than the commodity itself. Debates around oil raise profound questions not only about the ways in which the legitimacy of the Saudi royal family has been constructed, but also about how wealth is to be conceived and disbursed in a putatively Shari'a-centered society. A further argument is that al-Qaeda should be understood as an heir of Arab nationalist and anti-imperialist discourses on the subject of oil. One crucial difference between al-Qaeda and the earlier views, however, lies in al-Qaeda's replacement of pan-Arabism with a utopian pan-Islamism that conceives of these hydrocarbon reserves as the property of the entire Muslim nation (*umma*) to be exploited for the defense and propagation of the religion. Furthermore, with al-Qaeda's sanctification of violence, these reserves can be attacked, even destroyed, if they are not serving, let alone harming, the *umma*.

OIL IN POPULAR CULTURE

Oil has been a trope in poetry and literature as well as political discourse, official and otherwise, from the time of its discovery in Arabia in the late 1930s until today.[2] Perhaps the most well-known literary example of its invocation as a disruptive force is 'Abd al-Raḥmān Munīf's quintet *Cities of Salt* in which the author laments the demise of the old order with the coming of the age of oil and its nefarious western oil men.[3] An even more resonant expression of the disruptions wrought by the discovery of oil and its effects on the social and political order can be found in the poetry of the Saudi Nabaṭī poet Bandar bin Surūr, a bard of the 'Utayba tribe.[4] It seems that on at least two different

---

[2] Cf. Toby Craig Jones, *Desert Kingdom: How Oil and Water Forged Modern Saudi Arabia* (Cambridge, MA: Harvard University Press, 2010).

[3] 'Abd al-Raḥmān Munīf, *Mudun al-milḥ* (Beirut, 1985).

[4] Nabaṭī poetry uses the local vernacular Arabic, and Bandar bin Surūr is considered to have been a master of the form and to have addressed the modern transformations in Saudi culture in pithy and poignant terms. For a fuller exposition of Bandar bin Surūr's poetry and life see the chapter by Abd al-Aziz al-Fahad in this volume.

occasions Bandar declaimed a particular poem about the discovery of oil, whose key lines are

> Curse the Christian who found the oil // would that the gushing oil blind his eyes

> Without it you had to bear the unbearable to be considered a man // you would need to do heroic deeds that weaklings cannot do

> You would need resolve and determination to cross empty wastes // wastes that the unworthy [lit. sons of owls] cannot cross[5]

But oil not only ended the era of manly and tribal virtue and personal prowess, it also produced a government with hitherto unprecedented power to co-opt and enforce obedience. In another poem, Bandar describes the way in which political autonomy became constricted and the once independent tribal shaykhs were brought to heel through state handouts. His description of this new feature of the Saudi politics is encapsulated in the following lines:

> O, Abu Majid, our times have changed // rainy clouds turned into dust storms

> 'Utayba's chiefs are now worthless // do not seek justice from such quislings living on doles

> I yearn for the old chiefs who held Najd under their firm grip, as if nailed to their hands

> The chiefs of Najd's tribes who uprooted mighty armies // have become docile and content to feed, like chicken, on grain thrown to them on dirt[6]

---

[5] I would like to thank Dr. Saud al-Sarhan, Mr. Muhammad al-Sayf, and Prof. Saad Sowayan for providing me with different versions of Bandar bin Surūr's poems. Bandar's poetic oeuvre has not been established with any certainty, and there is some confusion over the content of many of his poems. It seems that numerous interpolations have been made that may not be his. For our purposes, it is sufficient to note that the lines mentioned here are widely considered to be his and to express a shared sentiment about the effects of the discovery of oil. Many of his poems can be found on the internet. See, for example, http://www.gsaidlil.com/vb/showthread.php?t=1263 (accessed Dec. 2012). Here is the transliteration of the quoted lines:

> ṣalliṭ 'alā naṣrānī allī ligā az-zet // ya 'all nab' az-zet yi'mī 'yonih
> lolah tiḥtāj al-marājil shifālīt // tiḥtāj shayyin yagṣir an-nadhil donih
> 'azmin 'alā l-firjih w-gaṭ' al-khalālīt // allī 'yāl al-bom ma yagti'onih

[6] gil li-bo mājid tarā wagtinā gher // tibaddalat siḥb al-mitar ba-l-'ajājī
> gomih 'tebah shyukhhin ma bahum kher // la yiddi'ī bi-shyukh rab' al-kharaji
> yabkī shyukhin sammarat najd tasmīr // tasmīr 'ūd al-'āj fī 'ūd sājī
> shyukh najd allī tihidd at-twābīr // yirma lihum habbin swāt ad-dijājī

Bandar is alluding to an Arabian practice, one that predates the Saudi state, which involves a patron giving a client what is referred to in Najdi Arabic as a *sharha*. This is a confusing word for an outsider because in classical Arabic it carries negative meanings such as ravenousness, gluttony, or covetousness, whereas in Najd it does not necessarily have these connotations. In Najdi colloquial *sharh* refers to a person who is hard to please no matter how much you give him or do for him, but it can also mean someone who is justifiably expecting another to do something for him. In other terms, *sharha* refers to something one expects from someone else either as reciprocating for the performance of a previous favor or because they are friends or relatives.[7] In the clientelist and highly personalized exchanges that characterize social and political relationships in Saudi Arabia, *sharha* refers to the gift of cash, land, cars, or camels that the higher status person or patron provides to the dependent and lower status person, who is in turn obligated to serve and respect the patron. It is common, for example, to hear a person attached to a prince claim that the prince provided a "gift" (*sharrahna*), which typically occurs at a specific time in the calendar year during a visit to the prince to receive a regular *sharha*. One can think of this as a grant (*minha*) or more appropriately an allowance, and as constituting part of a practice of patronage through largess.[8] The promise of financial largesse to his subjects by the king in Saudi Arabia is sometimes referred to as a *makrama malakiyya* (generosity of the king), and this has in recent times generated considerable resentment, expressed through social media (Twitter and YouTube). The resentment takes the form of denying the king's act as constituting true generosity because the funds being disbursed belong to the people and not to the royal family or the government.

Oil magnified the clientelist power of the Saudi rulers to unprecedented levels at a time when the modern centralizing state was also becoming the dominant institution in society. This then stripped many hitherto active agents in society, such as tribal shaykhs but others as well, of whatever autonomy they once had. The poignancy of Bandar's poem lies in the description he

---

7 In Najd the expression "so-and-so doesn't have a *sharhih*" (*flān mā 'alayh sharhih*) indicates that such person is not expected to rise up to the occasion and fulfill his obligations. This is either because he cannot, for whatever reason, or he is churlish or he is not a person of good and noble breeding who knows what his duties and obligations are. I would like to thank Prof. Saad Sowayan for explaining to me the different and contextual meanings of this term.

8 The Saudi state provides such allowances to tribal leaders not only inside the kingdom but also to those in Jordan and Yemen among other neighboring countries. Interestingly, the regimes (Jordanian and Yemeni) do not seem to regard this largess with suspicion or resentment. Rather, the acceptance of power by the Al Saud family, and the obligations for generosity that this implies, mean that this sort of practice is not only tolerated but deemed appropriate and correct.

provides of the overwhelming monetary power that the central government now acquired – and that later individual members of the royal family would also have – from oil revenues. Once proud shaykhs became domesticated chickens, living off the feed thrown to them on the ground.

Oil and power are intimately associated and on display in Saudi Arabia's political system. When I asked a Saudi who had recently received a *sharha* from the government whether he felt guilty for receiving money without actually earning it through work, the answer I received was: "this is my right" or "this is mine" (*hadhā ḥaqqī*). I then retorted that this money was from oil revenues, which instead properly belong to the public treasury. The response, as one can imagine, was that as a member of the public, my interlocutor had a right to this sum. This exchange raises the question of ownership of the resource and the methods of it disposal and use, a topic that is dealt with in the Islamic law of governance and to which I will turn to later. For the moment, it is important to note that such acts of "gift giving" are integral to the functioning of the Saudi political system, as are regular monetary stipends to numerous individuals both within and outside the kingdom. Furthermore, the relationship such payments have to notions of good governance and corruption is not straightforward, although a strong view is increasingly prevalent among Saudis that such acts have no place in a modern society that should be governed along rules of equity, accountability, and transparency. Such calls for political reform are often associated with the rise of an Islamist opposition in the 1990s and more recently with campaigns in the social media realm of Facebook and Twitter. However, from at least the 1960s, Arab nationalists and leftists have made arguments for a broader distribution of the oil wealth, albeit without success. Before we turn to the Arab nationalists, let us examine briefly how the scholars of Islam, the ulama, have discussed oil.

OIL AND THE ULAMA

Some Muslim scholars were wary of the negative influence that oil would have on Saudi religious life and culture. This sentiment was expressed by Shaykh 'Abd al-'Azīz b. 'Abd al-Laṭīf Āl Mubārak of al-Aḥsā, the province in which oil was first discovered, when he wrote:

O God preserve our religion from perdition //

For it has receded and blackest darkness now prevails

After the passing of those in whose folds we enjoyed blessings //

The enemy, in his deceit, has laid for us a net

And has trapped us with this Company [i.e., Aramco]

He spends money and with this captures men // and every day he raids us
without warning or cause and the hasty one has fallen for him

He has started telling us that money has // a secret that makes friends of the
wolf and lamb[9]

A wariness, even hostility, toward foreigners has long been prevalent among
the ulama of Najd. A pertinent example is when the leading Wahhabi scholars
wrote to King 'Abd al-'Azīz around 1928, warning him against entering into any
relationship or partnership with foreigners who live under Christian rule and
that involves prospecting for mineral deposits. They argued that such agree-
ments are forbidden under Islamic law because of the corruption (*mafāsid*),
both religious and worldly, that they will cause.[10] Some scholars, like the late
mufti 'Abd al-Azīz Ibn Bāz, allegedly established their credentials initially
by objecting to their presence in the kingdom.[11] The ulama, however, have
over time accommodated themselves to the foreigners' presence because the
government had final say on the matter and because these strangers brought
wealth to the country with the discovery of oil. The dominant tendency of
the Wahhabi scholarly establishment has been to view the government as its
protector and therefore to engage pragmatically with its demands and exigencies even if this has meant violating long-standing and cherished Wahhabi
principles. Thus, the Council of Senior Scholars, a body that represents this

---

9   There is some ambiguity about the authorship of this poem. Some of the lines may in fact
    belong to another scholar, Shaykh Sulaymān b. Siḥmān. I would like to thank Dr. Saud al-
    Sarhan for bringing this poem to my attention. A couple of lines of this poem can be found on
    the following site: http://www.al-jazirah.com/2001/20010610/w04.htm (accessed Dec. 2012):

    rabbi iḥfaẓ 'alaynā al-dīn min al-halaka // fa-qad taḍā'ala ḥatta 'ammat al-ḥalaka
    lammā maḍā man lanā fī ṭayyihim baraka
    madda al-'adūw lanā min kaydihi shabaka // ḥatta taṣayyadanā fī hadhihi al-sharika
    alqā al-danānīr fa-ṣṭāda al-warā fa-lahu // fī kulli yawmin ighārātin wa-in lahu
    dā'in lima da'ā habba al-'ajūl lahu
    aḍḥā yukhbirunā anna al-dīnāra lahu // sirrun yu'lifu bayna al-ḍabbi wa-l-samaka

10 See *al-Durar al-saniyya fī al-ajwiba al-najdiyya*, n.p. 2004, vol. 9, pp. 333–4. I would like to
    thank Cole Bunzel for pointing this text out to me.

11 Ibn Bāz, at the time a judge in al-Dilam, is alleged to have objected to an American mission
    in al-Kharj that was prospecting for water. He was imprisoned briefly for this by King 'Abd
    al-'Azīz, and this in turn helped make his reputation as an upright scholar for having criticized
    the ruler on the basis of the well-established Wahhabi principle of disassociating from the
    infidel (*al-barā' min al-kuffār*). See Guido Steinberg, *Religion und Staat in Saudi-Arabien:
    Die wahhabitischen Gelehrten 1902–1953* (Würzburg: Ergon Verlag, 2002), 604–06. There is
    another version of the disagreement between Ibn Bāz and King 'Abd al-'Azīz, which relates
    to a fatwa Ibn Bāz issued regarding the triple repudiation or divorce. Ibn Bāz upheld Ibn
    Taymiyya's view that its expression three times in one sitting constituted one divorce and not
    the irrevocable triple divorce. In this, Ibn Bāz opposed the dominant view of the Wahhābī
    religious establishment.

establishment, has regularly accorded the rulers the religious opinions or fat-was they have sought. This was the case when the scholars condoned the alliance with and stationing of U.S. military forces in the kingdom in 1991 to help defend against a possible Iraqi invasion, or when issuing a fatwa declar-ing all public demonstrations illegal in Islam in response to the Arab Spring uprisings in 2011.[12]

On less sensational matters, scholars like Ibn Bāz often issued fatwas in response to requests from the workers in the oil fields, which points to the fact that the ulama accepted this feature of Saudi life. In return for this religious sanction of government policies, the scholars have been accorded by the state control over the social, religious, and educational spheres in society and have been employed in a number of institutions such as government ministries, universities, and missionary organizations. Such supine acquiescence to and legitimization of the policies of the Al Saud has engendered a strong reaction from the 1980s onwards from a faction of dissident scholars as well as Islamists who see in this a betrayal of the Wahhabi mission and doctrines.[13] Al-Qaeda has been one such a faction, but before we turn to its views on oil and its critique of the Saudi royal family, we need to briefly look at how Arab nationalists have discussed oil wealth.

OIL AND THE ARAB NATIONALISTS

Well before an Islamist opposition coalesced against the rule of the Al Saud, an Arab nationalist movement emerged in the 1950s in Saudi Arabia and held oppositionist views about the rule of the monarchy, and more specifically made arguments about how oil wealth should be used. The most articulate proponent of these views was the late 'Abd Allāh al-Turayqī (d. 1997). A native of the town of al-Zilfī in Najd, al-Turayqī was the first Saudi citizen to obtain an advanced degree in petroleum engineering, and upon his return from the University of Texas at Austin in 1945 began working in the Saudi government administration. Through his efforts, he was able to improve Saudi Arabia's share of oil revenues from the American-controlled oil company Aramco and was ultimately rewarded with the Ministry of Petroleum. He was the first Saudi oil minister from 1960 to 1962 and also a cofounder of OPEC. Al-Turayqī

---

[12] See Abdulaziz Al-Fahad, "From Exclusivism to Accommodation: Doctrinal and Legal Evolu-tion of Wahhabism," *New York University Law Review* 79, no. 2 (2004): 485–519. For a transcript of the fatwa of March 5, 2011 banning demonstrations see http://www.aleqt.com/2011/03/06/article_511783.html (accessed Dec. 2012).

[13] See Madawi Al-Rasheed, *Contesting the Saudi State* (Cambridge: Cambridge University Press, 2006), Thomas Hegghammer, *Jihad in Saudi Arabia* (Cambridge: Cambridge University Press, 2010), Stéphane Lacroix, *Awakening Islam* (Cambridge, MA: Harvard University Press, 2011).

eventually had a falling out with King Faysal, no doubt due to his ideological inclinations and independent views. Because of this, he spent the 1960s, 1970s, and 1980s in exile largely between Cairo and Beirut where he founded a journal called *Arab Petroleum* (*Naft al-'Arab*) whose pithy slogan encapsulated his political program: "Arab Oil for the Arabs" (*naft al-'arab li-l-'arab*). Al-Turayqī devoted himself to the Arab nationalist cause and was enamored of its charismatic political leader, President Gamal Abd al-Nasser of Egypt.

The core of al-Turayqī's views on the question of oil was that Saudi Arabia and other Arab oil-producing countries were being unfairly exploited by Western oil companies and the Western powers backing them, and he strove to see the latter's stranglehold on these resources broken. He wanted to see the oil wealth used for the general welfare and the economic and industrial development of the Arab world. The means for accomplishing this was nationalization of the oil industry.[14] By way of example, I will discuss one of al-Turayqī's articles titled "Nationalization of the Arab Oil Industry is a National Necessity," which he wrote in 1965.[15] In this he argues that the production of petroleum in the Arab world represents an example of economic colonization (*isti'mār iqtiṣādī*) because the Western companies control the resources of the Arab people and thereby generate unprecedented profits from the national wealth of the Arabs that they then repatriate overseas. These profits are then used to explore petroleum reserves outside the Arab world, and these new discoveries are subsequently used to compete with Arab production with the aim of reducing the bargaining power of the Arabs and to reduce prices and revenues for the latter. Furthermore, the western oil companies have taken all the downstream activities (e.g., refining and petrochemical production) to their own countries to deny the producing countries the profits such activities generate as well as the expertise that would otherwise accrue to the local Arab workers. The Western oil companies deliberately keep the Arab workers in menial jobs and prevent them from attaining technical and executive posts. For all these reasons, al-Turayqī concludes, "we see that the nationalization of the petroleum production in the Arab countries is a requirement necessitated by the national interest of these countries."[16]

While al-Turayqī's Pan-Arab views and activism led to his ostracism by the Saudi government, his program of nationalization and industrial development

---

[14] Cf. 'Abd Allāh al-Turayqī, *'Abd Allāh al-Turayqī: al-a'māl al-kāmila*, ed. Walīd Khaddūrī (Beirut: Markaz Dirāsāt al-Waḥda al-'Arabiyya, 1999), and Muḥammad Sayf, *'Abd Allāh al-Turayqī: sukhūr al-naft wa rimāl al-siyāsa* (Beirut: Riyāḍ al-Rayyis, 2007).

[15] 'Abd Allāh al-Turayqī, *'Abd Allāh al-Turayqī: al-a'māl al-kāmila*, 158–78 originally published in *Dirāsāt 'arabiyya*, year 1, no. 7, May 1965, 11–32.

[16] 'Abd Allāh al-Turayqī, *'Abd Allāh al-Turayqī: al-a'māl al-kāmila*, 177.

became the official policy of the kingdom from the 1970s onwards. Aramco was nationalized, albeit in a gradual manner that eschewed the hard-edged nationalism espoused by al-Ṭurayqī. Saudi Arabia also developed downstream industries, such as refining and petrochemicals, and in which today it is a world leader. What the Saudi government did not do, however, was to espouse the view that the oil wealth was to be shared by all Arabs, and it is the government's discourse on oil and oil wealth that we will now examine.

THE STATE'S VIEW ON OIL

In its official pronouncements the government of Saudi Arabia invariably describes the discovery of the country's staggeringly large hydrocarbon reserves to be both a blessing from God and a sign of His favor for the regime. By way of example, the centennial celebrations of King 'Abd al-'Azīz's conquest of Riyadh, which were held in 1998, concluded with a remarkable special effects film that began with the big bang of the universe's creation and culminated with the establishment of Saudi Arabia, the discovery of oil, and the beneficent rule of the Al Saud, who use this wealth for the benefit of the country and Islam. The permanent exhibits at the National Museum in Riyadh underscore the same point – God has affirmed the righteousness of the country and its leadership with the stewardship of Islam's holiest sites and the hydrocarbon bounty. These reserves, much like the two holy sanctuaries of Mecca and Medina, give Saudi Arabia and its leadership a special and blessed status – the Al Saud are the divinely anointed rulers of both country and religion.

Official discourse continuously underscores that the country's leadership has custodianship over these resources and exploits them for the general welfare and benefit of the people through the funding of large-scale public infrastructure projects (roads, schools, universities, hospitals, etc.) and the provision of social services (health, education, water, electricity, etc.). The oil revenues are also used for the promotion and defense of Islam through the sponsorship of missionary activity (*da'wa*), the establishment and funding of pan-Islamic institutions (e.g., Muslim World League, World Assembly of Muslim Youth) and Islamic universities, the building of mosques, the provision of educational stipends and the publication, printing, and distribution of the largest number of Qur'ans, and the management of the two holy sanctuaries in Mecca and Medina as well as the annual Hajj and the lesser pilgrimage throughout the year (*'umra*). Furthermore, the government claims that the oil reserves are carefully managed for the benefit of both present and future generations of Saudis. King Abdullah, for example, has said that the recent discoveries of oil were to be kept in the ground for future generations and are not to be produced immediately. Here is how he put it:

> Praise be to God whose will is guiding this country. Its riches are plentiful and I give you good tidings that its [oil] riches are very very many. I won't hide from you that when [these] new discoveries were made, I said to them: No, leave it, leave it in the ground. This oil, may God be praised, is for our children and our children's children; they will need it and we are now sufficiently well off, God be praised.[17]

The government's position is one of benign and well-intentioned paternalism. Subjects are likened to children to be looked after and have no say in how the resources are to be allocated. Gratitude and obedience are what is expected of the subjects and no explicit social contract binds the rulers to the ruled, especially since both are ostensibly acting in accordance with God's law. Furthermore, embedded in this view is a system of entitlements, whereby the government uses the country's natural resources to provide for the needs of its subjects – wealth accrues through rents that are then distributed and not by dint of entrepreneurial innovation and economic activity in the private sector. Nurturing such expectations in the population is generating opposition from those who feel that they have either been left out of the system or are not getting a sufficient share of the country's oil wealth. And the opposition has become particularly vocal and acute through the use of social media because the country has been experiencing a boom in revenues since 2004 when oil prices rose significantly and have remained relatively high as of mid-2014.

In terms of ownership of the resources, the Saudi government, like all other states in the Arab world, asserts by law that all natural resources are the property of the state. However, unlike most other countries, the law explicitly proclaims that these are to be exploited for the interest of the state, not that of the people. Article 14 of the Kingdom's Basic Law states:

> All natural resources that God has deposited underground, above ground, in territorial waters or within the land and sea domains under the authority of the State, together with revenues of these resources, shall be the property of the State, as provided by the Law. The Law shall specify means for exploitation, protection and development of these resources in the best interest of the State, and its security and economy.[18]

---

[17] Badr al-Khurayf, "al-Malik 'Abd Allāh, ru'ā ṭamūḥa li-ḍamān istifāda muthlā min al-nafṭ lil-ajyāl al-muqbila", *al-Sharq al-awsaṭ*, May 20, 2008.

[18] Kingdom of Saudi Arabia, *The Basic Law of Government*, http://www.shura.gov.sa/wps/wcm/connect/ShuraEn/internet/Laws±and±Regulations/The±Basic±Law±Of±Government/Chapter±Four/ (accessed Dec. 2012).

Furthermore, the Saudi code of mineral resources (*niẓām al-taʿdīn al-Saʿūdī*) states that oil and natural gas, and all their derivatives, are to be considered minerals that are owned by the government. The Saudi government's view that all minerals (*maʿādin*) are owned by the state is not the standard Ḥanbalī school's ruling on the matter, but rather that of the Mālikī school of law. To be more precise, the Mālikīs hold that mineral resources are owned and disposed of by the ruler in accordance with his view of the general welfare and that ownership of the land in which the resources are located does not determine actual ownership of the resource.[19] The Ḥanbalī view, by contrast, is that mineral resources are the property of the owner of the land where it is found.[20] This distinction became moot since the Saudi state effectively, though not de jure, came to own most of the land in the country (outside the towns and villages) after it had abolished the tradition of tribal lands (*ḥimā*) in the 1950s. A little later, in the 1960s, the state went on to invalidate the long-held Islamic legal doctrine of ownership through the "revival of fallow land" (*iḥyāʾ al-mawāt*). As a result, individual ownership of land has become a function of receiving a grant from the government.[21]

The other official, and more technocratic, view on the kingdom's hydro-carbon resources is that of the Ministry of Petroleum and Mineral Resources and of the national oil company, Saudi Aramco. The central assertion the ministry makes is that Saudi Arabia is a reliable supplier of oil and plays

---

[19] Cf. Maʿdin [q.v.], *Mawsūʿat al-fiqh al-islāmī*, (1419/1998), 38: 194–5 (dhahaba al-Mālikiyya fī qawl ilā anna al-maʿādin amruhā li-l-imām yataṣarraf fīhā bimā yarā annahu al-maṣlaḥa wa laysat bi-tabʿin li-l-arḍ allatī hiya fīhā, mamlūka kānat aw ghayr mamlūka). There is, however, another Mālikī view that the right of exploitation is determined by ownership.

[20] Cf. Maʿdin [q.v.], *Mawsūʿat al-fiqh al-islāmī*, (1419/1998), 38: 196–7 (wa qāla al-Ḥanābila: inna al-maʿādin al-jāmida tumlak bi-milk al-arḍ allatī hiya fīhā ... wa ammā al-maʿādin al-jāriya fa-hiya mubāḥa ʿalā kulli ḥāll ... wa tumlak bi-milki al-arḍ al-latī hiya fīhā li-annahā min namāʾihā wa-tawābiʿihā fa-kānat li-mālik al-arḍ ka-furūʿ al-shajar al-mamlūk wa thamaratih).

[21] Land is a major source of wealth and influence, and its control by the government is an important factor in understanding the centralization of power by the Saudi state. The methods by which this process took place from the 1950s onward and its social and political ramifications remain relatively understudied. Next to oil and the disbursement of its revenues, the control of land and its distribution is perhaps the most important factor for understanding the political economy of Saudi Arabia. The Saudi social media networks (Twitter and Facebook) are full of alleged stories about the "unjust appropriation" of land by members of the royal family through land grants, a phenomenon referred to as *shubūk*, involving the practice of placing metal wire fences around large acres of land all over the kingdom with signs that the fenced-in area now belongs to a given prince or to an entity known to belong to one of the royals. The best work to date on the political economy of Saudi Arabia is Steffen Hertog's *Princes, Brokers, and Bureaucrats: Oil and the State in Saudi Arabia* (Ithaca, NY: Cornell University Press, 2010), but it unfortunately does not delve into this opaque question of land ownership and distribution.

a unique role in the management of this resource. In so doing, it pursues policies for maximizing the welfare of the country's citizens and their over-all strategic and economic interests. It also maintains a "fair" price for this commodity on international energy markets so as to benefit all consuming and producing nations. Here is how the ministry's website expresses this policy:

> The Kingdom's petroleum policy is in line with the government's moderate and balanced approach that considers the interests of all involved parties and balances the present with the future. The Kingdom's moderate approach emphasizes cooperation, peace, economic development and prosperity for all the world. The Kingdom's petroleum policy seeks to stabilize the inter-national oil market by balancing supply and demand depending on its huge reserves, high production capacity, and spare production capacity that enable the Kingdom to meet the world demand during the different seasons. . . . The Kingdom also wants to maintain prices at reasonable levels that serve the interests of both producing and consuming nations alike. This balance will contribute to the growth of the international economy, especially within developing countries, and generate adequate returns for the international oil industry so it can invest in the exploration and production of oil in order to meet the world's growing demand.[22]

The present Saudi oil minister, Ali al-Naimi, expresses the kingdom's energy policy in these terms:

> While Saudi Arabia is doing all that it can to provide sufficient supplies of crude oil and petroleum products to meet the world's growing demand for energy, it has more to offer than just access to greater supplies. We also strive to be a source of stability in world markets. It is a responsibility which we take seriously and one which we believe is vital to maximizing economic growth and prosperity.[23]

And, finally, Khalid al-Falih, Saudi Aramco's president and CEO, expressed his company's policy in the follow way:

> Given the combination of geology, geography, history, and economics, Saudi Arabia and Saudi Aramco have been fated to play a dominant role on the world's energy stage. This is a duty that we have embraced just as generations

---

[22] Cf. http://www.mopm.gov.sa/mopm/detail.do?content=sp_policy (accessed Nov. 4, 2009).
[23] Cf.   http://www.saudiaramco.com/irj/portal/anonymous?favlnk=/SaudiAramcoPublic/docs/At±A±Glance/Reliable±Supply&ln=en (accessed Nov. 12, 2009).

of Aramcons before us did, and it is a responsibility we take very, very seriously indeed. So we build with confidence today, knowing that tomorrow we will be able to meet our commitments to all of our various stakeholders.[24]

The technocratic views expressed above underscore the acceptance by those who manage the resource that Saudi oil is a globally traded commodity in a capitalistic economic system. This is a system that Saudi officials seek to preserve and not disrupt. By contrast with Arab nationalists like ʿAbd Allāh al-Ṭurayqī – who viewed oil and its nationalization by producing Third World states as a means to develop an import substitution industrial economy that would make the Arab world less dependent on the West and more equal in terms of power relations – the technocrats of the ministry and Saudi Aramco are fully invested in maintaining the existing system. The technocrats see oil as a means for developing Saudi Arabia's economy – for example, engaging in more downstream activities (e.g., petrochemicals) and helping to diversify the economy away from dependence on oil rents – but they do not con-ceive of using oil production in a zero-sum contest with the West. They have internalized the wisdom of years of selling this product on the inter-national market, including the many effects, positive and negative, of such events as the Arab oil embargo in 1973 and the steep fall in prices of the mid-1980s. This more seasoned view of oil marketing and pricing leads these technocrats to shun the idea that oil can be used as political weapon in so far as Saudi Arabia can deliberately adjust production levels so as to achieve political parity with a putative enemy (e.g., Iran or the West). The technocrats have "stakeholders," which include not only the Saudi government and peo-ple but also customers all over the world who benefit from a well-lubricated system because of a predictable supply and "moderate" prices. As such, the policy that they claim to follow involves the professional management of the resource by adopting moderate and responsible measures that seek to enforce market stability and general economic development, domestically as well as overseas. Opponents of the Saudi regime, most notably al-Qaeda to whom we will now turn, view this policy as emblematic of the subservience of the Saudi royal family to Western domination and in return for which the West guaran-tees the regime's survival and protection from all its enemies, domestic and foreign.

---

[24] Khalid al-Falih, "Powering Prosperity, Enabling Growth: Saudi Aramco's Perspective on Global Energy Security," The Center for Strategic and International Studies, May 6, 2009, 8 (http://csis.org/files/090506_khalid_al_falih_remarks.pdf accessed Dec. 23, 2013).

AL-QAEDA AND OIL

The topic of oil figures prominently in al-Qaeda's ideological production and strategic statements.[25] A search for the word oil (*naft*) in the most comprehensive online database of jihadi sources, *Minbar al-Tawḥīd wa-l-Jihād*, comes up with nearly one hundred hits in the form of treatises, poems, articles, and other written materials.[26] Usama bin Ladin often mentioned oil in his speeches and writings and saw it as the principal source of Muslim wealth and strategic power. He also averred that the United States is centrally interested in controlling this resource in order to maintain its political and economic hegemony over the world. His views on what to do about reversing this state of affairs evolved over time, however. Bin Ladin insisted that one of al-Qaeda's principal goals was to redress this imbalance of power, giving Muslims control over this resource. In this respect, bin Ladin was an heir of Arab nationalists like 'Abd Allāh al-Ṭurayqī, although his political program is much more radical in its advocacy of violent means as well as being much broader to encompass the entire Muslim world, not just the Arabs. As we shall see, bin Ladin was careful in his earlier statements to insist that oil wells, installations, and facilities were not to be attacked by al-Qaeda's forces because these belonged to the Muslim community. Later, however, his views changed, and he argued that these should become the targets of attacks because the West, and the United States in particular, could not be weakened otherwise.

AN EGALITARIAN FANTASY

One of the most fascinating al-Qaeda documents that the U.S. government was able to retrieve from Afghanistan after the fall of the Taliban regime is a diary from the year 2000 that belonged to either Usama bin Ladin or someone

---

[25] There is no comprehensive study on this topic but only a few policy-oriented papers and brief articles. Cf. Michael Scheuer et al., "Saudi Arabian Oil Facilities: The Achilles Heel of the Western Economy," Jamestown Foundation, 2006 (http://www.jamestown.org/uploads/media/Jamestown-SaudiOil.pdf); David Cook, "Oil and Terrorism," Working Paper Series, James A. Baker III Institute for Public Policy, Rice University, 2008 (http://bakerinstitute.org/media/files/Research/b5edc3ae/IEEJoilterrorism-Cook.pdf), and The International Institute for Counter-Terrorism, "Oil Installations as an Attractive Target for Terrorism," 2009 (http://www.ict.org.il/Portals/0/Internet%20Monitoring%20Group/JWMG_Oil_Installations_as_a_Target.pdf); Tim Pippard, "'Oil-Qaeda': Jihadist Threats to the Energy Sector," *Perspectives on Terrorism* 4, no. 3 (2010) (http://www.terrorismanalysts.com/pt/index.php/pot/article/view/103/html).

[26] Cf. www.tawhed.ws.

very close to him, such as his personal secretary.[27] The diary includes minutes of meetings of the al-Qaeda core leadership, drafts of sermons and letters by bin Ladin (such as one to the father of an imprisoned al-Qaeda fighter), and long lists of questions that al-Qaeda's recruits were requesting bin Ladin to answer. A number of the questions involved issues pertaining to oil, such as how patient do the jihadis have to be before responding to the "Jewish-Crusader invasion of the Muslim countries" that seeks to control the oil fields, and how is the price of oil determined and what is the role of OPEC.

The diary offers a peek into the world of bin Ladin before the attacks of 9/11, revealing some of his views and what issues consumed his time. One page is particularly fascinating because it reveals a recurring fantasy that a number of al-Qaeda ideologues – not just bin Ladin – had about oil revenues and what to do with these should oil production come under their control. On page 62 of the diary, corresponding to February 13, 2000, the page's title is "Every Muslim's Share of the Oil." Under this a series of calculations are made, based on certain assumptions, to arrive at the share that every Muslim would obtain daily from the sale of "Muslim oil." The assumptions are that the countries of the Muslim world produce 30 million barrels per day and that the barrel should be priced at $150. The resulting revenue of $4.5 billion per day is then divided by the number of Muslims in the world, which is estimated to be at 1.2 billion persons. This would give every Muslim $3.75 per day and the "average Muslim family," which is stated to consist of eight persons, would receive $30 daily.

Bin Ladin's radically egalitarian fantasy is shared by another important jihadi strategist and ideologue named Abū Muṣ'ab al-Sūrī (aka Muṣṭafā Sitt Maryam) who indulges in a similar vision about oil revenues and their equitable division among the world's Muslims.[28] In al-Sūrī's epistle to the people of Yemen entitled "The Responsibility of the People of Yemen Regarding Muslim Sanctities and Treasures"[29] he laments the fact that the oil wealth of the Arabian Peninsula, which represents the lion's share of the Muslims'

[27] See Harmony Document AFGP-2002-801138, "Various Admin Documents and Questions," https://www.ctc.usma.edu/wp-content/uploads/2013/09/Various-Admin-Documents-and-Questions-Original.pdf, and translation into English at https://www.ctc.usma.edu/wp-content/uploads/2013/10/Various-Admin-Documents-and-Questions-Translation.pdf.

[28] For a detailed study of Abū Muṣ'ab al-Sūrī see Brynjar Lia, *Architect of Global Jihad* (New York: Columbia University Press, 2008). Al-Sūrī advocated a strategy of forming autonomous cells that would engage in violent acts against enemy targets. These included oil facilities and installations as well as shipping (399–401).

[29] Cf. http://tawhed.ws/r1?i=3316&x=wksgfnyz (accessed July 21, 2011).

public treasury (*bayt māl al-Muslimīn*), is being stolen by the top four hundred princes of the Gulf's Arab countries, who rule "under the protection of the Americans,... Jews and other Crusaders." For al-Sūrī, who is attempting to rally the people of Yemen to the jihadi cause, the "natural" price of the barrel of oil is $260. He explains, however, that its price is much lower because the United States imposes a deflated price on the "apostate" King Fahd of Saudi Arabia, who always obliges. Here is how al-Sūrī envisages what Muslims would do if the revenue of oil was divided equitably among them:

> These [low] figures [for the price of oil] are unjust and fake and have been imposed by the People of the Cross. Imagine what the situation would be like if we owned our oil and marketed it according to its natural price and imposed it at $260 per barrel, just as the Americans impose their prices for cars, computers, weapons and American chocolates on the consumers of the Arabian Peninsula and other places in the world! No one competes with them on the price and no one can impose another! Is this a right reserved for the Christians alone and is it not a right for Muslims too? The figures [for the revenues] will be unimaginably large. Muslims would no longer need to work and toil and could liberate themselves to do missionary work and to do armed struggle (jihad) and to spread the light of Islam around the world.[30]

Despite being considered one of the more pragmatic and hardnosed strategists among the global jihadists, al-Sūrī describes above one of the movement's romantic ideals, which is to use oil revenues at inflated monopolistic prices so as to liberate Muslims for the task of spreading Islam globally. His desire is for the restoration of the period of the early Islamic conquests, when Muslims performed the jihad and the economy was for the non-Muslims to run.[31] However unrealistic this vision might be, he no doubt regarded this as good propaganda material for recruitment to the cause in economically blighted Yemen. Unlike al-Sūrī, bin Ladin understood that oil was a commodity whose price was determined by market forces, and he had a keen sense of the history of oil prices going back to the 1970s, based on personal experience in Saudi Arabia. The price of oil was low, according to bin Ladin, because the United States was obliging Saudi Arabia to maintain high production levels, which meant that the market was oversupplied.[32] Here is how he put it albeit in more colorful terms: "Despite the fact that the West is careful enough not to

---

[30] Ibid.

[31] I would like to thank my Princeton colleague Michael Cook for pointing out this echo to early Islamic history.

[32] Bruce Lawrence, ed., *Messages to the World: The Statements of Osama bin Laden*, 46.

slaughter the Saudi chicken that lays black gold for them, they are extremely cautious that the price tag on this egg remains at a minimum."[33]

That this characterization of the global oil market bore no relationship to economic reality is, of course, beside the point here. For bin Ladin the low price allows the United States to keep its industrial economy strong and reinforces its ability to project military force around the globe, and he described this phenomenon in hyperbolic terms as "the biggest theft ever witnessed by mankind in the history of the world."[34] The low price also prevents Saudi Arabia from buying good military equipment with which to defend itself from external aggression, and therefore the United States deliberately keeps it in a posture of absolute subordination (*tab'iyya muṭlaqa*) vis-à-vis the West. This point is made in a video on YouTube titled "Raid on Manhattan" (*ghazwat manhattan*) that al-Qaeda's media production unit (*al-Saḥāb*) produced to justify and commemorate the 9/11 attacks. Here a clip shows bin Ladin lecturing his recruits and discussing Saudi Arabia and oil in which he says:

> The country [Saudi Arabia] is occupied in every sense of the word. They [i.e., the United States and West] are taking the petrol for the last ten years [i.e., the 1990s] at an average of $9 dollars per barrel. The barrel is sold refined in Europe for $230 dollars per barrel while they take it from us for $9 dollars. And from these $9 dollars is deducted the cost of operation, extraction and maintenance. Nothing is left. As for the rest, the Americans bring their old scrapped aircraft and say: "You, [King] Fahd, buy these seventy planes for such and such price." And he [the King] says: "Yes Sir, may you live long![35]

Although bin Ladin became contemptuous of the Al Saud and their rule after he was expelled from the kingdom in 1994, he was careful in his earlier statements to underscore the importance of preserving the oil reserves for the future benefit of the Muslim community and their soon-to-be established caliphate. It was imperative that Muslims not attack the oil resources and facilities so as not to imperil this fortune. In his 1996 statement titled "Declaration of War against the Americans Who Are Occupying the Land of the Two Holy Sanctuaries," bin Ladin warns Muslims not to fight one another and to be cautious

---

[33] Usama bin Ladin, "Open Letter to King Fahd on the Occasion of the Recent Cabinet Reshuffle," 1995, 33 (www.ctc.usma.edu/wp-content/uploads/2013/10/Open-Letter-to-King-Fahd-from-bin-Laden-Translation.pdf).

[34] Lawrence (ed.), *Messages to the World*, 163.

[35] "Raid on Manhattan" at minute 3:20 (http://www.youtube.com/watch?v=sDUOVErmxYg, accessed Nov. 3, 2009).

in their warfare against the infidel American occupiers because this could
lead to:

> Destruction of the oil industries, because the military presence of the crusader
> and American forces in the Islamic Gulf countries, on land, in the air, and at
> sea, represents the greatest danger and harm and the greatest menace to the
> largest oil reserves in the world. This presence is a provocation to the people
> and an affront to their religion, feelings, and dignity, and has driven them
> toward armed struggle against the occupying invaders. A spread of fighting
> in these areas would carry the danger of the oil burning which would be
> detrimental to the economic interests of the Gulf states and the Land of the
> Two Holy Mosques, and in fact to the world economy. Here we pause and
> urge our brothers, the fighters from among the people, to preserve this wealth
> and not to involve it in the battle because it is a great Islamic wealth and a great
> and important economic power for the coming Islamic state, God willing.[36]

THE CONSEQUENCES OF 9/11

The events following the 9/11 attacks and the U.S. invasion of Iraq in
2003 changed al-Qaeda's tactics and in particular bin Ladin's views on the
question of targeting oil facilities. Harming the economic interests of the
United States has always been one of al-Qaeda's strategic goals, but how to
do this effectively was never obvious or easy. The first al-Qaeda attack on an
oil target took place off the coast of Yemen in October 2002 when a suicide
bomber targeted the *MV Limburg*, a French oil supertanker. This led to a brief
increase in the price of oil and to a significant hike in shipping insurance rates.
Yet this attack does not appear to have been preceded by a sustained internal
discussion or a strategic analysis among the movement's ideologues, nor were
its lessons fully appreciated. In fact, al-Qaeda's branch in Saudi Arabia began
a campaign in 2003 of attacks against civilian and security targets, with the aim
of mobilizing large segments of the population in favor of its cause.[37] The first
al-Qaeda attacks took place in May 2003 and later in November of the same
year, and this led to the death and injury of many civilians, including many
Muslims. Such casualties appear to have tarnished the reputation of al-Qaeda
within the kingdom, and the Saudi authorities, both political and religious,
capitalized on this by reacting swiftly in their condemnation and beginning a
security crackdown against the movement's followers.

---

[36] I have slighted revised the FBIS translation of this statement, and it can be found in Arabic
at http://www.tawhed.ws/r?i=1502092b. Cf. "Compilation of Usama Bin Ladin's Statements
1994-January 2004, *FBIS Report*, 2008, 20.

[37] For further information on al-Qaeda's violent campaign in Saudi Arabia see Hegghammer,
Jihad in Saudi Arabia.

One consequence of this was that discriminating between targets became an issue for al-Qaeda, and an internal debate among the movement's leaders in Saudi Arabia resulted in the view that oil installations and the foreigners who work in them were to become the focus of attack. Nonetheless, al-Qaeda continued to target, and be targeted by, the security forces. In May 2004 al-Qaeda launched two attacks on oil-related facilities in Yanbu and Khobar during which foreign workers were specifically targeted and many tens of these were killed. The culmination of these attacks on oil installations occurred in February 2006 when suicide bombers in two pickup trucks were thwarted and killed by security forces while attempting to blow up the Bqayq processing facility, which handles more than 60 percent of Saudi production.

In addition, the U.S. invasion of Iraq convinced al-Qaeda's core leadership that America was determined to control more directly and fully the oil resources of the Muslim world. This had to be stopped at all costs. The idea formed that the United States could be harmed economically by targeting the oil, and this was reinforced by the many attacks that began to take place against the oil pipelines by insurgents in Iraq after the invasion. Bin Laden, for example, issued a statement in December 2004 that pertained to the situation in Saudi Arabia and Iraq in which he declared that oil installations were to be attacked. This reversal of his view appears to be more than an ex post facto justification for the attacks that occurred in May of that year. He held that by attacking the oil installations al-Qaeda could harm the United States economically and also mobilize Saudis to its cause:

> *Mujahidin*, be patient and think of the hereafter... be sure to know that there is a rare and golden opportunity today to make America bleed in Iraq, in economic, human, and psychological terms. So don't waste this opportunity and regret it afterwards. Remember too that the biggest reason for our enemies' control over our lands is to steal our oil, so give everything you can to stop the greatest theft of oil in history from the current and future generations in collusion with the agents and foreigners. They are taking this oil for a paltry price in the knowledge that the prices of all commodities have multiplied many times. But oil, which is the basis of all industry, has gone down many times. After it was going for $40 a barrel two decades ago, in the last decade it went for as little as $9, while its price today should be $100 at the very least. So keep on struggling, do not make it easy for them, and focus your operations on it, especially in Iraq and the Gulf, for that will be the death of them.[38]

In mentioning the price of $100 per barrel bin Ladin was again betraying a profound misunderstanding of global demand for this commodity and how

---

[38] Lawrence (ed.), *Messages to the World*, 272.

the price is set. As his statement was issued oil prices were already rising and continued on an upward trajectory to reach well over the $100 mark on a sustained basis. The price increase has been driven by increased global demand, especially from such countries as China and India, and also because oil, like other commodities, had become a financial instrument that is traded on the futures market by speculative investors. The pricing system has become much more complicated than the older model that bin Ladin had in mind, which dates back to the 1950s and 1960s. During those earlier decades international oil corporations could dictate supply and therefore price. Furthermore, the U.S. and the global economy had become more immune to relatively high oil prices, and the example from the 1970s when oil shocks could cause economic recessions no longer obtained.

'ABD AL-'AZĪZ B. RASHĪD AL-'ANAZĪ AND THE DESTRUCTION OF OIL

By 2004 al-Qaeda's branch in Saudi Arabia had become engaged in a detailed internal discussion about the permissibility of and justification for attacking oil resources and facilities. This was the result of questions that arose within the jihadi community as a result of the attacks in May 2004. The central question for al-Qaeda's leaders was whether the oil in Arabia was an asset that belonged to Muslims and as such could not be targeted, or whether these reserves had become a liability for Muslims since their enemies were using these to destroy Islam itself. To provide religious and legal justification for attacking the oil resources and installations, 'Abd al-'Azīz b. Rashīd al-'Anazī, an important ideologue in the movement, penned a work entitled *The Rule [Regarding] Targeting Oil Installations and the Foundations of the Rulings of Economic Jihad.*[39] This is a detailed legal exposition that draws on pre-modern Islamic sources, especially traditional Salafi and Wahhabi texts, to answer questions about who actually owns the hydrocarbon resources, what are the rules of economic warfare, and what is to be done with oil installations and resources if an enemy is using them to cause harm to Muslims.

Al-'Anazi's treatise concludes by permitting the attacks on the resources and their installations since this falls under the required harm (*nikāya*) that

---

[39] 'Abd al-'Azīz b. Rashīd al-'Anazī, *Hukm istihdāf al-maṣāliḥ al-naftiyya wa ta'ṣīl aḥkām al-jihād al-iqtiṣādī*. This is available on www.tawhed.ws. The author, who often wrote for al-Qaeda in Saudi Arabia's online publication *Sawt al-Jihād*, often used the pseudonym 'Abd Allāh b. Nāṣir al-Rashīd. He was one of the more scholarly men in the movement and was arrested by the Saudi authorities in 2005. He remains in prison. Cf. William McCants, ed., *Militant Ideology Atlas* (West Point, NY: Combating Terrorism Center, 2006), 289.

Muslims must inflict on infidels in warfare. Here is how the author summarizes his study, which is worth quoting at length because it reveals al-Qaeda's justification for these acts of violence and how its leaders conceived of these resources:

> First, targeting the oil installations constitutes a legitimate form of economic warfare, which is one of the most important ways of causing harm to the infidels.

> Second, Islamic law does not permit for oil wells to be owned by individuals. If these are found in land that has no owner, it is impermissible for individuals to own them; and if these are found in land that is owned, then the owner has the right to take a share that suffices him after which he cannot prevent others from benefiting from them. As for the various oil-related concerns, some are owned by individuals and some are not. The controlling principle is that it is impermissible to own these oil-related concerns if they pertain to the needs of the generality of Muslims.

> Third, the unbelievers do not own that which they have seized from the Muslims. Rather such property remains owned by its Muslim owner.

> Fourth, destroying the property of the unbelievers in warfare is permissible whenever it is determined that harming the infidels through this trumps the harm caused from its destruction.

> Fifth, destroying the property of Muslims is permissible when this is captured by the unbelievers, or it is feared that it will be captured, if it is determined that the harm that will result from the enemy benefiting from this trumps the expected benefit from its [eventual] return to the Muslims.

> Sixth, oil-related concerns are divided into four types: 1) Oil wells. It is not permissible to target these if the desired harm [to the enemy] can be accomplished by targeting other things. This is due to the preponderance of the harm over the benefit that is caused by targeting these wells. But if the means for harming the unbelievers is very constrained in defensive warfare and the aim [of harm] can only be accomplished by destroying the wells, then this is to be done. The determination of the benefit from such an act is a matter of independent judgment to be undertaken by the jurists and those who know the reality of the matter. 2) Oil pipelines. These are the easiest targets militarily, and the benefit of targeting these is preponderant, and God knows best. 3) Oil installations. These are similar to the previous type, but it is not permissible to target these if they are the private property of a Muslim. 4) Oil personalities. These are the easiest of targets and the benefit [of doing this] does not contradict any acknowledged harm as long as the targeted person is one who can be legitimately killed. The person who cannot be killed and

targeted is the one who has no relationship to the oil concern unless there is no other means but to kill him when targeting such an installation. In such a case his fate falls under the well-known issue of human shields (*tatarrus*).[40]

The length and detail of al-'Anazī's work (it is nearly eighty pages long) underscore the extent to which such violent acts proved controversial in Saudi society and vexatious for al-Qaeda. His attempt to justify such targeting, including the wanton destruction of the wells and resources, proved unconvincing and appears to have turned the population increasingly against the movement, just as the targeting of Muslims had done. Furthermore, the chaos and instability that al-Qaeda's attacks caused was unpopular. Most Saudis work for the government in one capacity or another, as civil servants, teachers, bureaucrats, etc. Targeting the principal source of the people's livelihood did not bode well for the future. The mufti of the kingdom, 'Abd al-'Azīz b. 'Abd Allāh Āl al-Shaykh, was quick to capitalize on this sentiment in his condemnation of the attack on Bqayq. After describing al-Qaeda with the usual term as the "errant faction" (*al-fi'a al-ḍālla*) he went on to say that their views and actions contradict Islamic law, constitute a major sin, and spread "mischief in the land." The last phrase is Qur'anic and is the basis for applying penalties against rebels and brigands who are accused of causing social disorder and terror. The mufti goes on to criticize al-Qaeda for wanting to destroy the country's economy by targeting the oil and its facilities and states:

> Is this [oil] not God's bounty to the Muslims with which the Two Holy Mosques were built and the Qur'an printed and through which the message of Islam was spread! . . . And because of it the salaries of millions of Muslims, in this country and overseas, are paid, and mosques are built, and wells dug . . . and such conveniences as electricity, water, telephone, roads, sea ports, airports and other such things through which this community has a strong presence in these times when the enmity towards Islam and Muslims has become acute.[41]

Even though this mufti has little personal appeal or a following in Saudi Arabia because he is perceived to be a servile minion of the political authorities, his criticism here expresses a general sentiment that appears to have been widely shared in society. There simply was no religious justification for targeting the oil, and in so doing al-Qaeda had placed itself beyond the pale, not least because the population's livelihood depended on its continued production.

---

[40] al-'Anazī, *Hukm istihdāf al-maṣāliḥ al-naftiyya*, 4–5.

[41] For the mufti's statement see "al-Muftī al-'āmm yudīn al-'amaliyya al-takhribiyya fī Bqayq," *al-Riyāḍ*, Feb. 28, 2006 (http://www.alriyadh.com/134351).

In a final attempt to justify its acts and reasoning, al-Qaeda published an article by someone named Adīb Bassām in the last issue to appear of its online journal *Ṣawt al-jihād* in January 2007.[42] Titled "Bin Ladin and the Oil Weapon," the author tries to reiterate that oil and its installations must be attacked because these are being used by the United States to wage war on Islam and Muslims. He repeats some of same the legal and economic arguments that al-'Anazī made in his treatise, and finally insists that bin Ladin has given directives for these installations to be attacked. The ultimate aim is to cut off as much of the supply as possible to the United States. By this time, however, the effort proved to be in vain, not least because al-Qaeda in Saudi Arabia had been physically crushed by the government's security and intelligence services, and what remained of the movement's followers sought refuge in Yemen and elsewhere. In Yemen, al-Qaeda has gone on to attack oil pipelines and facilities, but with little effect on the international market because of the very limited amounts being produced there.

CONCLUSION

I have tried to illustrate that oil constitutes an important *leitmotiv* in the politics of Saudi Arabia: from the poets who lamented its discovery because it led to the end of the old ways of Bedouin chivalry and manhood to the ideologues of al-Qaeda who concluded that only by its destruction would their idealized caliphate be made actual and their enemies defeated. It would seem obvious that such a resource, in' such massive quantities and dramatic political and social effects, would become an important topic of discussion and debate in Saudi Arabia. By focusing on oil here – surveying the various ways through which different constituencies invoke it, make claims about it, and justify their actions by reference to it – I hope to have provided greater insights into Saudi culture, history, and society. As long as it continues to flow, oil will undoubtedly remain a trope, and a tool, to be invoked and used by a state seeking to dominate more fully and thoroughly its society, but equally a topic through which dissent and resistance are produced from below.

---

[42] Adīb Bassām, "Bin Ladin wa silāḥ al-naft," *Ṣawt al-jihād*, no. 30 (1428 AH), 28–33 (http://www .e-prism.org/images/S30_-_Feb07.pdf).

PART 3

Islam and Islamism

8

From Wahhabi to Salafi

David Commins

Naming the doctrine preached by Muhammad ibn ʿAbd al-Wahhab has never been a simple matter. Early foes classified it as a Kharijite sectarian heresy. The name that stuck, *Wahhabi*, stigmatized the doctrine as the ravings of a misguided preacher. Naturally, Ibn ʿAbd al-Wahhab and his disciples preferred other names for themselves and their movement: at first, the folk who profess God's unity (*ahl al-tawhid* and *al-muwahhidun*), later, the Najdi call (*al-daʿwa al-najdiyya*).[1] Naming, then, is part of arguments over Ibn ʿAbd al-Wahhab's doctrine. If the doctrine is known as Wahhabi, it cannot claim to represent correct belief. The tendency to refer to it as Salafi is a recent development that first emerged among Wahhabism's defenders outside Arabia well before Wahhabis themselves adopted the term.[2]

To say that a doctrine is Salafi is to ascribe it the authority of Islam's Pious Fathers. The claim has been part of theological discourse since the ninth century. In modern times, the Salafi label has attained a firm grip on the contemporary Sunni Muslim imagination as a marker for Islam in its pristine form. But variation in which beliefs and practices Muslims count as Salafi makes it difficult to define. It helps to distinguish between claiming to follow the way of the Salaf, which is a common trope in Sunni, especially, Hanbali discourse, and claiming to be Salafi as distinct from other Sunnis. In the former case, we have a set of positions on theology and worship. In the latter case, we have a set of claims that would reshape public institutions (through legal reform) and social identity (dressing a certain way). The first is an artifact

---

[1] Najd is the region of central Arabia where the movement was born.
[2] As awkward as it may be in a chapter about the rhetorical deployment of names, I use the terms Wahhabi and Wahhabism as a matter of convention to refer to Muhammad ibn ʿAbd al-Wahhab's teachings and the movement inspired by those teachings.

of classical Islamic thought; the second is an artifact of how Muslims fashion religion as a total way of life.[3]

One instance of Salafism in the second sense is the modernist project associated with Muhammad ʿAbduh and Rashid Rida. They believed it necessary for Muslims to break with their present condition of decadence and return to the glorious past of the Pious Fathers to overcome subjugation to Western powers. The modernist Salafis sought general principles in authoritative texts that permit flexible adaptation to novel forms of governance, law, and education. By contrast, Wahhabis focused on fidelity to what they construed as the creed and cult of the Pious Fathers. For those who regard the modernists as the true Salafis, the Wahhabis' claim to be Salafis is spurious. According to this view, Salafism stood for a modernist outlook until Saudi religious scholars decided to appropriate the Salafi mantle to validate their teachings, reducing Salafism to dogmatism.[4] Although such a narrative may gratify the urge to discredit Wahhabism, it overlooks three significant points. First, the initial impulse to classify Wahhabis as Salafis came from the modernists themselves. Second, the story of Wahhabism's "Salafi" turn raises questions about terminology that do not go away by deciding which group is truly on the path of the Pious Fathers. Considering the political contexts of shifts in meaning ascribed to Wahhabi and Salafi does help answer such questions. Third, the struggle over naming is part of the broader process of Saudi Arabia's incorporation into the Muslim world. These three points are essential to understanding the phases in Wahhabism's Salafi turn. In the late Ottoman period, modernist Salafis outside Saudi Arabia defended Wahhabis against their critics by referring to them as Sunni adherents of the Hanbali law school. Then, after the collapse of the Ottoman Empire, Wahhabism's defenders began to call it Salafi. Finally, in the 1970s, Saudi religious scholars adopted the Salafi mantle.

THE WAHHABIS AS SUNNIS

When Wahhabism emerged in the mid-1700s, Ottoman ulama formed a solid phalanx hostile to its teachings. The Wahhabi view of other Muslims as

---

[3] For a concise discussion of classical and contemporary manifestations of Salafism, see Bernard Haykel, "On the Nature of Salafi Thought and Action," in *Global Salafism: Islam's New Religious Movement*, ed. Roel Meijer (New York: Columbia University Press, 2009), 33–57.

[4] Hamid Algar, *Wahhabism: A Critical Essay* (Oneonta, NY: Islamic Publications International, 2002), 46–9. Khaled Abou El Fadl, *The Great Theft: Wrestling Islam from the Extremists* (New York: HarperSan Francisco, 2005), 74–94. Henri Lauziere proposes that the concept of modernist Salafism is the product of an Orientalist misconception. See "The Construction of *Salafiyya*: Reconsidering Salafism from the Perspective of Conceptual History," *International Journal of Middle East Studies* 42 (2010): 369–89.

idolaters infuriated Ottoman ulama, and the Saudi challenge to Ottoman rule in Hijaz alarmed Istanbul. The impetus to legitimize Wahhabism surfaced among modernist Salafi ulama in Baghdad and Damascus in the late 1800s. Like the Wahhabis, they opposed the cult of saints and wished to revive the intellectual legacy of Ibn Taymiyya. Given the taint of disloyalty attached to Wahhabism, it was natural for defenders of saint veneration to denounce the Salafis as Wahhabis.[5] Thus, the motive for rehabilitating Wahhabism's reputation stemmed from common religious convictions and a need to deflect charges of affiliation with heretics. The case for Wahhabism had two elements. First, its enemies circulated fabrications and distortions, ascribing beliefs that Wahhabis did not hold. Second, Wahhabis followed the Qur'an, the Sunna, and the teachings of the four Sunni imams: If one read their treatises, one would find nothing contrary to historical Sunni consensus and the Hanbali law school. It is noteworthy that Wahhabism's defenders described it as Sunni, not as Salafi. That was because in the Ottoman context, Sunni was synonymous with legitimate doctrine whereas Salafi represented a challenge to established authority.[6]

The dynamics behind the urge to depict Wahhabis as Sunnis are evident in the career of Mahmud Shukri al-Alusi, leader of Baghdad's Salafis.[7] He was a vocal critic of practices associated with Sufi orders as innovations (*bida'*). Defenders of such practices incited Ottoman officials against al-Alusi by accusing him of spreading Wahhabism. On one occasion, al-Alusi was deported from Baghdad on suspicion of supporting the revival of Saudi power in Najd.[8]

---

[5] For controversy over the cult of saints in Baghdad, see Itzchak Weismann, "The Naqshbandiyya-Khalidiyya and Salafi Challenge in Iraq," *Journal of the History of Sufism* 4 (2003–4): 229–40. For the Damascus setting, see David Commins, *Islamic Reform: Politics and Social Change in Late Ottoman Syria* (New York: Oxford University Press, 1990), 129–31. On connections among Damascus, Baghdad, and Najd, see David Commins, *The Wahhabi Mission and Saudi Arabia* (London: I. B. Tauris, 2006), 132–4. The same rhetorical dynamics operated in Egypt, where defenders of saint veneration labeled Muhammad 'Abduh a Wahhabi. *Fatawa al-Imam Muhammad Rashid Rida*, vol. 1, ed. Salah al-Din al-Munajjid and Yusuf Khuri (Beirut: Dar al-Kitab al-Jadid, 1970), 380.

[6] Commins, *Islamic Reform*, 109. On Ottoman promotion of Sunni Islam and the Hanafi law school as the official religion, see Selim Deringil, *The Well-Protected Domains: Ideology and the Legitimation of Power in the Ottoman Empire, 1876–1909* (London: I. B. Tauris, 1998), 44–92.

[7] Hala Fattah, "Wahhabi Influences, Salafi Responses: Shaikh Mahmud Shukri al-Alusi and the Iraqi Salafi Movement, 1745–1930," *Journal of Islamic Studies* 14 (2003): 127–48. Edouard Metenier, "Que sont ces chemins devenus? Reflexion sur les evolutions de la Salafiyya Irakienne de la fin du xviiie au milieu du xxe siècle," in *Le courant reformiste musulman et sa reception dans les societes arabes*, ed. Maher Charif and Salam Kawakibi (Damas: IFPO, 2003), 99–107.

[8] Fattah, "Wahhabi Influences," 138–9. Dina Rizk Khoury cites a source that ties al-Alusi's expulsion to a visit by Rashid Rida, allegedly to see if there might be backing for an Arab caliphate, tantamount to fomenting secession from the empire. Dina Rizk Khoury, "Fragmented Loyalties

His defense of Wahhabism contained religious and political threads. He rejected the charge that Wahhabis disrespected the Prophet and authoritative ulama, asserting that they were, in fact, *muwahhid*[9] Muslims upholding the beliefs of the Pious Fathers, adhering to Hanbalism, and respecting believers who followed the Sunni law schools.[10] Moreover, Al Saud deserved credit for their political achievements, such as ending tribal warfare and bringing security to Arabia. He admitted that they went astray in the early 1800s when they rejected Ottoman authority and interfered with the pilgrimage. Recent Saudi rulers, however, concentrated on their own domain and sent religious teachers to instruct Bedouin in correct religion.[11]

In Damascus, controversy over Wahhabism exhibited similar contours: debate over correct religious practice, ad hominem attacks for holding Wahhabi sympathies, and entanglement with Ottoman sensitivities over loyalty to the sultan. The Damascus setting differed from Baghdad's in one important respect: Young men educated in state schools represented a dynamic element in cultural and political discussions. As youths, they had come under the influence of the modernist Salafis, who blended the call for religious purification with a progressive outlook on education, science, and politics.[12] Modernist Salafis also transmitted a favorable disposition toward Wahhabism. For example, in 1909, one of the young educated set, Salah al-Din al-Qasimi, published an article about Wahhabism in a popular Egyptian magazine where he noted that "Wahhabi" had become a catchall term for denouncing reformist religious leaders, newspapers (such as Egypt's *al-Ahram* and *al-Muqattam*), and literary societies. In fact, he contended, the Wahhabis were merely pious Hanbali Muslims renowned for their moral rectitude and avoidance of idolatry in worship.[13]

Al-Qasimi belonged to a cohort of Syrians whose outlook took shape in late Ottoman institutions that naturalized the culture of nationalism.[14] They

---

in the Modern Age: Jamil Sidqi al-Zahawi on Wahhabism, Constitutionalism and Language," in *International Congress on Learning and Education in the Ottoman World*, ed. Ali Çaksu and Ekmeleddin Ihsanoglu (Istanbul: Research Centre for Islamic History, Art and Culture, 2001), 342–3.

9 That is, proclaimers of God's unity.
10 Fattah, "Wahhabi Influences," 145–6.
11 Mahmud Shukri al-Alusi, *Tarikh najd* (Cairo: al-Matba`a al-Salafiyya, 1929), 90–105.
12 Commins, *Islamic Reform*, 95–103.
13 Muhibb al-Din al-Khatib, *al-Duktur Salah al-Din al-Qasimi, 1305–1344: Safahat min tarikh al-nahda al-'arabiyya fi awa'il al-qarn al-'ishrin* (Cairo: al-Matba`a al-Salafiyya, 1959), 250–6. The Egyptian publication was *al-Muqtataf*.
14 James L. Gelvin, "Modernity and Its Discontents: On the Durability of Nationalism in the Arab Middle East," *Nations and Nationalism* 5 (1999): 71–89.

adopted the modernist Salafi outlook because it was congruent with the project for Arab national revival. Their chief concern was not the restoration of religion according to the Pious Fathers but the political destiny of the Arabs, freshly conceived as a national community. Religion mattered to them, but more as an emblem of national authenticity than the ground of thought and action.

WAHHABIS AS SALAFIS

The passing of the Ottoman Empire and deepening of European colonial domination altered the political context of the meanings ascribed to Wahhabi and Salafi in three ways. First, "Salafi" shed the connotation of opposition to legitimate authority embodied by the Ottoman sultan. Second, nationalist themes became salient in arguments over religious doctrine. Third, Al Saud gained respectability by virtue of their independence of foreign rule, a quality duly emphasized by their agents and supporters. Under these conditions, modernist Salafi writers outside Saudi Arabia shifted from calling Wahhabism an expression of Sunni Islam to claiming that it was Salafi. Their writings on Wahhabism juxtaposed and jumbled religious and political themes as the anticolonial climate pressed on writers to formulate arguments in terms of national interest rather than classical Islamic texts. These discursive shifts are conspicuous in Egypt, where Ibn Saud's agent Fawzan ibn Sabiq distributed Najdi historical and religious treatises to provide raw material for a new wave of Wahhabi apologetics.

The best-known defender of Saudi interests in Egypt for this period was Rashid Rida, publisher of the leading religious periodical of the era, *al-Manar*. Due to *al-Manar*'s reach in the Muslim world, with a readership from Java to Morocco, Rida essentially "owned" the Salafi brand. Therefore, his position on Wahhabism was bound to be influential. One of his first comments on the Wahhabis appeared in the late Ottoman period, in a 1904 issue. A reader wrote to ask about the standing of the Shiite, Zaydi, and Wahhabi *madhhabs*. Rida responded that they were all Muslim (contrary to the Wahhabi view of the others as idolaters). He added that the Wahhabis were the closest of all Muslims to acting according to the Sunna but he did not yet refer to them as Salafis.[15] During the 1920s, Rida's terminology shifted. He now supported the Saudi political cause against the Hashemites in the struggle over Hijaz. Consequently, he published more articles about the Wahhabis, casting them

---

[15] Article from *al-Manar*, 1904, cited in al-Munajjid, *Fatawa al-Imam*, 1:111–12.

in favorable light, speaking of them as Salafi in creed and Hanbali in law school, or as Salafi Sunnis.[16]

In addition to attaching new descriptors to Wahhabism, its defenders in Egypt inscribed new meaning in "Salafi" and "Wahhabi" to make them suit the rhetorical purposes of nationalist and state-building discourses. Such rhetorical sculpting is evident in an essay on the history of Wahhabism by Muhammad Hamid al-Fiqi, the founder of a pro-Wahhabi organization in Egypt. Al-Fiqi's essay is notable for its emphasis on nation building. He praised early Saudi rulers for establishing secure, lawful conditions in Hijaz. He also commended Muhammad ibn `Abd al-Wahhab for encouraging the spread of literacy so that each believer may understand God's word. Al-Fiqi attributed to Wahhabism the modern aspiration for mass education that would make it possible for each Muslim to have direct contact with scripture rather than relying on the mediated authority of religious experts. That notion became a commonplace in sympathetic writings on Wahhabism, but it was not part of writings by Wahhabi ulama. Along similar lines, al-Fiqi's discussion of the ills caused by *taqlid* (imitation of established legal opinions) asserts that it destroyed the spirit of independent thinking, leaving Muslims vulnerable to imperialist conquest. Instead of placing *taqlid* in the scales of Islamic legal theory, he related it to the nation's welfare, a common trope in modernist Salafi discourse.[17]

More extensive reshaping of Salafi and Wahhabi appears in a 1936 treatise with the striking title *The Wahhabi Revolution*. Its author, `Abdallah al-Qasimi, came to Egypt from Saudi Arabia to study at al-Azhar. He is better known for his later radical writings, but his first publications were fierce attacks on al-Azhar's ulama and arguments for Wahhabi strictures against innovations in worship.[18] His essay on the "Wahhabi revolution" embodies the assimilation of the Arabian religious purification movement to nationalist and state-building purposes. Al-Qasimi referred to Wahhabism as the *Najdi Salafi da `wa* and the modern *Salafi nahda*, mixing the nationalist emphasis on rebirth (*nahda*) with religious call (*da `wa*). In place of terms used in conventional Saudi-Wahhabi historical narratives to describe the old order in Najd – idolatry, innovations,

---

[16] "Al-Wahhabiyya wa-l-'aqida al-diniyya li-l-najdiyyin," *al-Manar* 27 (1926): 275–8; "al-Wahhabiyya wa da`wat al-Manar ila madhhab al-salaf," *al-Manar* 28 (1927): 3–5; "Rasa'il al-sunna wa-l-shi`a," *al-Manar* 29 (1928): 683. Hamadi Redissi, "The Refutation of Wahhabism in Arabic Sources," in *Kingdom without Borders: Saudi Arabia's Political, Religious, and Media Frontiers*, ed. Madawi Al-Rasheed (New York: Columbia University Press, 2008), 174–5.

[17] Muhammad Hamid al-Fiqi, *Athar al-da `wa al-wahhabiyya fi al-islah al-dini wa-l-`umrani fi jazirat al-`arab wa ghayriha* (Cairo: Matba`at al-Nahda, 1935), 6, 33, 43–6.

[18] On al-Qasimi's life, see Salah al-Din al-Munajjid, *Dirasa `an al-Qasimi* (Dir`awn, Lebanon: Dar al-Kitab al-Jadid, 1967). For his criticism of al-Azhar, see `Abdallah ibn `Ali al-Qasimi, *Shuyukh al-Azhar wa-l-ziyada fi al-Islam* (Cairo, 1932/33).

jahiliyya – he drew on nationalist concepts to characterize the old order as one of weakness, misery, and ignorance.[19]

Al-Qasimi's narrative of the Saudi-Wahhabi enterprise made it a nationalist saga. At a time when Christians were invading Muslim lands, Muhammad ibn 'Abd al-Wahhab established a model not just of zeal for religion, but of revolution against oppression and for democratic equality. Najdis became attached to Al Saud leadership, which enjoyed divine support in vanquishing Arabian foes to form a single kingdom out of petty principalities. Al-Qasimi called Ibn Saud the genius of the twentieth century, the first Superman, and compared him to Hitler and Mussolini, claiming his accomplishments were greater because they occurred in a backward land immersed in chronic warfare. Thanks to him and to Wahhabism, Saudi Arabia enjoyed complete independence of foreign influence. In nationalist terms, Ibn Saud personified the nation's integrity: He preceded speeches with citations from the Qur'an and the Sunna unlike other Muslim leaders who cite Mister so and so, or Monsieur so and so, as though memorizing the Qur'an and citing *hadiths* were contrary to modern civilization.[20]

Nationalist logic is also evident al-Qasimi's defense of the Wahhabi ban on tobacco. He stated that Wahhabism bolsters the believer's will to refrain from temptations like tobacco and drugs that harm body and mind, wealth and freedom. But rather than citing proof-texts from scripture, he argued that smoking is a waste of money, especially in poor developing countries. Workers who earn a few piasters a day cannot afford to squander them on rolled poison that burns their sick lungs when they have dependents to provide for. Furthermore, when Egyptians and Syrians buy cigarettes, they put money into the pockets of foreign companies at the expense of local enterprises.[21]

Besides putting a nationalist spin on Wahhabi Puritanism, he conflated Ibn Saud's efforts to introduce modern technology with the goals of Wahhabism, when, in fact, Ibn Saud had to overcome Wahhabi leaders' objections to technical advances. Al-Qasimi claimed that Wahhabism was open to benefits from industrial techniques and inventions because no religious text contradicts the natural sciences. In fact, that was a modernist Salafi position typical of the 'Abduh-Rida school. Al-Qasimi praised the Saudi ruler for the spread of hospitals, doctors, scholars, and schools, and for introducing scientific inventions like the telegraph, telephone, automobile, and aircraft. It is noteworthy that

---

[19] 'Abdallah ibn 'Ali al-Qasimi, *al-Thawra al-Wahhabiyya* (Cairo: al-Matba'a al-Rahmaniyya, 1936), 1, 3.

[20] Ibid., 15, 30–5, 44, 47, 70–1, 79–83.

[21] Ibid., 18–20.

modernist Salafis were not alone in making nationalism and technical progress criteria for judging the merit of Muslim rulers. Conservative ulama in Syria had used the same criteria in arguments for their religious outlook in the late Ottoman period.[22]

The tendency for Muslims outside Saudi Arabia to frame Wahhabism in terms of Salafism was partly a token of the incorporation of Al Saud's domain into the cosmopolitan Muslim sphere. That process moved in two directions. Ibn Saud's subsidies for publishing collections of Wahhabi treatises represented movement from Arabia to other Muslim lands, as Najdi texts became widely available outside their homeland for the first time. Traffic moved in the other direction as well, with foreign Muslims arriving in the 1920s to serve the dynasty. Ibn Saud's absorption of Hijaz, with its pluralist religious landscape, was yet another facet of the process. Through immigration and annexation, modernist Salafism became part of the religious landscape in Saudi-ruled Hijaz.

In three respects, Hijaz was a propitious site for the emergence of Salafism in the late Ottoman period. First, proximity to Yemen exposed religious scholars to Muhammad al-Shawkani's reformist teachings that upheld Salafism's theological positions and sympathy for the Taymiyyan legacy.[23] Second, as site of the holy cities, Hijaz attracted ulama from India, including members of the *Ahl-i Hadith* movement, which shared Salafism's puritanical thrust. Third, a handful of Wahhabi ulama resided in the holy cities. These factors converged in the career of a Meccan shaykh, Abu Bakr Khuqir (1867–1930).[24]

Khuqir's teachers included a Wahhabi shaykh, Ahmad ibn ʿIsa, and a leading *Ahl-i Hadith* scholar, Nadhir Husain.[25] In a treatise attacking intercessionary practices, he cited Ibn Taymiyya, Ibn al-Qayyim, al-Shawkani, and Siddiq Hasan Khan; and he gave the modernist rationale for denouncing intercession,

---

[22] Al-Qasimi, *al-Thawra*, 26, 66. On Wahhabi ulama opposition to wireless telegraphy at the time al-Qasimi was writing, see Hafiz Wahbah, *Arabian Days* (London: A. Barker, 1964), 57–60. On conservative ulama in Damascus deploying modern "proofs" to buttress religious arguments, see James Gelvin, "Post Hoc Ergo Propter Hoc? Reassessing the Lineages of Nationalism in Bilad al-Sham," in *From the Syrian Land to the States of Syria and Lebanon*, ed. Thomas Philipp and Christoph Schumann (Würtzburg: ERGON-Verlag, 2004), 127–44. Observing the ostensible paradox of positing compatibility between Wahhabism and nationalism, Werner Ende referred to a "mismatch of national consciousness and neo-Hanbalite convictions." Cited by Redissi, "The Refutation of Wahhabism," 174–5, n. 57.

[23] Bernard Haykel, *Revival and Reform in Islam: The Legacy of Muhammad al-Shawkani* (Cambridge: Cambridge University Press, 2003).

[24] Abu Bakr ibn Muhammad Khuqir, *Majmuʿat muʾallafat al-shaikh Abi Bakr ibn Muhammad ʿArif Khuqir*, 2 vols., ed. ʿAbdallah ibn ʿUmar al-Dumayji (Mecca: Umm al-Qura University, 2004).

[25] Abu Bakr Khuqir, *Hadha thabat al-athbat al-shahira* in *Majmuʿat muʾallafat*, 2:31–4, 55.

calling it a cause of intellectual and moral decline. He wondered whether defenders of seeking help from the dead ever read scientific publications. His affinity for Wahhabism surfaced when he noted that were it not for the ulama of Najd, graves would be crowded with worshipers. Like the Salafis of Baghdad, Damascus, and Cairo, Khuqir asserted that Wahhabis followed the Qur'an and the Sunna, the Hanbali law school, and the way of Ibn Taymiyya and Ibn al-Qayyim.[26]

Khuqir labored in obscurity during the Ottoman and Hashemite periods, when Mecca's religious establishment evinced little interest in the religious purification trend. In nearby Jidda, modernist Salafism found a foothold among merchants and educated youth. For example, Muhammad Nasif, the scion of a wealthy merchant family, participated in a letter-writing network of Salafi ulama and publicists, and recruited Saudi royalty to patronize publishing activities.[27] Another leading voice of educated youth, Muhammad Hasan `Awwad, expressed modernist Salafi ideas in the 1920s. In an essay condemning conservative ulama, he declared that they were incapable of giving straight answers to simple questions about the benefits of fasting; they had no comprehension of Western scientific thinking and technical advances; and their books on grammar and law were confused and full of contradictions. If Muslims wanted insight into such matters, they should ignore today's ulama and consult the books of Ibn Taymiyya, Ibn al-Qayyim, and al-Shafi`i among the ancients, the works of Muhammad ibn `Abd al-Wahhab, and the books of Muhammad `Abduh and Farid Wajdi among the moderns.[28]

With the Saudi annexation of Hijaz, Ibn Saud enlisted local and immigrant Salafis to the cause of Wahhabism by writing for the official Saudi newspaper, *Umm al-Qura*, under the direction of Yusuf Yasin, a Syrian comrade of Rashid Rida.[29] A common thread in the newspaper's early issues is "clarification" of the true nature of Najdi religious doctrine. The first issue reproduced a speech by Ibn Saud stating that Najdis followed Muhammad ibn `Abd al-Wahhab only to the extent that the Qur'an and the Sunna supported his ideas.[30] Six months later, the newspaper published an article explaining that few people knew the

---

[26] Abu Bakr Khuqir, *Fasl al-maqal wa irshad al-dall fi tawassul al-juhhal* in *Majmu`at mu'allafat,* 1:19–21, 33, 40, 42, 52, 70, 109, 113–14. Al-Manar Press published the treatise in 1906.

[27] Muhammad ibn Ahmad Sayyid Ahmad, *Muhammad Nasif: Hayatuhu wa atharuhu* (Beirut: al-Maktab al-Islami, 1994), 20–4, 199, 302–4.

[28] Muhammad Hasan `Awwad, "Khawatir musraha," and "Muda`aba ma`a al-`ulama'," in *A`mal al-`Awwad al-Kamila* (Cairo: Dar al-Jil li-l-Tiba`a, 1981).

[29] On Yusuf Yasin's connection to Rashid Rida, see Joseph Kostiner, *The Making of Saudi Arabia, 1916–1936* (New York: Oxford University Press, 1993), 105.

[30] *Umm al-Qura*, no. 1, Dec. 12, 1924.

truth about the religion of the Arabs of Najd; some imagined the Najdis to believe in a new *madhhab* or even a new religion. In fact, the Najdi *madhhab* adhered to the Qur'an and the Sunna, adding nothing and leaving nothing out, preserving the way of the Prophet and the Salaf. In short, the Arabs of Najd followed Islam; there was no other name for it.[31] During the pilgrimage of 1925, Ibn Saud gave a speech to Indian pilgrims, explaining that his folk were loyal to the doctrine and *madhhab* of the Salaf.[32]

Umm al-Qura was an official expression of Saudi Arabia's engagement with the outside. It propagated the state's conception of itself and of the religious ideas it championed; its articles included defenses of Wahhabi doctrine as the expression of Sunni Islam. Dynastic favor extended to private initiatives as well. A few months after Ibn Saud's forces took over Jidda, he met with Muhammad Nasif, Muhammad 'Awwad, and others to encourage them to establish an "Islamic Sciences" committee to improve schools. Among its tasks was to compose schoolbooks on theology and law according to the Pious Fathers.[33] Apart from direct backing, Nasif took advantage of the favorable political setting to advance his project to gather, edit, and publish classical texts deemed part of the Pious Fathers' legacy. From the 1920s until the 1970s, he was a pivotal figure connecting Saudi Arabia to Salafi scholars and publishers in Arab countries and South Asia. His most enduring associations were with Rida's Cairo associates and Muhammad Bahjat al-Bitar's circle in Damascus. On the Saudi Arabian side, Nasif was in touch with prominent scholars like Hasan ibn 'Abdallah Al al-Shaikh, head of the Hijazi religious estate for nearly thirty years, and Muhammad ibn Salih al-'Uthaimin.[34]

For several decades, Salafis and Wahhabis mingled on the pages of *Umm al-Qura* and in publishing and educational endeavors. But when it came to terminology, the official line of Saudi ulama maintained that their doctrine

---

[31] *Umm al-Qura*, no. 27, June 26, 1925. The same point is in no. 59, Feb. 12, 1926.

[32] *Umm al-Qura*, no. 28, July 10, 1925. He expressed the same idea in his annual address to pilgrims in later years. Muhammad ibn 'Abd al-Rahman al-Khamis, *'Inayat al-Malik 'Abd al-'Aziz bi-l-'aqida al-salafiyya* (Riyadh: al-Amana al-'Amma li-l-Ihtifal bi-Murur Mi'at 'Amm, 1999), 20–2.

[33] On the formation of al-lajna al-'ilmiyya al-islamiyya, see *Umm al-Qura*, no. 70, May 7, 1926. Nasif, 'Awwad, and committee member Hasan Abu al-Hamayil were subscribers to *al-Manar* and appear in its pages as seekers of its fatwa on various issues. For Nasif's letters seeking fatwas, see al-Munajjid, *Fatawa al-Imam*, 2:580–92, 2:630–1, 2:633–41, 3:832–3. For 'Awwad and Abu al-Hamayil, see al-Munajjid, *Fatawa al-Imam*, 5:1867–77. Another committee member, Muhammad Husain Ibrahim, was head of Jam'iyyat Ansar al-Muwahhidin and wrote a newspaper article for razing tombs over graves.

[34] An extensive sample of Nasif's correspondence is reproduced in Ahmad, *Muhammad Nasif*. Contacts with Rida, 20–4; Bitar, 431–8; 'Uthaymin, 331–2, 457–60, 525; Hasan ibn 'Abdallah, 505.

was the proper expression of Sunni Islam. Salafism and Wahhabism remained distinct currents, the former flourishing as a cosmopolitan tendency and the latter retaining a parochial Najdi accent, albeit with increasing influence outside Arabia. The cosmopolitan tenor of Salafism is reflected in the geographical reach of Nasif's correspondence and the range of his interests. In addition to promoting classical works in religious fields like exegesis, *hadith*, law, and theology, he collaborated on publishing books about modern agricultural techniques, improving journalistic Arabic, and the politics of Mandate powers in the Arab world.[35] That Nasif's outlook coincided with the modernist Salafi agenda is clear from his correspondence.[36] Wahhabism, on the other hand, still had the connotation of narrow-minded dogmatism. Nasif's grandson recalled that when he was growing up in Jidda, where a pluralist Sunni milieu, including Sufi orders, had long been the norm, classmates called him a Wahhabi. He also mentioned that his grandfather had welcomed and held discussions with all sorts of people, implying that a Wahhabi would have shunned others.[37] Suspicion on the part of the Wahhabi establishment toward the Salafis emerged in a plaintive letter Nasif wrote to the leading Wahhabi shaykh of the early 1960s, Muhammad ibn Ibrahim Al al-Shaikh. Nasif asked why the Syrian Salafi and defender of Wahhabism Muhammad Bahjat al-Bitar had been excluded from recent meetings in Mecca and Medina concerning the Muslim World League and the Islamic University in Medina.[38] It seems that Wahhabi ulama recognized the gaps between their doctrine and that of modernist Salafis and therefore wished to limit the latter's influence in Saudi Arabia's new religious institutions.

THE SALAFI TURN IN SAUDI ARABIA

In 1971, a leading member of Al al-Shaikh published a magazine article about Muhammad ibn 'Abd al-Wahhab's life and doctrine. In it he wrote that Ibn 'Abd al-Wahhab's followers preferred to be known as *al-Salafiyyun* or *al-Muhammadiyyun*.[39] Recent editions of older Wahhabi treatises exhibit

---

[35] Ibid., 216–17, 242–3, 531.

[36] Ibid., 160, 230–1, 260–3, 306–7, 339, 365, 368.

[37] Ibid., 398–9.

[38] Ibid., 232–3. On the Wahhabi shaikh Muhammad al-'Uthaimin's corrections to Bitar's monograph on Ibn Taymiyya, see 457–60. On Bitar's essays defending Wahhabism, see David Commins, "Wahhabis, Sufis and Salafis," in *Guardians of Faith in Modern Times: 'Ulama' in the Middle East*, ed. Meir Hatina (Leiden: Brill, 2009), 241–3.

[39] Hasan ibn 'Abdallah Al al-Shaikh, "al-Wahhabiyya wa za'imuha al-Imam Muhammad ibn 'Abd al-Wahhab," *al-'Arabi* (Kuwait) no. 147 (Feb. 1971), 26, 29. The author spent most of his career in Hijaz.

the same shift to calling the Najdi doctrine Salafi. For example, where a nineteenth-century Wahhabi treatise used the term "Najdi call" (*al-da`wa al-najdiyya*), the modern editor substituted "the Salafi call in Najd" (*al-da`wa al-salafiyya fi najd*).[40] The Wahhabi establishment now embraced the Salafi label. The underlying political context was Al Saud's decision in the 1960s to open the kingdom to foreign Muslims to develop public institutions, especially in the field of education. With the influx of Muslims came independent Salafi scholars and Islamic revivalist organizations. The cosmopolitan Salafi world was transplanted to Saudi soil.[41] Newly established religious universities were sites of contact and exchange among non-Saudi religious scholars, their Wahhabi counterparts, Saudi students, and foreign Muslim students.

The religious pluralism that accompanied the influx of non-Saudi scholars had the potential to undermine the authority of Wahhabi ulama, especially among pious youth. Nasir al-Din al-Albani came from Syria to the University of Medina in 1961. Known for his impressive command of *hadith* science, al-Albani differed with the Wahhabis on matters of principle, such as his rejection of following any law school as opposed to Wahhabi adherence to Hanbalism, and on practice, such as his view that women were not obliged to cover their faces. The leader of the Wahhabi establishment, Muhammad ibn Ibrahim Al al-Shaikh, allowed al-Albani's teaching appointment to lapse in 1963, compelling him to leave the country.[42] Such challenges to Wahhabi doctrine may have provided an incentive to reaffirm it in the rhetorical currency of the day.

In the 1970s, Saudi intellectual production took a new turn as students and graduates of the religious faculties constructed a Salafi patrimony for Wahhabism in three sorts of publications: (1) editions of classical texts, (2) topical monographs on facets of belief and practice "according to the Salaf," and (3) biographies of historical and contemporary luminaries in the Salafi tradition, as conceived by Saudi ulama. An early artifact of the Saudi project to trace a Salafi ancestry is a 1971 volume, *The Saudi Scholarly Anthology: From*

---

[40] Salih ibn Muhammad ibn Hamad al-Shithri, *Ta'yid al-malak al-mannan fi naqd dalalat Dahlan* (Riyadh: Dar al-Habib, 2000). The original phrasing is on 123; the modern alteration is in the list of contents on 144.

[41] On Syrian Salafis moving to Saudi Arabia, see Arnaud Lenfant, "L'evolution du salafisme en Syrie au xxe siècle," in *Qu'est-ce que le salafisme?* ed. Bernard Rougier (Paris: Presses Universitaires de France, 2008), 163, 167–9.

[42] Stéphane Lacroix, "L'Apport de Muhammad Nasir al-Din al-Albani au salafisme contemporain," in *Qu'est-ce que le salafisme?* 51–4. On the emergence of the Salafi Group and Juhayman al-`Utaybi's splinter group from al-Albani's following, see Thomas Hegghammer and Stéphane Lacroix, "Rejectionist Islamism in Saudi Arabia: The Story of Juhayman al-`Utaybi Revisited," *International Journal of Middle East Studies* 39 (2007): 103–22.

the Pearls of the Ulama of the Pious Ancestors.[43] The editor gathered together five classical creeds (by al-Tabari, al-Tahawi, al-Maqdisi, Ibn Qudama, and Ibn Taymiyya), presenting them in chronological order, followed by five essays by Ibn 'Abd al-Wahhab, including *The Book of God's Unity* (*Kitab al-Tawhid*). No modern authorities are included in the collection, implying a direct, exclusive line from the authoritative formulators of Salafi theological doctrine to Najd. The point is stated succinctly in the title of a 1999 monograph, *The Call of Imam Muhammad ibn 'Abd al-Wahhab: Salafi, not Wahhabi*.[44] During the 1980s, a series called "Creeds of the Pious Fathers" (*'aqa'id al-salaf*) published editions of works by classical theologians.[45] Topical monographs on belief and practice "according to the Salaf" dealt with public affairs in works on morality,[46] loyalty and dissociation,[47] political practice and Islamic law,[48] and ruling on the basis of secular principles and the causes of excommunication.[49] Biography comprises a third element of the Salafi turn's intellectual output. Saudi publishers issued books about early authorities of the Salafi theological tradition: Sufyan al-Thawri,[50] Ibn Rajab,[51] and al-Marwazi.[52] Monographs on the tradition's modern revivers include Siddiq Hasan Khan and his position

---

[43] 'Abdallah ibn Muhammad ibn Hamid, *al-Majmu 'a al- 'ilmiyya al-sa 'udiyya: Min durar 'ulama al-salaf al-salih* (Mecca: Matba'at al-Nahda al-Haditha, 1971).

[44] Ahmad ibn 'Abd al-'Aziz ibn 'Abdallah al-Husayyin, *Da 'wat al-imam Muhammad ibn 'Abd al-Wahhab Salafiyya la Wahhabiyya* (Riyadh: Dar 'Alam al-Kutub, 1999).

[45] 'Ali ibn 'Umar Daraqutni, *Kitab al-nuzul* (Saudi Arabia, 1983); 'Abdallah ibn Muhammad al-Harawi, *Kitab al-arba 'in fi dala'il al-tawhid* (Medina, 1984); Ahmad ibn 'Abdallah al-Isbahani, *Kitab al-imama wa al-radd 'ala al-rafida* (Medina: Maktabat al-'Ulum wa-l-Hikma, 1987); Salih ibn Fawzan Al Fawzan, ed. *al- 'Aqida al-wasitiyya li-Shaykh al-Islam Ahmad ibn Taymiyya* (Riyadh: Maktabat al-Ma'arif, 1987); Abu 'Abdallah Muhammad ibn Mandah, *Kitab al-tawhid wa ma 'rifat asma' allah* (Medina: al-Jami'a al-Islamiyya, 1989).

[46] 'Abd al-'Aziz ibn Nasir Jalil and Baha' al-Din 'Aqil, *Ayna nahnu min akhlaq al-salaf* (Riyadh: Dar al-Taiba, 1993).

[47] Muhammad ibn Sa'id ibn Salim Qahtani and 'Abd al-Razzaq 'Afifi, *al-Wala' wa-l-bara' fi al-Islam: min mafahim 'aqidat al-salaf* (Cairo, 1985); original Umm al-Qura University master's thesis.

[48] Khalid ibn Ali ibn Muhammad 'Anbari, *Fiqh al-siyasa al-shar 'iyya fi daw' al-Qur'an wa al-Sunna wa aqwal salaf al-umma; buhuth fi al-nizam al-siyasi al-islami* (Riyadh, 1997). This publication has an appendix containing fatwas by leading Saudi religious authorities, Ibn Baz, 'Uthaymin, and Fawzan.

[49] Khalid ibn 'Ali ibn Muhammad 'Anbari, *al-Hukm bi ghayr ma anzala Allah wa usul al-takfir fi daw' al-kitab wa al-sunna wa aqwal salaf al-umma* (Saudi Arabia, 1996).

[50] Muhammad ibn Matar Zahrani, *Safahat mushriqa min hayat al-salaf: Sufyan ibn Sa'id al-Thawri* (Riyadh: Dar al-Khudairi, 1998).

[51] 'Abdallah ibn Sulaiman al-Ghufaili, *Ibn Rajab al-Hanbali wa atharuhu fi tawdih 'aqidat al-salaf*, 2 vols. (Riyadh: Dar al-Masayyar, 1998).

[52] Mawsim ibn Munir Ibn Mubarak al-Nufai'i, *al-Imam Muhammad ibn Nasr al-Marwazi wa juhuduhu fi bayan 'aqidat al-salaf* (Riyadh: Dar al-Watan, 1996).

on the doctrine of the Salaf;[53] Muhammad al-Shinqiti and his affirmation of the doctrine of the Salaf;[54] Abu Bakr Khuqir and his defense of the doctrine of the Salaf;[55] and `Abd al-`Aziz ibn Baz, heir of the Salaf.[56]

The modernist legacy of Muhammad `Abduh and Rashid Rida is notably absent in the Saudi roster of Salafi revivers. In fact, according to a recent narrative, they fall outside the Salafi pale altogether. Instead, they belong to the ranks of Muslim thinkers who came under the spell of European thought, along with Rifa`a Rafi` al-Tahtawi, Khair al-Din al-Tunisi, and Jamal al-Din al-Afghani. These thinkers assumed that social justice and democratic rights were valid ideas, and they mined the Qur'an and the Sunna for texts to support that assumption. By contrast, the method of the true Salafis, like Ibn Taymiyya and Muhammad ibn `Abd al-Wahhab, was to base their views on the Qur'an and the Sunna. The adoption of European ideas infected Muslim political thought.[57] To make matters worse, Afghani and `Abduh joined the Freemasons and disguised their rationalist and modernist convictions in Salafi garb. It was therefore inevitable when Rida fell under `Abduh's influence that he would pass along his master's misguided views. They all promoted rationalism under the banner of Salafism, and Western writers gullibly credited them with reviving Salafism when in fact they exploited the call for returning to the Pious Fathers as a slogan for their purely political anticolonial agenda.[58] Thus today's Wahhabi-Salafis have turned against Rida, a spokesman for legitimizing Wahhabism as a Salafi revival.

This reconstruction of Salafism's patrimony is driven by rivalry with the Muslim Brothers and kindred activist organizations. For decades the Saudi government welcomed them as partners in the struggle against Arab nationalist and leftist currents. But since the early 1990s, Saudi religious dissidents, known as *sahwa* sheikhs, inspired by the Muslim Brothers' political analysis and activism, clashed with the government. The Wahhabi religious estate's tradition of polemic found a new target that it construed as a sort of innovation

53 Akhtar Jamal Luqman, *al-Sayyid Siddiq Hasan Qinnawji: ara'uhu al-i`tiqadiyya wa mawqifuhu min `aqidat al-salaf* (Riyadh: Dar al-Hijrah, 1996).

54 `Abd al-`Aziz ibn Salih Tuwayyan, *Juhud al-shaikh Muhammad al-Amin al-Shinqiti fi taqrir `aqidat al-salaf* (Riyadh: Maktabat al-`Ubaykan, 1998).

55 Badr al-Din Nadirin, "al-Shaikh Abu Bakr Khuqir wa juhuduhu fi al-difa` `an `aqidat al-salaf," thesis, Umm al-Qura University, Mecca, n.d.

56 Mani` ibn Hammad Juhani, *al-Shaikh Ibn Baz: Baqiyat al-salaf wa imam al-khalaf: Safahat min hayatihi wa asda wafatihi* (al-Ahsa': al-Nadwa, 1999).

57 "Historical Development of the Methodologies of al-Ikhwaan al-Muslimeen and Their Effect and Influence upon Contemporary Salafee Dawah," version 2.01 (Mar. 2003), www.salafipublications.com, Part One, 13–15.

58 "Historical Development," Part Eight, 2, 5.

(*bid`a*) stemming from European influence on nineteenth-century Muslims, an influence that ran straight from Afghani, `Abduh, and Rida to Hasan al-Banna to *sahwi* shaykhs Salman al-`Awda and Safar al-Hawali.

The embrace of the Salafi mantle was both tactically convenient in the contest against the Muslim Brothers and their offshoots, and substantially easy, given the Wahhabi ulama's conviction that their theology faithfully reproduced the doctrine of the Pious Fathers. They did not ascribe to Salafi the set of modernist, nationalist, and state-building meanings that prevailed earlier. Instead, Salafism was reworked once again to suit circumstances of time and place. In the Saudi context, it was natural that Wahhabi ulama redefined Salafism to legitimate the official creed through the construction of a narrative that emphasized their unique connection to the Pious Fathers' careers and creeds.

CONCLUSION

One hundred years ago, Ottoman religious reformers did not want to be called Wahhabis. Najdi Sunnis did not want to be called Wahhabis. One or two early twentieth-century exceptions apart, nobody wanted to be called a Wahhabi.[59] The connotations of fanaticism and heresy associated with that name had staying power. By contrast, Salafi became associated with purity and authenticity, giving it a positive connotation in modernist, nationalist, and contemporary religious discourses. But if Salafi can refer to a flexible conception of religion as a set of general principles that allow for adaptation according to time and place, or to a firmly fixed creed that allows for no tampering and regards change with suspicion, is it possible to define the term and classify Muslims who claim it? Without suggesting that Salafi is an infinitely elastic term, we might interpret its permutations as an instance of the ways political context shapes arguments over religious rectitude.

As notions of civilizations' progress and backwardness took root in the Muslim world, religious scholars looked to the Pious Fathers for principles that harmonized with the impulse to adapt to new conditions. Salafi shifted from a term in theological debates to a modernist temperament seeking a foundation for remaking education, law, and politics. In the emergent culture of nationalism, the call to return to the way of the Pious Fathers filled two purposes.

---

[59] Sulaiman ibn Sahman embraced the Wahhabi label in a 1916 essay, *al-Sawa`iq al-mursala al-shihabiyya `ala al-shubuh al-dahida al-shamiyya* (Bombay: al-Matba`a al-Mustawfiyya, 1916). In the essay, he gave the title as *al-Sawa`iq al-mursala al-wahhabiyya* and twice used the term "Wahhabi" as a positive referent defined as those who follow the Qur'an, the Sunna, the Pious Fathers, and the founders of the law schools. Ibn Sahman, 81, 196–7.

It anchored a narrative of the community's rebirth through rediscovering the values and virtues of the Pious Fathers, and it affirmed the community's special place in the world, in this instance, as bearer of a universal divine mission. The latest twist in the meaning of Salafi, its association with armed struggle (jihad) against the Muslim world's enemies, resulting in the "Salafi-Jihadi" neologism, also reflects the impact of political context on religious discourse.

Wahhabism's rebranding as Salafi accompanied Saudi Arabia's integration with the Muslim world. From its rise until the late Ottoman era, Wahhabism was a purely regional phenomenon, quarantined from the outside by the stigma of sedition and heresy, and from the inside by a strict view of other Muslims as idolaters. The fall of the Ottoman Empire removed the political structure sustaining the quarantine on Wahhabism. Ibn Saud's pragmatic outlook opened Saudi Arabia to other Muslims, taking down the internal quarantine and turning a new page in interactions between his domain and the Muslim world. Furthermore, during the interwar period, Saudi Arabia's independence was a rare quality that made it appealing to nationalists in the Arab world.

The charge that Wahhabism's claim to be Salafi is illegitimate is part of a struggle over who speaks for Islam. The urgency of the controversy owes something to the reversal in power relations between Saudi Arabia's Wahhabis and their Muslim critics. If we think of Muslim religious discourse operating in a political space, we could say that from the mid-1700s until the mid-1900s, Saudi Arabia was in a weak position, possessing sufficient resources to defend its native religious discourse but definitely in a defensive posture, deflecting a steady stream of polemical aggression from surrounding Muslim lands. Saudi Arabia's accumulation of wealth in the second half of the twentieth century altered the balance of power, making it possible to project its native religious discourse to other Muslim countries through proselytizing and hosting students from other countries at its universities.[60] The critics are correct that Saudi religious scholars have constructed an intellectual pedigree that runs from the early Islamic period to Muhammad ibn 'Abd al-Wahhab to themselves, excluding modernists like 'Abduh and Rida. But such rhetorical sleight of hand is not exceptional; it runs through the entire story of Wahhabism's Salafi turn.

---

[60] An overview of Saudi proselytizing is in Saeed Shehabi, "The Role of Religious Ideology in the Expansionist Policies of Saudi Arabia," in *Kingdom without Borders*, 183–97.

9

Understanding Stability and Dissent in the Kingdom

The Double-Edged Role of the jama'at in Saudi Politics

Stéphane Lacroix

It is a common idea in Western scholarship on Saudi Arabia that, except for clandestine jihad-oriented groups, the kingdom is devoid of influential non-state institutions and organizations, whose very existence is officially against Saudi law. As a consequence, only two kinds of groups have generally been considered able to counterbalance, to some extent, the power of the Saudi state. First are the tribes.[1] Yet, although it is true that the tribes have retained some of their cohesion, especially in the countryside, they are a much less significant reality in the cities where, among other things, the existence and diversity of competing affiliations have weakened them. Second is what some authors have referred to as the technocratic "new middle class,"[2] understood to constitute a distinctive social group harboring an inherently modernist agenda. However, I am not convinced that this group is necessarily modernist, nor do I find any indication that it has any cohesion, and so considering it as a counter-power to the state seems to me to be wishful thinking.

In contrast to those two kinds of groups, the religious forces are usually described as having been "bureaucratized"[3] and integrated to the state within what is largely referred to as the "religious establishment." As a consequence, they have generally been portrayed as a mere appendix of the regime, and never as a buffer between state and society. An exception is found in the literature on Islamism, which offers a more oppositional view of Saudi Islam. Yet, it focuses on individualities ("charismatic preachers" such as Juhayman

---

[1] See, for instance, Christine Moss Helms, *The Cohesion of Saudi Arabia* (London: Croom Helm, 1981).

[2] See William A. Rugh, "Emergence of a New Middle Class in Saudi Arabia," *Middle East Journal* 27, no. 1 (1973): 7–20; Nadav Safran and Mark A. Heller, *The New Middle Class and Regime Stability in Saudi Arabia* (Cambridge: Center for Middle Eastern Studies, 1985).

[3] Ayman Al-Yassini, *Religion and State in the Kingdom of Saudi Arabia* (Boulder: Westview, 1985).

al-'Utaybi, "dissident ulama" such as Safar al-Hawali) – as if contention was merely driven by individual moves – rather than on the structures and resources necessary for collective action. As a consequence, very little has been said of the role of religious networks in a society where Islam is agreed to play a central role in structuring social relations.

In this chapter, I will describe the emergence in the kingdom from the 1960s onwards of relatively organized and strongly cohesive networks harboring a discourse that can be described as Islamist. Because of the widespread acceptance of Islamist ideas in Saudi society due in particular – as shall be demonstrated – to the influence of the Muslim Brotherhood through the education system, there is no doubt that these groups' rhetoric quickly acquired popularity. Yet, in the Saudi context, the primary importance of the *jama'at* came from the fact that they constituted unique mobilizing structures, especially in urban settings where other possible structures – especially the tribes – were weakened.

Social movement theorists have long argued that harboring a political discourse that resonates with the grievances or the worldview of whatever large segment of the population, or even benefiting from a favorable political opportunity structure, is not enough for a movement to produce effective mobilization; to take place effectively, mobilization also needs to rely on cohesive and well-developed mobilizing structures.[4] These mobilizing structures, in authoritarian contexts where the public sphere is heavily constrained, cannot be created overnight.[5] As a consequence, because they are the only well-entrenched potential mobilizing structure in the Saudi kingdom (and especially, again, in the cities), my contention is that the Islamist networks I am about to describe hold the key to mobilization in Saudi Arabia.

Mobilization, however, is inherently twofold: It can be in favor of the regime, or against the regime. And these Islamist networks have indeed acted during the last decades, as we shall see, as what Guilain Denoeux calls "double-edged networks," playing both "stabilizing" and "destabilizing" roles according to the social and political context.[6] To illustrate this point, I will examine different episodes in recent Saudi history, and describe how, in each of them, the action of these Islamist networks can account for the stability or the instability of the

---

4 See, for instance, Doug McAdam, John McCarthy, Mayer Zald, *Comparative Perspective on Social Movements. Political Opportunities, Mobilizing Structures, and Cultural Framings* (Cambridge: Cambridge University Press, 1996), 3.

5 Maryjane Osa, *Solidarity and Contention: Networks of Polish Opposition* (Minneapolis: University of Minnesota Press, 2003), 21.

6 Guilain Denoeux, *Urban Unrest in the Middle East: A Comparative Study of Informal Networks in Egypt, Iran, and Lebanon* (Albany: State University of New York Press, 1995).

political system. First, I will look at the period from the 1960s to the 1980s, which, apart from the isolated attack on the grand mosque in Mecca by a few hundred rebels in 1979, was generally a period of stability. Second, I will examine the post–Gulf War Islamist contention (1990–4), which, in contrast, represented a period of dissent and instability. Third, I will analyze the post–May 2003 period, when a local section of al-Qaeda started a campaign of terrorism in the kingdom, creating relatively short-lived instability. Fourth, I will end with a few remarks on the 2005 municipal elections.

INTRODUCING THE JAMA'AT

The Islamist networks that are the focus of this chapter date back to the 1960s, and their emergence is closely linked to the arrival in Saudi Arabia of thousands of members of the Muslim Brotherhood, fleeing from their home countries where they were persecuted by the incumbent nationalist regimes (Egypt after 1954, Syria during the years of the United Arab Republic and after 1963, Iraq after 1958 and more so after 1963, etc.). These were the times of what is known as the "Arab Cold War," and the Saudi kingdom was trying to build a coalition of conservative regimes and political forces to counter the growing influence of the so-called progressives, led by Gamal Abd al-Nasser.

In this conflict, the Muslim Brothers were a key asset for the Saudi kingdom: The Saudis needed an Islamic ideology to systematically oppose to Nasser's Arab Nationalism, yet the Wahhabi ulama were too traditional to build one out of Wahhabism. So the Muslim Brotherhood were put in charge of the whole Saudi counter-propaganda apparatus, especially the Saudi media sector, which they would soon control.

But there is more to the Muslim Brothers' presence in Saudi Arabia. As a matter of fact, they came at a time of crucial changes for the kingdom. With the considerable increase in oil money, the Saudi state and its institutions were rapidly developing. Yet, at a time when very few were the Saudis who had studied abroad, the kingdom was severely lacking in individuals capable of playing any significant role in this process. So the Muslim Brothers would soon be chosen to become the backbone of the modernization of the kingdom, to the extent that one can say, as a Saudi intellectual puts it in a provocative (and indeed probably a little exaggerated) fashion, that "the Muslim Brotherhood literally built the Saudi state and most Saudi institutions."[7]

Among these institutions was a sector of very special importance: the education sector. It is out of this sector – especially the high schools and the

---

[7] Interview, Saudi Arabia, March 2005.

universities – that would emerge, in great part under the impulse of the Muslim Brotherhood, the mainstream Islamist trend that developed in Saudi Arabia from the 1960s onwards, and which is known as *al-Sahwa al-Islamiyya* – the Islamic Awakening (hereafter designated as Sahwa).

As a consequence both of its origins and of its environment, the Sahwa's ideology emerged as a mix between the religious culture traditionally found in Saudi Arabia and that is known, in Western scholarship, as Wahhabism after its early proponent, Muhammad bin 'Abd al-Wahhab, and the Muslim Brotherhood's ideology. Wahhabism was especially influential in religious and social issues: The Sahwa would adopt the extreme social conservatism of the Wahhabis, in particular when it came to women's role in society, but also the Wahhabis' hostility to non-Wahhabi Islamic groups, especially the Sufis and the Shia. At the same time, the Sahwa adopted the Muslim Brotherhood's views on most cultural and political issues, especially the Brotherhood's concept and vision of the Islamic State and its rejection of Western influence.[8] Within the brotherhood's ideology, Sayyid Qutb's radical ideas were especially influential. Qutb considered, in particular, that there could be no middle way between *hakimiyya* (the sovereignty of God), understood as the full implementation of the Shari'a, which characterizes the Islamic state, and *jahiliyya* (pre-Islamic ignorance). These ideas had a greater impact because of the more obvious correspondence between them and the basic principles of Wahhabism: Muhammad 'Abd al-Wahhab had a similar "black and white" vision, opposing *jahiliyya* to *tawhid*, the unicity, or transcendence, of God. Also, most of the early advocates of the Sahwa had themselves been Qutbists in their countries of origin. The most famous of them, who would later be dubbed in Saudi Arabia as "the Shaykh of the Sahwa" (*shaykh al-sahwa*), was Muhammad Qutb, Sayyid Qutb's brother and a professor at the Umm al-Qura University of Mecca from 1971 onwards, right after he was freed from the Egyptian jails.[9]

Although the Sahwa was indeed more of a trend than a movement in a strictest sense, its most organized and structured part was represented by the *jama'at islamiyya*, or the "Islamic groups" (hereafter designated as *jama'at*). They constituted relatively organized networks of religious study groups and had developed as an outgrowth of the Saudi education system, and especially of its extracurricular activities, including the summer camps, the Saudi scouts, the committees for raising Islamic awareness, and the Qur'an

[8] Stéphane Lacroix and Thomas Hegghammer, "Saudi Arabia Backgrounder: Who Are the Islamists?" *International Crisis Group Middle East Report* no. 31, Sept. 21, 2004.

[9] On Muhammad Qutb, see Stéphane Lacroix, *Awakening Islam: Religious Dissent in Contemporary Saudi Arabia* (Cambridge, MA: Harvard University Press, 2011), 53–6.

memorization circles, which served for recruitment purposes as well as to provide resources.

After a number of episodes too numerous to be recounted here,[10] two main *jama'at* emerged as dominant in the kingdom. The first called itself *ikhwan*, in reference to the Muslim Brotherhood (*al-ikhwan al-muslimun*) (to which it identified, without formally considering itself as a local section of the movement as it exists in Egypt)[11] and was made up of four loosely connected branches, each of which enjoyed support in a certain region or social group. The founding father of the Saudi *ikhwan* is generally considered to be Manna' al-Qattan, an Egyptian Muslim brother who had emigrated to the kingdom as early as 1953 to teach at the faculty of Shari`a (*kulliyat al-shari`a*), before eventually becoming the director of higher studies at Imam University. Whether al-Qattan's influence on the formation of this first *jama'a* was direct or indirect, however, remains a subject of debate.[12]

The members of the other dominant *jama'a* merely named themselves "the salafis" (*al-salafiyyun*), but their foes would generally refer to them as the "sururis" (*al-sururiyyun*) because the *jama'a* had emerged under the influence of a Syrian ideologue named Muhammad Surur Zayn al-'Abidin.[13] Muhammad Surur was born in Syria in 1938 and became an activist in the Syrian Muslim Brotherhood when he was a teenager. In the mid-1960s, when he had already become a second-rank figure in the Brotherhood, he started voicing increasing criticism of the movement on two grounds: On political matters, he subscribed to the still minority "qutbist" line. On religious matters, Muhammad Surur advocated a much more rigorist, Wahhabi-like, approach to creed (*'aqida*) and criticized the Syrian Muslim Brotherhood for tolerating Sufis within their ranks. In 1965, partly as a consequence of these disagreements, Muhammad Surur left for Saudi Arabia, where he worked as a teacher of mathematics and religion in the scientific institutes (*ma'ahid 'ilmiyya*) of Ha'il and Burayda. Not long after he established himself in the kingdom, he left the Brotherhood for good and decided to initiate what he described as "a new form of Islamic activism"[14] – that is, to create his own *jama'a*, within the ideological framework of the broader Sahwi social movement.[15] Although it has

---

[10] For more details, see Lacroix, *Awakening Islam*, 62–73.

[11] One of the signs of the Saudi *ikhwan*'s independence was that they did not pledge allegiance (*bay'a*) to the guide (*murshid*) in Cairo.

[12] Lacroix, *Awakening Islam*, 64.

[13] Most of the information presented here on the *jama'at* was collected during interviews conducted in Saudi Arabia from 2003 to 2007.

[14] Muhammad Surur Zayn al-'Abidin, "Al-wahda al-islamiyya 8," *al-sunna*, Jumada al-Akhira 1413 [Dec. 1992], no. 27.

[15] As for Surur, he was expelled from Saudi Arabia in 1974 and reestablished himself in Kuwait, before leaving to Birmingham (U.K.) in 1984. There he created the Center for Islamic Studies,

first been used as a derogatory term, I will use the name "sururi" to designate this group, because the label "salafi," which means faithful to the al-salaf al-salih ("pious ancestors"), that is, pure or authentic, has been used by so many actors both throughout Islamic history and in the contemporary world that it has become ambiguous.

The strength of these jama'at came from the fact that, despite the fact that their organization structures remained somehow informal, they were very cohesive. There were several reasons for this. First, Saudis who belonged to a jama'a had usually been recruited at an early age, through the Qur'an memorization circle of their neighborhood mosque or the society for raising Islamic awareness of the school they attended. By intervening in the primary socialization of children, the jama'at gave themselves the means to exercise deep influence. Young people later joined study groups and were expected to attend one or more sessions a week led by the member in charge of the group, the murabbi (educator), sometimes also called emir (amir). On weekends and during vacation periods, members of the group, under the supervision of their emir, often went to a camp together or took part in similar activities. Soon, the study group became a second family, and the emir a second father. Emotional ties developed, which made any exit from the group unlikely. These ties usually remained, even when the member of the jama'a became an adult. There were also material incentives for the young member to stay with his jama'a. In certain universities, for instance, it was common that this or that jama'a controlled student housing – and reserved priority there for its members.

Despite its origins, the Sahwa – and, within it, the jama'at – did in no way, at the time of their emergence, constitute an opposition to the Saudi regime. Indeed, although its political worldview was largely shaped by the Brotherhood's teachings, the Sahwa mainly applied these teachings to other parts of the world, while it insisted – just like the traditional Wahhabi ulama – that, in principle, the Saudi state was the only true Islamic state in the contemporary world. In other words, while the Sahwa – and within it the jama'at – kept their oppositional potential intact in theory, they voluntarily neutralized it in practice.

THE STABILIZING ROLE OF THE JAMA'AT

The development of the Sahwa and its networks was even encouraged by the state, as a means of countering the influence of leftist militants in secondary

described by one of Surur's followers as "the main think-tank of the jama'a" throughout the 1980s and 1990s (interview with a sururi, Saudi Arabia). Surur left the United Kingdom late 2004 and has been living in Jordan ever since. See Lacroix, Awakening Islam, 70.

schools and university campuses. Indeed, one has to remember that the 1960s and 1970s were marked by leftist and Arab nationalist unrest in Saudi Arabia. Baathists, communists, and Nasserites were then active in the kingdom, and several coup attempts against the royal family took place, culminating in a 1969 attempt by a group of officers in the Saudi air force, organized in an "Organization for National Revolution" (*munadhdhamat al-thawra al-wataniyya*).[16] With the growth of the Sahwa, however, the leftist and Arab nationalist influence dramatically decreased during the 1970s.

In late 1979, after Juhayman al-'Utaybi and his group of followers stormed the *haram* of Mecca – where they remained for two weeks before being expelled with the help of French special forces – the regime reinforced the influence of the Sahwa by channeling more funding to those activities that were known to be the Sahwa's facade, especially the summer camps and the Islamic scouts. As a result of this influx of money, their numbers grew quickly. The reason for this increased support is that the Sahwa had had no involvement whatsoever in the Mecca incident; Juhayman and his group were a radicalized faction of a low-class pietistic movement called *al-Jama'a al-Salafiyya al-Muhtasiba* (The Salafi Group That Commands Good and Forbids Wrongdoing, or JSM), which had emerged in Medina in the 1960s, partly as a result of a non-Muslim Brotherhood influence, that of the Syrian scholar Muhammad Nasir al-Din al-Albani.[17] Juhayman's group therefore represented a completely distinct trend within Saudi Islamism, which T. Hegghammer and I have referred to as rejectionist, and which is characterized by a strong focus on ritual practices, and a declared disdain for politics yet active rejection of the state and its institutions.[18] As a consequence of their diverging worldviews, rejectionists and Sahwis largely disagree and strongly dislike each other; opposing the Sahwa's influence was even one the main objectives of the JSM in the 1970s. As it had done with the leftists in the 1960s and 1970s, the state therefore used the Sahwa, and its networks, to counter the influence of the rejectionists in the 1980s.

The 1980s also saw the emergence of a new actor on the Saudi Islamist scene: the Jihadis, followers of Palestinian shaykh Abdallah 'Azzam and later of Usama bin Ladin, who argued that fighting the Soviets and their communist

[16] Falah al-Mudayris, *Al-ba'thiyyun fi-l-khalij wa-l-jazira al-'arabiyya*(*The Baathists in the Gulf and in the Arabian Peninsula*) (Kuwait: dar al-qurtas, 2002), 58.

[17] On al-Albani, see Stéphane Lacroix, "Between Revolution and Apoliticism: Muhammad Nasir al-Din al-Albani's Influence on the Shaping of Contemporary Salafism," in *Global Salafism: Islam's New Religious Movement*, ed. Roel Meijer (New York: Hurst/Columbia University Press, 2009).

[18] Thomas Hegghammer and Stéphane Lacroix, "Rejectionist Islamism in Saudi Arabia: The Story of Juhayman al-'Utaybi Revisited," *International Journal of Middle East Studies*, 1, no. 39 (2007): 103–22.

allies in Afghanistan was an individual religious duty (*fard 'ayn*) for all Muslims. From the beginning, the Sahwa's shaykhs opposed Azzam's calls, to which – like the ulama of the official Saudi religious establishment, including shaykhs Abd al-Aziz Ibn Baz and Muhammad Ibn Uthaymin – they preferred a more traditional interpretation: Jihad in Afghanistan was, as they argued, an individual religious duty only for Afghan Muslims, and a collective religious duty (*fard kifaya*) for non-Afghan Muslims – which meant that non-Afghan Muslims should indeed support the Afghan *mujahidin* by prayers and donations, but that they should not necessarily go fight on their side.

There were two main reasons to this stance: First, the Sahwa repeatedly argued that the focus of its activism should be the "land of the two holy places" (*bilad al-haramayn al-sharifayn*), as they called Saudi Arabia, and not "some faraway land whose inhabitants are barely Muslims," as one interviewee put it.[19] The second reason for the Sahwa's opposition to 'Azzam was that the *jama'at* saw him as a competitor trying to break their monopoly on the hearts and minds of Saudi youth – and they did not want their members to escape their grip.

Although the Saudi regime first decided to officially encourage the departure of young Saudi fighters to Afghanistan as a way of boosting its Islamic legitimacy, it backed down in 1988 when it started hearing reports about how young Saudis in Afghanistan were increasingly falling under the influence of Egyptian and Middle Eastern radicals whose rhetoric was deeply hostile to the Saudi royal family. At this stage, then, the Saudi regime became very happy to offer discrete support to the Sahwa in its opposition to the jihadis. And it is obvious that the Sahwa's direct or indirect control over much of Saudi youth, sections of which were embedded within the *jama'at*, prevented the jihadis from recruiting more Saudis than they actually ended up doing: Several thousand young *mujahidin* from the kingdom went to Afghanistan, but, given the prevalence of the culture of pan-Islamist nationalism in Saudi Arabia in the 1980s,[20] the figures could arguably have gone much higher.

For all these reasons, then, it appears that, from the 1960s to the late 1980s, Sahwi networks played what can be described as a "stabilizing role" in Saudi politics, acting as a conservative force whose mobilizing potential was largely put at the service of the regime.

19 This stance is explained by the fact that the Afghans are not *salafi* but *maturidi* in creed ('*aqida*); they subscribe to the hanafi school of law, while Saudis *salafis* are either *hanbalis* or hostile to all schools, and they tend to have, or tolerate, Sufi tendencies
20 Thomas Hegghammer, *Jihad in Saudi Arabia* (Cambridge: Cambridge University Press, 2010).

FROM DESTABILIZATION TO RESTABILIZATION: THE GULF WAR

In 1990, in the wake of the Iraqi invasion of Kuwait, the royal family's call for Western troops to protect the kingdom from a potential Iraqi invasion prompted a wave of Islamist criticism, which led to the emergence of an Islamist reform movement, spearheaded by a number of lay and religious personalities. At a grassroots level, this movement manifested itself by the mobilization of thousands of young religious people every time a reformist religious figure would deliver an oppositional *khutba* (a Friday sermon at a mosque). At a more elite level, hundreds of prominent Sahwa figures drafted a couple of petitions, *khitab al-matalib* (the letter of demands) and *mudhakkarat al-nasiha* (the memorandum of advice), which were submitted to the king in 1991 and 1992. The demands of the movement were basically twofold: First, its proponents wanted Western forces out of the country; second, they asked for a comprehensive and radical reform of the Saudi political system, to make it more in line with their conception of Islam.

As I mentioned earlier, most of the research on this period focused on the role of charismatic leaders – Salman al-Awda, Safar al-Hawali, and others – who were presented as literally "mesmerizing" a population described as Wahhabi and conservative – and much of the literature seems to consider this a condition sufficient for this population to mobilize.[21] The dominant approach was therefore a mix of the sociopsychological and the cultural approaches to mobilization. Yet social movement theorists have long criticized these approaches and have recommended paying more attention to the presence and availability of structures, considered a condition essential for mobilization.

In this case, the mobilizing structures were the *jama'at*. After lengthy debates, oral sources indicate that, around late 1990, the reformist leaders were successful in convincing some of the *jama'at*'s leaders to support the movement, breaking with the *jama'at*'s traditional nonoppositional stance.[22] From one day to another, then, the *jama'at* started applying to the Saudi state the same Muslim Brotherhood rhetoric that they had applied to every state except Saudi Arabia for decades, thereby effectively transforming theory into practice. Rapidly tens of thousands of young Saudis became involved in the opposition's activities. More than the charisma of the leaders or the political culture of the followers, it is then the existence and availability of these *jama'at*

---

[21] See, for instance, Mamoun Fandy, *Saudi Arabia and the Politics of Dissent* (Baginstoke: Macmillan, 1999).

[22] Interviews, Saudi Arabia. See also *Awakening Islam*, 225–31.

as ready-made mobilizing structures that explains why the mobilization process was initially so quick and successful.

Yet, the movement's very dependence on the *jama'at* also explains why the mobilization declined very quickly after a couple of years, around late 1992 to early 1993. The *jama'at*, having benefited significantly – and still benefiting today – from the system and its institutions in which, as we have seen, they are somehow literally embedded, started to fear the consequences of the mounting tension between the regime and the opposition. And when the costs of mobilization started to rise, the *jama'at* basically withdrew their support from the opposition, returning to their earlier noninterventional stance. Long before the first big wave of repression against the movement that led in 1994 to the arrest of the main reformist figures, Salman al-Awda and Safar al-Hawali, the movement had therefore lost most of its mobilizing potential.[23] One could even argue that it is precisely because the regime knew the movement had lost its mobilizing potential and had become weak that it resorted to repression, without fear of the consequences.

In the case of the 1990–4 Islamist contention, then, Sahwi networks started by playing a "destabilizing role," before eventually switching sides and putting their stabilizing potential at the service of the regime.

AL-QAEDA IN THE ARABIAN PENINSULA AND THE JAMA'AT

The aftermath of the Taliban's defeat in Afghanistan in late 2001 prompted al-Qaeda's central leadership to reconsider the movement's strategy. One of the decisions taken at this stage was to launch a violent campaign in Saudi Arabia, explicitly directed against the Western presence, and implicitly against the regime. From mid-2002, returnees from Afghanistan started creating cells in Saudi Arabia, which would end up forming the basic infrastructure of "al-Qaeda in the Arabian Peninsula" (*Tanzim al-Qaida fi Jazirat al-Arab* – which I refer to as QAP). The QAP started a campaign of terrorist attacks in May 2003, and this campaign kept some momentum until 2005, after which only isolated attacks continued to occur.[24]

From the onset, the Sahwa denounced the QAP's campaign, and, more importantly, just as they had done in the 1980s with the earlier jihadis, the *jama'at* maintained a firm grip on their members to prevent them from joining the QAP. The strategic importance of the *jama'at* for the QAP's recruitment

---

[23] Ibid.
[24] For an outstanding account of the QAP's campaign, see Hegghammer, *Jihad in Saudi Arabia*.

was acknowledged by the QAP leadership in several statements that were published in Sawt al-Jihad, the QAP's mouthpiece. In June 2004, for instance, QAP leader Isa al-'Awshan published a letter entitled "Letter to the Youth of the Summer Camps" (*risala ila shabab al-marakiz al-sayfiyya*) ("youth of the summer camps" is one of the common circumlocutions used to designate *jama'at* members) in which he tried to convince *jama'at* leaders and followers to support al-Qaeda's cause by relying on a mix of Wahhabi and Muslim Brotherhood rhetoric deemed attractive to Sahwa-minded youth. In his text, al-'Awshan tries to take advantage of the fact that, in contrast with most other QAP members, he himself was a mid-ranking *jama'a* figure, using this to better connect with his audience: "By God's will, I was, in the past, in charge of several summer camps, and I lived among the youth of the summer camps for many years. Because I know many of them personally, and I am convinced of the sincerity of their intentions, of their attachment to religion, of their care for Islam, I seize this opportunity to address a message to every young person who participates or has participated in the summer camps, as well as to the supervisors and the individuals in charge of these summer camps." Then he adds, playing on his audience's emotions: "Didn't we study together the biography of the Prophet (Peace be upon him) and his companions? ... Didn't we spend all our time talking about the suffering of Muslims here and there ... ?" Before concluding: "Then what about today when we see the Cross and its soldiers spreading corruption on earth, while we remain silent and passive?"[25]

The *jama'at*'s cohesion, however, was stronger than this kind of rhetoric. Thus, the QAP's efforts failed, and very few *jama'at* leaders and followers ever supported or joined al-Qaeda. It can even probably be said that the *jama'at*'s opposition to the QAP, and the control the *jama'at* maintained over much of the Islamic youth, partly accounts for the QAP's growing inability to recruit followers after late 2003,[26] and, to some extent, for the eventual failure of the QAP's campaign. Sympathizers of the QAP easily recognized this fact, as did the anonymous author of a pamphlet published in 2008 on the internet called "Islamist Movements in Saudi Arabia at the Service of the Secret Police – The Sururis as an Example."[27]

Again, Sahwa networks played a "stabilizing role" in Saudi politics, by keeping firm control over youth who could otherwise have become potential

---

[25] 'Isa al-'Awshan, "Risāla maftūha ilā shabāb al-marākiz al-sayfiyya" (Open Letter to the Youth of the Summer Camps), *Sawt al-jihad*, 1 Jumada I 1425 (June 19, 2004), no. 19.

[26] Figures indicate that the QAP recruited very few individuals in Saudi Arabia after late 2003. See Hegghammer, *Jihad in Saudi Arabia*.

[27] *Al-harakat al-islamiyya fi-l-sa'udiyya fi khidmat al-mukhabarat*, http://www.almedad.com/vb/showthread.php?t=10474&page=1.

al-Qaeda recruits. As a sign of gratefulness, the regime allowed the same Sahwi shaykhs who had spent the second half of the 1990s in jail a greater presence in the Saudi public sphere, especially in the media. Since 2004–5 Salman al-Awda has, for instance, presented a weekly talk show on MBC, and his foundation, al-Islam al-Yawm (in English, *Islam Today*), after several years of presence on the internet, has been allowed to publish a monthly magazine. Other Sahwi shaykhs such as Safar al-Hawali and Nasir al-'Umar have also been authorized to open websites, some of which now attract a wide readership.

THE MUNICIPAL ELECTIONS AND THE JAMA'AT'S "BARGAINING POSITION"

Between February and April 2005, Saudi Arabia, under pressure from within and from abroad to reform itself, held what was presented as the kingdom's first municipal elections.[28] At these 2005 elections, male voters were to elect half of the municipal councils (the other half being appointed by the king).

The *jama'at*, again, played a key role in the process, especially in the urban settings:[29] In the kingdom's major cities, the two leading candidates were a *sururi* and an *ikhwani*, with scores very far above all other candidates. Although voter registration was relatively low (for instance, around 25 percent in Riyadh, with a turnout of 73.6 percent), most of the voters gave their voice to *jama'at* candidates. This is all the more significant given that, in each district, there were tens of candidates with a salafi beard and other obvious signs of religiosity, and that the candidates' programs were all very similar, since the regime had set the condition that candidates could campaign only on local issues (roads, infrastructures, etc.) and that no ideological stances would be permitted. In addition, on no occasion did any of the candidates publicly identify himself as part of a *jama'a* (and some, when asked, even denied it very strongly). However, there is no doubt that their followers and sympathizers – some of whom were interviewed for this study – knew precisely who they were.[30]

In Riyadh, for instance, five out of the seven winners are known to belong to the Saudi *ikhwan*, while the two remaining are considered close to them.[31] This *ikhwani* victory in a city reputed as a stronghold of the *sururis* is mostly

---

[28] This is only partly true: In the early decades of the twentieth century, elections were held for some municipal councils in the Hedjaz.

[29] Interestingly, tribal leaders won in the countryside, where the *jama'at* are weak. This showed that, as we previously argued, although the tribes have ceased to represent a major political force in the cities, they still maintain a strong mobilizing potential outside the urban areas.

[30] Interview with *jama'at* members, Saudi Arabia, February–April, 2005.

[31] Ibid.

explained by the fact that the *sururis* were first hesitant in participating in the elections; the *ikhwan*, in contrast, started mobilizing their resources and followers straight away and were much better prepared. The *sururi* victory in Dammam – seven candidates elected out of seven, while the *ikhwan*, though they are known to have a sizeable presence in the region, got none of their affiliates onto the municipal council – is then portrayed as a revenge for the humiliation suffered in Riyadh.[32] In Dammam, the *sururis* used every means at their disposal to support their candidates against the *ikhwan*, from sending large amounts of SMS to intensive posting on Islamist forums; also, most of the major shaykhs of the region being *sururis* or close to them, they wrote fatwas supporting the *sururi* candidates. In other cities, the results were more mixed with, always, however, a dominance of *ikhwan* and *sururis*.

There are two readings of these results: First, they illustrate the rivalry that exists between the two leading *jama'at*. This is nothing new: Since the 1960s *ikhwan* and *sururis* have actively competed for positions and resources in all sectors of influence, especially the schools and universities, the Islamic NGOs, the ministries, etc. Interestingly, however, the municipal elections offer – with some exceptions due to local circumstances, as we just saw – a useful map of the two groups' presence in the different regions of the kingdom. Second, they represented a triumph for the Sahwa in general, regardless of the different affiliations within it. Indeed, the municipal elections offered the *jama'at* a key opportunity to demonstrate their strength and to confirm what we have argued in the introduction of this chapter: that they are, in the cities, the only nonstate structures with a real mobilizing potential.

The role played here by the *jama'at* was ambiguous: On the one hand, their aim, by strongly encouraging their followers to vote, no doubt was to prove their strength and influence – which could be understood as something potentially destabilizing. Yet, the *jama'at* were very keen on playing by the rules. As we have already mentioned, one of the conditions set by the regime was that the candidates campaign only on local and nonpolitical issues, ranging from housing to roads, etc. – but do not address national or ideological issues. This is precisely what the Islamist candidates did, and the only candidates excluded for taking political stances were liberals, as in the case of that liberal candidate who explicitly wrote in his program that he was in favor of women driving.[33]

In the election process, therefore, instead of playing a straightforward stabilizing or destabilizing role, the *jama'at* adopted a middle way, what we could call a bargaining position: By encouraging their followers to participate and

---

[32] Ibid.
[33] The candidate's name is Sulayman al-Salman, who ran in Riyadh.

play by the rules, they helped to legitimize the process initiated by the regime. Yet, this had a price, and by showing their strength and influence, one of their main aims was to put pressure on the regime to prevent it from moving further on the way of social liberalization – on women's issues, for instance – as Saudi liberals, and the West, have constantly been asking. Another key issue for the *jamaʿat* is the reform of the Saudi education system and of Saudi school and university curricula – and here again, they oppose any change, because it would threaten was they see as their vital base.

The pressure put on the regime by the Sahwa and the *jamaʿat* partly explains why Abdallah, although he himself and his close advisors are known to be personally favorable to social liberalization and education reform, has taken a very careful approach to these issues since he became king in August 2005. One can imagine that he and his entourage are well aware both of the stabilizing role the *jamaʿat* can play as long as they are appeased and of their tremendous potential for destabilization, should they decide to mobilize against the regime.

CONCLUSION

Saudi Arabia has long been portrayed as an exception in the Middle East, if not in the whole world: a country with no forms of popular organization. This has prompted a heavy focus on culture and psychology to explain Saudi political dynamics – and especially Saudi Islamist dynamics. In the literature, never is the question of mobilizing structures asked. Yet, as demonstrated here, there exist informal nonstate structures that possess strong cohesion: the networks of religious study groups known as the *jamaʿat*. In the cities, they are the only mobilizing structures with a large following, which gives them tremendous importance. Depending on the political context and the perceptions their leaders may have of their interests, they can play either stabilizing or destabilizing roles. Understanding their attitude goes a long way in accounting for the periods of stability and dissent experienced by the kingdom. It also sheds new light on some of the constraints currently faced by the regime and partly explains some of the political options recently taken by King Abdallah.

10

The Struggle for Authority

The Shaykhs of Jihadi-Salafism in Saudi Arabia, 1997–2003

Saud Al-Sarhan[1]

I

Introduction

Toward the end of the 1990s a new group of religious scholars emerged in Saudi Arabia. These scholars, who embraced a similar ideology and were well connected to each other, offered religious justification and support to all Jihadi groups throughout the world, and their fatwas, statements, and books provided the ideological justification for the Jihadi-Salafis, including al-Qaeda. It was the first time in the modern history that Saudi scholars found themselves becoming global ideologues for the jihadis, who began referring to this group of scholars as the "shaykhs of Jihadi-Salafism" (*shuyukh al-Salafiyya al-Jihadiyya*).

In this chapter I propose to examine how these shaykhs sought to establish their religious authority, and how they interacted with other centers of power, such as the Saudi king's office, the official Saudi ulama, and with the "Islamic Awakening" (*Sahwa*) leaders, who represented a Saudi movement influenced by the Muslim Brotherhood. I have selected for study three of Jihadi-Salafism's most important Saudi shaykhs: Humud b. Abd Allah al-'Uqla al-Shu'aybi (1927–2002), Nasir b. Hamad al-Fahd (b. 1969), and 'Ali b. Khudayr al-Khudayr (b. 1955). These were the most active and influential shaykhs in the new movement and were prolific in expressing their opinions on domestic and international matters. Although several lesser important Jihadi-Salafi scholars are worth noting, such as Sulayman al-'Ulwan, 'Abd al-'Aziz al-Jarbu', and Ahmad al-Khalidi, the three aforementioned shaykhs – al-Shu'aybi, al-Fahd, and al-Khudayr – constitute a cohesive group that held

[1] I would like to thank Bernard Haykel and Robert Gleave for their assistance with this chapter. I also want to thank Eman Alhusain and other colleagues at KFCRIS for their comments on the final version of this study.

the same views and acted in unison from 1999 to 2002. As such, they can be understood as constituting a unit in addition to being the most important Saudi scholars for the Jihadi-Salafi movement.

Despite the confusion, especially among Western scholars, about the meaning of "Salafi", "Jihadi," and "Takfiri,"[2] I use the term "Jihadi-Salafis" in this study to mean the following: In theology, Jihadi-Salafis follow the creed of *al-salaf al-salih* (early pious Muslims), especially as interpreted by Ibn Taymiyya (d. 1328); and in jurisprudence, they claim *ijtihad* (independent reasoning) for themselves and reject the *taqlid* ("imitation") of one of the four *madhahib* (schools of Islamic Sunni law). At the same time, Jihadi-Salafis believe jihad is the only way for Muslims to deal with unbelievers (*kuffar*). They use *al-wala' wa-l-bara'* ("friendship and enmity") as one of the main principles of their ideology.[3]

Biographies

Humud b. `Abd Allah al-`Uqla' al-Shu`aybi[4]

Al-`Uqla' was born in 1927 in the small village of al-Shiqqa,[5] close to the city of Burayda (in central Saudi Arabia). At the age of six he had learned to read, write, and count, but he became blind when he was seven years old. In 1948 he traveled to Riyadh to study, initially under shaykh `Abd al-Latif b. Ibrahim, then under the shaykh's brother, the then Grand Mufti Muhammad b. Ibrahim.[6] At the college in Riyadh, al-`Uqla' was introduced to the writings of Sayyid Qutb through Egyptian teachers. Al-`Uqla' became enamored with Qutb's ideology and remained loyal to him until his death.[7]

---

[2] See, for example, Thomas Hegghammer, "Jihadi-Salafis or Revolutionaries? On Religion and Politics in the Study of Militant Islamism," in *Global Salafism: Islam's New Religious Movement*, ed. Roel Meijer (London: Hurst & Company, 2009), 244–66.

[3] Saud al-Sarhan, "al-Wala' wa-l-Bara': al-aydiyulujiyya al-jadida lil-harakat al-Islamiyya" (Al-Wala' wa-l-Bara': The New Ideology of the Islamist Movements), *al-Sharq al-Awsat*, no. 9192, Jan. 28, 2004.

[4] More information concerning al-`Uqla' is available at www.al-oglaa.com.

[5] Hegghammer and Lacroix incorrectly name it Shaqra', which is another city in Saudi Arabia. See Thomas Hegghammer, *Jihad in Saudi Arabia: Violence and Pan-Islamism Since 1979* (Cambridge: Cambridge University Press, 2010), 84; Stéphane Lacroix, *Awaking Islam: the Politics of Religious Dissent in Contemporary Saudi Arabia* (Cambridge, MA: Harvard University Press, 2011), 169.

[6] There is no doubt that al-`Uqla' was a student of Mufti Muhammad b. Ibrahim. One of the early sources confirming this connection is the collection of Ibn Ibrahim's works in which al-`Uqla' is listed among Ibn Ibrahim's students. See Muhammad b. `Abd al-Rahman Ibn Qasim, *Majmu` Fatawa wa-Rasa'il al-Shaykh Muhammad b. Ibrahim*, (Riyadh: Matba`at al-Hukuma, 1979), 1:9.

[7] See, for example, Humud al-`Uqla', *Kalimat haqq fi Sayyid Qutb* (The Right Word about Sayyid Qutb).

The first institute of religious scholarship (*al-ma`had al-`ilmi*) and the first college of Arab and Islamic studies in Saudi Arabia were established in 1952 in Riyadh. Al-`Uqla' studied there until he graduated from the Shari`a College in 1957, where he then taught from 1958 until 1984. Following his retirement, he worked as a lawyer and at the same time resumed teaching at the Shari`a College in al-Qasim province until 1995 (this institution was known as Imam Muhammad b. Su`ud Islamic University and is now al-Qasim University). In 1995 al-`Uqla' was arrested and imprisoned for forty days. He died on January 19, 2002.

Nasir b. Hamad al-Fahd[8]
Nasir al-Fahd was born in Riyadh in 1969 and graduated from Imam Muhammad b. Su`ud Islamic University in Riyadh in 1992. He worked as an assistant professor in the college of the Faculty of Theology (*usul al-din*), Department of Theology and Modern Sects (*al-`aqida wa-l-madhahib al-mu`asira*) until August 1994. He was arrested in that month and was released from prison three years later in November 1997. Al-Fahd was arrested again on May 27, 2003, and remains in prison as of this writing.

`Ali b. Khudayr al-Khudayr[9]
Al-Khudayr was born in 1955 in Riyadh. On graduating in 1984 from Imam Muhammad b. Su`ud Islamic University in al-Qasim, he became a teacher, and subsequently director of a school in Burayda. He was arrested in Burayda in September 1994, released in 1999, and rearrested in May 2003. He remains in prison.

II

Historical Background

Before 1994
Although al-Fahd took up political activism only after he had been imprisoned in August 1994, both al-`Uqla' and al-Khudayr had been politically active before 1994, due to the influence of the Sahwa and their own political activities. Both had supported the Sahwa against the Saudi state's policy of using international troops to defend Saudi Arabia and to free Kuwait from the Iraqi army's invasion in 1990–1.

---

[8] Al-Fahd's biography (of which the writer has a copy) is available on his website: http://www .al-fhd.com. See also Madawi al-Rasheed, *Contesting the Saudi State: Islamic Voices from a New Generation* (Cambridge: Cambridge University Press, 2007), 139–55.

[9] Al-Khudayr's biography is available at http://www.tawhed.ws/a?i=13.

Saud Al-Sarhan

During the early 1990s the conflict between the state and *Hay'at kibar al-'ulama'* (the Council of Senior Scholars) on the one side and the Sahwa leaders on the other became more clearly defined and more aggressive. In May 1991, more than 450 Islamists signed a petition addressed to King Fahd (d. 2005) known as "The Letter of Demands" (*Khitab al-matalib*). In this, they asked the king to respond to their demands, including matters pertaining to governance.[10] Al-'Uqla' and al-Khudayr both signed this petition, and in July 1992 they both signed a second petition known as "The Memorandum of Advice" (*Mudhakkirat al-nasiha*),[11] which was also addressed to the king and was signed by 106 Islamists who sought political reform and criticized the government.

When the government's Council of Senior Scholars issued a written state-ment criticizing the Memorandum of Advice,[12] Humud al-'Uqla', 'Abd Allah b. Jibrin (d. 2009), and 'Abd Allah al-Mas'ari (d. 2005) wrote a refutation of this. This became known as the "Triple Letter" (*al-Khitab al-thulathi*).[13]

'Ali al-Khudayr and some of his students roamed the towns and villages of Saudi Arabia (especially in the southern region) to spread the statements of the Committee for the Defence of Legitimate Rights (CDLR).[14] He also wrote a harsh letter to the governor of al-Qasim, protesting against the organization of a large sporting event in Burayda, which allowed non-Muslim players to come to the city.[15]

Along with some others, al-Khudayr also participated in several events in Burayda in support of the Sahwa scholar and activist Salman al-'Awda and his colleagues. During these events, hundreds of Sahwa followers crowded the streets around al-'Awda's house, and speeches were given by many of the Sahwa shaykhs, including Humud al-'Uqla' and al-Khudayr,[16] who declared the establishment of the "Committee to Defend the Scholars of the Muslim World" (*Hay'at al-difa' 'an al-'ulama' fi al-'alam al-Islami*). On September

---

[10] For this letter, see Mansoor Jassem Alshamsi, *Islam and Political Reform in Saudi Arabia: The Quest for Political Change and Reform* (New York: Routledge, 2011), 99–102; Tim Niblock, *Saudi Arabia: Power, Legitimacy and Survival* (London: Routledge, 2006), 95; Stéphane Lacroix, "Islamo-Liberal Politics in Saudi Arabia," in *Saudi Arabia in the Balance*, ed. Paul Aarts and Gerd Nonneman (London: C. Hurst, 2005), 41.

[11] For *Mudhakkirat al-nasiha*, see: Alshamsi, *Islam and Political Reform*, 102–10; Niblock, *Saudi Arabia*, 95–6; Lacroix, "Islamo-Liberal," 41–2.

[12] On Sept. 27, 1992 (the author has a copy of this).

[13] This letter is available at http://www.al-oglaa.com/?section=subject&SubjectID=134, accessed Nov. 1, 2009.

[14] The author heard this in 1994 from al-Khudayr himself and also from some of his students.

[15] Al-Khudayr allowed the author to read the letter after it had been sent to the governor of al-Qasim.

[16] Telephone interview with Hasan ba Shammakh (Jan. 21, 2008).

15, 1994, following the arrest of Salman al-ʿAwda, the well-known leader of the Sahwa, ʿAli al-Khudayr, Ibrahim al-Dubayyan, and his younger brother Dubayyan met the governor of al-Qasim to voice their opposition.[17] Al-Khudayr was arrested the following day.[18]

Nasir al-Fahd had been arrested three weeks earlier,[19] along with a group of Salafis, most of whom were from his home town, al-Zulfi. Before being imprisoned, al-Fahd had not been interested in political Islam. He was, however, an adherent of Wahhabi doctrine and teachings. During this time he wrote two significant books, the first being "The Ottoman Empire and the Position of the Leaders of the [Wahhabi] Mission towards It" (*al-Dawla al-ʿUthmaniyya wa-mawqif aʾimmat al-daʿwa minha*).[20] His devotion to Wahhabism is evident in this book because he declares the Ottoman Empire to have been an infidel state. He also refuted Muslim intellectuals who admired the Ottoman Empire and declared its leaders to have been Sufis and enemies of Shaykh Muhammad b. ʿAbd al-Wahhab's mission.

In his second book, "The Truth about Islamic Civilization" (*Haqiqat al-hadara al-Islamiyya*),[21] al-Fahd asserts that true civilization consists of religious scholarship, which is what the early pious Muslims believed in and practiced. He rejects all the temporal or secular sciences,[22] such as philosophy, architecture, music, engineering, astronomy, and chemistry. He then lists twenty-seven Muslim scientists and travelers, such as Avicenna, Alpharabius, Alkindus, Ibn Tufayl, al-Jahiz, ʿAbbas b. Firnas,[23] Ibn Battuta, and Ibn Jubayr, all of whom he labels infidels or reprehensible innovators.

Although al-Fahd did not engage in politics during this period, his attitude toward the Saudi state was decidedly unfriendly. He wrote a fatwa forbidding the army salute, labeling this action an innovation that led to apostasy (*bidʿa mukaffira*), and he conducted a debate with one of Ibn Baz's students about this matter.[24] Subsequently, he was involved in a trial concerning a poem that insulted a princess, and he was arrested in August 1994.

---

[17] Lajnat al-difaʿ ʿan al-huquq al-sharʿiyya, *al-Huquq: al-Ahdath al-rahina, nashra istithnaʾiyya tasdur ʿan lajnat al-difaʿ ʿan al-huquq al-sharʿiyya* (London, 1994), no. 2.

[18] For the date of his arrest see Lajnat al-difaʿ ʿan al-huquq al-sharʿiyya, *al-Huquq: al-Ahdath al-rahina*.

[19] On Aug. 24, 1994.

[20] Available at http://www.tawhed.ws/r?i=zdntfe5u, accessed Nov. 1, 2009.

[21] Available at http://www.tawhed.ws/r?i=oo8j8m2r, accessed Nov. 1, 2009.

[22] In practice, al-Fahd uses technology without hesitation. He was among the earliest users of computer software in writing his books.

[23] Al-Fahd described ʿAbbas b. Firnas as having a small brain because of his attempt to fly.

[24] Interview with Fahd al-Shafi.

The Birth of a Movement (1994–1997)

In Ha'ir prison, al-Fahd and his Salafi friends encountered the Sahwa leaders, with whom they discussed Islamic issues, both religious and political. At this time, Salman al-'Awda arranged a weekly meeting in the prison between all the shaykhs of the Sahwa and the Salafis; however, al-Fahd was excluded from attendance at these meetings,[25] possibly on account of his age (he was only twenty-five years old), or perhaps because of his strong personality and opinions. This exclusion angered al-Fahd, who hated al-'Awda and became increasingly critical of him. The two men clashed frequently, and al-Fahd challenged al-'Awdah on a number of occasions.[26]

While in prison, al-Fahd also became a close friend of 'Ali al-Khudayr, who admired the young scholar and was influenced by his knowledge and opinions. Although al-Khudayr was also close to al-'Awdah and the Sahwa more generally, he gradually moved away from their ideologies and came to favour the more Salafi views of al-Fahd.

The Dragon (1997–2003)

When the leaders of the Sahwa in Saudi Arabia were released from prison in June 1999, they found the scene had changed dramatically. Since their imprisonment there had been great changes in society, including politics as well as the arrival of the internet and various new information technologies. At the same time, the Islamic opposition based in London became divided in March 1996, and the influence of "The Movement for Islamic Reform in Arabia" (MIRA) began to fade as a result of the conflict between Muhammad al-Mas'ari and Sa'd al-Faqih, the leaders of the movement.

The 'Ulayya bombing in November 1995, which was carried out by some extremists and was followed by another bombing in 1996 in al-Khobar, provided Saudi intellectuals with an opportunity to criticize fundamentalism and extremism. Furthermore, satellite television channels, especially al-Jazeera,[27] allowed people inside Saudi Arabia to hear different perspectives from religious scholars such as Yusuf al-Qaradawi and Ahmad al-Kubaysi, among others. Furthermore, people in Saudi Arabia have been able to access the internet since 1998. All of these developments resulted in the government and the Salafi religious scholars losing their monopoly on information and fatwas and

---

[25] Interview with Fahd al-Shafi who heard this from Nasir al-Fahd himself.

[26] Hegghammer, *Jihad in Saudi Arabia*, 87.

[27] For the al-Jazeera channel, see Mufid al-Zaydi, *Qanat al-Jazira wa-kasr al-muharramat fi al-fada' al-i'lami al-'Arabi* (Beirut: al-Markaz al-Thaqafi al-'Arabi, 2003); Hugh Miles, *Al Jazeera* (London: Abacus, 2005); Sam Cherribi, "From Baghdad to Paris," *Harvard International Journal of Press/Politics* 11, no. 2 (2006): 121–38.

signaled the end of "the Islamic cassette" era as well as that of the facsimile communiqué.[28]

Such change was followed by the death of the most senior scholars in Saudi Arabia, Ibn Baz (d. May 1999), and Ibn 'Uthaymin (d. January 2001). A new critical Islamic movement appeared at this time and began to challenge the statements of the Sahwa from an Islamic point of view. This movement was known locally as the Rationalists or the Modernists, but was labeled "Islamo-Liberal" by some Western scholars.[29]

In Afghanistan, a new Islamic government (the Taliban) succeeded in taking over the country in 1996. This new state applied its understanding of Islamic law and ruled the country very strictly. Consequently, Afghanistan became an idealized state for fundamentalists and for a great number of the Sahwa follow-ers in Saudi Arabia.[30] The leader of the Taliban, Mulla Muhammad 'Umar, declared himself to be the Commander of the Faithful (amir al-Mu'minin) in 1996, and Usama bin Ladin gave him his allegiance. In 1998, Usama bin Ladin and Ayman al-Zawahiri, among others, declared the establishment of the "World Islamic Front for War against the Jews and Crusaders" (al-Jabha al-Islamiyya al-'alamiyya li-qital al-Yahud wa-l-Salibiyyin). This effectively was a declaration of a global Jihad by al-Qaeda – an organization formed in the late 1980s by bin Ladin – against the United States and a series of attacks ensued, including the U.S. embassy bombings in 1998 in Dar al-Salaam (Tanzania) and Nairobi (Kenya) and the suicide bombing of the USS Cole in 2000 while it was refueling in the Yemeni port of Aden. The American response to these events was to counterattack with a series of cruise missiles targeted at the Sudan and Afghanistan in August 1998. Al-Qaeda's operations, the American response, and emotive reports by al-Jazeera television ignited support for jihad among young people in Saudi Arabia and other countries.

This was the state of affairs when the Sahwa leaders were released from prison and they were unable or unwilling to take on any political initiative. In

---

[28] For the importance of the Islamic cassette and the great role that it played in disseminating religious information, see Muhammad Hamid al-Ahmari, Malamih al-Mustaqbal (Riyadh: Maktabat al-'Ubaykan, 2005), 53–4; for the end of the Islamic cassette phenomenon see Majallat al-Majalla, no. 1056, May 7–13, 2000.

[29] See Stéphane Lacroix, "Islamo-Liberal Politics in Saudi Arabia." However, it is possible to date the formation of this trend to the second half of the 1990s.

[30] For example, see Humud b. 'Abd Allah al-'Uqla' al-Shu'aybi, Hawl mashru 'iyyat hukumat Tal-iban, available at http://www.al-oglaa.com/?section=subject&SubjectID=180; Nasir b. Hamad al-Fahd, al-Tibyan fi kufr man a 'ana al-Amrikan, 1:31–34, available at [http://www.tawhed.ws/r?i=np2ks5ge]; 'Abd Allah al-Ghunayman, Fatwa fi munasarat Taliban wa-l-qunut laha (Oct. 16, 2001), available at http://www.saaid.net/fatwa/f7.htm; interview with Nasir al-'Umar in al-Ra'y al-'Amm, Nov. 26, 2004.

part, this was due to the fact that their strategies and views had changed during their years in prison: Politically they had become much more quietist, and their passive attitude toward the Islamic issues of the day disappointed many followers. For example, the Sahwa leaders did not support the Taliban when it destroyed the two statues of the Buddha at Bamiyan, and they also refused to support al-Qaeda's operation against the United States on September 11, 2001.

By contrast, the new Saudi Jihadi-Salafi leaders (including al-`Uqla', al-Fahd, al-Khudayr, and others) became more active and provided new ideas for the Sahwa's erstwhile followers (*Sahwiyyun*). These ideologues provided an ideology that allowed these followers to retain their dissident political identity and engage more effectively with what was happening in the world. Because `Ali al-Khudayr was a second tier Sahwa leader, he did not have a large number of supporters within the movement, and al-Fahd had never been a member of the Sahwa. To attract the Sahwa's followers, they each needed the legitimacy that only Humud al-`Uqla' could provide because of his previous association with the Sahwa. Al-`Uqla' was therefore designated the nominal leader of this group of ideologues, but in fact the main drivers of ideas were al-Fahd and al-Khudayr.[31] Al-Fahd was full of energy upon his release from prison. He wrote on several internet forums under the pseudonym Shunkhub,[32] and he and al-Khudayr read many newspapers and wrote a large number of fatwas and books against journalists, writers, scholars, intellectuals, and others.

The End of the Myth

On Wednesday May 29, 2003, Prince Nayif b. `Abd al-`Aziz (d. 2012), then the Saudi Minister of the Interior, announced the arrest of eleven wanted individuals, including `Ali al-Khudayr, Nasir al-Fahd, and Ahmad al-Khalidi. After a skirmish in Medina, these shaykhs of Jihadi-Salafism were arrested, along with several members of al-Qaeda and some women.

Six months later (in November 2003) Saudi TV held interviews with al-Fahd, al-Khudayr, and al-Khalidi during which they were shown declaring their repentance and regret for having excommunicated Saudi intellectuals and the government. They also withdrew their support from al-Qaeda and

---

[31] For example, Nasir al-Fahd used to write fatwas and attribute them to Humud al-`Uqla' to give them more legitimacy. Muhsin al-`Awaji reported that he was told by al-`Uqla' that the letter of advice about his internet forum (al-Wasatiyya) was written by Nasir al-Fahd, and then attributed to him (i.e., al-`Uqla'). See also Hegghammer, *Jihad in Saudi Arabia*, 85–6.

[32] According to al-Fahd, he chose Shunkhub because it was the name of one of his great-great-grandfathers.

Usama bin Ladin, and they censured al-Qaeda for its military operations in Saudi Arabia.

The repentances of al-Fahd and al-Khalidi were not sincere. On February 16, 2004, al-Fahd issued a new statement revoking his original repentance. The main points in the new statement are the following:

1. Al-Fahd strongly regrets his repentance on TV because he mistakenly thought that in so doing he could deceive the Saudi government. This was a mistaken assumption, and the government was not duped.

2. He asserts his belief in the excommunication of the Saudi state, stating that:

   > If force and imprisonment are the bases for the excommunication of the government, then the government is certain to win because it monopolizes these, and I do not. But if what proves the excommunication of the government are the Qur'an, the Sunna, knowledge (*'ilm*), and proof (*burhan*), then I will certainly be victorious. I challenge all the government's scholars, including their leader the grand mufti, to an open debate about this matter. I swear by God that I will prove the apostasy of the government from proofs in the Qur'an, the Sunna, the consensus (*ijma'*), and sayings of the scholars from all the schools of law, indeed, from the sayings of the scholars of this regime itself, beginning with Shaykh Muhammad b. 'Abd al-Wahhab, may God have mercy upon him, right up to shaykh Ibn Baz, may God have mercy upon him. I have written the third section, entitled "The Participation of the Saudi Government in the Global Crusader Campaign," of a book called "The Explanation of the Excommunication of Whoever Assists the Americans" (*al-Tibyan fi kufr man a'ana al-Amrikan*). In this section I have listed more than thirty quotations from the scholars of the [Saudi] state – the first, second and the third – all of which establish its infidel character and its apostasy from the religion of Islam. The draft of this book is with the investigative police (*mabahith*).

3. He affirms his belief in all the books he has written, for example, "The Explanation of the Excommunication of whoever assists the Americans,"[33] "The Explanation of the Danger of Normalization for Muslims" (*al-Tabyin li-makhatir al-tatbi' ala al-Muslimin*), and "The

---

[33] Two volumes are available at http://www.tawhed.ws/r?i=3b5bzov8%Ao;and http://www.tawhed .ws/r?i=np2ks5ge. For a study of this book see al-Rasheed, *Contesting the Saudi State*, 141–6. Interestingly, Jihadis all over the world pay attention to this book, and it has been translated into English and Urdu.

Ruling on the Use of Weapons of Mass Destruction" (*Hukm isti 'mal aslihat al-damar al-shamil*).

4. He proclaims his support for his hero Usama bin Ladin.
5. He asserts his support for the use of violence against the Saudi state.[34]

Despite their repentance, the shaykhs of Jihadi-Salafism remained in prison, and the movement declined relatively quickly in Saudi Arabia. This had to do, in part, with the defeat of al-Qaeda's branches and cells all over the world, but also with the Saudi government's domestic efforts at weakening this movement.

Careful examination of the history of al-Qaeda in the Arabian Peninsula and that of the shaykhs of Jihadi-Salafism shows that the two movements formed separately from one another. Several factors brought them together, however. These include various socio-political changes within Saudi Arabia and the fact that both movements were drawing support from the followers of the Sahwa, which in turn was being weakened. Al-Qaeda and the shaykhs of Jihadi-Salafism adopted identical political views on issues within and beyond Saudi Arabia (e.g., the United States as the enemy of Muslims and the House of Saud as apostate rulers that should be toppled through violence). The events of September 11, 2001, cemented the union between these two groups. Within Saudi Arabia, the shaykhs of Jihadi-Salafism provided the ideological justification for violence, and al-Qaeda engaged in the violent acts. If Islamic history is any guide, it points to the fact that such extremist movements have a very limited shelf life because their violence either consumes them or engenders a violent and swift reaction from the mainstream.

III

The Sources of Religious Authority

Religious authority in Saudi Arabia can be found in two institutions: the political (with the king at the top) and the official ulama. The official religious institution is represented by the traditional shaykhs (mainly from urban Najdi families). This institution is hierarchical, with the Council of Senior Scholars at the top of the hierarchy.

The relationship between the two official institutions has settled into the pattern that the king has the exclusive prerogative to appoint the head as well as the members of the Council of Senior Scholars, and he has the sole right to dismiss from the council whomsoever he wishes. This effectively means that the institution obtains its sanction from the king.

---

[34] The letter is available at http://www.tawhed.ws/r?i=1502093y, accessed Nov. 1, 2009.

The political institution, on the other hand, gains its religious legitimacy from applying Islamic law. Ibrahim al-'Awaji notes that:

Islam is the source of political legitimacy, the basis of the judicial system and the moral code of society. Islam is the primary political and social frame of reference. On the one hand, it is the formal religion of the state and therefore its principles are the supreme authority. On the other hand, it is a social and cultural institution whose system of social conduct and spiritual force penetrate every aspect of Muslim life.[35]

The King's Religious Authority

The caliphs and sultans in traditional Islamic history claimed two authorities: the temporal and the religious.[36] The Saudi monarch makes similar claims. The Basic Law of Saudi Arabia declares the king as the point of reference for all branches of government (judicial, executive, and regulatory).[37] Furthermore, many politico-religious matters rely exclusively on his choice or judgment. Some of the religious matters that pertain to the ruler's authority are declaring jihad, issuing fatwas, commanding right and forbidding wrong (al-amr bi-l-ma 'ruf wa-l-nahy 'an al-munkar), and qunut al-nawazil (special supplications made aloud in prayers when calamities strike). The shaykhs of Jihadi-Salafism challenged the religious authority of the Saudi monarch and argued that he was not the point of reference for the various branches of government. For them, it was the scholars (ulama) who were the point of reference, and the king was understood to operate under the scholars' guardianship, and not vice versa.

In the following discussion I provide some examples that illustrate how these shaykhs of Jihadi-Salafism challenged and rejected the king's religious authority.

Fatwas

The fatwa is not simply a legal opinion that is issued by a competent authority. Embedded in the fatwa is also a conception of political authority. In the Sunni

---

[35] Ibrahim al-'Awaji, "Bureaucracy and Society in Saudi Arabia" (Ph.D. thesis, University of Virginia, 1971), 67–8.

[36] For the religious authority of the Caliph in medieval Muslim thought, see Patricia Crone and Martin Hinds, God's Caliphs: Religious Authority in the First Centuries of Islam (Cambridge: Cambridge University Press, 1986).

[37] See Article No. 44. For an explanation of this article, see the interview with Dr. Muhammad al-'Isa, Minister of Justice, in the al-Riyadh newspaper, May 3, 2010.

tradition, the mufti provides a fatwa on God's behalf, which is why fatwas are understood to be "signed on God's behalf" (al-tawqi` `an rabb al-`alamin).[38] In this same tradition, the monarch is seen to be God's deputy and His shadow on earth.[39] In theoretical terms, this means that the king *and* the mufti share God's temporal authority and both constitute together the category of "those in authority" (ulu al-amr).[40] However in practical terms, if the mufti consents to being appointed by the monarch, then he gives up his authority and acts on behalf of the ruler.

One of the aims of the shaykhs of Jihadi-Salafism was to liberate the fatwa-issuing authority from that of the ruler. Another aim was to place the ruler under the supervision of the ulama. In a sense, what these shaykhs were attempting to achieve was a Sunnified version of the Shiite doctrine of the Guardianship of the Islamic Jurist (wilayat al-faqih).

By way of illustrating this, al-`Uqla' disagrees with certain scholars in his written work "The Requirements of the ifta'" (shurut al-ifta') as to whether the mufti must be appointed by the ruler (wali al-amr). Al-`Uqla' asserts that all the Sunni schools of law clarify the requirements of the muftis, and that none of these requires the permission of the ruler in matters of appointment. Moreover, he argues, this requirement cannot be found in the Qur'an or the Sunna. Al-`Uqla' then discusses the religious authority of rulers and insists that the rulers are not legislators; rather, they merely execute the prescriptions of the Shari`a, which, indeed, requires the interpretation of the ulama. According to al-`Uqla', the ruler is only to be obeyed in rightness (ma`ruf), and there is no obedience to him in the case of sin.

---

[38] See, for example, the famous book by the Hanbali Salafi scholar Ibn Qayyim al-Jawziyya entitled I`lam al-muwaqqi`in `an rabb al-`alamin.

[39] See Patricia Crone, God's Caliph and Usama al-`Absah, Zilluh `ala al-Ard: Alqab hukkam muslimin fi ruqum muqaddasa (Beirut: Dar Qudmus, 2004). Ibn Taymiyya also approves of describing the sultan as "God's shadow on earth"; see Ibn Taymiyya, Majmu` Fatawa wa-rasa'il Shaykh al-Islam Ibn Taymiyya, ed. `Abd al-Rahman Ibn Qasim (Riyadh: Majma` al-Malik Fahd li-Tiba`at al-Mushaf al-Sharif, 2004), 35:45–6.

[40] The official Saudi religious literature asserts that "ulu al-amr are the rulers and the religious scholars." Interestingly, some Saudi royals wrote newspaper articles to refute the notion of regarding religious scholars as ulu al-amr. They insist that ulu al-amr (sing. wali al-amr) were merely the rulers. See Talal b. `Abd al-`Aziz Al Su`ud, al-Sharq al-Awsat, Jan. 29, 2002, and Turki Al Faysal Al Su`ud, Sharq al-Awsat, Jan. 20, 2002. For the official scholars' interpretation of "wali al-amr" see Sulayman b. `Abd Allah b. Muhammad b. `Abd al-Wahhab, Taysir al-`Aziz al-Hamid fi sharh Kitab al-Tawhid (Riyadh: Dar al-Sumay`i lil-Nashr wa-l-Tawzi`, 2007), 944; Salih Al al-Shaykh, al-Tamhid fi sharh Kitab al-Tawhid (Riyadh: Dar al-Tawhid, 2002), 414; and Muhammad Ibn `Uthaymin, al-Qawl al-mufid fi sharh Kitab al-Tawhid, ed. Sulayman Aba al-Khayl and Khalid al-Mushayq (Riyadh: Dar al-`Asima lil-Nashr wa-l-Tawzi`, 1994), 2:255.

Jihad

In classical Islamic jurisprudence there are two types of Jihad: offensive Jihad, when Muslims declare war against non-Muslims, and defensive Jihad, when Muslims and Muslim lands come under attack. In the former case, according to the classical jurists, the ruler's permission is required for this kind of war to be recognized as a legitimate jihad. In the latter case, jihad is a personal obligation (*fard 'ayn*), which means that every individual may engage in jihad without permission of the ruler or a guardian. A son might march forth without his father's permission, a wife without her husband's consent, or the people without the ruler's sanction.

The shaykhs of Jihadi-Salafism insist that Muslims are under attack by Jews and "Crusaders," by which they mean specifically the Israelis and the Americans. Because of this jihad is deemed to be defensive and therefore not requiring the permission of the ruler for engagement in battle against the enemy.[41] In making this argument, these ideologues are clearly following the doctrine of the Palestinian 'Abd Allah 'Azzam who argued that jihad is now a personal obligation because it is defensive.[42] Traditionally, Muslim jurists identified this obligation as pertaining only to the people in the cities and the countries that are being attacked. For the modern jihadis and the shaykhs of Jihadi-Salafism the scope of the obligation has been broadened considerably so that all Muslims, wherever they may be, are now obligated to defend any and all Muslim lands. Thus, for example, people in Saudi Arabia are not required to seek the permission of their ruler to defend such Muslim lands as Afghanistan, Chechnya, the Philippines, and all other Muslim territories.

Supplications in Times of Distress (*Qunut al-nawazil*)

On January 11, 2001, Humud al-'Uqla' sent his "Letter on the legitimacy of *qunut al-nawazil*"[43] to Salih Al al-Shaykh, the Saudi Minister of Islamic Affairs, when the latter decided to forbid the imams in the mosques from undertaking *qunut al-nawazil* without the explicit permission of the ruler (*wali al-amr*). Al-'Uqla"s argument has two features. The first is legal when he claims that the permission of the ruler is not required for *qunut al-nawazil* and insists that this is the opinion of the vast majority of the jurists. The second feature is political. Al-'Uqla' argues that those who require the ruler's permission are actually referring to the caliph (*al-imam al-a'zam*) and today there is no person

---

[41] Humud al-'Uqla', *Hukm isti'dhan al-walidayn fi al-Jihad.*
[42] 'Abd Allah 'Azzam, *al-Difa' 'an aradi al-Muslimin ahamm furud al-a'yan*; 'Abd al-Qadir 'Abd al-'Aziz, *al-'Umdah fi i'dad al-'udda lil-jihad fi sabil Allah*, 307–8.
[43] Humud al-'Uqla', *Risala fi mashru'iyyat qunut al-nawazil*, available at http://www.al-oglaa .com/?section=subject&SubjectID=140, accessed Nov. 1, 2009.

holding such a position. The most important point in al-`Uqla"s letter is his warning that if the *qunut* pertains exclusively to the ruler's permission, then this would make all general Muslim matters subject to politics and therefore open to abuse by the rulers. And moreover since rulers today are mere politicians who do not care about Muslim causes, they will not give their permission for *qunut* and thereby cause grievous harm to the community.

Qunut al-nawazil is not merely a religious matter. It is a politically significant institution since through its practice Islam's enemies are identified and a determination is made as to which party deserves the support of the community. For example, when the second war in Chechnya broke out in 1999, many prayer imams conducted *qunut* in their mosques to support the Chechens against the Russians, and they did this without the government's permission.

Nasir al-Fahd holds the same beliefs as al-`Uqla' on this question. Thus such issues as jihad, *qunut*, and helping the Muslims in Iraq and Afghanistan through money, the media, and even military support do not require the permission of the ruler. According to al-Fahd, although politics does not control the Shari`a, politicians must declare their repentance for any policy that contradicts its principles.[44]

`Ali al-Khudayr has also paid significant attention to this matter in his answers to questions from the members of al-Salafiyyun Forum.[45] He argues that there is a new trend whose adherents relegate all Shari`a matters and religious issues to the rulers. Al-Khudayr is uncompromising and insults this new trend by labeling its adherents as "modern Imamis Shi`is."[46] A noteworthy point in al-Khudayr's analysis is his extensive use of Salafi and Wahhabi scholars to support his arguments and to refute those of his opponents. Using fatwas from Ibn Taymiyya, Muhammad b. `Abd al-Wahhab, `Abd al-Rahman b. Hasan (grandson of Ibn `Abd al-Wahhab), `Abd Allah Aba Butayn, and Muhammad b. Ibrahim, al-Khudayr denies that political leaders and rulers have any religious authority. His selective use of quotations is illustrative of his claims, so that he cites Muhammad b. `Abd al-Wahhab stating the following: "It is unknown [to us] that any scholar has claimed that religious judgments are not valid unless [permission is obtained] from the ruler (*al-imam al-a`zam*)." Another quotation from `Abd al-Rahman b. Hasan asks: "where in the Qur'an and what evidence [can be adduced that] jihad is not required except with the presence of a leader (*imam muttaba`*)?"

44 Nasir al-Fahd, *al-Tibyan*, 1:131.
45 `Ali al-Khudayr, *Ajwibat Muntada al-Salafiyyun*, q 45, available at http://www.almeshkat.net/books/open.php?cat=28&book=776, accessed Nov. 1, 2009.
46 Presumably al-Khudayr was influenced by `Abd al-Qadir `Abd al-`Aziz, who states that linking jihad to the permission of the rulers is a Shii doctrine. See `Abd al-`Aziz, *al-`Umda*, 65.

Despite these views, the shaykhs of Jihadi-Salafism do not support a separation between the temporal and religious authorities, nor do they accept any version or form of secularism in governance. What they believe firmly is that the authority of rulers should fall under the control of the ulama, and they insist on the right of the ulama to participate in determining the policies of government in international affairs to ensure that *wala'* and *bara'* are properly adhered to and applied.[47]

By way of further illustration of the views of the shaykhs of Jihadi-Salafism, it is useful to present and analyze a statement they issued in which they challenged the authority of the rulers, the "Declaration of Support for the Wanted and Forbidding Divulging of Information about them" (*Bayan fi munasarat al-matlubin wa-tahrim al-iblagh 'anhum*).

On May 7, 2003, the Saudi Ministry of the Interior released the names of nineteen alleged terrorists, seventeen of whom were Saudis. Claiming that these individuals were planning terrorist attacks in Saudi Arabia, the ministry requested the public to inform the nearest police station if anyone had information that could lead to the arrest of the wanted suspects, and it warned people against giving refuge to these alleged terrorists. The shaykhs of Jihadi-Salafism responded by issuing a statement in support of the wanted persons, and this was signed by Nasir al-Fahd, 'Ali al-Khudayr, and Ahmad al-Khalidi.[48]

Here are some of the statement's most salient and revealing points:

1. The shaykhs personally knew some of these wanted persons and expressed admiration for their jihad in Afghanistan.
2. It was stated that the *mujahidun* (i.e., the wanted individuals) would not target Muslims or Muslim property, but only the "Crusaders".
3. The shaykhs asserted that these nineteen individuals were wanted by the American government only, and that the Saudis were simply carrying out American orders.
4. They declared that it was absolutely forbidden to betray these *mujahidun*, oppose them, discredit them, inform on them, report them, publish their photographs, or track them down. Any such act would, in fact, be rendering assistance to America.
5. The shaykhs asked other Saudi scholars, students of religious knowledge (*talabat al-'ilm*), and missionaries (*du'at*) to support these wanted persons in any way possible. This, they stated, was a duty incumbent on all Muslims.

---

[47] Al-Fahd, *al-Tibyan*, 1:131.
[48] The statement is available in *Rasa'il al-Matlubin al-19* (The Letters of the 19 Wanted), 8–11.

6. Finally, people were asked to post this statement on all internet forums, and to print, copy, and disseminate it anywhere possible.

This statement appeared widely in Saudi Arabia, and especially among the Sahwa followers. I saw its impact at Imam Muhammad b. Su'ud University (the Qasim branch) where it appeared all across the campus, and in some classes it was read aloud by teachers. Subsequently, the shaykhs were thanked for their support by the nineteen wanted men.[49] The political situation quickly changed when on May 12, 2003, sixteen suicide bombers detonated three large car bombs inside three compounds housing Westerners. The attacks killed twenty-six people and left 160 injured. Five of the suicide bombers were from the list of the nineteen wanted individuals: 'Abd al-Karim al-Yazaji, Hani al-Ghamidi, Muhammad al-Shihri, Khalid al-Juhani, and Jibran al-Hakami. If anything, these attacks underscore that the government had lost control over a section of the religious sector of society, and its authority was being undermined. Furthermore, these attacks also indicate that a new center of authority had emerged and that was represented by these shaykhs. Ultimately, the aim of the shaykhs of Jihadi-Salafism was to arrogate authority to scholars like themselves and to alter the relationship between the rulers and the ulama. To clarify matters further, the nature of this relationship is illustrated in the figures that follow, which offer three different perspectives, that of the ruler (Fig. 10.1), the official ulama (Fig. 10.2), and the Jihadi-Salafis (Fig. 10.3).

IV

The Relationship of the Shaykhs of Jihadi-Salafism with the Official Ulama

The official ulama consists of the mufti and the institutions he controls, the Council of the Senior Scholars and its committees, and finally the various court judges. These ulama are known for their alliance with and allegiance to the Saudi state and, as shown above, derive their legitimacy from the king.

When the shaykhs of Jihadi-Salafism started their activities and released fatwas, statements and letters in which they attacked certain Saudi intellectuals and offered support for the Taliban, the official scholars made no move either to confront them or to refute these fatwas. Their posture could be described as one of deliberate avoidance. Later, after 9/11 and the "war on terror" that followed, the Jihadi-Salafis became harshly critical of the Saudi government for its alliance with the United States. In response to this, the official ulama

[49] Ibid., 20.

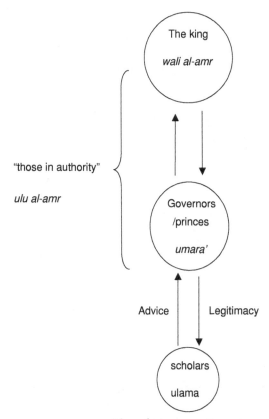

FIGURE 10.1. The ruler's perspective.

sought to support the Saudi government by among other things casting doubt on the qualifications of the shaykhs of Jihadi-Salafism. This posed a serious challenge to latter's legitimacy and claims to authority.

On October 16, 2001, the Saudi newspaper *Okaz* released a statement in the name of the secretary of the Council of Senior Scholars that challenged al-'Uqla"s qualifications and his fatwas. *Al-Watan* newspaper republished this same statement on January 20, 2002, following al-'Uqla"s death. 'Ali al-Khudayr and others[50] responded by writing two separate statements in defense of al-'Uqla"s credentials and authority.[51] Al-Khudayr stated that even though al-'Uqla' had not been a member of the Council of the Senior Scholars he

[50] Such as Ahmad al-Khalidi and 'Abd al-'Aziz al-Jarbu'.
[51] See 'Ali al-Khudayr, *Difa 'an al-Shaykh Humud b. 'Uqla' al-Shu'aybi*, available at http://www.tawhed.ws/r?i=jz2oj2bd, accessed Nov. 1, 2009.

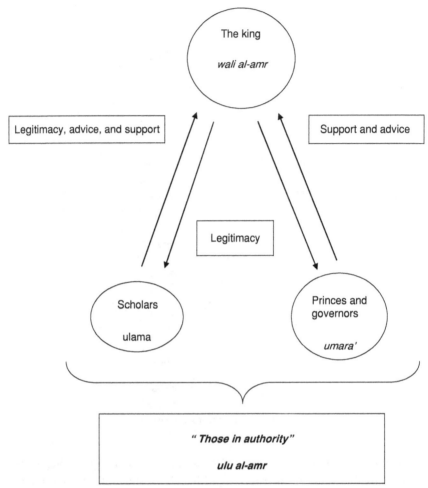

FIGURE 10.2. The official ulama's perspective.

had taught most of its members, including the mufti himself. As a professor, al-'Uqla' had taught at universities, where he reviewed the work of other
scholars, including Ibn 'Uthaymin, and professors such as Muhammad Aman
al-Jami, Rabi' al-Madkhali, Abu Bakr al-Jaza'ri, and 'Abd al-Qadir Shaybat
al-Hamd. All of these are considered among the luminaries of the official
Wahhabi religious and legal establishment. In addition, al-Khudayr pointed
out that Humud al-'Uqla' had been a student of Muhammad b. Ibrahim, a
former grand mufti and a perhaps Saudi Arabia's most influential scholar of
the twentieth century. Al-Khudayr further stated that Muhammad b. Ibrahim

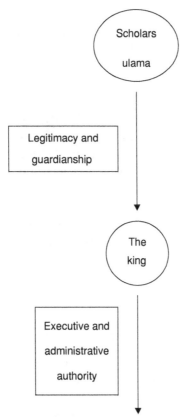

FIGURE 10.3. The Jihadi-Salafi movement's perspective.

and late Ibn Baz both trusted al-ʿUqla', had asked him to teach in the mosques, and considered him a mufti.

Al-Kudayr's claims are based on strong grounds. In religious terms, al-ʿUqla' was well qualified. He had been a student of the most respected scholars who trusted him and regarded him highly by asking him to undertake religious teaching and to issue his own legal opinions. Moreover, al-ʿUqla' had taught leading scholars in his time, such as the chief mufti ʿAbd al-ʿAziz Al al-Shaykh and Salih al-Luhaydan (a former chairman of the High Council of Justice). This meant that al-ʿUqla' had been a member of the top scholarly institutions and was also a university professor. He was, in other words, a successful and top member of the Wahhabi scholarly establishment. What distinguished al-ʿUqla' from the official scholars was simply the recognition of the political authority, something the scholars of Jihadi-Salafism accorded no value to and did not seek.

Once they had proved al-ʿUqla"s credentials as a top scholar and the legitimacy of his views, al-Khudayr and al-Fahd went on to exploit fully this point. They would go on to write books, fatwas, statements, and letters and attribute them to al-ʿUqla', who approved of this and willingly put his name to these works. This was important because neither al-Khudayr nor al-Fahd had al-ʿUqla"s stature and therefore could not effectively rally support for their views without his name. Al-ʿUqla' also gave al-Khudayr and al-Fahd a boost in the prefaces of their books in which he praised their religious knowledge and described them as highly qualified scholars. Al-Khudayr and al-Fahd further tried to bolster their stature by presenting their movement as the only one faithfully upholding the tradition of the pre-modern Salafis, in particular Ibn Taymiyya and the Wahhabis. On any given matter these shaykhs of Jihadi-Salafism would gather as many citations as they could from the Sunni legal schools, but especially from the Salafis so as to underscore the claim that they are the only true heirs of this tradition.

V

The Struggle with the Sahwa's Leaders

In the early 1990s the leaders of the Sahwa movement derived their legitimacy from the wide support they garnered from many religious people in Saudi Arabia, especially the youth. This was because they were seen to have spoken the truth of religion to the power of the rulers. However, after their release from prison in 1999 the Sahwa leaders became closer to the Saudi government and can even be described as consisting of "semi-official" shaykhs.[52] Although this change in the relationship between the Saudi authorities and the Sahwa leaders happened quite gradually, it did affect subsequent dealings between the leaders of Sahwa and the shaykhs of Jihadi-Salafism.

Relations between the Jihadi-Salafis and the Sahwa movement's leaders deteriorated rapidly. At first, the two parties did not reveal their disagreements, and it seems that Humud al-ʿUqla' and Sulayman al-ʿUlwan, a major Sahwa leader, tried to keep the conflict private. However, shortly after al-ʿUqla"s

---

[52] It is worth noting that the good relations between the Sahwa leaders and the government did not last for more than a decade. The wave of revolts, which started in 2011, in the Arab world has led to the rise to power of Islamist parties in a number of Arab countries. This has led various Sahwa leaders to attempt to exert pressure on the Saudi government in the hope of gaining influence domestically and regionally. In response to this, the government has withdrawn the privileges it had granted to some of the Sahwa's leaders, most notably Salman al-ʿAwda who lost his television show, for example.

death, the Sahwa leaders openly declared their disagreement with the Jihadi-Salafis and openly aligned themselves with the Saudi government. This was done because the Sahwa leaders understood that once the Saudi government had declared war on terrorism, they needed to distance themselves from the Jihadi-Salafis to preserve the gains that they had made over many years. For the Sahwa, al-Qaeda and the Jihadi-Salafis were through their violent acts and writings reversing the Sahwa's achievements over at least two decades.[53] The second reason for the conflict had to do with the appeal of the Jihadi-Salafis among the supporters of the Sahwa – the struggle became over the Sahwa's attempt to preserve its constituency in Saudi society.

In response, the Jihadi-Salafis began to criticize publicly the Sahwa leaders. `Ali al-Khudayr, for example, set out to refute what he described as the new Sahwa in an essay entitled *Usul al-Sahwa al-jadida* (The Principles of New Sahwa).[54] In this work, he claimed that it was in fact the Jihadi-Salafis who represented the real continuation of the Sahwa movement, whereas the traditional leaders of the Sahwa had deviated from its true message. Al-Khudayr begins his essay by stating that "the principles of the Sahwa are the same principles as those of Sunnis in matters pertaining to faith, monotheism, excommunication, jurisprudence, jihad, politics, the attitude toward unbelievers and those who go astray, innovators, as well as the rejection of coexistence [with unbelievers] and all secular projects." Al-Khudayr continues that two groups deviated from the principles of the Sahwa:

1. The Defeatists (*inhizamiyyun*), by which al-Khudayr means the Sahwa leaders who have neglected the true belief in excommunication, *al-wala' wa-l-bara'* and jihad. This can be seen because this group refuses to excommunicate the nominal Muslims who have deviated from true belief and to stand against the tyrants and secularists. Instead, they call for coexistence with the unbelievers, neutralizing the jihad, and advocate a jurisprudence of tolerance.

2. The Modernists (*`asraniyyun*), who, according to al-Khudayr, have abandoned Islam altogether and have adopted the values and views of the secularists.

The real struggle between the Jihadi-Salafis and the Sahwa emerged most clearly over the response to a statement dated February 12, 2002, which was

---

[53] See `Ali al-Khudayr's *Usul al-Sahwa al-jadida* in which he mentions that the Sahwa had criticized the Jihadi-Salafis in these terms.

[54] Available at http://www.tawhed.ws/r?i=w38eazd, accessed Nov. 1, 2009.

signed by about sixty American intellectuals and entitled "What We're Fighting For."[55] The aim of this U.S. statement was to provide moral justification for America's war on terrorism, but it also called on Muslims to stand with them and accept American values. The U.S. statement prompted a collective response from Saudi intellectuals, including a number of the Sahwa leaders, who issued a statement in April 2002 under the title "How Can We Coexist?" (*'Ala ayy asas nata'ayash?*). This called on the West to replace war with an open dialogue between the Muslim and Western worlds. It was signed by 153 Saudis[56] and expressed their opinion about Muslim relations with non-Muslims as well as their views on the war on terrorism.

The shaykhs of Jihadi-Salafism reacted violently to this statement. Al-Fahd and al-Khudayr succeeded in rallying some well-known religious scholars to refute it, including such figures as 'Abd al-Rahman al-Barrak, Sulayman al-'Ulwan, Sa'd al-Humayd, 'Abd al-Rahman al-Mahmud, Bishr al-Bishr, and 'Abd Allah al-Sa'd.[57] Books were also written in refutation of the statement. Al-Fahd, for example, wrote a work entitled "Castigating the Falsehoods in the Intellectuals' Statement" (*Tali'at al-tankil bima fi bayan al-muthaqqafin min al-abatil*), while al-Khudayr, for his part, wrote "Reviving the Religion of Abraham and Refuting the Defeatist Traitors" (*Ihya' millat Ibrahim wa-l-radd 'ala al-mukhadhdhilin al-munhazimin*). Both al-Fahd and al-Khudayr accused the Sahwa leaders of being "defeatists" and listed all the errors in their statement, especially the following points:

1. The statement negated the belief in *al-wala' wa-l-bara'*, which requires hatred for and antagonism toward infidels. In other words, the statement undermined the cornerstone of Islamic monotheism (*al-tawhid*)
2. It negated the doctrine of armed struggle (*jihad*) against the unbelievers
3. It perverted the *Shari'a*'s rulings (*ahkam al- Shari'a*)
4. The signatories consist of defeatists, modernists, and secularists.

---

[55] Institute for American Values, "What We're Fighting For: A Letter from America." The institute is a neo-liberal and socially conservative organization based in New York. For this statement see Ridwan al-Sayyid, "Hal yasluh shi'ar al-harb al-'adila li-tashkil majal mushtarak lil-hiwar wa-l-tadamun? ijaba 'Arabiyya 'ala risalat al-muthaqqafin al-Amrikiyyin," *al-Ijtihad*, 54 (2002), 267–80; al-Fadl Shalaq, "Radd 'ala risalat al-harb al-'adila," *al-Ijtihad*, 53 (2002), 215–30; Antwan Sayf, "Risalat al-Sittin muthaqqaf Amriki al-harb al-'adila 'ala ard al-ghayr wa-l-hiwar ghayr al-mutakafi," *al-Ijtihad*, 54 (2002), 255–66.
[56] The statement is available in Arabic and English at www.Islamtoday.com; and see "Muthaqqafun Su'udiyyun yaruddun 'ala al-risala al-Amrikiyya "'Ala ayy asas nata'ayash'," *al-Ijtihad* 54 (2002): 231–43.
[57] Nasir al-Fahd, *Tali'at al-tankil bima fi bayan al-muthaqqafin min al-abatil*, 2.

One consequence of the Jihadi-Salafi reaction was that some of the state-ment's signatories withdrew their names from the April 2002 statement.[58] Moreover, it became clear that the Sahwa leaders were losing the battle for alle-giance of their followers.[59] Under pressure, some of them (Salman al-`Awda, Safar al-Hawali and Nasir al-`Umar) were forced to write an explanatory state-ment (*bayan tawdihi*) in which they retracted some of the assertions of the April statement. For example, they now insisted on upholding the centrality of jihad, the doctrine of *al-wala' wa-l-bara'*, and antagonism toward unbeliev-ers. They continued to insist, however, that their new statement in no way contradicted the first statement but merely offered further clarification.

The obvious inconsistency of the Sahwa leaders provided Jihadi-Salafi the opportunity to exert additional pressure. Al-Khudayr duly wrote "Refuting the Explanatory Statement" (*al-Radd `ala al-bayan al-tawdihi*), and al-Fahd took this opportunity to publish his book "Castigating the Falsehoods of the Intellectuals' Statement" on the internet.

Al-Fahd and al-Khudayr, among others, also insisted that not only had the Sahwa leaders abandoned the false beliefs expressed in the first statement, but their aim was to deceive their followers as well as their critics. Because of this the Sahwa leaders had resorted to language in both statements that was vague and open to various interpretations. Thus, they were dishonest opportunists who were not to be trusted.[60]

It is worth detailing Nasir al-Fahd's *Tali`at al-tankil* to fully appreciate the Jihadi-Salafi position at this juncture. The work is divided into six parts. In Part I, al-Fahd emphasizes the "correct" understanding of *al-wala' wa-l-bara'*, jihad, and the forms that enmity toward the infidels should take. Part II consists of a series of comparisons, such as the views of the Sahwa leaders in the past versus those expressed in the April statement. Another comparison pertains to the language in the U.S. statement versus that used in the Sahwa's response. Nasir claims that the February American statement used proud and powerful language, whereas the Sahwa's response was feeble and obsequious. In Part III, al-Fahd claims to use "rational evidence" whereby he details the past and present of U.S. foreign policy to argue that relations between the Muslim world and the West is based on conflict and struggle, and not coexistence.

---

[58] There were more than five signatories. See Nasir al-Fahd. *Tali`at al-tankil*, 9.

[59] See Lacroix, "Islamo-Liberal," 47.

[60] The Sahwa leaders did not disseminate their second statement as widely as the first, and it was available only in Arabic. Moreover, it was removed after a few days of being posted on the *Islam Today* website. See Nasir al-Fahd, *Tali`at al-tankil*, 9–10; and Lacroix, "Islamo-Liberal," 50.

In Part IV, al-Fahd uses arguments from the Shari'a, providing twenty-two proof-texts to refute the Sahwa's statement and thirteen other texts to illustrate how the Sahwa leaders deliberately misrepresented Islamic law. In Part V, al-Fahd offers further refutation of the Sahwa's claims, which he labels specious arguments (shubuhat). And in the final section, al-Fahd attacks the Sahwa for using the principle of "welfare" (maslaha) to base their arguments, and he calls this the "Idol of the [religiously] bankrupt" (taghut al-muflisin). The welfare of the Muslims cannot lie in making compromises on matters of creed and principle, but rather it can be found only in an uncompromising devotion to the exclusivist doctrine that rejects all toleration of the unbelievers and foregrounds jihad.

The main strategy of the Sahwa leaders was to avoid a public confrontation with the Jihadi-Salafis, while secretly attempting to convince the latter of the validity of their claims. In the event this should fail, the Sahwa would then seek to destroy the Jihadi-Salafis. This is what eventually transpired. Although the Sahwa leaders were not involved in debating with the Jihad-Salafis, they encouraged others, such as journalists and Islamic modernists, to attack al-Fahd and al-Khudayr, and to challenge their books and opinions. The Sahwa also sought to have their statement of "How can we coexist?" defended by many intellectuals and journalists.

After the Jihadi-Salafi leaders were imprisoned in 2003, Safar al-Hawali, one of the principal Sahwa leaders, claimed to have had a dialogue with them before their arrest. Al-Hawali alleged that the exchange became aggressive once the Jihadi-Salafis accused him of being an infidel, and he claimed that they had issued a fatwa against him.[61] The Jihadi-Salafis responded to al-Hawali from prison when Ahmad al-Khalidi wrote a letter repudiating al-Hawali's claims.[62] In this letter, al-Khalidi denied that they had any debate with al-Hawali or that they had called him an infidel.[63] Al-Khalidi further claimed that after al-Fahd and al-Khudayr wrote refutations of the Sahwa statement "How can we coexist?" both al-Hawali and al-'Awda traveled to Riyadh to declare their repentance and regrets to Shaykh 'Abd al-Rahman al-Barrak. The Sahwists also promised to write a new statement clearly refuting the first that they had signed. Moreover, al-Hawali had requested al-Fahd to delay the publication of his book "Tali'at al-tankil," again so as to attempt a reconciliation between the two leadership groups. Al-Fahd, however, refused to meet with al-Hawali until

---

[61] 'Uqaz newspaper no. 1432, May 19, 2005.
[62] The letter is available on: http://www.tawhed.ws/r?i=3452.
[63] In his interview, al-Hawali referred to the Jihadi-Salafi books, although nowhere in these is he accused of being an infidel.

his refutation had been published. Clearly, and regardless of different versions of events, the Jihadi-Salafis were a group that posed a real challenge to the Sahwa, and the latter did try to attempt a reconciliation that ultimately failed.

VI

Conclusion

All dissident religious groups and movements have had to contend with the official religious scholars since the latter form part of the state in Saudi Arabia. And although the official scholars have faced challengers over the years, the pressure and threat has never been as acute as it has been since about the year 2000. The stance and authority of the official scholars were sufficiently strong during the government's confrontation with the Ikhwan movement (1919–30), the Juhayman al-'Utaybi group (1977–79), and the Sahwa (1990–4) even though by the 1990s this authority was clearly in decline. With the events of 9/11, however, the Salafi-Jihadis posed the strongest challenge yet to the government in Riyadh. This was in part due to the successive death of the chief mufti 'Abd al-Aziz Ibn Baz (d. 1999) and Muhammad Ibn 'Uthaymin (d. 2001), which represented a significant loss to the prestige of the official religious establishment. Because of this, the Saudi state recruited some of the Sahwa leaders in an effort to weaken the Jihadi-Salafis ideologues and political movement they supported, al-Qaeda. This effort proved to be effective, and the Sahwa leaders rose to the challenge.

The Sahwa not only responded ideologically to the Jihadi-Salafis, they also mobilized their social base against al-Qaeda, especially after the suicide attacks of May 12, 2003. To do this the Sahwa relied on the credibility it had garnered in opposing the Saudi state in the 1990s and was able to use its extensive social network with Islamists of various orientations in turning people against al-Qaeda. Some of al-Qaeda's recruits were even persuaded by the Sahwists to turn themselves in to the Saudi authorities. The challenge posed by the Sahwa greatly upset al-Qaeda's leaders, who then labeled the Sahwists traitors and renegades.[64] The pro-government role that the Sahwa played also strengthened the authority of the official scholars, who were vilifying the Jihadi-Salafis as

---

[64] For example, see Yusuf al-'Uyayri, *Hamsa fi udhun al-shaykh Salman al-'Awda*; idem, *Difa'an 'an al-Mujahidin: Risalah maftuhah ila al-shaykh Safar al-Hawali*, idem, *Fadlan inbatihu sirran*, idem, *Hal yakdhib al-rasikhun fi al-'ilm*; Lewis, 'Atiyyat Allah, *al-Munazara al-kubra: al-Qa'ida wa-l-Harakiyyun wajhan li-wajh*; Ibrahim al-Rubaysh, *Dr. Salman al-'Awda khilal 'ishrin 'aman*; 'Abd Allah al-Rushud, *Risala hawl Nasir al-'Umar wa-da'wa lil-munazara aw al-mubahala*; Yahya al-Ghamidi, *Sanawat khadda'a: Dirasa li-waqi' du'at al-Sahwa*.

members of the "errant group" that had strayed from the true teachings of Islam. Thus, the Sahwa served the government in two ways.[65]

Whenever the Sahwa leaders had challenged the Saudi state (e.g., "Letter of Demands" and "Memorandum of Advice," the formation of the Committee for the Defence of Legitimate Rights), they always appealed to the authority of the official ulama or that of well-known shaykhs, such as Ibn Jibrin and 'Abd al-Rahman al-Barrak, who were on good terms with the government. The scholars of Jihadi-Salafism, by contrast, appealed to their own authority and ultimately sought to diminish the standing of the official scholars. The Sahwa never broke completely from the religious establishment, whereas the Jihadi-Salafis condemned this unequivocally.

A close examination of the books and statements of the Jihadi-Salafi scholars leads to the conclusion that these offered the theoretical justification for the violent operations of al-Qaeda. There is little by way of new strategic or tactical vision in the works of these ideologues, except perhaps when Nasir al-Fahd was asked in May 2003 by a member of al-Qaeda in the Arabian Peninsula whether the use of nuclear weapons was permissible. His answer was that they were. The arrest in 2003 of these Salafi-Jihadi scholars limited their influence considerably. Nonetheless, whatever influence they did have came less from their ideas and was due to the relative weakness of the state's institutions, both political and religious in Saudi Arabia and beyond. This insight has not been lost on the Saudi political leadership, and it has sought to strengthen considerably the religious institutions, especially after the various Arab Spring uprisings. Since then, the Saudi monarch has issued several royal decrees, which include a prohibition against defaming or criticizing the Chief Mufti or the Council of Senior Scholars. In addition, the king has established offices throughout the kingdom for the General Presidency for Religious Research and Fatwas. He has also created thousands of new government jobs as well as allocated SAR 200 million ($53 million) for the religious sector.[66] It remains to be seen whether these policies will sufficiently bolster the government's religious institutions to contend with the next group that emerges to challenge the status quo.

---

[65] The challenges that face the official ulama institution are not confined to Saudi Arabia, but are in fact a general phenomenon in the Muslim world. See Ridwan al-Sayyid, *al-Sira' 'ala al-Islam* (Beirut: Dar al-Kitab al-'Arabi, 2004); and Basheer M. Nafi, "The Rise of Islamic Reformist Thought and Its Challenge to Traditional Islam," in *Islamic Thought in the Twentieth Century*, ed. Suha Taji-Farouki and Basheer M. Nafi (London: I. B. Tauris, 2004), 28–60.

[66] See Saudi royal decrees no. A/71, A/72, A/73 in 13/04/1432 AH (=May 18, 2011).

11

"Classical" and "Global" Jihadism in Saudi Arabia

Thomas Hegghammer

INTRODUCTION

The presence of fifteen Saudis among the nineteen hijackers on September 11, 2001, earned Saudi Arabia a reputation as "al-Qaeda country." However, this reputation has also blinded observers to an interesting puzzle, namely, the question why there have not been *more* Saudi al-Qaeda members. Since the 1980s, many thousands of Saudis have fought as mujahidin in foreign conflicts such as Afghanistan, Bosnia, Chechnya, and Iraq. Given this large pool of activists, one would have expected al-Qaeda to be very strong in Saudi Arabia. However, recent research has shown that al-Qaeda has found it notoriously difficult to recruit and operate in the kingdom.[1] The group's first and last major offensive there, the campaign launched by "al-Qaeda on the Arabian Peninsula" in 2003, was crushed by the government after a couple of years. Moreover, Saudi operatives have not been involved in major attacks in the West since 2001. This chapter seeks to explain the paradoxical weakness of al-Qaeda in Saudi Arabia by documenting an important ideological split in the Saudi jihadist movement, namely, between two ideological schools I term "classical" and "global" jihadism, respectively.

The inquiry raises a broader conceptual issue, namely, the extent to which transnational Islamist militancy is a homogenous political phenomenon. I argue here that it is not; observers have long conflated two partly distinct forms of transnational militancy, namely, foreign fighter activism and anti-Western terrorism. While al-Qaida has sought to perpetrate mass-casualty attacks against Western noncombatants, most foreign fighters in Afghanistan, Bosnia, and Chechnya used relatively conventional tactics in confined theaters of war.

---

[1] Thomas Hegghammer, *Jihad in Saudi Arabia: Violence and Pan-Islamism since 1979* (Cambridge: Cambridge University Press, 2010).

This, I argue, was not a minor tactical dispute, but a deep-seated ideological disagreement that has shaped entire organizations and inspired numerous debates, some of them public and acrimonious. At the core of the dispute were two different jihad doctrines: The "classical jihad doctrine," articulated by Abdallah Azzam in the 1980s, advocated restricted military involvement in other Muslims' wars of national liberation. The "global jihad doctrine," developed by Usama bin Ladin in the 1990s, prescribed unrestricted global war against the United States and its allies.

The split between classical and global jihadists is not Saudi-specific; it is operational across the Muslim world. However, in few places have the political implications of this ideological divide been as consequential as in Saudi Arabia. This is partly because the kingdom has had the largest community of transnational jihadists of any country since the mid-1980s. I argue here that the analytical distinction between classical and global jihadism is crucial for understanding the evolution of militancy in post-1990 Saudi Arabia. A closer look at the Saudi jihadist community in the 1990s and 2000s will show that most militants were classical jihadists and that global jihadism was a much more marginal phenomenon than previously thought.

The chapter is divided into three parts. The first looks at theory and examines the principal differences between four ideal types of modern jihad doctrine, which I call "orthodox," "revolutionary," "classical," and "global," respectively. The second part portrays the principal Saudi actors associated with classical and global jihadism, and the third part examines the relationship between them.

DOCTRINES

What characterizes the classical and global jihad doctrines, and how do they relate to other views on jihad? Before we can address this question, some clarifications are in order. First, I focus here on jihad in the military sense. I am not concerned with the debate on what jihad means, but rather with Muslim views on what constitutes legitimate violence. Second, I define "doctrine" loosely as a set of normative principles on a given issue. I do not mean to suggest the existence of discrete and static manifestos or rule-books on jihad. The doctrines I talk about are to some extent academic constructs; the actors themselves do not necessarily conceptualize and organize views on jihad in the way that I will do below. However, such constructions are scientifically necessary, if only to organize the vast and diverse body of Muslim writings on jihad.

The Islamic literature on jihad can be described in different ways. In this chapter I am concerned with those issues on which activists demonstrably disagree, and that have practical consequences for their behavior. I therefore focus on five core issues. First: What is the rationale for the violence? Second: Against which enemy should the violence be directed? Third: To what extent should Muslim governments control the use of violence? Fourth: For which Muslims is fighting an inescapable duty? And fifth: Which tactics can be used?

Although not always articulated in this way, these issues have been recurrent themes in the Islamic legal literature since the first treatises on jihad were composed in the eighth century AD. The questions have inspired continuous legal debate, because the Qur'an and the *hadith* provide few clear answers and because political circumstances have changed. Partly for the same reasons, modern militant Islamist groups have disagreed between themselves on the same issues. Indeed, every militant group, if not every individual ideologue, has its own way of answering them. This does not prevent us from speaking of a limited number of ideal type positions that have proved more popular or influential than others. In this section I shall highlight three such positions that I call the revolutionary, the classical, and the global jihad doctrine.

"Orthodox" Views on Warfare

To understand the distinctive features of these doctrines and how they resonate among potential recruits, it is necessary to have an idea of "orthodox" views on warfare in Islam, as reflected in the opinions of medieval jurists and contemporary official ulama. Of course, this task is complicated, to say the least, by the absence of a commonly agreed upon Islamic legal code. Instead we have what Roy Mottahedeh and Ridwan al-Sayyid have described as "an accretional body of legal thinking in which minority opinions are preserved and in which there may be more than one widely held normative position."[2] To speak of an orthodox jihad doctrine in this context is obviously problematic. What we can do is acknowledge the existence of a variety of opinions and try to identify mainstream positions on the five questions listed above, first among medieval jurists and then among contemporary ulama.[3]

---

[2] Roy P. Mottahedeh and Ridwan al-Sayyid, "The Idea of the Jihad in Islam before the Crusades," in *The Crusades from the Perspective of Byzantium and the Muslim World*, ed. Angeliki E. Laiou and Roy P. Mottahedeh (Washington, DC: Dumbarton Oaks, 2001), 23.

[3] For more detailed surveys of the variety of opinions, see Majid Khadduri, *War and Peace in the Law of Islam* (Baltimore: Johns Hopkins University Press, 1966); Alfred Morabia, *Le Ğihad dans l'Islam médiéval: Le 'combat sacré' des origines au XIIeme siecle* (Paris: Albin Michel, 1993); Rudolph Peters, *Jihad in Classical and Modern Islam* (Princeton, NJ: Marcus Wiener, 1996); Reuven Firestone, *Jihad: The Origin of Holy War in Islam* (Oxford: Oxford University Press, 1999); David Cook, *Understanding Jihad* (Berkeley: University of California Press, 2005); and

On the first issue, medieval jurists mostly did not deal with the issue of
political justification because they took the legitimacy of jihad against non-
Muslims for granted.[4] There was nevertheless an implicit understanding that
the immediate political purpose of jihad was territorial conquest (offensive
jihad) or reconquest (defensive jihad). Second, most medieval scholars understood jihad as warfare against non-Muslims.[5] Rebellion against a nominally
Muslim ruler was generally not considered *jihad*, but *baghy*, a practice subject
to a separate set of rulings (*ahkam*).[6] However, the opposite phenomenon, that
is, caliphal repression of Muslim rebels, *was* sometimes referred to as jihad.[7]
An important minority view was that of Ibn Taymiyya, who ruled that rebellion
against a nominally Muslim, but de facto un-Islamic government, constituted
legitimate jihad.[8] On the third point, most writers assumed the existence of a
caliphate and considered the war a prerogative of the caliph. Only he could
declare jihad; indeed, he was obliged to do so at regular intervals.[9] On the
fourth issue, jurists considered jihad a collective duty (*fard ʿala al-kifaya*, or
fard kifaya) if its purpose was to acquire new territory through offensive jihad.[10]
Jihad could become an individual obligation (*fard ʿala al-ʿayn* or *fard ʿayn*)
for some people in two situations. First, if the caliph appointed people for
offensive jihad, these had to fight.[11] Second, if a particular region was invaded
by infidels, all capable men in that region were required to fight. If the local
Muslims were unable to resist, the individual duty extended outward in concentric circles to Muslims nearby, potentially applying to all Muslims.[12] We
will come back to this "concentric circles principle" below. On the fifth and
final issue, medieval jurists developed detailed guidelines for conduct in war
that reflected a concern for proportionality and discrimination.[13] However,
for certain situations, many scholars approved of indiscriminate tactics, such

Michael Bonner, *Jihad in Islamic History: Doctrines and Practice* (Princeton, NJ: Princeton
  University Press, 2006).
4 Peters, *Jihad*, 119.
5 Morabia, *Ğihad*, 255 and 259; Bonner, *Jihad*, 10; Ella Landau-Tasseron, "Jihad," in *Ency-
  clopaedia of the Qurʾān*, ed. Jane Dammen McAuliffe (Leiden: Brill, 2005).
6 Khaled Abou El Fadl, *Rebellion and Violence in Islamic Law* (Cambridge: Cambridge University Press, 2001).
7 Morabia, *Ğihad*, 256; Firestone, *Jihad*, 17; Bonner, *Jihad*, 10–11.
8 Cook, *Understanding Jihad*, 6.
9 Morabia, *Ğihad*, 207–9; Peters, *Jihad*, 3 and 5; Cook, *Understanding Jihad*, 164; Bonner, *Jihad*,
  12.
10 Morabia, *Ğihad*, 215; Peters, *Jihad*, 3; Bonner, *Jihad*, 115.
11 Peters, *Jihad*, 3–4.
12 Morabia, *Ğihad*, 215–16.
13 John Kelsay, *Arguing the Just War in Islam* (Cambridge, MA: Harvard University Press, 2007),
  97–124.

as the use of catapults (*manjaniq*) against besieged cities or the launch of night raids (*qatl al-bayat*) in which low visibility put noncombatants at risk.[14] Attacks on enemy armies that used Muslims as human shields (*tatarrus*) were also generally considered legitimate.

In the nineteenth and twentieth centuries structural political changes – such as the disappearance of the caliphate, the rise of the nation state, and the emergence of a system of international relations – rendered some of the rulings of the medieval jurists highly impractical. The medieval jihad doctrine was thus gradually adapted by modern scholars to the new political realities. Pointing to the absence of a caliphate and to the need for pragmatic relations with the non-Muslim world, modern jurists stripped jihad of its offensive dimension and reshaped it into something close to a just war doctrine.[15]

Needless to say, twentieth-century ulama disagreed on many things regarding jihad, but there nevertheless emerged something that we might call a contemporary Islamic legal orthodoxy on jihad. On the five key issues of concern to us, most contemporary ulama share a relatively clear position.[16] First, military jihad can be declared only in situations where non-Muslims occupy Muslim territory.[17] Second, it follows from this that the violence can be directed only against the non-Muslim aggressors. Third, for citizens of a given country to participate in jihad somewhere, the government must give its permission and preferably organize its citizens' military activities.[18] Fourth, violent jihad is an individual duty only for the people directly touched by occupation; for all other Muslims, fighting is a collective duty. Fifth, jihad should be waged with a strict concern for proportionality and discrimination.[19] There is a broad consensus against the targeting of noncombatants, although some scholars have condoned indiscriminate tactics, for example, by widening the definition of "combatant" to include off-duty military personnel.[20]

These general positions are shared not only by most official ulama, but also by many moderate Islamists, such as ideologues of the contemporary

---

[14] Morabia, *Ǧihad*, 227–30.

[15] Peters, *Jihad*, 6–7; Bonner, *Jihad*, 160–61.

[16] For an overview, see Ahmad ibn Salim Misri, *fatawa al-'ulama' al-kibar fi'l-irhab wa'l-tadmir: wa dawabit al-jihad wa'l-takfir wa mu'amalat al-kuffar [Fatwas of the Great Scholars on Terrorism and Destruction: And the Principles of Jihad, Takfir and Dealing with Infidels]* (Riyadh: Dar al-Kayan, 2005). For sample divergent opinions, see Cook, *Understanding Jihad*, 123–27.

[17] Peters, *Jihad*, 104 and 125; Cook, *Understanding Jihad*, 122–3.

[18] Rachel Scott, "An 'Official' Islamic Response to the Egyptian al-jihad Movement," *Journal of Political Ideologies* 8, no. 1 (2003): 54.

[19] Peters, *Jihad*, 145–7.

[20] Kelsay, *Arguing the Just War in Islam*, 140–1.

Muslim Brotherhood and its various sister groups.[21] In Saudi Arabia, the so-called Sahwa movement has always espoused a relatively orthodox view on jihad, although it often advocated more state support for jihad abroad. At times, nonviolent Islamists and independent scholars have held slightly more radical or deliberately ambiguous positions, but on the whole, the Muslim Brotherhood and similar groups have held relatively orthodox positions on jihad. However, starting in the 1960s, radicalized Islamists would challenge this orthodoxy in a number of different ways.

Revolutionary Jihadism

The first modern activists to articulate a substantially new jihad doctrine were militants in 1960s and 1970s Egypt and Syria who sought to topple the regime and implement an Islamic state. They developed a revolutionary jihad doctrine which departed from orthodoxy on almost all the five issues mentioned above.

First, for the revolutionaries the principal purpose of jihad was not to liberate occupied Muslim territory, but to topple nominally Muslim regimes and forcibly establish Islamic states.[22] Of course, the revolutionaries also viewed the liberation of occupied territory as a legitimate cause for jihad, but the fight against regimes had priority. Second, for the revolutionaries the main target of the violence in the short term should not be original infidels but nominally Muslim regimes. In their parlance, the fight against the "near enemy" had priority over the fight against the "far enemy."[23] Third, since the ruler was the enemy, his permission was obviously not required.[24] Fourth, war against the tyrant was an individual duty on all Muslims.[25] Fifth, virtually any tactics could be employed so long as the intended target was a representative of the regime.[26]

The revolutionary jihad doctrine represented a major departure from orthodoxy, most of all because it opened for the use of violence against nominal

---

[21] For example, in October 1978, the editor of the Egyptian Muslim Brotherhood magazine *al-Daʿwa*, Umar al-Tilimsani, envisaged jihad against Israel, but only under the command of the head of state; Firestone, *Jihad*, 159. See also Yusuf al-Qaradawi, *Fiqh al-Jihad* (2009), cited in Nelly Lahoud, "Qaradawi on Jihad", www.jihadica.com, Oct. 25–27, 2009.

[22] Johannes Jansen, *The Neglected Duty: The Creed of Sadat's Assassins and Islamic Resurgence in the Middle East* (New York: Macmillan, 1986), 6.

[23] Ibid., 192.

[24] Revolutionaries also considered that if they had to participate temporarily in a territorial struggle against non-Muslims, it should be outside any state framework; Emmanuel Sivan, *Radical Islam: Medieval Theology and Modern Politics* (New Haven, CT: Yale University Press, 1985), 16–20.

[25] Jansen, *The Neglected Duty*, 21.

[26] Ibid., 25–9.

Muslims. Of course, intra-Muslim warfare was nothing new. The term jihad had been applied by various scholars to rebellion against Muslim rulers, to the repression of Muslim rebels, and to the purification of other nominal Muslims (e.g., in eighteenth-century Arabia and nineteenth-century Nigeria). However, these were the exceptions that proved the rule. For most Muslims, jihad has been about warfare against infidels. The jurisprudential "trick" of the revolutionaries was to widen the definition of "infidel" (*kafir*) to include select groups of Muslims. The right to declare nominal Muslims as infidels (*takfir*) was traditionally reserved for the ulama, but the revolutionaries, most of whom were laymen, claimed the right to do it themselves.

The controversial nature of the revolutionary jihad doctrine was reflected in the relatively small number of people it mobilized. In some times and places, such as 1970s Syria and 1990s Algeria and Egypt, severe regime repression and local conflict dynamics helped produce relatively large communities of revolutionaries. But in most other countries the number of active revolutionaries arguably never exceeded a thousand. Moreover, by the late 1990s, popular support for revolutionary jihad in the Muslim world had been significantly undermined by the failures and violent excesses of militants in Algeria and Egypt.[27]

Classical Jihadism

In the meantime, activists promoting foreign Muslim participation in the 1980s Afghan jihad had articulated a discourse on jihad that differed from both that of the ulama and that of the revolutionaries. For lack of a better term I call this doctrine "classical jihadism," not because it is identical to medieval or modern orthodoxy, but because it is *closer* to orthodoxy than the two other doctrines prevalent in the Islamist community, namely, revolutionary and global jihadism. The principal ideologue behind the classical jihad doctrine was the al-Azhar-trained Palestinian ideologue Abdallah Azzam (d. 1989). A brief look at his answers to our five questions reveals the main characteristics of this doctrine.

First, jihad was again primarily about the liberation of occupied Muslim territory.[28] Azzam did not rule out a future struggle against secular regimes, but he explicitly dismissed it as utopian under the current political conditions.[29]

---

[27] Gilles Kepel, *Jihad: The Trail of Political Islam* (Cambridge, MA: Belknap, 2002), 366.
[28] Abdallah Azzam, *al-difa' 'an aradi al-muslimin: ahamm furud al-a'yan* (The Defence of Muslim Lands: the Foremost of Individual Duties), chapter 1 (available at http://www.religioscope.com/info/doc/jihad/azzam_defence_1_table.htm, accessed Oct. 15, 2009)
[29] Abdallah Azzam, *ilhaq bi'l-qafila* (Join the Caravan), part 1 (available at http://www.religioscope.com/info/doc/jihad/azzam_caravan_1_foreword.htm, accessed Oct. 15, 2009).

Second, the jihad envisaged by Azzam was to be directed against any non-Muslims directly involved in the occupation of Muslim land.[30] Third, he dismissed the notion that the waging of jihad was subject to authorization from the heads of state.[31] Politicians could and should help the jihad effort, he argued, but they had no authority to stop it. Official ulama, on the other hand, should be listened to and preferably be enlisted into the jihad effort. However, if they failed to support jihad, they should be ignored. This view was related to his position on the fourth point, which was that jihad was an individual duty for all Muslims so long as any piece of Muslim land was under occupation.[32] On the issue of tactics, Azzam emphasized the need to follow Islamic rules for warfare, though wherever medieval scholars had disagreed, he systematically espoused the least restrictive (i.e., most radical) interpretation.[33] Crucially, however, he did not condone out-of-area operations; warfare was to be conducted primarily by and against soldiers on the battlefield. He also did not advocate suicide bombings, although he did articulate a flowery discourse on martyrdom that paved the way for the adoption of suicide bombings by Sunni militants in the 1990s.[34]

Classical jihadism was less controversial than revolutionary jihadism because the purpose of the struggle was the same as in orthodox doctrines, namely, the liberation of territory from non-Muslim occupation, something that in principle did not require the killing of Muslims. The fact that classical jihadism was more palatable to the masses is evidenced by the scale of the Arab mobilization to Afghanistan in the 1980s, to Bosnia in the 1990s, and to Iraq in the 2000s.

However, Azzam's doctrine was not uncontroversial from an orthodox perspective, because Azzam presented a new and radical view on the question of who had a duty to fight. In the 1980s, virtually all ulama considered military participation in the Afghan jihad as an individual duty only for the Afghans; for other Muslims, fighting was a collective duty, that is, optional for individuals and subject to the authorization of their respective rulers. Azzam, on the other hand, viewed military participation as an individual duty for all Muslims worldwide. Both parties pointed to the "concentric circles principle," but they interpreted it differently. For official ulama, this principle had long been a

---

30 Azzam, *The Defence of Muslim Lands*, chapter 1.
31 Ibid., chapter 3.
32 Ibid.
33 Abdallah Azzam, *fi'l-jihad adab wa ahkam* (Manners and Rules in Jihad) (available at http://tawhed.ws/r?i=5ghypwb2, accessed Oct. 15, 2009).
34 See, e.g., Abdallah Azzam, *ayat al-rahman fi jihad al-afghan* (Signs of the Merciful in the Afghan Jihad) (available at http://tawhed.ws/dl?i=kzj4tots, accessed Oct. 15, 2009).

way to limit responsibility for fighting to the local population under attack. Theoretically, if the locals were unable to resist, others should join the fight; but in practice scholars would never declare the locals unable to resist. Azzam did; for him the very existence of an occupation somewhere was proof that the locals were unable to resist, so the individual duty logically extended to the entire umma.[35]

A number of Islamist figures such as Hasan al-Turabi, Safar al-Hawali, and Yusuf al-Qaradawi publicly criticized this interpretation, describing it as highly impractical for Muslims and, in the case of Afghanistan, beneficial to the United States.[36] Official ulama, on the other hand, generally did not criticize Azzam, mainly because it was politically costly for them to do so, given the popularity of the Afghan jihad. Instead they used ambiguous language, saying, for example, that "supporting the jihad in Afghanistan is a duty for all Muslims," without specifying whether the support should be military or if the duty was individual. It was only later, when states sought, in vain, to curb transnational jihadist activism, that the implications of Azzam's doctrinal privatization of jihad became clear.

It is important to note that classical jihadism was a doctrine for involvement in *other Muslims'* struggles of national liberation, not their own. Local resistance to occupation – for example, by Palestinians in Palestine and Chechens in Chechnya – did not require any doctrinal innovation because it was covered by orthodox jihad doctrine.

Global Jihadism

Azzam's insistence on the urgency of liberating Muslim territory stemmed from a pan-Islamist worldview in which the all the woes of Muslims around the world were the product of a global conspiracy by non-Muslims to weaken Islam. In the early 1990s, some activists began to view America as the leader of this conspiracy and to consider other tactics than the ones prescribed by classical jihadism. Thus in the mid-1990s, Usama bin Ladin articulated a justification for a global military campaign against the United States with the aim of evicting Westerners from Muslim lands, especially Saudi Arabia, where

---

[35] Azzam, *The Defence of Muslim Lands*, chapter 2. Similarly, in early 2003, the Chechnya-based Saudi ideologue Abu Umar al-Sayf wrote "If the US invades Iraq, jihad will be an individual duty on the people of Iraq, and the people around them as needed, mujahidin have to head to Iraq until sufficiency is reached and the enemy repelled." Abu Umar al-Sayf, *maqasid al-jihad wa anwa'uhu* (Principles of Jihad and Its Forms) (available at http://tawhed.ws/r?i=dmem6wk7, accessed Oct. 15, 2009).

[36] Hegghammer, *Jihad in Saudi Arabia*, chapter 2.

TABLE 11.1. *Characteristics of Ideal Type Contemporary Jihad Doctrines*

	Orthodox	Revolutionary	Classical	Global
Rationale	Territorial occupation	Malgovernance	Territorial occupation	Territorial occupation
Immediate enemy	Non-Muslim occupiers	Muslim rulers	Non-Muslim occupiers	America and allies
Need for authority?	Yes	No	Partly	No
Duty for all?	No	Yes	Yes	Yes
Discriminate tactics?	Yes	No	Partly	No

the United States had deployed large numbers of troops in 1990. The global jihad doctrine developed in stages, but it emerged in final form in the 1998 "Statement of the World Islamic Front for Jihad against Jews and Crusaders."[37] Returning to our five core issues, we can summarize the doctrine as follows.

First, the primary declared objective of the military effort was the liberation of occupied Muslim territory everywhere, especially on the Arabian Peninsula and in Palestine. Second, the violence should primarily be directed against America and its non-Muslim allies. Third, Muslim state leaders had absolutely no authority of the jihad effort because they were illegitimate, and official ulama should not be heeded because they were corrupt. Fourth, jihad was an individual duty on all Muslims. And, fifth, all means in all places are permitted.

It may now be time to step back and look at the four ideal type doctrines side by side (see Table 11.1).

The doctrines of classical and global jihad shared two features that have led to their conflation. Both were articulated in pan-Islamist discourse, that is, they focused on the fight against external enemies, and they highlighted instances of Muslim suffering at the hands of non-Muslims. Moreover, both classical and global jihadists viewed the armed defense of the Muslim nation as the individual responsibility of every Muslim on the planet. The jihad effort was therefore an inherently transnational and private enterprise in which nation-states had no role to play.

---

[37] Available at http://www.fas.org/irp/world/para/docs/980223-fatwa.htm (accessed Oct. 15, 2009). See also Bruce Lawrence, ed., *Messages to the World: The Statements of Osama Bin Laden* (London: Verso, 2005).

However, classical and global jihadist doctrines also differed on three key points. First, although classical jihadists considered all non-Muslim occupiers equally worth fighting, global jihadists prioritized the United States and the West. Second, classical jihadists paid somewhat more attention to the opinions of senior official ulama than did global jihadists. Classical jihadists preferred to get involved in areas considered as jihad fronts by at least some senior ulama. Global jihadists, on the other hand, did not heed the ulama but operated where they wanted. Third and most important, global jihadists undertook out-of-area operations and targeted civilians, something classical jihadists tried to avoid.

Crucially for this analysis, the two doctrines produced different views on Saudi Arabia as an area of operations. For classical jihadists, the U.S. military presence in Saudi Arabia was unacceptable, but it did not merit violent resistance so long as virtually all ulama were opposed to the idea and so long as more brutal occupations were taking place elsewhere. For global jihadists, the fight against the United States had priority, and the opinions of the ulama did not matter.

So far we have stayed in the realm of ideology and doctrine. Let us now look at how these differences played out in practice in the Saudi context.

ACTORS

Who exactly in Saudi Arabia were the classical and the global jihadists? What was their relative size and power? And how neat was the distinction between the two communities?

The classical jihadists were the people who went abroad to fight in specific combat zones where Muslims were confronting non-Muslims. This type of activity began in earnest with 1980s Afghanistan; it later brought Saudis to 1990s Bosnia, Chechnya, Philippines, and Kashmir, and it continues today, not least with Syria. Generally speaking, the classical jihadist community has been relatively decentralized and unorganized, but ad hoc organizational structures developed in the context of particular mobilization efforts, especially to Afghanistan in the 1980s, Bosnia and Chechnya in the 1990s, and Iraq in the 2000s. Each mobilization produced a community of veterans with a particular identity and culture: Thus we can speak of the "Afghans," the "Bosnians," or the "Chechens" as subsets of the classical jihadist community. These subcomponents were partially overlapping, because some people participated in more than one jihad, and because veterans from different conflicts tended to socialize when at home and between wars.

The global jihadists were those who sought to carry out operations against Western targets in places other than the abovementioned jihad zones. This type of activism started in the mid-1990s and was closely associated with the al-Qaeda organization. Most, though not all, Saudi global jihadists were linked in some way to Usama bin Ladin and al-Qaeda. As such, they were more tightly organized than the classical jihadists, no doubt reflecting the difference in the risks associated with their respective projects.

The classical jihadists were always much more numerous than the global jihadists. Reliable numbers do not exist, but a conservative estimate would put the number of Saudis involved in classical jihadism at some point between 1985 and 2005 to around 8,000, broken down as follows: 1980s Afghanistan: at least 5,000; 1990s Bosnia: at least 500; 1990s Chechnya: at least 100; post-2001 Afghanistan: at least 500; post-2003 Iraq: at least 1,500; post-2006 Somalia: at least 50; the minor fronts (Kashmir, Philippines, Eritrea): at least 100.[38] In addition, many of the at least five hundred Saudis who joined al-Qaeda camps in Afghanistan in the late 1990s were initially motivated not by global jihadism but by classical jihadism, as we shall see below.

By contrast, the number of Saudis involved in global jihadist activity in the same period probably does not exceed a thousand.[39] In the 1990s, the al-Qaeda presence in the kingdom was very weak. As late as 1997, there were only a few tens of Saudi al-Qaeda members, and up until 1999, bin Ladin's network in Saudi Arabia probably counted fewer than a hundred people. Between 1999 and 2001 Saudi recruitment to al-Qaeda camps in Afghanistan increased dramatically, so that by mid-2001 between five and seven hundred Saudis were in Afghanistan. In 2002 those who had not been killed in the U.S.–led invasion or been sent to Guantanamo returned to Saudi Arabia, where they would build an organization known as "al-Qaeda on the Arabian Peninsula" (QAP), which at its largest may have included some three to five hundred people, depending on how one defines campaign involvement.

This difference in size reflected two important realities. The first was a difference in Saudi popular support for the two political projects in question. The global jihadist agenda was much more controversial than the classical jihadist one, by virtue of being theologically les orthodox and militarily less conventional. The global jihadist doctrine ultimately involved bombings inside Saudi Arabia, which – however, sharply focused on Western targets – was less palatable to ordinary Saudis than conventional combat abroad. The second and related reason was the difference in state attitudes to the two projects.

---

[38] Hegghammer, *Jihad in Saudi Arabia*, passim.
[39] Ibid.

Because the global jihadists envisaged operations in the kingdom, they faced much higher constraints in the form of police repression than did the classical jihadists. The latter enjoyed the tacit support of most of the religious establishment and parts of the political establishment (although the latter became less sympathetic to classical jihadism after 1993 as a result of events in Bosnia and Islamist contestation at home).

But why was there so much Saudi support for classical jihadism, and why was there any support for global jihadism at all? This had to do with the peculiar role of pan-Islamism in Saudi politics. In the course of the 1980s and early 1990s, declared sympathy for suffering Muslims abroad had become a very important source of political and religious legitimacy for both the state and its Islamist opponents. This created an environment with a relatively high tolerance for activism that could be framed as support for the umma, including various forms of assistance to Muslim rebel groups waging wars of national liberation. The global jihadists also benefited from this, because the discursive theme of their rhetoric was the same as that of the classical jihadists, namely, the suffering of the umma at the hands of infidels.

A less intuitive, but very important reason why global jihadism prospered in late 1990s Saudi Arabia was that al-Qaeda's recruiters systematically concealed the most controversial parts of its program from prospective recruits. Bin Ladin knew that it was difficult to recruit Saudis directly off the streets for international terrorism. It was much easier to convince recruits once they were in the training camps. To get people to the camps, al-Qaeda recruiters cunningly marketed the training camps as a necessary station on the way to a classical jihad front such as Chechnya or Palestine.[40] These two conflicts were particularly prominent around the turn of the millennium due to the outbreak of the second Chechen war in 1999 and the second Palestinian intifada in 2000. In this period, global jihadist recruiters essentially piggybacked on the strong classical jihadist current in Saudi Arabia to lure people to the camps, where they were socialized and indoctrinated into the more radical bin Ladin doctrine.[41]

The ease with which global jihadism could be concealed as classical jihadism illustrates the close relationship between the two ideologies and communities. Indeed, the distinction between the two types of activism was

---

[40] See *The 9/11 Commission Report*, 233; and Sharon Curcio, "Generational Differences in Waging Jihad," *Military Review* 85, no. 4 (2005): 84; "Testimony of Detainees – CSRT," 1274; "Testimony of Detainees – CSRT," 2655; *Sunday Times*, Nov. 25, 2007; and Dexter Filkins, *The Forever War* (New York: Alfred A. Knopf, 2008), 62–3.

[41] *New York Times*, Oct. 12, 2003.

never clear-cut. For a start, the ideological similarities between the two doc-trines means there was a significant overlap between the rhetoric of the two communities. Classical jihadists were also hostile to the West in general and to the U.S. military presence in the kingdom in particular. Conversely, global jihadists routinely spoke of the need to support the mujahidin in Palestine, Chechnya, Iraq, and elsewhere. Both communities had a shared interest in raising awareness of issues supporting the worldview that Islam was under attack by non-Muslims.

Second, there were numerous personal links between individuals in the two communities, because most global jihadists had started their militant careers as classical jihadists. For all intents and purposes, global jihadists were radi-calized classical jihadists. As a result, the two communities were often socially quite closely intertwined.

Third, individuals sometimes displayed ambiguous behavior and thus escaped easy categorization as either classical or global jihadists. Because individual behavior is also shaped by nonideological factors such as social dynamics, temperament, or contingencies, individuals might move in and out of networks and causes in ideologically inconsistent patterns.

A fourth and related point is that sometimes there emerged politically ambiguous conflicts that could be framed both as a classical and as a global jihad front. This was notably the case in post-9/11 Afghanistan when there was a classical jihad front with the United States as the occupier. In these cases the interests of the two communities coincided and inspired direct collabora-tion. Classical jihadists were also very supportive of the Taliban and the Arab presence in Afghanistan prior to 2001, but they did not mobilize militarily for it to the same extent, because there was no non-Muslim occupier (although some viewed the Northern Alliance as such).

However, these factors are not sufficient to invalidate the analytical dis-tinction. For all their ideological similarities, the classical and global jihadist differed on issues of crucial operational importance, namely, where, how, and against whom to deploy military resources. The global jihadists rhetori-cally supported the idea of jihad in Palestine and Chechnya, but they did not spend their resources there. Moreover, cases of ambiguous individual behav-ior do not invalidate ideal type distinctions so long as the former are greatly outnumbered by cases of unambiguous behavior. Most classical and global jihadists behaved in patterns consistent with their respective doctrines. The vast majority of people who fought in 1980s Afghanistan and 1990s Bosnia and Chechnya never attacked Westerners; Saudis in post-2002 Iraq may have attacked Western forces, but few if any did so "out of area."

One of the reasons why classical and global jihadists have long been con-flated is that it was rarely in either of the two camps' interest to highlight differences between them. However, at times they entered into competition and outright polemics.

RELATIONS

In this third section I shall look more closely at the relationship between the two communities since the rise of global jihadism in the mid-1990s. I shall focus on two particularly tense periods in this relationship: the tensions in the late 1990s between Chechen Arabs and Afghan Arabs, and the 2003 debate over whether to fight in Iraq or in Saudi Arabia.

Khattabists versus Bin Ladenists

In the second half of the 1990s, when Usama bin Ladin started recruiting Saudis to the global jihadist cause from his base in Afghanistan, the unofficial leader of the classical jihadist community was Ibn Khattab, the Saudi leader of the Arab fighters in Chechnya. Tensions would soon develop between the two leaders as they competed for Saudi money and recruits to their respective projects.

Ibn Khattab, whose real name was Samir al-Suwailim, was a veteran of the Afghan jihad who had traveled to the Caucasus in 1995 as one of the first foreign volunteers to get involved in the Chechen war.[42] To classical jihadists, the conflict between the Chechens and the non-Muslim Russian military represented a clear-cut case of jihad requiring the involvement of Muslims worldwide. Together with his close associates, including the Saudi ideologue Abu Umar al-Sayf (Muhammad al-Tamimi) and the Chechen commander Shamil Basayev, Khattab set up camps for foreign volunteers and established a logistics chain through Turkey and Azerbaijan as well as a recruitment network in the Gulf. They also set up a religious school in Chechnya for which they recruited religious teachers from Saudi Arabia.[43] Between 1995 and 1999, hundreds of Arabs, including around a hundred Saudis, joined the jihad in Chechnya.[44]

As a result of these efforts, there soon emerged a community of activists in Saudi Arabia preoccupied with the Chechen jihad. These "Chechens" or "Khattabists" constituted a largely separate network from that of the "Afghans"

---

[42] *Arab News*, May 4, 2002.
[43] Al Awshan, "*khalid bin abdallah al-subayt.*"
[44] Murad al-Shishani, *The Rise and Fall of Arab Fighters in Chechnya* (Washington, DC: Jamestown Foundation, 2006); Julie Wilhelmsen, "When Separatists Become Islamists: The Case of Chechnya," *FFI Report* (Kjeller: Norwegian Defence Research Establishment, 2004).

or the "bin Ladenists" that developed around the same time.[45] The separation had some social and historical roots. Bin Ladin and Ibn Khattab were born thirteen years apart in two different parts of Saudi Arabia (Hijaz and the Eastern Province, respectively), so they drew on different social networks in their respective mobilization efforts. Moreover, the two leaders had never been in close contact. In the Afghan jihad, they fought at different fronts (bin Ladin in the east and Khattab in the north), and in the early 1990s bin Ladin was in the Sudan while Khattab was in Tajikistan. However, the main reason for the separation between Khattabists and the bin Ladinists was ideological. Khattab and his followers did not approve of bin Ladin's America-first strategy, and although they denounced the U.S. military presence in the kingdom, they disapproved of the idea of jihad at home.[46] Moreover, the Khattabists prided themselves in the use of relatively clean tactics; unlike al-Qaeda, they did not target civilians or undertake out-of-area operations.[47] It is worth noting that all the most controversial out-of-area terrorist operations conducted by Chechen militants, such as the Dubrovka and Beslan operations, occurred after Khattab's death in April 2002.

Despite the tendency of some observers to describe Khattab as a part of al-Qaeda, the relationship between Khattab and bin Ladin seems to have been less than cordial. Khattab in fact always denied having any direct connection with bin Laden, and although he did describe the latter as a "good Muslim," he is not on record as having publicly praised or endorsed him.[48] More important, the two argued over ideology. Around 1998, bin Ladin allegedly wrote to Khattab, inviting him to collaborate more closely and support bin Ladin's global jihad. Khattab politely declined, stating his more limited regional ambitions. More letters followed, and the exchange allegedly developed into an extensive debate over strategy in which neither party made concessions.[49]

---

45 Author interviews with Nasir al-Barrak and Faris bin Huzzam.
46 Paul Tumelty, "The Rise and Fall of Foreign Fighters in Chechnya," *Jamestown Terrorism Monitor* 4, no. 2 (2006).
47 Author's interviews with Nasir al-Barrak and Faris bin Huzzam. Abu Umar al-Sayf wrote that "Islam forbids the killing of noncombatants such as the elderly, women and children. This is unlike the Jews and the Christians, who till this day have used collective punishment and targeted women, children and the elderly in Bosnia, Chechnya, Palestine, Kosovo, Afghanistan and Iraq"; Abu Umar al-Sayf, "*hal al-umma wa'l-irhab al-mafqud*" (The State of the Umma and the Lost Terrorism), Feb. 2003 (available at http://tawhed.ws/r?i=4yd2i00y, accessed Oct. 15, 2009).
48 Tumelty, "The Rise and Fall."
49 Ibid. See also Cerwyin Moore and Paul Tumelty, "Foreign Fighters and the Case of Chechnya: A Critical Assessment," *Studies in Conflict and Terrorism* 31, no. 5 (2008): 412–33.

If bin Ladin had initiated this correspondence, it was probably because he realized that the Khattabists represented a serious competitor for political support and material resources in Saudi Arabia. In fact, bin Ladin's success in recruiting Saudis to Afghanistan was partly contingent on the failure of Khattab in Chechnya. In the period between 1995 and 1999, when the Arab mobilization to Chechnya occurred, bin Ladin had serious problems recruiting Saudis to al-Qaeda.[50] However, the outbreak of the second Chechen war in 1999 proved a stroke of good fortune for the global jihadists, because the accompanying Russian blockade made Chechnya virtually inaccessible for foreign volunteers. At the same time, images of Russian atrocities broadcast on al-Jazeera and disseminated on the internet increased pan-Islamist fervor in the kingdom, a sentiment al-Qaeda was able to exploit through the deceptive recruitment strategy mentioned above. This development, along with several other factors, contributed to an exponential increase in Saudi recruitment to al-Qaeda camps in Afghanistan between 1999 and 2001. In this first major contest between classical and global jihadists, bin Ladin had prevailed. Soon the tables would turn.

Jihad in Iraq versus jihad on the Arabian Peninsula

In May 2003, al-Qaeda finally implemented the project it had been planning for seven years, namely, a large-scale violent campaign against Westerners in Saudi Arabia. After initial successes, the campaign eventually failed, in part because of the presence of a classical jihad front in Iraq next door.

In early 2002, after the U.S.-led invasion of Afghanistan had deprived al-Qaeda of a safe haven, bin Ladin sent his Saudi foot soldiers back to the kingdom with orders to start preparing for a campaign. The returnees spent a year building an organizational infrastructure that became known as "al-Qaeda on the Arabian Peninsula" (QAP). On May 12, 2003, they launched a major terrorist offensive, the longest and bloodiest in the country's history.

This time, it was the global jihadists' turn to experience bad luck. In the year that passed between bin Ladin's strategic decision to open the Saudi front and the launch of the campaign, the United States invaded Iraq, creating a classical jihad front on Saudi Arabia's northern border. Because resources for violent Islamist activism were scarce in Saudi Arabia after 9/11 and even more so after May 2003, classical and global jihadists quickly found themselves in a state of competition over recruits and money. This drove the two camps

---

[50] Hegghammer, *Jihad in Saudi Arabia*, 117–18.

into a heated ideological debate over whether it was best for Saudis to fight in Iraq or in Saudi Arabia.

Almost immediately after the May 2003 bombings, critics suggested that people should go to Iraq if they really wanted to fight the Crusaders.[51] In the first issue of QAP's magazine *Sawt al-Jihad* (*SJ*) in October 2003, senior QAP leader Abd al-Aziz al-Muqrin felt obliged to explain why he had not gone to Iraq.[52] The controversy escalated further in December 2003, when Abu Umar al-Sayf publicly criticized QAP and called on Saudis to fight in Iraq instead.[53] Al-Sayf and others argued that the violence in Saudi Arabia diverted attention and resources away from the jihad in Iraq. QAP countered with articles in *SJ* stating that the jihad in Saudi Arabia was not at all incompatible with the jihad in Iraq and that Saudis should fight the crusaders close to home, where they would have a stronger impact.[54] QAP also wrote articles attempting to mobilize "retired" classical jihadists – that is, people who had been to Afghanistan, Bosnia, and Chechnya in the past – but to little avail.[55]

During this period, the classical and global jihadists constituted partly separate organizational networks. People involved in recruitment and fundraising to Iraq seem to have held QAP at arm's length for fear of attracting police attention. QAP, on its side, had little to gain from interacting with activists who were sending recruits and money out of the country. The split in the Saudi jihadist movement greatly undermined support for and recruitment to QAP. Aspiring Saudi jihadists keen on fighting in defense of the Islamic nation saw Iraq as a vastly more attractive and legitimate battleground than the streets of Riyadh and Mecca. Few Saudi donors would pay for weapons that would be used literally outside their doorstep when they could support the mujahidin in Iraq instead.

The political victory of the "Khattabists" over the "bin Ladinists" manifested itself very clearly in the outcome of their recruitment efforts. While QAP

---

[51] See, e.g., Abdallah al-Rashid, *intiqad al-i'tirad 'ala tafjirat al-riyadh* (Criticism of the Objection to the Riyadh Bombings), July 2003 (available at http://tawhed.ws/dl?i=hiyd550g, accessed Oct. 15, 2009).

[52] *"liqa' ma' ahad al-matlubin al-19"* (1) (Interview with one of the 19 wanted men), *Sawt al-Jihad*, no. 1 (2003).

[53] "Al-Qa'ida Leader Calls for Attacks on Americans in Iraq Rather than on the Saudi Government in Saudi Arabia," *MEMRI Special Dispatch*, no. 635 (2003).

[54] See, for example, Muhammad al-Salim, *"la tadhhabu ila al-'iraq!"* (Don't Go to Iraq!), *Sawt al-Jihad*, no. 7 (2003); and Muhammad al-Salim, *"labayka ya 'iraq"* (Woe to You, Iraq), *Sawt al-Jihad*, no. 11 (2004).

[55] See, e.g., Abd al-Aziz al-Muqrin, *"risala ila man taraka al-silah"* (Letter to Those Who Have Left Their Weapons), audio message, 2004 (transcript available at http://tawhed.ws/r?i=vkiboxea, accessed Oct. 15, 2009).

recruited only a small number of relatives and acquaintances, the classical jihadists mobilized an entire new generation of Saudis volunteers to Iraq.[56] However, the sinking ship of global jihadism would soon take classical jihadism with it.

Post-2003 Developments

The QAP campaign gradually petered out as the organization proved unable to replace the personnel lost in arrests and shootouts. For all intents and purposes, the jihad in Saudi Arabia was over by mid-2005. Perhaps more important, the violence had turned popular opinion firmly against al-Qaeda and severely delegitimized the global jihadist doctrine. Since 2006, the global jihadist community in the kingdom has been very weak, although not eradicated.

Classical jihadism, on the other hand, remained relatively popular. The old conflicts in Palestine, Chechnya, and Kashmir remained, the U.S.-led occupations in Iraq and Afghanistan continued, and new jihad fronts opened up in Somalia and elsewhere. Classical jihadist mobilization was facilitated by the proliferation of other symbols of Muslim suffering, such as the Abu Ghraib and Guantanamo prison controversies and the Israeli bombardments of Lebanon and Gaza in 2006 and 2008, respectively.

However, after an initial spike in recruitment to Iraq, the classical jihadist community seems to have suffered a marked decline in recruitment after about 2005.[57] This was in part because the QAP campaign had prompted the government to start cracking down on all forms of militant activism, including foreign fighter activism. Up until 2003, classical jihadist recruiters and fundraisers had enjoyed relatively low constraints in the kingdom, because the government did not want to pay the political price of cracking down on networks involved in supporting "suffering Muslims abroad." With the 2003 violence, the public discourse on religious extremism changed significantly, reducing the political cost, for the regime, of police measures against classical jihadists. From 2003 onward, the authorities began arresting people involved in recruitment and fundraising to Iraq and other foreign jihad fronts. Such crackdowns had occurred in the past, but it was only after 2003 that they became systematic. This change of policy, combined with dramatic improvements in intelligence

---

[56] Thomas Hegghammer, "Saudi Militants in Iraq: Backgrounds and Recruitment Patterns," *FFI Report* (Kjeller: Norwegian Defence Research Establishment, 2007).
[57] Kenneth Katzman, "Al Qaeda in Iraq: Assessment and Outside Links" (Washington, DC: Congressional Research Service, 2008), 16.

capability of the domestic security services, has taken a heavy toll on the organized classical jihadist community in Saudi Arabia.

The government has also sought to undermine the religious legitimacy of classical jihadism by having official scholars such as Abd al-Muhsin al-Ubaykan rule that the situation in Iraq is so chaotic it cannot be considered a jihad at all.[58] However, this is undoubtedly a minority opinion. The mainstream scholarly opinion is closer to the orthodox one, which is that there is a jihad in Iraq, but that only Iraqis have a duty to fight. This was essentially the view expressed in the statement published in late 2004 by a number of prominent semiofficial scholars including Salman al-Awda and Awadh al-Qarni.[59] The statement caused heated debate, with Saudi liberals and outside observers publicly accusing the signatories of supporting terrorism, forcing the signatories to issue follow-up declarations explicitly discouraging Saudis from going to Iraq.[60] In substance, their statement was no different from fatwas issued by more senior scholars in the past on other conflicts. The 2004 controversy was indicative of a tectonic shift in government attitudes to Islamist militancy. Although this political climate makes it difficult for Saudi scholars to publicly condone Saudi participation in Iraq and other battle fronts, there are undoubtedly scholars who do. For example, Abdallah bin Jibrin is known to have been regularly paying his respects to families of Saudis "martyred" in Iraq.

The government now treats classical and global jihadists somewhat more evenly, although there is still a degree of differential treatment. This relates partly to capabilities and partly to intentions. It is extremely costly to monitor the entire jihadist community equally closely – so the government focuses on those it considers the biggest immediate threat to internal security. Still, the days of the government's glaring differential treatment of foreign fighters and al-Qaeda seem to be over.

It remains to be seen how this leveling of the playing field will affect relations between classical and global jihadists. It may bring the communities closer together, as the classical jihadists are radicalized by repression, lose their partial respect for religious authority, and warm to the idea of operating in the

---

[58] *al-Sharq al-Awsat*, Nov. 4, 2004.

[59] "*jam' min al-'ulama al-sa'udiyyin yuwajjihuna khatiban maftuhan li'l-sha'b al-'iraqi*" (Group of Saudi Scholars Direct Open Letter to the Iraqi People), www.islamtoday.net, Nov. 5, 2004. Similar views have been expressed by other senior scholars such as Salih al-Luhaydan; see, e.g., Lisa Myers, "More Evidence of Saudi Doubletalk," *Newsweek*, Apr. 26, 2005.

[60] See Ayidh al-Qarni's statement on *al-Jazeera* on Nov. 14, 2004, Salman al-Awda's article in *al-Riyadh* newspaper on Nov. 20, 2004, and Safar al-Hawali's interview with *al-Ukaz* on May 19, 2005.

kingdom. It may also divide them, as classical jihadists fear that association with global jihadists will bring further state repression.

CONCLUSION

The distinction between classical and global jihadism in Saudi Arabia was never clear-cut, but as far as analytical distinctions go, it was highly operational. It had observable and significant effects on the behavior and fate of organizations. Disaggregating transnational jihadism helped us solve several puzzles in the history of Saudi Islamism.

The people who joined other Muslims' wars of national liberation were not of the same ideological persuasion as the ones who planned terrorist attacks against Westerners in Saudi Arabia and elsewhere. Luckily for Western expatriates, the former were always more numerous than the latter. Until the late 1990s, most Saudi militants were classical jihadists, not al-Qaeda operatives, which explains why, for so long, there were many Saudi militants yet little violence in the kingdom.

When the global jihadists became a sizeable community around 1999–2000, it soon became clear that their interests conflicted with those of the classical jihadists, prompting competition for resources. In the early 2000s the global jihadists enjoyed a monopoly due to the Russian siege on the principal classical jihad front, Chechnya. In 2003, however, the near simultaneous outbreak of the terrorism campaign in Saudi Arabia and the insurgency in Iraq placed the two communities in direct and fierce competition for recruits and money, one that the global jihadists were bound to lose given their lack of popular support.

For al-Qaeda, the existence of a strong classical jihadist community in the kingdom was a mixed blessing. In 1999–2000 global jihadists had been able to exploit popular outrage over Chechnya and Palestine to their own benefit by selling al-Qaeda's training camps in Afghanistan as a station on the way to classical jihad. Once in the camps, recruits were socialized into global jihadism. However, they were able to do this only so long as they themselves had camps and Chechnya and Palestine were sealed off. As soon as a classical jihad front became available in Iraq, al-Qaeda suffered.

After experiencing a certain boost in the early 2000s, the popularity of al-Qaeda's global jihad doctrine now seems to be in decline in large parts of the Muslim world. The many Muslim casualties of al-Qaeda's attacks have caused public resentment, and a growing number of former militants and Islamist ideologues have authored elaborate refutations of the global jihad doctrine. Classical jihadism has brighter prospects. Undermining Abdallah

Azzam's doctrine is a formidable challenge for Muslim states, because international politics play to its advantage, and because it is too close to orthodoxy to be easily discredited. For Saudi Arabia, which spent decades promoting Islamic solidarity, it is an even greater challenge. As a Saudi official recently observed, "We encouraged our young men to fight for Islam in Afghanistan. We encouraged our young men to fight for Islam in Bosnia and Chechnya. We encouraged our young men to fight for Islam in Palestine. Now we are telling them you are forbidden to fight for Islam in Iraq, and they are confused."[61]

[61] Robert Windrem, "Saudi Arabia's Ambitious al-Qaida Fighter," *NBC News*, July 11, 2005.

PART 4

Social Change

Raiders and Traders

A Poet's Lament on the End of the Bedouin Heroic Age

Abdulaziz H. Al Fahad

"Najd belongs to him who possesses the longest lance."
Bedouin proverb
"Poetry is the register of the Arabs."
Arabic proverb

No country is identified with the Bedouin as much as Saudi Arabia.[1] This identification is understandable, as the Bedouin presence has been a hallmark of its society both numerically and culturally. Yet, the prevalent association of the Saudi state (in its more than two-century history) with the tribe and nomads represents a serious misreading of the political history of the state and its nature.[2] What follows is a study of a particular poet, Bandar bin Srur[3] (1937–84), hailing from a Bedouin background, who captures, perhaps better than anyone, the fact that the Saudi state (and the associated manifestations of modernity it wrought) represents the antithesis of what "Bedouinism" stood for, and reflects the fundamental alienation of traditional nomads from the state and its moral order.

My earliest memories of the Bedouin and their values are related to a particular desert knight, Dghaylib bin Khnaysir, of the Bedouin Asa'ida clan

---

[1] Earlier versions of this paper were presented at the Yale Middle East Legal Studies Seminar in Istanbul, January 2008, and a seminar on the State of the Saudi State in Princeton in 2009. I wish to express my gratitude to several colleagues and friends who read and commented on earlier drafts of this paper.

[2] A summary of references to this literature is found in Abdulaziz H. Al-Fahad, "The 'Imamah vs. the 'Iqal: Hadari-Bedouin Conflict and the Formation of the Sa'udi State," in *Counter-Narratives: History, Contemporary Society, and Politics in Saudi Arabia and Yemen*, ed. Madawi Al-Rasheed and Robert Vitalis (London: Palgrave Macmillan, 2004), 56, n. 4.

[3] The transliteration used, while adhering for the most part to the standard Arabic, is modified to reflect the reality of vernacular pronunciation, especially the dropping of certain vowels.

of the `Utayba tribe, who died an old, impecunious man in the 1950s. Dghaylib led a nomadic existence to his last days and engaged in raiding (*ghazw*) and counter-raiding until the state imposed its authority while he was still a vigorous warrior. Dghaylib took a liking to staying close to our hometown, al-Zilfi, whose main inhabitants belonged to the same clan, albeit all were *hadar*, as the sedentary population is called. He was much admired and managed to develop strong friendships (including with my grandfather) that lasted for the rest of his life. Over time, a repertoire of his deeds and sayings became part of the local lore.

The anecdotes about Dghaylib are plentiful.[4] Two should illustrate many of the themes addressed here. He always feared dying in bed "like an old lady," a fate he considered ignominious and unbecoming of a warrior of his caliber, whose natural end should come with a blow of the sword. Alas, the state outlawed raiding and deprived him of the prestige of a warrior's death; he died in bed just as he had feared.[5] Of violence, he simply could not understand the hadar point of view. When they good-naturedly chastised him for raiding, killing other men, and stealing their property by telling him that God would throw him into hell for his sins, he refused to accept that fate. He retorted by saying that he could not believe God would punish him for "the killing of [a mere] fifteen Mutayri and three Harbi tribesmen, while not punishing King Abd al-Aziz for the killing of thousands of men." For him, there was no superior moral sanction for killing in the name of God or the state over

---

4 He was clearly recognized to be a warrior of the first order. He engaged in violence until prohibited by the newly established state and was admired and feared by both friends and foes. Yet other than among a dwindling circle of men and occasional mentions on websites, he is hardly known. Contrast that with another `Utaybi warrior, Shlaywih al-`Atawi. Local chronicles refer to the latter; his poetry is regularly recited and documented, and the events of his life are well known. He finally made it to the western reader when a whole tome was dedicated to his poetry and life (see P. Marcel Kupershoek, *The Story of a Desert Knight, The Legend of Slewih al-`Atawi & Other `Utaybah Heroes*, Oral Poetry & Narratives from Central Arabia 3 [Brill, 1995]). Like Shlaywih, Dhgaylib had a brother (Mnawi) of equal accomplishment to the former's own brother (Bkhit). In addition, Shlaywih propelled his family (and descendants to this day) into a chiefly position, which never happened for Dghaylib's descendants. There is no reason to believe that Dghaylib's life and deeds were by any measure inferior to those of Shlaywih, yet history remembers them differently largely due to two factors. For Shlaywih (and his brother), born and killed in the nineteenth century, nomadic life was not constrained by any central authority, and both were poets. Not being poets and living many of their vigorous years in the shadow of a centralizing modern state, Dghaylib and Mnawi were deprived of the recognition befitting their deeds.

5 Upon his death, a hadari man performed the ritual body washing, reporting that he counted "ninety marks left by cauterization," the traditional medical procedure in Arabia. He found it difficult to believe that they were in fact the scars of wounds sustained by a lifetime of *ghazw*.

killing in the name of traditional Bedouin values. He was one of the last men to profess and practice such a sensibility.

This now defeated sensibility was forged through millennia in the crucible of the Arabian Desert. For at least since the domestication of the dromedary, a central feature of life in the Arabian Peninsula, especially its hinterland, Najd, has been the great socioeconomic division of its inhabitants into two distinct, if not separate, communities. The Bedouin were politically organized along tribal lines and engaged in pastoral nomadism as their main economic activity. The hadar, the sedentary population, while exhibiting some tribal traits, lived in settlements with a mixed economy centered on agriculture, commerce, and the crafts.[6] Living in a land with little rain and sparse vegetation, both communities eked out a meager existence and life was generally precarious, with periodic droughts and famines ravaging the population. In this ecologically harsh landscape, the Bedouin and the hadar exploited their own somewhat separate ecological niches and developed elaborate systems to mitigate the vicissitudes of their environment, including mechanisms to contain dangers posed by both communities to each other. This usually took the form of the hadar's attempts to form a central government that would channel the resources of the settled townsmen and villagers against the nomadic tribes, both for protection against the latter's depredations and to impose hadar rule and collect taxes from the fiercely independent tribes. For the Bedouin, on the other hand, maintaining their tribal independence vis-à-vis other tribes as well as the hadar polities was the sine qua non of a nomadic tribal existence. The balance of power was generally in favor of the mobile and warlike nomads, and central authority was seldom successfully instituted, and when formed never of long duration, until the advent of the modern Saudi state.

It is generally acknowledged that the last and decisive encounter between the two conceptions of political organization, that of hadar central authority and Bedouin tribal independence, took place on the plains of Sbila in central Arabia on March 30, 1929.[7] Subsequently only sporadic skirmishes occurred, and the Bedouin's military, fiscal, judicial, and territorial autonomy was decisively ended. In its place, the idea of one supreme leader (later to be named king), Shari'a law, payment and collection of tax (i.e., zakat or alms tax), and monopoly of the legitimate use of force by the central authority were firmly established.

---

[6] On the Hadar/Bedouin dichotomy, see the useful anthropological work of Sa'd 'Abd Allah al-Suwayyan, *Al Sahra al Arabiya, Thaqafatuha wa Shi'ruha 'abr al 'Usur, Qira'a anthrubulujiyya* (Beirut: Arab Network for Research and Publishing, 2010), 345–402.

[7] For a description of the battle by one participant, see Mohammed Almana, *Arabia Unified: A Portrait of ibn Saud* (London: Huchinson Benham, 1980), 103–11.

INTRODUCTION

Not long after that watershed battle in Sbila, a poet was born (1937).[8] Bandar
bin Srur bin Khdayr al-Qassami al-'Utaybi[9] grew up an orphan in a typical
Bedouin 'Utaybi tribal family in Upper (*'Aliyat*) Najd, in Mahazat al-Sayd, a
large desert in the heart of his tribe's traditional territory. Although he could
read and write, everything in his poetry points to a thoroughly traditional
Bedouin sensibility. It is clear that Bandar was comprehensively schooled
in the traditions and narratives of his tribe, a mastery of which is readily
apparent in his poems. In due course, he had to contend with the limitations
imposed by that life style under the hegemony of the state. Deprived of the
bedrock on which the Bedouin moral order was based, namely raiding, which
became a crime in the new state-centered universe, and constrained by an
omnipotent (and omnipresent) government, tribesmen had few avenues open
to them. Bandar's generation drifted, and some enlisted in the armies of the
new polities that had formed in the region (Jordan, Iraq, Saudi Arabia, Kuwait,
etc.). Serendipitously, and at age fifteen,[10] Bandar bin Srur was granted help
by the government as an orphan to travel to Ta'if for study until he finished

---

[8] According to his older brother Dayf Allah, Bandar was born in the late summer of the year the
    Bedouin named (in the manner of the inhabitants of central Arabia who were mostly illiterate
    and knew little about formal dating) "Riblan," the year of plenty of the grass called *ribla*, i.e.,
    a year of good rains, which corresponds to the year 1937. A copy of his national card indicates
    the year 1360 AH (1940/41), but as people of that generation (and mine) well knew, these dates
    were generally arbitrary. Despite its hagiographic bent, I have found much useful information
    in a four-hour series of interviews with his brother, uncle, cousins, and many of his friends
    broadcast by the satellite station, al-Sahra, and available on the internet at http://www.youtube
    .com/watch?v=vwo2hI2v7_Y.
[9] In addition to the source cited above, biographical information about Bandar bin Srur is based
    on interviews held in the fall of 2007 and summer of 2011 with 'Adhi ibn 'Id al-Ghannami
    al-'Atawi al-'Utaybi. The latter befriended Bandar starting in 1964, when he left his job with the
    Frontier Forces and participated with Bandar in many of his desert adventures. I wish to thank
    'Adhi and his son Khalid for their generous hospitality and willingness to share information
    about Ibn Srur. Some of Bandar's biographical data and adventures are recounted by a friend
    of his, Sultan ibn Mhanna al-Nahawi, in a long interview with an Arabic satellite station,
    al-Amakin, which is available in five parts on the web, at http://www.youtube.com/watch?
    v=bP4wIFElfIE. I have also spoken with Sultan by phone through a mutual friend to confirm
    certain aspects of Bandar's life and poems. Some of the information about his life as well as
    his poems were presented in censored versions.
[10] A childhood friend of Bandar interviewed by al-Sahra television cited above stated that Bandar
    went to Ta'if to attend school in the "Year of the [Solar] Eclipse." I consulted with my father,
    and he confirmed that central Arabia did have a total eclipse in the early 1950s. Relevant NASA
    charts indicate that such an eclipse did indeed occur in central Arabia on February 25, 1952.
    It should be noted that at that time a teenager would be able to receive the equivalent of six
    years of education in three.

sixth grade – quite an achievement for boys of his generation, especially those hailing from a Bedouin background. He served in the military for a year in Ta'if and then enlisted in one of the 'Utayba brigades (*fawj*, the so-called tribal levies) in the National Guard under the command of Shaykh Majid ibn 'Umar ibn Rubay'an. He was stationed in al-Ahsa in eastern Saudi Arabia, where he was appointed a clerk. There, he developed a passion for trucks and was allowed to become a driver by his commander. This new arrangement apparently lasted for three years,[11] and he eventually returned to a life of roaming, adapting to the exigencies of modernity, a modernity that while wreaking havoc on his traditional culture also provided unusual opportunities for those able to adjust. Bandar became an independent truck driver, with the romance of the truck[12] replacing that of the camel, a romance enshrined in a multitude of splendid odes by many poets, including him. Unable to raid, he found his calling in the closest approximation to the heroic past, smuggling and running the gauntlet of armed government forces and the deadly deserts not yet conquered by superhighways and GPS.

But his real love, as gleaned from his poems, was clearly for the by-then defunct Bedouin heroic age, in which violence, especially raiding, was central to a man's sense of virtue. Men lived in constant peril, always on the verge of extinction by natural as well as human forces, and thus reacted by elaborating a system of complex rules to minimize the daily dangers faced. In the maze of this complex Bedouin code, men found space for a path to excellence. Egalitarianism was both believed and practiced, and men felt equal and acted in a classless society where wealth, even if acquired, could not be accumulated for long as it would naturally attract raiders. In addition, "meritocracy"

---

[11] According to al-Ghannami, Bandar spent many years trucking between Kuwait and Saudi Arabia. The police on occasion sought Bandar, but there is no indication whether his infractions were related to smuggling activities or his subversive poems. At least on one occasion, he had to be smuggled out of Saudi Arabia by his friend (Abu Bandar, see below) and eventually moved to the UAE in 1966 or thereabouts. He did not permanently return to Saudi Arabia until around 1977.

[12] The advent of the truck strongly influenced the poetry of the last generation of traditional poets. The truck replaced the camel as mounts carrying the messenger entrusted with the poet's message, which typically occupied the first few verses, with a full description of the truck and its parts replacing those of the camel. Of all trucks, the Ford F-250 and F-350 assumed pride of place; Bandar's occasional references to the Dodge are a reflection of his experience with that vehicle, which was used by the National Guard. Ford trucks ceased to be imported in 1967 when an embargo was imposed by most Arab states, but second-hand Ford vehicles were still available. In the 1970s, Toyota's Land Cruisers replaced the Ford as the preferred desert vehicle. By then, the traditional Nabati *qasida* had undergone dramatic transformations whereby the messenger disappeared and the Toyota is rarely mentioned in any significant odes. Given Bandar's love affair with the Ford, it is ironic that he was driving a Land Cruiser when he died.

was rewarded, and those men brave of heart and talented enough could successfully propel themselves (and their families or even their larger lineages)
into prominence. Although bravery and courage were amply rewarded in both
material and symbolic ways, if the successful warrior was gifted with versifying,
a talent seemingly in abundant supply, he would be the embodiment of excellence in Bedouin society, a "warrior-poet." Bandar recognized that he was a
talented bard, and indeed, in clearly provocative language, he held himself
to be *the* poet of his age[13] and challenged anyone to match his odes. But he
could never meaningfully show or test his "warrior" skills, skills that would
have allowed him to acquire both fame and prestige as well as quench his
thirst for material wealth, which he would have spent in the legendary desert
"occupation" of boundless (nay, reckless) generosity. His considerable talents
and restless spirit combined with a spendthrift[14] proclivity resulted in a hard
material existence that led him to a vagabond's life, feeling deeply alienated
from his environment, a misfit betrayed by a world that had little room for a
man of his sensibilities. It is perhaps no surprise that he should die a lonely,
childless[15] death, asleep next to his truck in Upper Najd in early September
1984. He left, however, a powerful legacy as the preeminent Bedouin critic of
the modern moral order, that of the Saudi state and its nationalist narratives,
as well as its notions of what constituted the moral and the virtuous.

The world against which Bandar rebelled is a place where we all live and
with which we are familiar. But his "lost paradise," constituted of a moral
system in which violence and heroism (both physical and otherwise) reigned
supreme, is gone forever, displaced by a modernity manifested in an all-
powerful state that obliterated all opposing moral, legal, and political claims.
In this modernity, violence is both contained by elaborate codes and yet
freewheeling, shorn of the moral constraints of the Bedouin code. In this new
world, competing for excellence did not take place in the open field of the
desert where Bandar's sensibility would have acquitted him well. Modernity
required men to pursue excellence in different ways and for different ends.
Physical courage has little space in the new order of the nation-state, in which
violence abounds but is organized and mechanized, leaving little room for
traditional warriors. Traditional "hospitality" also retreated despite the surfeit
of resources many modern citizens managed to accumulate. To be successful

---

[13] For example, in one line he states: "I say there are no poets in Najd [other than myself]; and
if there are any, no one has informed me."

[14] His brother, in the interviews cited above, states more than once that Bandar was able to
accumulate and squander much wealth.

[15] According to al-Ghannami, Bandar never married. His brother, on the other hand, indicates
that Bandar married his cousin.

in the modern era, a man had to negotiate his way through the challenges of the bureaucracy and commerce, speak strange tongues, and defer to men one held to be of inferior character. Education and excellence in the classroom and fancy degrees became a currency far superior to Bedouin mores. The hadar were apt to take advantage of the new opportunities more readily than the Bedouin. Although it is debatable as to whether the Bedouin have recently caught up in terms of education and can compete for the rewards of good citizenship, Bandar belonged to that generation that fell in between. He is in a real sense an interstitial or liminal person, caught between the moral and social values and attitudes of two distinct eras. Bandar's generation had a sensibility that was unacceptable to the new order and largely failed to adapt fully to the requirements of modernity. Because of this and because of his wit, he became the critic par excellence.

Bandar, however, is also different from most of his contemporaries. Other poets busied themselves with criticizing aspects of modernity and loss of the older, nobler ways, but clung fiercely to the notion of tribal loyalty that sought to lift their tribe above the others. In contrast, Bandar, while intensely proud of his tribe and convinced of its superiority, devoted much of his criticism of modernity to a condemnation of his *own* tribe, specifically its chiefs, or shaykhs, for their failure to uphold the old values and for succumbing to the new ways. Here we should perhaps say a word about this lost, much-lamented world.

PREMODERN ARABIA: AN OVERVIEW

Geographically, Arabia is described as a huge peninsula over one million square miles in size, with modern-day Saudi Arabia occupying about 80 percent of this mostly arid landmass of vast expanses of sandy deserts. Populations tend to be concentrated in the more hospitable and relatively fertile uplands of the western and southwestern mountains. These igneous mountains, the Arabian Shield, form the watershed of the peninsula and slope gently toward the east and north until the low plains of the Arabian Gulf and the Syrian/Iraqi deserts. In the western area lies the Hijaz, the abode of the holy Islamic places, inhabited by a large hadar population of mixed tribal and nontribal background living in towns and villages and a nomadic population of considerable size. The southeast mountains, the `Asir, are inhabited mostly by settled tribal communities with few if any nomadic components. Both the Hijaz and the southern regions have historically served as incubators of nomadic groups that would regularly erupt and violently move into the Najdi hinterland, in the process causing much disruption and displacement of the nomadic inhabitants of the central region, with ripple effects reaching as far as the Jazira (Upper Mesopotamia) near the borders of Anatolia.

Immediately to the east of the Hijaz mountains is the Najd (plateau), which is geographically divided into western Upper Najd ('Aliyat Najd) and eastern Lower Najd (Safilat Najd). Upper Najd is one of the richest pasturelands in Arabia, and it is here that much of Bedouin history and lore have been made. Most of the hadari towns and villages are located in the Lower Najd.

The Hadar

The hadari communities of Najd lived in scattered villages and small towns, usually in proximity to water, sustaining a subsistence economy. Although income disparities existed, stratification was limited and accumulation of wealth was rare, the latter mostly represented by merchants who engaged in long distance caravan trade. In their social structure, the hadaris maintained their tribal identities. But unlike the Bedouin, such an identity did not take the form of "tribal" organization, and influential families generally ruled towns and villages with no necessary connection between the size of their clan and their ability to rule. Indeed, one of the most striking aspects of Najdi hadari society was its detribalization. This emerged in part because of the constant turnover of the Najdi tribes, where every century or so a new tribal confederation would arise and displace older ones, which, in due course, caused the structure of the Najdi hadar to be so mixed as to render it meaningless in terms of tribal organization. Hadaris also engaged in exogamous practices, coupled with the right of women to inherit – a right that many Muslim communities seem to have breached (such as the tribes of the western and southern areas of Arabia) – which led to an alignment of interests that may not have always coincided with tribal lines. This detribalization and constant failure in political organization, coupled with incessant Bedouin political and military pressures, proved crucial to the subsequent emergence and success of the Wahhabi reform movement and the formation of the Saudi state.

Although town chiefs, or amirs, could collect taxes, they were rarely large enough to sustain an organization beyond the most rudimentary structure of a small retinue, and certainly not a standing army, police force, or any of the panoply of institutions typically associated with successful central governments. Indeed, hadari politics exhibited such divisiveness that in many towns and villages in central Arabia, even neighborhoods would boast of their own amirs and enter into direct competition with other sections of the same town. Succession to rule was more often accomplished through regicide than through peaceful means. This violent, fissiparous tendency in hadari politics was apparent throughout its known history and was not extinguished until the 1930s by the Saudi state.

Socially, the hadar maintained certain tribal features. For example, the notion of a "pure" Arabian genealogy was part of hadari social organization. Typically hadaris trace themselves to one of the "pure," or *asil* Arabian tribes, and intermarried only with families deemed *asil*. Rule in villages, towns, and larger polities was always held by the *asil* groups. The non-*asil* were considered socially inferior, but did not necessarily suffer economically. The non-*asil*, or *khadiri* among other designations, were an amalgam of individuals and groups with no distinct racial, social, or economic background. Thus anyone who immigrated into central Arabia and was not recognized to descend from an *asil* tribe, or those who practiced certain crafts and professions, including smiths, tanners, tailors, butchers, barbers, leather workers, and other handicrafts, were held to be non-*asil*. If an *asil*, due to blood feuds or for any other reason, hid his pedigree and intermarried with non-*asils*, he would be categorized as a non-*asil*, and his progeny would find it difficult to reclaim their *asil* status. Economically, however, this group could boast of powerful interests in premodern Arabia, and many of the successful individuals and families with large wealth hailed from this background. This group also stood to benefit the most from the successful formation of the state, and they were certainly its most ardent supporters. This fact became a real, if unspoken, point of contention in the Bedouin confrontation with modernity.

The Bedouin

The division of the hadari community into *asil* and non-*asil* is a direct replica of Bedouin genealogical structures. But although it is somewhat difficult to understand the rationale for the hadari distinction between *asil* and non-*asil*, this feature is more readily comprehensible in the Bedouin milieu. For "purity" of genealogy is nothing more than a reflection of power relations among the constantly warring, adversarial tribal groups. Once a tribe is defeated and agrees to pay tribute to the more powerful tribe, the notion emerges that this vanquished tribe is paying tribute not because of contingent power relations but because of an eternal defect in its status – that it was created to become a vassal. That one can reasonably trace the histories of the lower status tribes (at least as reasonably as that of the *asil* tribes) and show that they are genealogically no less pure than the *asil* seems to have been irrelevant to the social structure of premodern Arabia. Thus a group called the Hutaym, consisting of five well-known Arabian tribes, became the Bedouin's equivalent of the khadiris among the hadar. The "caste" system is more pronounced with the tribe called the Salab, who were nomads serving as craftsmen, hunters, and guides in the desert. Their low status in the social ranking of the desert Arabs provided them with the unusual advantage of being essentially inviolable in their person and property. No self-respecting Bedouin would dare molest a member of the Salab or rob him of his belongings.

Unlike the hadar communities, the Bedouin of central Arabia suffered from constant flux; a tribe rarely stayed long in any one place. In typical fashion, a tribe would "descend" from the mountains of the Hijaz or the south, compete for pasture in Najd, and displace older tribal formations, which in turn would push north and eastward, dislodging other tribes. Every two centuries or so what used to be a pure Najdi tribe would end up pasturing in the Fertile Crescent. Although tribal waves are difficult to date with any precision, it is nonetheless possible to give a sketch of the tribal landscape over the last few centuries.

Most of the pre-Islamic and early Islamic tribal confederations in Najd have disappeared, with those remaining having been effectively merged into later tribal formations. Thus traces of old tribes and clans are discernable more through guesswork than real evidence. Starting in the fifteenth century CE, we hear of a new confederation, the Bani Lam, that ruled over most of Najd. They were soon challenged by a new emerging tribe, the Zafir, which managed to displace the Bani Lam, who made their way into Iraq. By the eighteenth century, the 'Anaza ascended and extended its hegemony over most of central Arabia, again pushing the Zafir into the northeastern regions. Like its predecessors, 'Anaza's hegemony did not last long and was eventually eclipsed by the Mutayr, with large sections of 'Anaza moving into the Levant. The late eighteenth and early nineteenth centuries saw the emergence of Qahtan as the most powerful tribe in Najd, during the same period as the rise of the Wahhabi movement and the Saudi state, of which the Qahtan was principal ally. By the time of the demise of the first Saudi state in the aftermath of the Ottoman-Egyptian invasion and the destruction of the Saudi capital, Dir'iyya, in 1818, the sources report the intrusion of the 'Utayba tribe into Upper Najd. By the early twentieth century, 'Utayba was the main tribe occupying the choicest lands in central Arabia. The story of the rise of this tribe is illustrative of the Bedouin "cycle" and still deserves scholarly attention, some of which I will provide below.

As typical of Arabian tribes, 'Utayba originated in the highlands of the Hijaz. Its core group, Bani Sa'd, has inhabited the mountains south of Ta'if since pre-Islamic times. The name 'Utayba started cropping up in historical chronicles in the fifteenth century CE, but the tribe remained confined to the Hijaz until the late eighteenth and early nineteenth centuries when the first groups started migrating into Najd.[16] The genealogy of the tribe is problematic because tribal purists insist that all of the clans are related to each other by blood, whereas sufficient evidence exists that, like other Arabian tribes, it is actually composed of varied groups forged more by a process of political/military alliance building than by biological bonds. Indeed, one cannot find an agreed upon "genealogical tree" for the tribe. Hijazi genealogists have their version, which divides the tribe into three sections, which are in turn subdivided into clans and lineages. The Najdi genealogists have a simpler notion made less complicated by the fact that other than the Asa'ida, all the Utayba of Najd were Bedouin. Thus the tribe is divided into two main sections, Barqa and Rawq, the former being more numerous than the latter. Rawq in turn consists of the moieties of Talha and Mizhim, each of which is composed of a number of clans. Mizhim's many clans include the Dhawi Thubayt from which descend the Rubay'an, the paramount chiefs of Rawq, as well as Dhawi 'Atiyya, which in turn is divided into many lineages, including the Qasasima, to which Bandar belongs. From Barqa hails the Humayd family, the main shaykhs of that section, as well as other chiefs of the various Barqa clans. As in most tribes from Najd, there is no acknowledged paramount chief of the whole tribe, and the claims are contested between the Rubay'an and the Humayd.

The rise of this tribe in the politics of Najd can be traced with some accuracy because it is relatively more recent. Thus we see references to actors from 'Utayba in early nineteenth-century chronicles such as the leader of the Saudi-Wahhabi cavalry. We also begin to notice small groups moving into Upper Najd for pasture, perhaps driven by drought or population pressures in their original areas of the Hijaz. By the middle of the nineteenth century, reports about 'Utayba dominate the chronicles as they appear on the scene in great numbers, wresting control over much of the territory from Mecca all the way to Riyadh and its environs. Qahtan, Harb, and Mutayr are displaced from their historical territories, and water wells and pasturelands come under the control of the various 'Utaybi clans until the modern Saudi state decreed the abolition of tribal territories in the middle of the twentieth century.[17]

---

[16] An earlier group, the Asa'ida, migrated from Ruhat (close to Mecca) in the seventeenth century and settled in several Najdi towns. But this migration is not relevant to the tribal politics of that era as the migrants never formed themselves into a nomadic tribe and instead conducted their affairs in the typical hadari fashion in Najd.

[17] In addition to Upper Najd, northern Arabia/southern Syrian and Iraq were the other major theaters of Bedouin politics. These territories were similar to each other ecologically though the northern areas tended to offer the nomads richer pastures and lucrative contacts with the more affluent societies of the Levant. It also exposed them much earlier to the pressures of modernity and the powers of centralized governments. These territories nonetheless present very similar economic and cultural systems. With minor variations, what applied to the Bedouin of inner Arabia is equally valid for the northern tribes.

POETRY AND POETS

It is no exaggeration to say that the history of Najd is to a substantial degree poetic – literally. The little written history that exists about central Arabia after the first Islamic centuries is mostly devoted to the hadari community; the Bedouin and their tribes are hardly mentioned. To overcome this paucity of material on the history of Najd, heavy use is made of the vernacular, or Nabati, poetry, the odes (sing. *qasida*) much beloved and easily memorized and transmitted over the generations. These odes supplement what little is known about the history and culture of the area and its inhabitants, both nomadic and sedentary. This poetry[18] is the direct descendant of the pre-Islamic Arabic tradition[19] with little change beyond the transformation of language from classical Arabic to a vernacular that, although not easily understood by other Arabic speakers, nonetheless maintains the old Arabian linguistic and poetic tradition practically intact. Although many local differences in the dialects of the various regions and tribes existed, a lingua franca of sorts evolved that kept the variations to a minimum and ensured a standard vernacular that allowed for mutual comprehensibility both linguistically and culturally. Indeed, not only were regional linguistic variations not an obstacle, but hadari and Bedouin poetry show little difference in terms of language.

The role of poetry goes much beyond the problematic documentation of historical events. Like ancient Arabic poetry, it is a register of social events as well as a codification of the moral principles and cultural values prevalent in premodern Arabia. It is neither epic nor legendary, but rather topical and lyrical, chiefly composed in response to real events. Poets were not a special class, and much of the society took to composing poetry, although first-class poets were rare. Nabati poetry, like ancient Arabic odes, is predominantly boastful, panegyric, elegiac, and amatory. Both the hadar and the Bedouin produced and consumed this oral literature voraciously. However,

> [t]he most stirring are the compositions of nomadic chiefs and desert knights who employed their poetic skills not to amuse or entertain, but to press for

---

[18] The best study, whose summary is presented here, is Saad Abdullah Sowayan, *Nabati Poetry* (Berkeley: University of California Press, 1985), where a full discussion is to be found, esp. 51–66.

[19] If one Biblical scholar is to be believed, the earliest "Bedouin" *qasida* would be Deborah's Ode. He argues that the ode is "no psalm but a typical nomadic war song imbued with the manly virtues of the desert, and as such sets out to eulogize such desert virtues as bravery on the field of battle and the nobility attaching to the dispensing of hospitality generously and unstintingly at one's hearth and home. . . . What we have here are not the ordinary moral and religious values of the Bible which we know so well, but the manly virtues of the desert." Morris S. Seale, "Deborah's Ode and the Ancient Arabian Qasida," *Journal of Biblical Literature* 81, no. 4 (Dec. 1962): 343–7.

a course of action, to reveal a plan, to declare war, to deliver a threat, to challenge a foe, to sue for peace, to appeal for assistance, to celebrate a victory, to document an honorable deed, or to boast about a chivalrous act. Their verses are records of their heroic adventures and the roles they played in shaping the events of their time.... The language they employed is terse, dignified, and to the point. The appeal of their poetry lies in the fact that it faithfully depicts in a rich language a nomadic existence that was heroic, chivalrous, and free.

In addition to the knights and chiefs, each tribe had a host of poets. Just as heroes unsheathed their swords to deal death blows to the men of enemy tribes, the poets unleashed their tongues with verses that flew like sharp arrows to strike enemy tribes and symbolically conquer them. Tribal poets fought their own battles of words, which were fueled by tribal feuds. The tribal poet drew the material for his compositions from tribal life and his role was to record in verse the honorable deeds of his tribe, to sing its praises, and to defend it against antagonist poets. To perform his task most effectively, the tribal poet had to have a thorough knowledge of tribal history and genealogies. In big assemblies, it was the alert and quick-witted poet who cogently and eloquently argued the case of the tribe.[20]

Although the odes tend to differ depending on the subject – for example, panegyric, lampoon, elegiac, amatory – the typical prelude often begins with an address to a (usually phantom) messenger who is entrusted with the communication of the message the poet is sending to its proper recipient. Also, typically, a number of verses are composed describing the mount, with only the best chosen – a young, barren she-camel, used strictly for the speedy conveyance of messengers and for no other chores.[21] The poet would devote some verses to a description of the road, noting the length it would take to traverse it, and highlighting the landmarks the messenger expects to pass – villages, *wadis*, water wells, hills. The body of the ode would then address the recipient, giving him his due in respect and praise followed by the message itself. Usually the ode would conclude by invoking God's blessing upon His Messenger, Muhammad.

In that vein, the story of 'Utayba's ascent can be viewed through the prism of the various poetic duels that took place between two chiefs, Turki bin Humayd of Barqa and Muhammad bin Hadi of Qahtan (both died in the 1860s), odes that document the sensibilities and values of the heroic age perhaps better than any other source. The story begins with occasional 'Utayba groups coming to pasture in Upper Najd, thus intruding on the tribal territory (*dira*) of Qahtan.

---

[20] Sowayan, *Nabati Poetry*, 51–2.
[21] See, for example, Sowayan, *Nabati Poetry*, 57.

In accordance with the Bedouin code, the newcomers would appear before the chief of Qahtan and offer gifts in the form of one or more Arabian horses, a token of their acknowledgment of his supremacy in this *dira*, and the fact that they enjoy the right to graze their animals at his sufferance. After a few seasons, legends surrounding the odes have it that the shaykh of Qahtan sensed that the newcomers could pose a serious threat to his tribe's hegemony. So in one season, when both Qahtan and 'Utayba were pasturing under a truce that included terms compelling each chief to return any animals seized by his tribesmen to the other party, the chief of 'Utayba fulfilled his obligation and returned "four horses and a fifth one [called] al-Tum." However, a camel owned by an 'Utaybi called Zabn was pilfered by Qahtan and their shaykh declined to return it. This incident thus became a *casus belli*. The stories around the poems become a bit confused: We hear another ode addressed to the chief of Qahtan in which Turki objects to the change in the treatment of 'Utayba such that a symbolic gift is no longer enough. Qahtan's chief retorted that when 'Utayba showed up to pasture, it did so prior to the offering of the gifts, and because of this its tribesmen should return without pasture or pay a "penalty" (*khafara*). This was a request no *asil* tribe could accept. Whatever the chronology, the poems show that these frictions led to major warfare between the two tribes with 'Utayba eventually taking over the water wells of Qahtan as well as associated pasturelands.[22]

THE HEROIC MILIEU

These poetic duels cogently capture the tenor of the times, its intricate codes – chiefly diplomacy, mutual respect, expectations, the notions of the honorable, virtue, and the values that made life bearable in an otherwise harsh environment. For tribal existence was premised on the presumption that tribes and tribesmen lived in a state of war, a Hobbesian world where life was short, nasty, and brutish. Life under such conditions, where all were mutual enemies, where deserts offered very little sustenance and physical mobility was a fundamental requirement for the economic survival of the tribes, led to the emergence of a transtribal code that considerably mitigated the consequences of this permanent state of war. In pre-Islamic times, this code was embodied in the concept of *muru'a*, which the later Bedouin called *marjla*, literally

---

[22] The poems are widely available in popular collections of Nabati poetry. A convenient reference is found in Abu 'Abd al-Rahman ibn 'Aqil, *Diwan al-shi'r bi-lahjat ahl Najd* (Riyadh: Dar al-'Ulum, 1982), 1:115–94, and Muhammad ibn Dakhil al-'Usaymi, *Shu'ara' 'Utayba*, (Dammam: Matabi' al-Mudawkhal, 1995), 2:125–76.

manliness (both etymologically the same as the English virtue). The code was successful because of the unavoidable need for men to live in some sort of peace, to be productive and to counter the harsh circumstances of their ecological niche. It also worked because of deterrence, whereby violators would suffer the consequences of the infringement of the rules both physically, through the sacred institution of vengeance (*thar*), and symbolically through ill repute.

This Bedouin code at its core was a humanist creed, and God, while prevalent in speech, actually played a minor role in Bedouin life. Among the nomads, Islamic rituals were minimally observed, if at all. Shari`a was ignored, and the Bedouin resorted to their own judges, men who inherited their position within the same family for generations. Their judgments tended to bind both their own tribe and other tribesmen who wished to resort to their services. The customary rules (*slum*, sing. *salm*) were faithfully remembered and applied. Precedents – a *stare decisis* of sorts – were critical to the system, and adverse parties were able to win their cases through citation of earlier tribal judges' rulings. The enforcement of these awards was accomplished by nothing more than the force of public opinion. These judges, the `awarif (sing. `arfa), performed their functions successfully even in the shadow of the nation-state in the Middle East, and only in Saudi Arabia were they totally delegitimized as *taghut*, or those who apply laws other than the Shari`a.

The most prized possession of the nomads has always been their camels and their *dira*. Although there were pastoral nomads who herded sheep and goats (cows, on the other hand, were an exclusively hadari business), it is the camel herders who sit at the top of the social and military order, as such beasts offered both a store of wealth and an instrument of war.[23] A Bedouin with a camel herd had to be able to replenish it through raiding and to protect it against other raiding parties. Raiding and counter-raiding became the preeminent occupation of the Bedouin; only the less capable did not partake in this endeavor. But the nomads also recognized that such constant raiding would make life impossible in the desert, and complex rules evolved that allowed raiding to be almost exclusively for the acquisition of wealth (i.e., camels) and not for the purpose of killing. The Bedouin conceived of his enemy in equal terms, and he would find no pride in fighting someone inferior. Thus the Bedouin warrior usually addressed his enemy in the most

---

[23] In the desert, the most critical war instrument was arguably the camel. The horse, while extensively used, could not survive in the harsh, arid environment without the camel. Horses were fed camels' milk as nourishment. When traveling on a raid, a horseman would have his own camel to ride and an extra camel and its cameleer (*zammal*) to carry provisions for the horse, especially water, horses being less able to withstand thirst. The *zammal* performed his functions in return for a share of the booty won by the horseman.

respectful terms, allowed him his due, and always regarded him as a worthy adversary. There is no honor in calling your opponent a coward or many of the sobriquets hurled at the enemies of the modern state. The Bedouin warrior, furthermore, conceived of combat in intensely personal terms, not something to be engaged in anonymously. The true desert knight was not interested in hiding his identity under most circumstances, and he would wear distinctive dress (usually bright red coats) to alert his enemies to his whereabouts during major battles and would accept a duel with the enemy.[24]

Generally, an attack would be preceded by a declaration of war (*radd al-niga* or *al-bara*), sometimes sent in a poem. Women, children, the elderly, and the sick were not to be molested. The more honorable chiefs would not raid water haulers or provision carriers. When actually engaged in warfare, several customs and rules evolved to preclude excessive killing. Somewhat paradoxically, the Bedouin believed very little was worth dying for; hence he had little incentive to fight to the death, and fleeing when the odds were against you was not considered cowardice. Indeed, one of the best epithets is to call someone "the protector of the last fleeing man." It is also perfectly acceptable for someone who is under attack to negotiate his surrender (*man'*) under mutually agreed terms, usually saving his life in return for surrendering his mount and/or weapons. Once a warrior grants *man'*, he was under the obligation to ensure the safety of his captive and to allow him to leave unharmed. Indeed, the "playful" nature of raiding led some observers to consider it nothing more than a bloody sport, and sufficient evidence exists to back up this observation. One story recounts that Muhammad bin Hindi (d. 1915), a chief of 'Utayba, during an engagement with Qahtan warriors was fearful that he would miss the late afternoon prayer and asked for a truce to perform it, which he did with members of the opposing party. Afterwards, he noticed a valiant fighter who impressed him, and upon learning that he was so-and-so of Qahtan, could not help but pray to God that he be saved ("O God, He who saves birds in the sky,

---

[24] In reality, warfare in the desert was not of one type. Major battles (*manakh*) took place between large sections of opposing tribes when engaged in competition over the control of territory and wells. They could last weeks or months, and casualties would be relatively high. It is in these and similar major battles that a young maiden, usually from the chiefly house, would mount her camel, bare her face and hair (and some claim even her breasts), and shout encouragements to her tribesmen to defend her and her camel ('*itfa*). Other major battles usually would involve conflict with hadari rulers and tribesmen. But the majority of violence in the desert was perpetrated by small marauding parties, usually busy in springtime, which went out to plunder livestock. A raiding party would have its own leader ('*agid*) and elaborate rules applied to the division of booty. More resourceful warriors who kept their identity concealed engaged in a type of theft that depended on stealth and steady nerves (*hayif*). They would prowl at night, silence the guard dogs, make their foray into the pen where the animals were kept, and then walk away with one or more camels or horses, all during the dead of the night. If they were caught, they could be killed.

please save this horseman"). Another recurrent event/theme is of the warrior who, on the point of thrusting his lance at a fleeing enemy, pauses to ask his foe, "Do you wish it to hit you or your horse?" The aim of the question is to spare the man's life by killing the horse instead.

The possession of camels provided nomads with wealth, power, land in the form of tribal *dira*, pasture, and this also allowed the Bedouin to extract rents and supplement their meager income. The most lucrative of these *dira*s would be lands straddling major trade or pilgrimage routes, where large caravans would pass through regularly. Any traveler traversing a tribal *dira* was subject to confiscation of property or even death unless he obtained a covenant of safe conduct from the tribe, which could usually be granted by any member of the tribe who would undertake to protect the traveler from attack by his co-tribesmen in return for a tribute, an *akhawa*.[25] This companion, or *khawi* (a name given both to the protector and his ward), would be subject to powerful social condemnation along with his lineage if he failed to protect his *khawi*; granting such protection became one of the paramount virtues and a source of great pride for the nomadic tribesman. For larger caravans, the more powerful chiefs would usually offer protection in return for large amounts of money, which they would presumably share with their kinsmen. For many centuries, the tribes astride the pilgrimage routes received large subventions from the powers of the time, be they Ottoman, Egyptian, or Iraqi. Occasional failures to pay the tribute would lead to bloody attacks by the nomads and the pilfering of the pilgrims' belongings. Control over the *dira* also allowed the tribesmen to control access to water, a commodity without which no desert could be traversed. Once again, rules evolved to allow for the peaceful access to wells, usually controlled at the clan level. When a tribal territory enjoyed more rain than elsewhere, self-interest dictated that that tribe would permit other tribal groups access to its *dira* in return for token gifts. This constituted recognition by the fortunate tribe that one day it might need access to *dira*s of other tribes, such as during a drought. When the tribes congregated in this fashion, a general truce would be observed, disallowing any attacks and outlawing the settling of old scores;[26] warfare could be resumed only ten days after dispersal.

---

[25] This tribute was also imposed on hadari towns and villages. Any settlement within the tribal *dira* would be subject to raiding by this tribe (if its inhabitants were not genealogically related to the dominant tribe) unless the town or village retained its own *khawi*, who, in return for regular payment, would ensure that none of his tribesmen plundered the settlement, and, should one do so, he undertook to return the booty. Larger towns may have been able to defend themselves, but smaller ones had no choice than to pay to avoid constant harassment.

[26] A story describing these arrangements and how tribesmen dealt with conflicts under such conditions can be found in Fahd al-Marik, *Min Shiyam al-'Arab* (Riyadh: Maktabat al-Shiqri, 4th imprint, 2000), 1:61–96. B. Ingham studied the poems made on that occasion, "The Pool of Oaths – A Comparative Study of a Bedouin Historical Poem," in *A Miscellany of*

If a man found himself in a situation where the rules changed and he became or was remembered as an enemy, customary law required that the target be given "three days of flight." Not to grant this, that is, not to allow him to flee where he had a chance to fight, was deemed dishonorable, a stain very few could afford on their record.

Other sacred rules in the desert include the institution of offering refuge to the innocent and the offender alike (*dakhil*). When a man perpetrated a crime, usually homicide, he could seek shelter with a powerful Bedouin warrior, usually from another tribe, who would protect him from his enemies' attacks for at least one year and two months, a period reckoned long enough for passions to cool and for payment of blood money to be arranged and accepted in settlement. This prevalent practice offered renowned warriors and chiefs opportunities to enhance their prestige, and indeed the more powerful would find it insulting if someone with a minor infraction or a weak enemy were to seek their protection; they preferred to dedicate their energies to really challenging affairs as befit their reputations. Truly intricate rules governed this institution in particular, including what is considered the proper residence of the protector. Seeking protection generally succeeded if the fugitive was able to enter the area between the tent and the animal pen before his pursuers caught him.

The "neighbor," *jar*, is likewise another sacred institution that creates mutual obligations for the host and his guest. On numerous occasions intra-tribal, clan, or family disputes or other matters might compel an individual, alone or with family or lineage, to move away from his tribe and stay with another, even an avowed enemy. He would be extended all the protection usually accorded to the host's own tribesmen. Reciprocally, if the tribesmen of the guest were to raid and take away any of the host's belongings, tribal custom obligated the guest to recover it for his host, and failure to do so would impugn the reputation of the former.

The rules directed at the amelioration of this constant state of war are also elaborated toward the protection of "guests" (sing. *dayf*). A guest in the desert is inviolable in his person as well as his property. Thus while traveling, if a Bedouin greets another and the latter offers greetings in return, this constituted an acceptance of a truce between the two while they were in the same place. The tradition of "*milha*," or "sharing salt," requires that sharing food or drink creates mutual obligations for the host and guest alike. If a traveler of the Mutayr tribe drinks milk offered to him by an 'Utaybi, for example, and the

Middle Eastern Articles, ed. A. K. Irvine, R. B. Sergeant, and G. Rex Smith (Harlow, England: Longman, 1988), 40–54.

host is subsequently robbed by a Mutayri tribesman, the Mutayri *dayf* must make his host whole and recover his property. The duration of this protection depends on the food or drink consumed by the guest. If it is milk, it is accepted that the obligations extend for a full twenty-four hours; if it is a meal, it will last for the period it takes to have two meals; and if meat was eaten, protection lasts for seven days, on the theory that it would take this long for the body to digest the food and drink. The protection is reciprocal; both the host and the guest are obligated to make the other whole in case one is robbed by the other's tribesmen. In another practice, a tribesman may offer his protection through imparting his lineage brand on the walking stick of his guest; violation of such protections usually engenders dangerous consequences, with hands or noses of the co-tribal offenders being cut off in retribution and to restore the full honor of the protector.[27]

Moreover, the tradition of hosting in the desert is one of the most remarkable institutions in premodern Arabia, with both the hadar and the Bedouin. A reputation of generosity and hospitality was something greatly cherished, and those who showed such qualities enjoyed extraordinary social prestige, with odes composed in their honor traveling far and wide – transmitted and recited to this day. In fact, certain conceptions and practices of generosity border on the incomprehensible. Abd al-Karim al-Jarba, of the Shammar in Iraq, was nicknamed *Abu khudhah*, or "father of take it [it is yours]," and he was renowned for never saying no to any request. Turki bin Muhayd, of the Fid`an of the `Anaza of Syria, was called *msawwit b'l-`asha*, "he who cries out 'come for dinner'." This was because he would regularly send his servants to the surrounding hills at dinnertime, crying at the top of their lungs that food was being served just in case there was anyone in the neighborhood. A Bedouin is reputed to have heard the howls of a wolf, and upon discovering that it was old and could not feed for fear of the dogs, he slaughtered a sheep and left it for the wolf to feast on. Hadaris also practiced hospitality with equal abandon.

Essential to the rules of hospitality both in the desert and the sown had been the permanently lit hearth. Although meals required special preparations and animals would be slaughtered at the arrival of guests, whether known or not (although the host had to judge the worth of his visitors and accord them the

---

[27] There is no published reference for these desert rules. See Alois Musil, *The Manners and Customs of the Rwala Bedouin* (American Geographical Society, 1928), esp. 438–641; Sa`d `Abd Allah al-Suwayyan, *al-Sahra' al-`Arabiyya: thaqafatuha wa shi`ruha `abr al-`usur, qira'a anthrubulujiyya* (Beirut: al-Shabaka al-`Arabiyya li-l-Abhath wa al-Nashr, 2010), 655–797 and references therein. For the reader familiar with the Arabian vernacular, much of the Bedouin code is found among the numerous stories in Sa`d `Abd Allah al-Suwayyan, *Ayyam al-`Arab al-Awakhir* (Beirut: al-Shabaka al-`Arabiyya li-l-Abhath wa al-Nashr, 2010).

appropriate level of hospitality), truly hospitable men always had coffee ready, day or night. Competition was fierce to acquire the reputation for renowned hospitality, a virtue as coveted as bravery. Thus when Dghayyim al-Zalmawi (d. circa 1906), a Bedouin in north Arabia, composed what became the classic hospitality ode,[28] legend has it that the ruler at the time, Muhammad ibn Rashid of Ha'il, became so jealous that he decided to verify the claims himself. Ibn Rashid arrived at midnight to find the hearth ablaze and coffee pots full and ready. Prudently, the poet composed an apologetic poem full of praise for the amir!

FORMATION OF THE STATE AND THE END OF
THE BEDOUIN ERA

The political chaos that characterized much of modern Najdi history was a major factor in the birth of the puritanical religious reform movement, known as Wahhabism, in the middle of the eighteenth century. The tenets of this movement were theologically simple – a return to the original Islamic beliefs, shorn of the prohibited innovations, accretions, and syncretism of the later Islamic centuries. Wahhabism's founders opined that "polytheism" was rampant in Arabia among both the hadar and the Bedouin, with the latter receiving harsher condemnation (some did not even believe in the essential tenet of the resurrection). The reformers launched a campaign to cleanse the land of errant beliefs while simultaneously using the hadar as their power base under the leadership of the House of Saud (not even the largest of the myriad of rulers in central Arabia at the time). They fought to unify the various towns and regions as well as compel the Bedouin under one unified political leadership. The Wahhabis outlawed raiding, imposed and collected the *zakat* in the desert and sown, attacked tribal judges and appointed Shari'a-trained ulama to adjudicate disputes, and imposed an era of order and security throughout the land not seen since the early Islamic centuries. Their zealotry and inexperience in international affairs led them to commit fatal mistakes, eventually forcing the major Islamic power of the period, the Ottoman Empire, to delegate the task of destroying the new Wahhabi-Saudi state to its Egyptian vassal and to bring the holy Islamic cities of Mecca and Medina back under

---

[28] This poem is well known. For an English translation see Alois Musil, *The Manners and Customs of the Rwala Bedouin* (American Geographical Society, 1928), 68–9; for a short study of the poem see Semha Alwaya, "Formulas and Themes in Contemporary Bedouin Oral Poetry," *Journal of Arabic Literature* 8 (1977): 48–76. It has also inspired many poets to emulate it (the classical *mu'arada*). For the text of the poem and two imitative odes see Humud al-Nafi', *Shu'ara' min al-Zilfi*, 1:194–6 (Riyadh: Matabi' al-Nahda, n.d.).

the control of Istanbul. The invaders struck alliances and bribed local forces, both settled and nomadic, and the nascent state was duly crushed by 1818. Bedouin Arabia reverted to its merry old ways for one more century despite the repeated attempts of the Saudi and other rulers to impose a semblance of order in the country.

Until the rise of Wahhabism, the Bedouin order remained unchanged from pre-Islamic times. The eighteenth century, however, witnessed two developments that would prove fatal to the continuity of traditional tribalism with its associated customs, practices and institutions, and overall ethos. The ideological war launched by the Wahhabi ulama continued actively for more than two centuries and sought (eventually successfully) to undermine the nomadic order by imposing Islamic concepts, beliefs and practices, largely antithetical to traditional nomadism, especially the proscriptions of raiding, theft of cattle, and vengeance. The latter, for example, was premised on the notion that the aggrieved party may kill the killer or *any* of his male relatives, up to the perpetrator's great-grandfather and his descendants, a notion rejected in Islamic practice, which holds that crime is the personal responsibility of the culprit. In due course, the Bedouin began to observe Islamic rituals, especially prayer, and ultimately many of their chiefs conceded that it was "dishonorable" to raid the hadar, and thus confined their raiding to other nomads only. Coupled with these campaigns to impose Islamic beliefs and rituals on the Bedouin was the equally aggressive drive to establish a unified state with one ruling family over both the nomads and the hadar, which included by the twentieth century strong efforts to settle the nomads and engage them in agricultural activity. The Wahhabi campaigns were ultimately successful with the formation of the modern Saudi state in the early twentieth century.

The other development that impinged on Bedouin life has been technological. Although the impact on the nomadic order was very slow to materialize until the middle of the twentieth century, the disruptive effects of technology were being felt even before, especially by the northern tribes. Modern weapons, the telegraph, the steamship, the railroad – all helped shift the balance of power from the martial nomads to central governments. One particular invention may have contributed most to a slow transformation of the Bedouin system of values and practices – firearms.[29] Whereas the nomads acquired various types of guns quite late in the day, a sufficient number was available to

---

[29] For a historical review of the introduction of firearms among the Bedouin, see Benjamin Adam Saidel, "Matchlocks, Flintlocks, and Saltpetre: The Chronological Implications for the Use of Matchlock Muskets among Ottoman-Period Bedouin in the Southern Levant," *International Journal of Historical Archaeology* 4, no. 3 (2000): 191–216.

them to produce the marksman (*bwardi*) as a new category of desert warrior. Slowly, firearms allowed for impersonal warfare, where even a coward could anonymously kill the bravest of the brave, as happened frequently enough during the nineteenth and twentieth centuries. It may have also led to a rise in casualties in Bedouin raids, which further contributed to the disruption of the traditional order. Indeed, many chiefs pointedly refused to carry firearms, considering them to be fit only for cowards. Thus, when an 'Utaybi chief (variously reported to be Muhammad bin Hindi or Mnahi al-Haydal) was presented with a Martini-Henry rifle, he tried it; unimpressed, he composed the following ditty rejecting the new invention and reasserting the old values:

> There is nothing manly in shooting Mawarit [i.e., Martini-Henry rifles]; It is a shot by a fleet-of-foot, thrusting it from far away,
>
> For me, it is holding her [i.e., the horse's] reins and head; And God may do what he will,
>
> I want the one [i.e., horse], swift in maneuver; For life must expire anyway.[30]

The rise of the modern state in Arabia rendered traditional Bedouin life simply impossible. Ideologically, the new state imposed Islamic law and outlawed many of the institutions that underpinned the nomadic political and moral order, especially raiding, without which no meaningful "Bedouinism" could exist. If the extinction of the buffalo was the main culprit in the collapse of the moral order that sustained the lives of some Native Americans,[31] it is equally valid to assert that the "disappearance" of raiding rendered Bedouin life meaningless: Bedouin history simply came to an end. In addition to outlawing raiding, *akhawa* disappeared as an independent source of income, and instead government subventions for some chiefs and tribal activities were dispensed according to rules beneficial to the state, and mostly directed toward curbing tribal autonomy. To compound the losses, the *dira*[32] as an exclusive tribal territory was abolished by the 1950s, and animals could graze anywhere without fear or need to pay[33] (incidentally contributing to the ecological destruction of pasturelands).

[30] Khayr al-Din al-Zirikli, *Ma Ra'ayt wa ma sami't*, ed. 'Abd al-Razzaq Kamal (Maktabat al-Ma'arif, Ta'if, n.d.), 203.

[31] See Jonathan Lear, *Radical Hope: Ethics in the Face of Cultural Devastation* (Cambridge, MA: Harvard University Press, 2006).

[32] An earlier attempt by the state to outlaw exclusive control over wells in the desert was aborted after countless feuds erupted.

[33] On the other hand, the *hima*, or exclusive pasturelands surrounding towns and villages, remained legally protected on the basis that settlements needed to graze their animals nearby without competition from the nomads who were mobile and could therefore move elsewhere.

The discovery of oil was a singular event in the transformation of the relationship between the state and citizen, especially the nomads. With rents accruing to the public treasury independent of taxation and unrelated to overall economic productivity, the state acquired a degree of autonomy from its own society unmatched in modern history. And with the rise of modern economic sectors, traditional pastoralism and animal husbandry became less competitive activities and poverty befell the nomads, unlike the urbanite hadar who had skills better suited for the modern economy.

The state has been cognizant of its Bedouin "problem" and sought ways to cushion the collapse of the nomadic order. One institution developed in part for that purpose has been the National Guard, which tribes and tribesmen could join as either full-time or reserve soldiers, a nod to the centrality of the martial ethos to the nomads. Major clan shaykhs would command their own brigades (*fawj*) in which their clansmen would enlist and receive regular stipends for their services. Although most of the major nomadic tribes in Saudi Arabia formed their own brigades, none could form more than three, except for `Utayba, which boasts eight brigades. One of the Rubay`an commanders in the National Guard became a patron of the poet Bandar and helped save him from many difficulties, both financial and with the authorities, and would therefore occupy an honorable position in the poet's odes.

However, even the National Guard was ultimately run by hadari officers and civilians, and the Bedouin role was greatly curtailed. To make matters worse from the nomad perspective, the *khadiris* would be allowed to form their own brigade on an equal footing with the *asil* tribes (they are the only hadar with their own military units within the National Guard). This inversion of the historical relationship between the hadar and the Bedouin would not pass unnoticed and led to resentment. For, historically, the Bedouin and the hadar always held to mixed views of each other. While a symbiosis evolved between the two communities allowing for peaceful coexistence and for noncoercive economic exchange, the fact remained that as individuals the Bedouin were always in a militarily superior position vis-à-vis the hadar, the latter being held in contempt by the former for their failure to engage in raiding and for "hiding" behind the walls of their towns.[34] Equally, the hadar, while respectful of the centrality of courage in the nomads' ethos, regarded them in mostly unflattering terms. The following is a poem that faithfully illustrates these attitudes, composed by the `Utaybi hadari poet

---

[34] For a classic story, probably from the seventeenth century, that is still being told on this score in which the hadari villager bests his Bedouin friends, along with a translation of the poem composed by the hadari on that occasion, see Sowayan, *Nabati Poetry*, 22–3.

from the Hijaz Bdaywi al-Waqdani (d. 1879) and addressed to his son, `Abd al-`Aziz, when he saw him being too friendly with the Bedouin:

1. `Abd al-`Aziz, the lion, predator of the bush; Young man, what on earth got you involved with the Bedouin,
2. How foolish is the man who seeks benefits from the Bedouin; For the Bedouin shall rob you of anything you have,
3. Abandon the Bedouin, may they be gone; For their ways are different from your ways,
4. Be careful and do not go alone lest they rob you; And do not travel with them as they will obliterate your provisions,
5. Upon meals they are like wolves; Over food their paws displace yours,
6. The rooster, even if it calls for prayer [i.e., crows], is still ritually unclean; And the dog cannot be trusted even if it is your friend,
7. Their man loves praise; If you hear him sometimes he would impress you,
8. But if you mention the Prophet and his Companions; Not one of them would invoke blessings upon them,
9. He does not respect or appreciate you; And if you speak, the least of them would call you a liar.[35]

It is in this landscape, where old ways disappeared and the measure of men was transformed under the overbearing direction of the modern state, that Bandar grew up and against which he rebelled.

BANDAR BIN SRUR: THE REBEL-POET

No standard collection of Bandar's poetry exists,[36] in part because of the issues he chose to address and the viciousness with which he composed some of his verses (including occasionally the scatological). But a collection recorded in his own voice is widely available, including on the internet. His subjects are those covered by most Arabian Nabati poets, such as amatory poems that show good command of the craft but hardly passionate feelings, employing generic

---

35 al-`Usaymi, *Shu`ara `Utayba*, 1:63–4.
36 I was able to obtain a number of cassette tapes with most of his poems recorded in his own voice as confirmed by al-Ghannami. The tapes are of poor quality with many gaps, perhaps due to the reluctance of the original owners to share all of his subversive poems. In addition, I have consulted written collections, some published and others owned privately, but they were less useful than the tapes. Many of the poems and his recordings are also widely available online. I am grateful to `Abd Allah ibn Bjad al-`Utaybi for providing me with a number of these tapes.

female names that did not seem to correspond to real persons. He passed through the obligatory religious phase, where he authored a number of poems pietistic in nature, again not very stirring. He shows superior skills, however, in his (uncharacteristically sycophantic) panegyric odes, several of which exist, devoted to the late Shaykh Zayid ibn Nahayyan, the late ruler of Abu Dhabi and president of the United Arab Emirates. Although impressive, he clearly composed them in pursuit of material gain, expecting royal largesse in return for the shameless praise and for which he was presumably well rewarded.[37] His need to seek rewards in this fashion left an indelible mark and was reflected in his other more passionate odes.

By contrast, the panegyrics devoted to Bandar's patron, Turki ibn Fayhan ibn Rubay'an, a major Utaybi chief and commander in the National Guard, are not only artistically beautiful but do convey genuine feelings of affection and respect. It is said that this shaykh assisted Bandar during many difficulties, mostly due to his smuggling activity and constant need for money. For Bandar seems to have been unable to settle down and keep a regular job. Most reports show a man on the move, driving a truck and engaging in smuggling of unspecified contraband (mostly tobacco, which was "banned" until the late 1960s, and even after lifting the ban attracted high duties). Smuggling in the 1950s and 1960s was an activity available to any enterprising individual familiar with the desert and its treacherous ways, and both hadar and Bedouin took to this trade with much gusto. The moral ambiguity regarding the legal status of paying custom duties – about which the ulama held simultaneously

---

[37] It is noteworthy that as far as can be determined, he never authored any poems praising members of the Saudi royal family except for King 'Abd al-'Aziz, whom he seems to have genuinely admired. He had openly told al-Ghannami that "I do not praise these Royals but 'Abd al-'Aziz fully deserves praise." Indeed, other than King 'Abd al-'Aziz, the closest reference to Saudi royalty that I was able to find is a negative one addressed to the late Muhammad al-Sudayri, a maternal uncle of the late King Fahd and his full siblings, a governor of the northern province, and a ranking poet in his own right. Through his 'Utaybi friend, Fayhan, Bandar was invited after his return from the UAE to meet al-Sudayri, who reportedly commented after the meeting that "it was better to hear of him than to meet him." Sensing his mistake, al-Sudayri feared that Bandar "would cause him a scandal among Rawq," the main branch of 'Utayba to which Bandar belonged. Upon hearing the comment, Bandar indeed composed three verses, mocking Rawq, al-Sudayri, Fayhan, and a Rawq chieftain to boot:

> Two shits to Rawq, and one shit to Fayhan; and ninety, tightly packed shits to al-Sudayri,
> If you are burdened, oh Muhammad [al-Sudayri], by the presence of guests; I carry your burden eighty times over,

At this point in his extemporaneous composition Kwaytan al-Did, a man of chiefly background, interjected to stop him, and he lambasted him with further scatological references:

> And you, Kwaytan, you belong in the midst; for you neither bring benefit nor cause harm.

that collecting such duties from Muslims was illegitimate and disobeying the command of the leader of the community (i.e., the king) was equally illegitimate – helped many adventurous spirits (and those inclined to quick gains) to enlist in this "trade." But enterprising as he may have been, Bandar still failed to acquire the material security he sought, and his poems reflect a man in dire financial straits.[38] One of his odes is addressed to the chief's daughter when he heard her shouting to her father that "his unstable friend" (*marjuj*) (i.e., Bandar) was at the door. This ode is full of complaints about bad luck and misfortune but generous with praise for this patron.

He also became enthusiastically engaged in intratribal lampooning, again defending the Rubay`an chiefs against what he considered worthless would-be `Utaybi shaykhs. His lampoons were both powerful and vicious, with the target called many epithets, including the derogatory (in *asil* culture) "son of meat butchers." He was alternatively reminded that he hailed from a family of small adventurers whose best exploits were to steal a camel, as opposed to the Rubay`ans who led tribal armies in major showdowns with other tribes as well as rulers, taking care to enumerate the battles they led.[39]

Whatever the occasion for his poems, Bandar rarely fails to lament his bad luck and boast about his superior morals and character. Combining intense personal pride with a clearly wounded spirit, his verses show a man experiencing many trials and tribulations and generally mistrustful of life. He would invoke his ancestry and tribe in the most immodest terms, even going so far back as to remind listeners that a woman of his tribe was the Prophet's wet nurse. He would repeatedly stress that he was an exceptional man, not lowly or worthless. He reminds his listeners of his extraordinary poetic skills, only to return to complaints about his misfortunes. The nature of these misfortunes is unclear, but, as alluded to above, he was a spendthrift; no matter what amount of money came his way, he still managed to waste it and remain in constant need.[40]

---

[38] He was jailed more than once, and it was the Rubay`an chief who regularly bailed him out, but his imprisonment was denied by his friend al-Ghannami. Al-Nahawi, however, confirms that he was jailed on more than one occasion due to his smuggling activities.

[39] It is remarkable that for such a cantankerous man, I have been able to find only one poem in which he was critical of another tribe (Harb) as opposed to his own.

[40] If rumors are to be believed, his misery was due in part to "substance abuse," i.e., the tragic affliction of many Saudis who habitually use certain stimulant pills (Captagon). This was originally introduced by truck drivers who used it to keep awake in order to meet delivery deadlines. According to al-Ghannami, when Bandar returned from the UAE around 1977, he was clearly a "changed" man, different from the man he knew before. Bandar continued to visit him in his house in Riyadh until about 1980 when he last saw him. Al-Ghannami stated that he was not aware of any such abuse.

But his best odes are those devoted to his resentment of the new state-sanctioned order and morality. In language reminiscent of the best Nabati poetry produced in the Bedouin milieu, Bandar composed odes that kept faith with the original style of the poetry and content of a bygone age. But it is also true that Bandar uses certain modern references, such as to Lipton tea (instead of the traditional coffee), and we may catch the occasional contemporary slang word or note a reference to modern institutions (e.g. high school) or inventions such as the telephone. Nonetheless, his style was traditional, and with the exception of one *qasida*, all his messengers employed trucks, with the camel as means of transport disappearing forever. The physical description of the famous mounts of old was replaced by inventive depictions of the modern truck, with Ford and Dodge occupying the pride of place.

His most famous poems are two, one dedicated to the critique of his own tribe and what became of its chiefs, and the other devoted to venting his resentment and disapproval of the modern Saudi order based on oil rents. I have been unable to ascertain the occasion of the first poem, which is addressed in the typical Nabati fashion to a companion[41] whom he tells to get ready to convey his message by ensuring that the truck is set to cross the desert wastes with all deliberate speed. He is sending his poem to his friend Abu Bandar,[42] who is praised as a man who spares no expense to honor his guests. The poet complains about the change in circumstances by condemning the 'Utayba shaykhs as worthless, salaried retainers of the state, with no power and no prestige – counterfeit chiefs. His yearning for the older days of the true 'Utayba chiefs, ancestors of the current illegitimate ones, comes through clearly in the seventh through ninth verses, a nostalgia for an order where tribes were independent and could determine their destiny through their own military prowess.[43] Instead, Bandar found himself seeking patronage from the

---

[41] Mnir al-Dalbihi al-'Utaybi is a friend and fellow truck driver who met the same fate as Bandar a few years later. He was found dead next to his truck in Upper Najd, a fate he eerily foretold to al-Ghannami not long before his death.

[42] This is 'Abd al-Muhsin ibn Hasan al-Shu'ayfi al-'Usaymi al-'Utaybi whose family had been settled in al-Ahsa, in eastern Saudi Arabia, for a few generations. He was a close friend of Bandar to the point that he apparently named his eldest son after him, hence his teknonym (*kunya*) Abu Bandar. He was always helpful to Bandar and on at least one occasion smuggled him to Qatar to avoid arrest, a prospect variously attributed to his smuggling activities and subversive poems.

[43] His pride may have been historically inaccurate. 'Utayba did resist payment of tax to polities, especially the nineteenth-century Rashidi rulers. It nonetheless had its share of accommodations with the rulers of various periods and regions. Although Turki ibn Humayd always insisted that his tribe was independent of the surrounding polities, his contemporary Bdaywi al-Waqdani found pride in a panegyric ode dedicated to the Sharif ruler of the Hijaz. This ode contains the lines "We are the rulers' stick from the days of our ancient ancestors; We are

ruler of Abu Dhabi, referring obliquely to a UAE tribe (Manasir) in less than complimentary terms. Bandar resented having to do this:

1 O Mnir, take the Ford [truck] and collect the invoices; Take it to the repair garage and have it checked,

2 Make sure gasoline pipes are clear; And for ignition, make sure the spark plugs are working,

3 When it is ready to steal distances with speed; Such speed as that of the peregrine chasing the bustard chick,

4 Take it to him who is oblivious to expenses; He who erects poles for the slaughtering of lambs for his guests,

5 Tell Abu Bandar that our times have changed; For the rainy clouds have been replaced by sandstorms,

6 The shaykhs of his tribe, `Utayba, are worthless; For a salaried shaykh is not a legitimate shaykh,

7 Our times yearn for the swords that nailed their hegemony over Najd tightly; Tightly as the nailing of ivory to teak planks,

8 They chased Ibn Hadi [chief of the Qahtan tribe] beyond [Mount] al-Nir; And Mihsin al-Firm [chief of the Harb tribe] they expelled beyond Swaj [Mountain],

9 A people, O Mnir, who firmly held their ground in the midst of warring tribes; And refused to pay tribute to the tax collector,

10 Today we come to Najd like shepherds searching for lost cattle; We discharge our business and scurry away,

11 We move aimlessly and want to be part of the Manasir [a tribe of Abu Dhabi]; And walk the land without interest in anything.

12 When will some changes take place in Najd;
    So that patient men may be relieved?[44]

13 The Shaykhs of Najd, who used to shake large armies;
    Now, seeds are thrown to them like for chicken][45]

`Utayba, the weapon of kings." Most likely Bandar would have dismissed him as a hadari, even if what he said was correct on certain occasions.

44 In a similar vein, he composed another poem, addressed to the same Abu Bandar, and dispatched with the same Mnir, but this time on a Boeing jet, where he laments his luck, declares his superiority, condemns the age and the character of its men, but saves the most biting words for the chiefs of `Utayba when he says: "His [Abu Bandar's] people, `Utayba, boasts of numb shaykhs; vultures hovering above looking to scavenge."

45 This verse does not exist in any the recordings I reviewed but it is widely quoted. Bandar's friend, al-Nahawi, confirmed to me that the verse is authentic. It should be noted that one of his friends, in the third installment broadcasted by al-Sahra television, states that Bandar sought the intercession of a Saudi prince with King Faysal, insisting that while he composed some of the objectionable verses, "some were forged" and not authored by him.

And the second seminal poem:

1 O, Mhammad, my mood has been disturbed and I turned away;[46] He who turns far away will have fewer worries,

2 I, Bandar, am not a worthless son of a worthless man; A worthless man polite with a bunch of people who dislike him,

3 Because my ample experience, and my goings and comings taught me that; greeting someone who does not respect you is an insult,

4 Curse the Christian who discovered oil; Would that the gushing of oil blind his eyes,

5 Were it not for that, only tough men would attain manly virtues; Virtues that require merits lowly men do not have,

6 The resolute's will to traverse desolate expanses; That the offspring of the [lowly] owls cannot cross,

7 Of all virtues, I have chosen three; For the rest, all humanity are able to accomplish,

8 I wish for no reward except from God; For whoever honors them should not expect to be rewarded by people.

Although the occasion for this poem is obscure, one legend speaks of Bandar appearing for some business at the offices of the oil company Aramco when he ran into someone he knew, perhaps a *khadiri*, or even the son of a manumitted slave of the chiefs of a certain clan of 'Utayba. As the story goes, this employee apparently offended Bandar, hence the poem.[47] Whatever the circumstances, this short poem best embodies the attitude of some social groups of Bandar's generation among the Bedouin who saw their prestige decline relative to the hadar and felt that they were unable to partake in the modern economy as successfully as the urbanites. The first hemistich of the fourth verse is already a classic; it encapsulates a powerful (if simplistic) conviction that were it not for oil, brought about by the West and its know-how (hence the Christians), power, economic, and social relations would have evolved in a different direction. Although there is perhaps some truth to such a claim, it is farfetched to assert that the old ways could have been preserved, because the overwhelming power of modernity and the state as its main agent in Arabia were destined to crush the old order. Bandar's unsustainable position, as reflected in this poem, is

[46] In another recording, this hemistich is changed where the name of the person is removed. It reads: "I am the one who suffered calamities and turned away." It is unclear why it was deleted, but perhaps this person (whose identity I could not ascertain) was real and Bandar had later deleted his name after a falling out.

[47] Al-Ghannami is not aware of this story. He believes Bandar composed the poem in response to the superiority displayed by some Aramco employees toward him, not a specific individual.

clearly evident in verses six and seven. The virtues and values he espouses
are irrelevant to the modern era. The belief that manliness was tested in the
crossing of desert wastes was certainly valid for most of Arabia's history, but
with modern transport (and certainly with today's highways and the advent of
GPS), even the most effete men can accomplish the feat with ease. That the
poet still believed the three "values" or "virtues" to be paramount is a clear
indication of the extent of his disorientation and disenchantment.

The three virtues Bandar refers to are what have traditionally been called
the "Three Whites"[48] (*al-thalath al-bid*), white indicating a positive value. The
Three Whites are the virtues we have already mentioned in the old order, the
"neighbor" (*jar*), "guest" (*dayf*), and "companion" (*khawi*). How can one be
faithful to such values in modern society? No visiting guest dares show up
uninvited or at least without an advance phone call. In our urban setting, the
idea of anonymous visitors showing up on the doorstep uninvited is simply
incomprehensible. Likewise, the notion of *jar* is radically different today; your
neighbor is merely the person who inhabits the house next door and no other
criteria apply. Although respect for the *jar* is enshrined in Islamic morality, this
embodies none of the connotations and expectations of the Bedouin culture
of protection. The same disjunction is more evident still with the institution
of the *khawi*, a complex arrangement where the Bedouin imposed tribute
on hadari towns and villages, caravans, and individual travelers in return for
protection from their own tribesmen. Private protection was one of the first
functions that was eradicated or "nationalized" by the modern state.

All of these virtues are based on certain conceptions of power and structures
of a political and moral order for which Bandar longed. In the universe he
longed for, even the opportunity to feed one's guests was dependent on one's
ability to raid and acquire from others the wealth and animals to slaughter.
Ultimately what the poet hoped for was a halt to modernity and the preservation
of the old order. He was able to grasp and enjoy certain manifestations of
modernity, mostly as reflected in the automobile and the mobility it afforded.
He variously attributed this invention to the "Christian," the "Jew," "beer
drinkers," or even the White House. Bandar, however, failed (or refused) to
grasp the irreversible nature of our condition and the final death of the old
order he so clearly cherished. The poet's early death was perhaps the strongest

---

[48] Countless poems refer to these three values, the most famous is the following: "Let it be known
that the *jar*, *khawi* and *dayf* are like religious rituals, both obligatory and supererogatory." Musil
in *The Manners and Customs of the Rwala Bedouin*, 466, has a longer version of this poem.
For a summary of the importance of these values, see al-Zirikli, *Ma Ra'ayt*, 199–200; 'Abd
'Allah ibn Bulayhid, *Sahih al-akhbar 'amma fi bilad al-'Arab min al-athar* (third impression,
n.p., 1979), 5:192.

message of his rejection of a world he did not appreciate and did not wish to live in longer than necessary.

Bandar's critique is not simply confined to harking back to a bygone age. He was astute enough to recognize that other forms of "injustice" were present in the modern state, such as those associated with the uneven distribution of resources. On this matter, however, he opted to use cryptic language, averting the frontal attack he usually employs. Thus in an ode of several verses, in which he complains about the deficient character of many of his contemporaries and proudly proclaims his own superiority, he poses, in forceful, metaphorical language, the following question:

1 I ask you who do all things well; You read the Book [i.e., Qur'an], and perform daily prayers to your God,

2 What is the [worth of the] well that is gushing with water; Whose plants do not enjoy the benefit of its water and whose irrigation ditches are dry,

3 Do name the cause, please do, you who know about it; Do name the cause, you who know it, before I do.

These three verses are generally recognized to be a critique of the injustice of the state, which, despite its plentiful resources, has failed to distribute to the deserving, presumably including Bandar and his tribe.

CONCLUSION

Today, the tribal ethos is gone, and the emasculation of the traditional Bedouin tribe is complete. In late October 2007, 'Utayba held a one-week "Camel Pageant" festival in the desert within its traditional territory in Upper Najd. The tribe was able to obtain the necessary government permits in emulation of earlier pageants held by other tribes. The scene was truly impressive: huge tent pavilions, costing millions of riyals, were erected on the sandy plains of al-Sirr. Yet, when we drove through, we were simply unable to identify who was who among the participants. Although pavilion size may have been indicative of the importance of the shaykh (more likely a reflection of his wealth or that of someone in his clan), no other indication allowed a determination of his identity or that of the clan. As it turned out, the attempts to identify the shaykhs by plaques and signs had engendered strong conflicts, as the chiefs clashed over claims of who were the real shaykhs of the various clans. Living in the modern state, the shaykhs were told that they must accept anonymous numerals as identifiers over their pavilions, nothing more. On TV, the shaykhs looked, behaved, and spoke as typical hadaris, with very few traces left in their diction of their historically distinct dialects. If it were not for the names, invoking a magnificent warrior past, these men would hold no particular distinction. In the presence of the symbols of the state, the modern 'Utaybi shaykhs behaved in typical hadari fashion, fawning publicly over the good graces of the state and its representative, both royal and commoner. This was a scene Bandar would have found both painful and abhorrent. To add insult to injury and in a sign of the total emasculation of the traditional tribe, the state dictated that a hadari 'Utaybi from the old Asa'ida clan be made the chairman of the organizing committee because of the endless and unresolvable competition among the chiefs. Moreover, when the tally of contributors was published in the local newspapers, it was the merchants who had made the event possible.

Ironically and concomitant with the festival, a poem was widely disseminated and hugely admired for its aesthetic beauty. The poem was composed by one Fayhan al-Raqqas, an 'Utaybi tribesman, in the twilight of the Bedouin era, sometime before 1930. Although his poem is boastful and invokes the traditional virtues befitting an illustrious tribe, it avoids belittling other tribes and makes no mention of the state. That it was sung using a traditional musical instrument, the *rababa*, by a well-known "singer" and was easily available online or on cassette tapes only helped promote its popularity. The poem, however, uses the old bloody, warrior language that is utterly incomprehensible to the overwhelming majority of listeners and reciters alike.

In the world of the nation-state, the oddity of tribesmen invoking the poem's images of warfare, when now all enemies have become fellow citizens, underscores that the tribal ethos is devoid of content. This is further testimony of the collapse of the traditional notions of the "tribe" and its transformation into a genealogical holdover shorn of its historical and political relevance. Bedouin-origin shaykhs and their followers today are no better than the historical hadar, a fate much lamented by Bandar bin Srur. No longer able to make history, these tribesmen now confine their fights to the telling of their histories on websites. *Ghazw* has gone "virtual" – a fate that Bandar would have rejected equally vehemently.

13

Rootless Trees

Genealogical Politics in Saudi Arabia

Abdulaziz H. Al Fahad

Arabian genealogies (*nasab/ansab*) are unique.[1] As one scholar put it, commenting on the earliest compendium of Arabian genealogy,

> The great genealogical work the *Jamharat al-nasab* [A Collection of Genealogies] of Hisham b. Muhammad al-Kalbi (d. c. 204 AH/819 CE) marks the completion of the codification of Arabic genealogies and forms the basis of most later work. This vast compilation has no parallel in other cultures. The aristocratic families of Western Europe certainly produced elaborate genealogies, sometimes tracing their ancestry back to the Trojans or other figures of classical antiquity. Such genealogies often included collateral branches as well and were not simply the direct stem of the leading branch. The Arabic genealogies, as recorded by Ibn al-Kalbi, remain, however, in a class of their own. In part this is because of the sheer size of the material. The Register of the *Jamharat al-nasab* contains some 35,000 names, all of people, real and imaginary, most of whom died before the end of the first century *hijri* [7th CE]. No other genealogies can produce an onomasticon on this scale.
>
> The second distinguishing feature is that this compilation attempts to provide the paternal lineages of an entire nation.... [T]he aim seems to have been to provide as complete account as possible of at least the most important lineages of all the Arab tribes. Written genealogies from other cultures tend to concentrate on the distinguished ancestry of one family or group rather than attempting to portray the structure of a whole nation. Both in size and scope, the written genealogies of Ibn al-Kalbi are unique.[2]

---

[1] An earlier version of this paper was presented at the Yale Middle East Legal Studies Seminar in Marrakech, January 2010.

[2] Hugh Kennedy, "From Oral Tradition to Written Record in Arabic Genealogy," *Arabica* 44, no. 4 (Oct. 1997): 531–2.

The new "science" initiated by Ibn al-Kalbi would thrive over the next several centuries in lands under Arab and Muslim influence. Spurred by diverse needs, Arab/Muslim communities maintained a steady production of genealogies in various forms, written and oral, official and personal. The mixing of Arab tribes and foreign elements in the conquered lands under the banner of Islam starting in the seventh century led to the spread of this tradition to newly converted communities with the Arabs trying to maintain genealogical separation from the new converts. The politics of the time eventually lead to further evolution of the genealogical tradition. In due course genealogies would translate into strong currents of political affiliation within the early Arab-conquering groups with tribes joining political coalitions under a variety of genealogical devices. The fact that genealogies were reduced to writing transformed their nature, rendering them less adaptable to changing circumstances, a distinguishing characteristic of the earlier oral tradition. Gradually the Muslim communities, especially in the great Islamic urban centers, seem to have become less concerned with genealogies as a *lived* reality, identifying more with notions of Islamic egalitarianism. Beyond a rehashing of the old genealogical information and various attempts to graft an Arab pedigree for the newly converted Muslims, one genealogical interest flourished: tracing the genealogies of numerous families to that of the Prophet's descendants, the *Ahl al-Bayt*. Despite the dubious nature of many claims to Prophetic descent, the fact that under Islamic law and tradition they enjoyed certain privileges, including financial entitlements, turned these genealogical pretensions into a thriving cottage industry; large communities throughout the Islamic world made claims to such descent, and attempts at grafting new ones are still going apace.

While outsiders dedicated their energies to maintaining or inventing an Arab or a Prophetic descent, in the cradle of Islam, the Arabian Peninsula, and outside the holy cities, the old genealogical tradition survived and remained essentially in oral form. For the middle Islamic centuries, the recorded genealogies that survived came mostly through chronicles of the rulers' courts in adjacent lands in the Levant and Egypt where chanceries maintained records of visiting Arabian dignitaries and their clans as well as a full list of Bedouin tribes living astride the pilgrimage routes to the holy cities who had to be paid regular subventions to secure safe passage of the Muslim pilgrims. Occasionally local authors would record events in short chronicles that would contain some interesting genealogical information, but what survives is limited. The earliest genealogical record extant in central Arabia[3] comes from the seventeenth

---

[3] Jabr ibn Sayyar (d. 1664), *Nubdhah fi Ansab Ahl Najd*, ed. Rashid Al 'Asakir (Riyadh, 2001).

century, and a few other tracts were subsequently authored, most of them not more than a few pages. The first[4] major modern written exposition on central Arabian (known as Najd) genealogies was published in the 1978 by a well-known jurist as a biographical dictionary of Najdi 'ulama, all of whom hailed from hadari (sedentary) background.[5] A trickle of books, about both Bedouin and hadari genealogies, started appearing, turning into a flood by the 1980s. Genealogical studies, books, family trees, and associations, as well as quarrels over pedigree, were now in full bloom.

Although it is ubiquitous, investigating this phenomenon of genealogical resurgence is challenging. While written products are abundant, the underlying causes of the disproportionate preoccupation with genealogies are difficult to discern, and there has been no serious analysis of the phenomenon of which I am aware. The emergence of this phenomenon simultaneously with the consolidation of the modern Saudi state appears, at minimum, to be counterintuitive. With the steady bureaucratization of the state and the process of rationalization generally associated with modern economic systems, this ascriptive status should have diminished in importance if not disappeared outright. The genealogical boom belies such expectations, and it seems that the consolidation of the Saudi state may have been a direct contributor to the entrenchment of genealogical identities. It is also clearly influenced by the spread of education and the replacement of a premodern, mostly oral, culture with a literate society. It is true that this genealogical phenomenon is not unique to Saudi Arabia, and some studies of similar developments in the Arab east suggest that economic factors are dominant in its emergence, but in the Saudi case economic issues do not seem to be very significant. The Saudi case does contain an element of economic redistribution, but genealogical "associations" appear to serve mostly noneconomic interests. Of the several possible explanations, the best is to view genealogies and their modernization as a general reaction against the decline of traditional modes of social and

---

4 Two earlier works were published. The first, by Abd al-Rahman Al-Mughiri (d. 1944), *Al-Kitab Al-Muntakhab fi Dhikr Qaba'il Al-Arab* (Dar Al-Mada, Jidda, 1998), was written in the early twentieth century and first published in the 1960s; most of it was dedicated to historical information about ancient tribes and attempts to link modern clans and families with the early formations. The other is a summary of genealogical information about some Najdi hadari families by the nineteenth-century historian Ibn Lu'bun (d. after 1841) (*Tarikh Hamad ibn Muhammad ibn Lu'bun* [Taif: Dar Al Ma'arif, 1988)]. They did not stir as much debate as the later works.

5 Abd Allah ibn Abd al-Rahman Al Bassam, *'Ulama Najd khilal Sittat Qurun* [The 'Ulama of Najd during Six Centuries] (Mecca: Dar al-Nahda, 1978). The first edition was published in three volumes. Later a revised edition, *'Ulama Najd khilal Thamaniyat Qurun* ['Ulama Najd during Eight Centuries] (Riyadh: Dar al-'Asima, 1999), was published in six volumes.

political organization, the atomization of society, the homogenizing powers of the modern state, and the failure of civil society to take root.

INTRODUCTION

Perhaps more than any other in modern times, the Saudi state was consciously built on a puritanical interpretation of Islam, and Islam has always been ambivalent toward genealogies, an ambivalence, although not necessarily reflected in Saudi official or social practice, that has certainly been echoed in scholarly works. For equality among the faithful (at least men) is clearly enshrined in the sacred texts, where only "piety" determines a person's worth. The Qur'an unequivocally states, "O mankind, We have created you from man and woman and made you into peoples and tribes that you may recognize one another; verily before God the noblest is he who fears God most." The Prophet further emphasized this point in many well-known traditions, *hadiths*, one of which, the "Farewell Address," was given during his last pilgrimage: "O people of Quraysh [his tribe], God has taken from you the boastings of *Jahiliyya* [pre-Islamic ignorance] and its pride in ancestors. All men descend from Adam and Adam was made of dust. O mankind, We have created you from man and woman . . . [reciting the Qur'anic verse above]. An Arab is not superior to a non-Arab except through the fear of God." Early Muslim converts, from non-Arab or genealogically inferior Arab background, played major roles in the rise of Islam and were and remain highly venerated. Yet an element of the old tradition still survived within the new Islamic moral order. The Prophet encouraged knowledge about one's genealogy to ensure knowing one's kin to maintain familial ties. The second caliph, 'Umar, is reported to have encouraged the Arab conquerors in the Levant to preserve their genealogies and to avoid becoming like the inhabitants of the Iraqi countryside, who when asked their names, used toponyms.[6] The fact that the descendants of the Prophet were accorded a special status in Islamic tradition also ensured the survival of genealogical interests throughout history as the claimants to this honor proliferated and had to be accommodated or excluded. The early Islamic genealogical production was thus maintained by scholars, many of whom carried unimpeachable religious credentials, although the introduction to their works always carried the appropriate disclaimers – and many of the writers were non-Arab to boot.

---

[6] A contrary tradition attributed to the Prophet says about genealogy that it is "a knowledge by which none profits and ignorance of which does no harm." Ali ibn Hazm, *Jamharat ansab Al'arab*, ed. E. Levi-Provencal (Cairo: Dar al-Ma'arif, n.d.), 3.

Perhaps no name has been associated with the new renaissance in codi-fication and general scholarship on genealogies in Saudi Arabia more than that of the late Saudi scholar Hamad al-Jasir (1908–2001).[7] By 1981 al-Jasir had finished publishing his great life's work, monumental volumes on the histor-ical geography of Saudi Arabia, a dictionary of its tribes, and a dictionary of the genealogies of the hadari families of Najd. The first work, *al-Mu'jam al-Jughrafi li-l-Mamlaka al-'Arabiyya al-Sa'udiyya* (*The Geographical Dictionary of the Kingdom of Saudi Arabia*), is an impressive, encyclopedic compendium on the historical and present geography of the country, which was started in 1968 and was not finished until the early 1980s.[8] A collaborative work involving scores of authors in some thirty volumes, al-Jasir single handedly edited and published the work through his own publishing house, Dar al-Yamama, and directly authored several volumes covering different parts of the country. The second publication, *Mu'jam Qaba'il al-Mamlaka al-'Arabiyya al-Sa'udiyya* (*A Dictionary of Tribes in Saudi Arabia*, 1980), was directly complied by al-Jasir and covered all tribes in Saudi Arabia that were still "nomadic" (Bedouin) at the time of the formation of the modern Saudi state in 1932. Both works could be seen, paradoxically, as something of a conscious effort at a "nationalist"

---

7 Born in western central Arabia (al-Sirr) in 1908 and educated in the traditional ways of religious learning in the circles of Wahhabi 'ulama, al-Jasir started his long and productive career as religious preacher, then a judge, an educator, a journalist, and finally an editor of his own bimonthly journal, *Al-Arab*, probably the most influential Saudi scholarly publication. He published and edited numerous works on Arabic and history, both general Islamic and Arab as well as local. He edited many manuscripts in these fields. Despite being the product of this traditional environment, he was clearly not bound to it, and he was regularly removed from the positions he filled. He was fired as a judge because he had his own interpretations of the Shari'a rules he was applying. He was then entrusted with part of the newly established "secular" education department that the late King Abd al-Aziz introduced in the country, only to be fired again. He then published the first "magazine" in Riyadh in the early 1950s only to run afoul of the powers that be, both religious and political. He moved in the 1960s to Beirut where he launched his *Al-Arab* journal, devoted to the study of Arabic, history, and geography pertaining to the Arabian Peninsula. He had the dedication of the true scholar to his craft and seemed to be able to resist the blandishment of power and access. By the time he passed away in a Boston hospital in September 2001, still actively editing his journal, he had accomplished what few scholars could: a legacy of books, articles, and contributions that in many respects define what Saudi Arabia is, and not just in the three works mentioned above. Most of his life is covered in a two-volume memoir, *Min Sawanih al-dhikrayat* (Riyadh: Dar al-Yamama, 2006).

8 To appreciate the importance of this work, a few facts have to be kept in mind. For many of the geographical maps and place names in Saudi Arabia, even Arabic references and works resorted to translations of western produced maps which invariably corrupted the names, rendering their Arabic confusing. More importantly, an understanding of much pre-Islamic and early Islamic Arabic literature (both poetry and prose) is difficult to achieve without correct knowledge of the geography of Arabia. This *Dictionary* aimed, inter alia, to cure these deficiencies.

project on the part of a scholar imbued mostly with a prenationalist sensibility. His third work, *Jamharat Ansab al-Usar al-Mutahaddira fi Najd* (*A Collection of the Genealogies of the Sedentary Families of Najd*, 1981; hereinafter referred to as *Jamharat*),[9] is a much more problematic book, which could be viewed as furthering more parochial norms contrary to the nationalist aims of the former two.

It is remarkable that a man of his generation and sensibility would, for example, choose to work on the historical geography of Saudi Arabia and not the Arabian Peninsula. He uncharacteristically accepted the artificial lines of the modern nation-state as legitimate demarcations for this scholarly work; the same could be said of the tribal dictionary. He looked at the tribes with an eye not only to making them accessible to both researchers and laity, but also with a conscious agenda of rehabilitation. Never an easy or straightforward subject to start with, Arabian tribal genealogies are fraught with explicit and implicit taboos about pedigree or "purity" (*asil*) and lack thereof. The preeminent authority of his generation, al-Jasir lent his considerable prestige and learning not only to accepting what "non-*asil*" tribes said about their own ancestry, but devoted pages and books to "proving" their historically *asil* genealogies. He systematically attacked derogatory designations and only used names accepted by the concerned tribe. His tribal dictionary includes *all* "Bedouin"[10] tribes of Saudi Arabia, and anyone reading it not familiar with the country and its social landscape would simply see a great collection of tribes with no distinction in status, contrary to lived reality. But the great author would brook no challenge as it seems his own traditional sensibility (he was a hadari of the Harb tribe, one of the great *asil* tribes straddling western and central Arabia) was assimilated into the process of nation building of the Saudi state, where a notion of equal citizenship has been emerging over the last few generations.

Thus that al-Jasir would write and publish the *Jamharat* is surprising as it goes against his apparent commitment to a "national" project of equal citizenship as reflected in his two other scholarly dictionaries. The first public

---

9 Recall the *Jamharat* (meaning a collection or majority of something) of Ibn al-Kalbi; this evocative title was probably chosen to place the new *Jamharat* squarely within the old Arabian, comprehensive tradition.

10 His definition of the tribes included in his *Dictionary* is problematic. He clearly states that he would include only tribes that were at least partially "nomadic" on the eve of the establishment of the Saudi state. However, he proceeded to include *sedentary* tribes of the southwest while excluding, for example, the great Tamim tribe in Najd, whose members have been settled for centuries. Implicitly, al-Jasir was not using the Bedouin/hadari distinction for inclusion and exclusion in his *Dictionary*, but rather the degree of tribal organization, which was very high with the sedentary tribes of southern Hijaz and the southwest and practically nonexistent among the hadari tribes in central Arabia and the rest of the country.

intimation of his intention to produce a collection on hadari *ansab* came in an issue of his *al-Arab* journal in 1980 where he published a study, prepared at his request, by a writer familiar with the original inhabitants of the city of Riyadh, purporting to enumerate the *asil* families of the town at the inception of the modern state in the early twentieth century. Over a long career, he managed to amass an impressive body of information on the *asil* families of central Arabia, which he compiled from personal knowledge and historical records (especially local chronicles, genealogical tracts, and modern studies on various towns with records about families' genealogies). When he published the *Jamharat* in 1981 it went quickly through a second revised edition, which is now the standard reference. With this publication, a torrent of genealogical "studies," feuds, questions, challenges, and outright fabrications were unleashed, much of which found an ambivalent reception in his *al-Arab* journal. This flood, which occupied many pages in each issue, was to continue until shortly after al-Jasir's death in 2001. And the genealogical production did not stop with al-Jasir and his books and journal; indeed, a veritable industry had emerged by the 1970s in which families, towns, tribes, and communities produced books, genealogical trees, and family associations, transforming *ansab* into a major point of friction both socially and politically. It is no exaggeration to describe what has been transpiring over the last generation as nothing short of a genealogical revolution.

ARABIAN SOCIETY

Saudi Arabia covers about four-fifths of the Arabian Peninsula currently with a population of around 20 million natives and a large expatriate community of about 9 million. But until the 1970s, the total native population of the country was probably not more than four million inhabitants.[11] Prior to the great urbanization wave of the 1970s (spurred, inter alia, by the oil boom of that decade), the small Saudi population was thinly dispersed over the large country with varying socioeconomic characteristics. The southwest mountains and plains were inhabited by strongly tribal but sedentary communities subsisting mostly on agriculture; it was probably the most densely populated area in the country but also the most insular. Western Arabia, the Hijaz, the abode of Islam's holy places of Mecca and Medina, boasted a mixed population of nomadic and sedentary tribes as well as concentrations of sophisticated cosmopolitan communities centered around the major urban areas. The central, northern, and eastern regions were inhabited by large Bedouin (nomadic) tribes spread over

---

[11] In 1963 a census, never recognized by the government, put the total population at 3.2 million.

huge expanses of arid deserts and by sedentary communities living in small towns, settlements, and villages.

Genealogical traditions varied over regions and over time. In the southwestern mountains, old tribal formations remained stable during the last millennium or so and changes were not significant. The *asil* tribes maintained their status and controlled their territories with minimum interference by outsiders, and those of non-*asil* background were excluded from their ranks. Scholars generally do not find much difficulty in tracing these tribes to the early tribal formations in pre-Islamic and early Islamic times. The coastal lands in the southwest seem to have been less stable tribally and have been heavily influenced by the rich Islamic tradition of seeking a pedigree that associates tribes with the family of the Prophet, resulting in the emergence over time of a significant number of clans claiming the holy lineage, claims that did not always go unchallenged. This quest to associate the *nasab* of various families with the *Ahl al-Bayt* was also prevalent in the great urban communities of the Hijaz, where claims abound to such lineage, both genuine and made up. As in the rest of the Islamic world, the fabricated claims typically stem from the desire of successful families (through learning or trade) to acquire a prestigious pedigree, and such families were usually able to achieve this goal.

In the rest of the country the story is somewhat different. Especially in Najd, most of the tribes were always in a state of flux and old formations were replaced by new ones. Hadari society was practically detribalized, and incentives, both material and symbolic, to associate the *nasab* with that of *Ahl al-Bayt* seem to have been absent. Although the genealogical obsession is national in character, it is in this central region (the subject matter of the *Jamharat*) that most manifestations are felt. A quick look at the historical and social background of this region is thus in order.

THE HADAR

The hadari communities of Najd lived in scattered villages, settlements, and small towns, usually concentrated in areas with more reliable water resources. The hadaris led mostly a subsistence existence, engaged in agriculture, commerce, and the crafts. There were richer and poorer hadaris, but stratification was limited and accumulation of wealth was rare, the latter mostly represented by merchants engaged in long-distance caravan trade. In their social structure, the hadaris still maintained tribal identities. But unlike the Bedouin, such an identity did not take the form of tribal organization, and towns and villages were generally ruled by influential families with no necessary link between their ability to rule and the size of their clan. Indeed, one of the most striking aspects of Najdi hadari society was its detribalization. This came about in part because of the constant turnover of the Najdi tribes, where every century or so a new tribal confederation would come onto the scene and displace older ones, which in due course caused the structure of the Najdi hadar to be so mixed as to render it meaningless in tribal terms. That hadaris held to more exogamous practices, which coupled with the right of women to inherit, a right that many Muslim communities seem to have breached (such as the tribes of the western and southern areas of Arabia), ensured an alignment of interests that may not have always corresponded with tribal lines, as attested by many of the land and *waqf* disputes.[12] It is this community that would form the backbone of the Wahhabi religious movement as well as provide the foot soldiers in the process of state formation.[13]

Socially, the hadar would still maintain certain tribal characteristics. For example, the notion of an *asil* Arabian genealogy was and remains part of hadari social identity. Typically hadaris trace themselves to one of the *asil* Arabian tribes and would intermarry[14] only with equally *asil* families. Historically, rule in villages, towns, and larger polities was always held by the *asil* groups. The non-*asil* families, or khadiri among other designations, perhaps as many as 30 percent of the population, were held to a generally inferior *social* position, but did not necessarily suffer economically. The *khadiris* are an amalgam of individuals and groups with no single racial, social, or economic background. Thus anyone who immigrated into central Arabia and was not recognized to come from an appropriately *asil* tribe, or people who practiced various crafts and certain professions, including smiths, carpenters, tanners, tailors, butchers, barbers, leather workers, and other handicrafts, were held to be non-*asil*. If an *asil*, due to a blood feud or some other reason, hid his ancestry and intermarried with non-*asils*, he would be recognized as non-*asil*, and his progeny would find it difficult to reclaim their *asil* status. Economically,

---

[12] My own family history is a testimony to this misalignment between genealogies and property interests; a feud that spanned generations and was legally partially resolved in the early 1960s produced over a century of conflicts many shifting alliances that were inconsistent with genealogical affiliations.

[13] On the *asil/non-asil* dichotomy, see Abdulaziz H. Al-Fahad, "The 'Imamah vs. the 'Iqal: Hadari–Bedouin Conflict and the Formation of the Sa'udi State," in *Counternarratives: History, Contemporary Society, and Politics in Saudi Arabia and Yemen*, ed. Madawi Al-Rasheed and Robert Vitalis (London: Palgrave Macmillan 2004), 38–9.

[14] "Equivalency" (*kafa'a*) in marriage, although a social issue, is legally sanctioned by Islamic tradition. Theoretically, relatives of a woman married "below" her social and economic station (including *asil/non-asil* distinctions) could petition a court to dissolve the marriage. There was recently such a case in Saudi Arabia that has achieved international notoriety. See *Alsharq Alawsat* [London], no. 10327, Mar. 8, 2007.

nonetheless, this group would boast of powerful interests in premodern Arabia as well as under the Saudi state, and many of the successful individuals and families with large wealth hailed from this background. This group also stood to benefit the most from the successful formation and consolidation of the state, and they were certainly its most ardent supporters.

It is these *asil* hadari families and clans that would form the core of the *Jamharat*, and it is the khadiris, among others, who would challenge their differential status. This battle continues to this very day.

THE BEDOUIN

The stratification of the hadari community into *asil* and non-*asil* is a direct replica of Bedouin genealogical structure. But although it is somewhat difficult to understand the rationale for the hadari distinctions between *asil* and non-*asil*, this feature is more readily understandable in the Bedouin milieu. For "purity" of *nasab* is nothing more than a reflection of power relations among the warring, adversarial tribal groups. Once a tribe is militarily defeated and agrees to pay tribute to a more powerful tribe, the notion emerges that this vanquished tribe is paying tribute not because of contingent power relations but because of an eternal defect in its status – that it was created to become a vassal. That one could trace histories of these tribes and show that they were genealogically not less pure than the *asil* seems to have been irrelevant to the social structure of premodern Arabia. Thus a group called Hutaym, consisting of five well-known Arabian tribes, became the Bedouin's equivalent of the khadiris among the hadar. The "caste" system is more pronounced with the Arabian tribe of the Salab, who were nomads serving as craftsmen, hunters, and guides in the desert. Their low status in the social ranking of Arabians provided them with the unusual advantage of being essentially inviolable in their person and property. No self-respecting Bedouin would thus molest a Salabi or rob him of his property.

Unlike the hadar communities, the Bedouin of central Arabia suffered from constant flux, and a tribe rarely stayed long in any one place. In typical fashion, a tribe would "descend" from the mountains of the Hijaz or the south, would compete for pasture in Najd, and dislodge older tribal formations, which in turn would push north and eastward, displacing other tribes. Every two centuries or so what used to be a purely Najdi tribe would end up pasturing in the Fertile Crescent. Genealogical manipulations, however, allowed an otherwise unstable social and political structure to survive these incessant pressures. Patrilineal genealogy was inherently political and served as the ideological foundation on which alliances necessary for survival in the harsh desert were forged. With the nomadic tribes, *nasab* was a genealogical idiom for the allocation of natural resources and territory, and little more of it is remembered than is needed for the organization of tribal political life. The genealogy of the smaller unit, that of the *khamsa* or "fifth," the descendants in an extended family up to the great-great-grandfather, was certainly based on clear biological affinity, but not necessarily the larger tribal groupings. The *khamsa* would be agglomerated into the lineage where biological connections would exist within it but not necessarily for all members. Traditional rules would permit outsiders to become allies and join the lineage, and in due course the new group would be completely assimilated. It is also the case that larger units are formed almost always, especially at the level of the tribe or confederation, through this process of alliance building. For example, the Harb tribe clearly includes remnants of ancient Arabian tribes from the Hijaz, even though the core of the tribe emigrated from Yemen in the tenth century CE. The same could be said about practically all tribes in central, eastern, and northern Arabia. The suppleness of the genealogical ideology permitted the formation of these coalitions, providing an effective way for survival in a rather unstable environment, ecologically, socially, and politically. The intrusion of the modern state with its literate citizens effectively put an end to this *dynamic* political genealogy, but genealogy as a social construct endured in a different form, serving different purposes.

STATE MAKING AND SOCIOECONOMIC CHANGE

Like all modern nations, Saudi Arabia embarked on a process of state making characterized by the introduction of the usual panoply of "measurements" and their standardization to help ensure state control. The national flag was decreed. Instead of the various foreign currencies used by the inhabitants, a standard coin (later a paper currency) was introduced. The bewildering assortment of measures used in various regions, be they for weight, volume, or distance, were abolished and replaced by a "rational" metric system that allowed for ease of commerce *and* simultaneously enhanced the reach of the state. But, like in the modern West, state making could not succeed without the imposition of a standard naming system, and the Saudi state slowly but surely introduced such a system that allowed state authorities to have full "legibility" of its citizens and society.

ARABIAN ONOMASTICS, GENEALOGIES, AND THE STATE

Naming practices in traditional Arabia were, at their core, genealogical. Typically, a person would have an *ism*, a personal name such as Muhammad, followed by the name of his father, which is preceded by ibn/bin (or bint for a woman), or son of, followed by the name of the grandfather, again preceded by ibn/bin, and so on, depending on the circumstances and the degree of clarity needed. Usually a "surname" would appear at the end, signifying an ancestor or a lineage, a physical feature (e.g., tall, short, lame), a profession, or a toponym. In addition, the *kunya*, or teknonym (calling a person the father of his first-born son, *Abu Fulan*), was widely used as an honorific. This system prevailed in the small, prestate communities, both nomadic and settled, and the limited size of each community rendered any elaborate naming system unnecessary. Indeed, until a generation ago, in most of the Arabian villages and small towns, people were known to belong to certain families and a full name could be produced at will, but the quickest way of identification was "nicknames," *'iyara* or *mi 'yara*. The nicknames were of varied types, and many if not most were derogatory, but such names tended to be unique, rendering any resort to the elaborate genealogical names superfluous. The nicknames were made all the more necessary because of the penchant in premodern Arabia for the use of a relatively limited number of names, especially within the hadari families.

The naming practices among the Bedouin and the hadar, although similar, were different in certain respects. The genealogical name prevailed within both communities, but the hadar resorted to more religiously inspired names, especially theophoric ones. The nomads, on the other hand, who used fewer Islamic names, had a more pronounced inclination toward "exotic" names, not least of which those taken from the animal world (e.g., Mlayhan (little black camel), Hanash (snake), Hmayyir (little donkey), J'aylan (little dung beetle)). Another distinguishing feature in Bedouin naming was the fondness for alliterative names in a given family (thus brothers would be called Faraj, Mfarrij, Farraj). Unlike the hadar who did not usually use their tribal identity in names, the Bedouin tended to keep their lineage and tribal *laqab*, which signified their tribal affiliation to outsiders.

With the emergence of central authority, the varied naming practices were slowly jettisoned, and a standard naming system was uniformly imposed. Nicknames, so effective in a small community, were now neither practical nor socially acceptable, and the full genealogical name was firmly instituted. As the state started to intrude more and more into society with many of today's social, educational, employment, and general economic needs impossible to obtain without interaction with its organs, the legibility question became preeminent, and citizens wishing to partake of the services provided by the bureaucracy had no choice but to conform to the new requirements. Identity papers (*tabi'iyya*) were a necessary requirement for each citizen (exclusively for males until recently), and to obtain them a name had to be provided,

among other things. Two witnesses would be procured before the local government office who would testify that the person requesting the *tabi'iyya* was
so-and-so.[15] And here the requirements for the hadar and the Bedouin would
diverge.

For the Bedouin have always presented unique challenges to the establishment of central authority in central Arabia. The nomadic tribes maintained a
life style that depended on mobility and possessed the means to defend their
independence against any efforts to bring them under the control of outsiders.
In the formation of the modern Saudi state in the early twentieth century, a
principal cause for its success has been the elaborate effort not only to contain
the Bedouin tribe as a political unit, but actually to destroy it as a political
entity, a goal the state achieved within a short time. The measures used to
curtail the autonomy of the Bedouin nomads are myriad and most fall outside
the scope of this chapter, but "naming" has been one of the most effective tools
used to bring the nomads under the control of the state. It was thus decreed
that for the Bedouin, a person seeking his *tabi'iyya* had to provide *five* names:
his first name, followed by his father's, followed by his grandfather's, then the
name of his lineage, and finally the name of his tribe. In this fashion, if a
nomadic citizen (even if he is settled) is sought by the authorities, a review of
his full name would give the bureaucracy a quick source for his location: his
lineage chief, who was expected to use his position and contacts within his
own community to enable the state to locate his co-tribesman. This naming
system originally designed to ensure state control would eventually bring about
its own unintended consequences with which the state has been grappling so
far unsuccessfully, especially since the nomads are all settled now.[16]

For the hadar, the requirements were different; only four names were
required: the *ism*, or given name, the father's name, the grandfather's name,
and the "surname." For the hadari names a problem arose that had to
be dealt with to ensure legibility. For in certain parts of the country, and

---

[15] A lingering problem with legibility has been the lack of definite birth dates on identity papers.
With very few exceptions, no records were kept of births, and until recently the need to produce
a birth date only came up when applying for the *tabi'iya* or in some instances at the sixth grade
level if a child was enrolled in school. The determination of the birth date was delegated to
physicians who were supposed to come up with an accurate number. Only a year was required,
and, regardless of its accuracy, every citizen born in a certain year would be allotted the middle
of the year as his birthday. All Saudi citizens above certain age were thus "born" on the same
date of the same year. This increased reliance on names as the most effective identity device.

[16] For example, by insisting that all members of a given tribe use the tribal marker as a last name,
with some tribes running into the hundreds of thousands, statistically it would be impossible
not to have a large number of names, even if five, appearing identical, making identifying
individuals problematic.

partaking of the practice that prevailed in adjacent Arab lands, the naming system dropped the "ibn/bin" particles, giving a string of sequential names with no clarity as to progeny. This problem was compounded further by the habit in certain families of giving their sons *two* personal names (akin to western practice), mostly associated with the name Muhammad, for example, Muhammad Anwar. With such names, it was not clear who was father and who was son, and a new decree required that the "ibn/bin" be introduced between the name of the son and the name of each ancestor. Thus was uniformity achieved, and all names in the Saudi state were rendered in a standard fashion, allowing for instant identification of each citizen. This was capped by the introduction of a "national" card by which each citizen was expected to obtain an electronically sophisticated card that carried vital metrics, not just his or her full name. The grip of the state on all relevant information concerning its citizens became complete.

A STATE TRIUMPHANT, A SOCIETY ATOMIZED

The success of the modern Saudi state at penetrating and controlling all aspects of society is no less impressive than any of the older, more advanced nations of Europe. This was made possible for many reasons, not least of which is the ability of the Saudi state to import and impose modern technologies and systems that allowed it to dominate society and make its presence felt in all walks of life. The combination of a modern bureaucracy, strong security services, advanced technologies, and elaborate systems have permitted the state to dominate in every field. Starting with the Bedouin, the state gradually, but decisively, destroyed any semblance to any independence the tribe might have. Their traditional tribal territories, the *dira*, where a tribe held the functional equivalent of sovereign powers, such as control of the pastures, water wells, movement within it, and adjudication of dispute through customary law, were abolished, and any citizen, nomad or otherwise, could come and go and freely have equal access to the land (except water wells, which remained in private hands or under lineage control). The traditional *ghazw*, or raiding of Bedouin against the hadar and among themselves, was banned, and killing became the crime of homicide punishable under the Shari'a rules by death. Cattle theft was reduced from the manly heroics of Bedouin lore to a crime, large or small depending on the circumstances, and appropriate punishment was swiftly meted out. The modern advances in war and information technology ensured that the state had a permanent, unchallengeable advantage over the Bedouin and rendered their political organization, the tribe, obsolete. Here the tribe maintained its genealogical structure, enhanced by the prevalence of literacy and writing as well as by the government naming requirements, but lost everything else. Shorn of control over its own territory, deprived of raiding, and its judges no longer enjoying power or prestige, the tribe could no longer perform the functions it provided so effectively throughout history. Furthermore, the dynamic process that allowed mobility in alliance formation and the production of leadership was stunted. Tribes were literally frozen, and no shift in tribal identity was possible under the glaring gaze of the state, which fixed their boundaries. Leadership became ossified with the established shaykhly families in ascendance at the inception of the state simply maintaining their positions through the power of the bureaucracy, which decreed who and who was not a shaykh; the "meritocracy" of old disappeared. Genealogically defined but politically emasculated, the modern tribe in the Saudi state was rendered a shell of its old self and could offer its members very little beyond certain privileges that the state would bestow as it saw fit, usually through the traditional shaykhs of the clans.

The forces brought about by the modern state that sealed the fate of the traditional Bedouin tribe did not spare the hadari forms of social and political organization either. In most of the interior of Arabia, detribalized, sedentary groups comingled in small towns or villages and developed over the course of several centuries relatively strong *territorially* based identities, overshadowing any lingering tribal affiliations. Spatially contiguous communities had common defensive interest vis-à-vis outside forces and despite the internal divisions characteristic of these towns and villages they still would act to defend their collective interests such as ensuring open trade routes, protecting harvests, or maintaining the exclusivity of their pasturelands. These regions also developed their own local dialects and occasionally their specific dress codes, thus enhancing a sense of distinct identity, again separate from clan and lineage and from other regions as well. Some regions in certain periods of their history even managed to achieve some degree of political unity, such as the domination of Hayil in the north of its adjacent villages and Burayda over most of Qasim province. This territorially anchored identity manifested itself in rudimentary notions of participatory governance where the elders of the community (without regard to the asil/non-asil distinction) were regularly involved in making important decisions concerning the welfare of their villages, towns, and regions. Never institutionalized, the practice nonetheless was widespread to the degree that when they Saudi state was established the tradition continued and was manifested in two distinct ways. First, the "governors" of towns were invariably chosen from among the influential local families. In addition, the town's elders had regular and meaningful access to the governor, who himself was privileged with access to the highest authority in the land, the king. Slowly and with the proliferation of state organs, population growth, and the ascendancy of state-based institutions over everything else, the local governors, effectively political appointees, were gradually removed and replaced by bureaucrats or simply downgraded in their ability to affect important decisions. Concurrently, the formerly acceptable practice of allowing *collective* petitions of the king and his major assistants were frowned upon and effectively stopped. For both the hadar and Bedouin, the citizen now stood alone before Leviathan; neither tribe nor town could act as buffer between the individual and the state.

The 1970s saw the first oil boom that led to a transformation of the living standards in Saudi Arabia. The dominance of the state over society and economy, which was steadily on the rise during the preceding decades, now experienced a quantum leap. The state was able to intrude everywhere. Geographically, old, isolated communities were connected with the rest of the country through roads and telecommunications. Schools proliferated and a national curriculum was made available to all citizens, not just for those in major urban areas. Both radio and television broadcasting was extended throughout the country, where all citizens were offered a steady diet of information dictated by the state. Newspapers, magazines, and soccer teams were established in the main cities, and national teams represented the county in international arenas. A national anthem that was just music now included poetic praise of the county and its leadership. The "imagined community" of Saudi Arabia came of age during this period, where urbanization exceeded 80 percent and a national dress, a uniform dialect, and high literacy finally replaced the isolated, separate localities with their own parochial practices and sense of identity. The homogenous citizenry was thus born.

National homogenization and the standardization of dialect, dress, education, cuisine, and the emergence of a national identity were not the only processes at play, for simultaneously status and class differentiation was also taking root. With few exceptions, Arabian society was characterized by a credible degree of egalitarianism in part due to uniform poverty. The "tribal" ethos viewed all tribesmen of *asil* background to be of equal status, and the failure of the local economy to generate meaningful surplus for any sustainable length of time ensured that an ideology of equality prevailed. The consolidation of the state and the economic growth brought about by the integration of the national market and the influx of oil rents into the coffers of the state would eventually lead to the erosion of egalitarian norms. By the 1980s a sizeable middle class took form and a merchant class was thrust more pronouncedly onto the national scene; none of these new formations coincided with the old lines of the status groups, as the *asils* enjoyed no better access to the modern market or government resources than the rest. Instead, class differentiation would take place within the same genealogical group, and wide gaps emerged among close kin.[17]

Status differentiation also became more prominent. The traditional egalitarianism allowed for a degree of deference to the traditional "aristocratic" families of Arabia and men of rank, but society by and large did not view their status to be much different from the rest of the *asil* groups. Formal titles, for example, were rudimentary, reflecting this sensibility, and other than typical designations such as imam, shaykh, and amir, very little else was used. Men of whatever background had the right of access to the powers that be, and the latter's doors were expected to be open to petitioners and visitors alike. Addressing the imam, shaykh, or amir was not a complicated matter in terms of protocol as more or less any man would simply show the proper respect in his demeanor and could address the person by his title (oh, shaykh), or if more gifted with etiquette would address him by his teknonym, perhaps the most respectful form of address in premodern Arabia (and still prevalent to this day). With the consolidation of the modern state and the unleashing of economic forces, this simple sensibility no longer obtained, and inflation in titles ensued. Royalty slowly imported Egyptian and European court titles, the rich wanted to be recognized and felt deserving of a special type of esteem reflected in the forms of address, and the rest resorted to the use of equivalent designations such as *sayyid* or *ustadh* (Mr.), not to mention also the proliferation of academic titles.

THE PRINCE IS BORN

In 1993 major reforms were decreed by the late King Fahd. A constitution, dubbed the "Basic Law of Governance," was promulgated along with a law for an appointed parliament and another law for provincial administration.[18] Although the first two laws did usher in some new ideas about governance and relations among the organs of the state and attempted ever so slightly to advance notions of participatory politics, the provincial law had fewer pretentions. The law did seek to streamline certain administrative practices and to clarify relations between the center and the provinces, but it is arguable that the most lasting impact of the law was on titles.

The Arabic word *amir* is an extraordinarily rich and versatile appellation. For ages it was a simple functional (noninheritable) designation that came

---

[17] It is easily observable that essentially all affluent families had large numbers of less well-off kin in all parts of the country.

[18] A translation of these laws is available at http://www.servat.unibe.ch/icl/sa00000_.html.

with a given role and did not necessarily signal an inherited status, although it did carry the airs of an ambiguous honorific title. An *amir* was just a leader or a commander. Thus the Prophet is reported to have admonished that even when only two people were to travel together, one of them should be appointed an *amir*, or a leader of the trip. A commander of a military contingent was an *amir*, and so was the caliph, *Amir al-Mu'minin*, or Commander of the Faithful. In local Arabian parlance this elastic notion of the *amir* prevailed. Among the Bedouin there were shaykhs who were also the *amir*s. In each town, indeed even little villages, the headman enjoyed the title of the *amir*. This traditional term survived in the practice of the early Saudi state as each province was headed by an *amir*, each subdivision was also headed by an *amir*, the state-appointed heads of villages were also so designated, and Bedouin shaykhs of all degrees of seniority also carried the title. But this functional designation coexisted with another, status-associated conception of the *amir*, the prince of the royal family. This harks back to 1926 when Abd al-Aziz assumed the mantle of the King of the Hijaz after the conquest and for the first time introduced modern royal protocol to a land innocent of such trappings. Members of the royal family became eligible to the title of prince, or *amir*, now a liminal designation straddling two, potentially incompatible, worlds, Europe of ancient status and class consciousness, and an Arabian egalitarian sensibility. For a while, the two notions of *amir* would coexist until the advent of the provincial law.

Within the royal family a differentiation process also came into play. The core of the family, the sons and daughters of the founder of the modern state, King Abd al-Aziz, and their descendants would now enjoy the further appellation of "his/her royal highness" whereas the collateral branches would have to settle for a mere "his/her highness." Further down the line, collateral branches of the royal family who never carried the princely title were enfranchised and permitted to use the designation. The new (i.e., post-1932 appellations) obviously set royalty apart from the rest of the commoner *amir*s, but it seems that the distance between the two stations as reflected in the use of the same title was seen as not sufficiently large, and that was remedied with the new provincial law. Henceforth all positions within the administrative apparatus of the state would not use the title *amir* except at the major provincial posts, which were to be the exclusive domain of princely appointees. Other designations, honorifics, and titles proliferated, reflecting actual hierarchy, both social and bureaucratic. But now only princes could be called *amir*.

The problem of honorifics and titles were not just within the ranks of who is and who is not royal but extended farther down the various social strata. Newly empowered merchants and major bureaucrats were not happy with the simple new titles equivalent to the nondescript "Mr."; they wanted to be shaykhs, which etymologically mean an older man and later became a designation of two influential social groups, religious ulama and tribal leaders. Disturbed by the intrusion of the nouveau riche on their historical domain, the state duly protected these titles and issued a decree restricting their use to members of the two groups. As demands for titles in this affluent society could not be satiated, the newly successful continued to use the title of shaykh anyway even if in official circles and pronouncements they were barred from the privilege. Government decrees would not stem the entrepreneurship of the successful, and many of them would seek to acquire, legitimately or otherwise, the newest fad, a doctorate, which bestows the much sought-after title of "Doctor."

The New Genealogies

The struggle over titles and their evolution in official and social practice was not the only response to the transformations wrought by a powerful state and a thriving economy. Titles were mostly the domain of personal rivalry and ambitions; genealogies, on the other hand, where a collective endeavor, and they too had to respond to the new pressures of modernity. The genealogical response to these pressures took various forms, depending on the social group involved, with marked differences between Bedouin and hadari reactions.

THE BEDOUIN

Within the Bedouin communities, state naming practice ensured that the tribe survived as a genealogical appellation. All Bedouin, as well as the tribally organized communities of the southwest and the Hijaz, maintained their tribal identity, and there was little room for dispute over who belongs. True, there are a number of small instances in which the tribal name would be carried by genealogically non-*asil* families, but the numbers were not significant, and it was usually not associated with serious claims to being genealogically related to the tribe. One tribe, however, significantly "suffers" from this misapplication of the tribal label. For the Dawasir of southern Najd, a large number of non-*asil* sedentary families adopted the name over the course of the last half century or so, on the theory they were affiliated with the tribe (a large number were former slaves) and hailed from the area *named* after that tribe (i.e., a toponym). Still, as there were no serious claims to genealogical affinity, the issue seems to be moot. It is noteworthy, however, that a state that saw fit to ensure the exclusivity and sanctity of many titles has taken a hands-off attitude toward tribal surnames in this context, declining to police them for the tribe.

One of the main battle lines in the new genealogies is the intrusion of literate high culture into the realm of traditional Bedouin genealogies. From time immemorial the Bedouin were aware of and maintained their genealogies in oral form, which was very well suited to the political functions genealogies were expected to perform. The preliterate, oral culture permitted a degree of genealogical suppleness that was indispensable for the alliance formation on which Bedouin survival depended. The early Islamic codification of the tribal genealogies "fixed" those relationships permanently and reduced them to a scholarly endeavor divorced from their original tribal purposes. Where it was still required in the Arabian hinterland and the deserts of the Levant, genealogies endured in the old fashion: oral, flexible, and changing according to the political exigencies of the time. Bedouin, among other things, were illiterate, cared only about the immediate genealogical unit, and understood the larger tribal identity sufficiently to know it and had no reason to care about the useless information of who came from where a thousand years ago.

This indifference witnessed a tangible shift with state consolidation and rising educational levels and the transformation in the sources of prestige, and the old *mufakhara* (boastings) were reintroduced in different forms. Genealogical writing, whether or not about historical roots of current kinships and leaders, was no longer the exclusive domain of the select literate of old; tribesmen now commanded the means and had access and participated in the debates with much enthusiasm. Tribesmen would issue books and write articles purporting to document current and historical genealogies and glorious deeds, which invariably were contested issues. Bedouin within each tribe had their own internal frictions and debates, but when these were confined to gatherings around a hearth in a small encampment, the repercussions were limited. Publishing contested tribal claims in public in written form, however, is a different order and requires a response in kind. There are generally two contested issues within Bedouin discourse: affiliation and leadership. As many of the lineages and tribes were composed through alliances, a method of "tribe building" that was well recognized, it seems that not many tribesmen would accept being described as outsiders grafted onto the stem of tribal genealogy, and written speculations about these origins more often than not elicited strong reactions. But more significantly, leadership claims have been the most contested. Although in the old days the battlefield provided the arena to acquire and maintain leadership of a lineage, a clan, a moiety, or a tribe, today determination of leadership is essentially a bureaucratic act that may or may not be consistent with current qualifications, let alone the historical record.[19]

---

[19] Examples are numerous. One memorable incident was the announcement several years ago by the ranking shaykh of the Barqa moiety of the ʿUtayba tribe and published as an advertisement

Deprived by the state of the resources that historically underpinned its viability
and determined the process of producing its leaders, the tribe now acquired
the leadership that is anointed by the state and whose powers is more the result
of its proximity to the state and its resources than the leadership's affinity with
their kin. Some historical leaders may have run afoul of the new political order
by joining the losing coalitions of the past and were consequently sidelined by
the authorities, enjoying no powers except the trappings of past glory. Publicly
protecting their ancient legacy became the only course available to them, and
ensuring their story is told in the modern age became important business.

Another significant genealogical debate centered on attempts to link sur-
viving tribes to ancient Arabian formations, an interesting scholarly quest that
more or less has little to do with today's tribal life. As mentioned above, the
ancestry of the southwestern tribes and some in the Hijaz was relatively easy
to trace, but the rest posed practically insurmountable challenges to research,
and claims consist more of speculation than history. Some elements of this
debate can be viewed as a manifestation of something other than literary interest. For one, there is still some prestige in a literate milieu to be garnered
from a close association with the ancient, illustrious tribes, a sort of testimony
to a distinguished history (especially as pertains to their role in early Islamic
campaigns) and a confirmation of an *asil* pedigree. The other element is
the determined efforts of the non-*asil* tribes to acquire/reclaim their *asil* status. For, let us recall, the general tribal structure divided tribes into *asil* and
non-*asil* groups, a division reflective of the "correlation of forces" in premodern times. By the early twentieth century, several major tribes were generally
viewed as being of inferior status, and the *asil* tribes would not intermarry
with them. In the old days, these tribes had the opportunity to reclaim an *asil*
status through challenging power relations with other tribes and, by marshal-
ing enough resources and with some luck, would duly establish their military
prowess and be freed of paying tribute and eventually achieve the *asil* social
status. Indeed, the Huwaytat of northwestern Saudi Arabia/southern Jordan
managed to achieve just such a transformation, including intermarriage with
the *asil* groups. The Banu Rashid, on the other hand, were just starting to
make their military might felt by other tribes when the state came onto the
scene and froze the dynamism inherent in the traditional Bedouin system.
The battlefield no longer an option, what was left for these tribes were textual
campaigns. In this campaign the state and *public* discourse were sympathetic

in local newspapers in which the elder described himself as the "paramount shaykh" (*shaykh shaml*) of the tribe. This elicited strong objections in the form of counter-advertisements contesting the designation by the leaders of the other moiety, the Rawq. It is generally understood
that local newspapers are admonished to be careful with such claims, and perhaps as a result
we do not see these statements in such stark public display.

to their quest. For not only did these tribes produce and commission the production of genealogical works seeking to show their ancient *asil* roots, they
also had open support from state authorities, not least of which is the prohibition against any publication of works that would stigmatize these tribes.
Furthermore, various learned authorities participated in these textual battles
and lent their prestige to the rehabilitation project, a prime example of whom
is our distinguished scholar Hamad al-Jasir in his *Dictionary of the Tribes* and
in other works.[20] The only tribe that has not been yet rehabilitated is the Salab,
but it is probably a matter of time until their turn comes.[21]

THE HADAR

Ours is the age of globalization in its various manifestations, including notions
of political correctness. One reflection of this in Saudi Arabia is the newly
developed taboo in respect of asking other people about their genealogical
background. This new sensibility does not affect men of Bedouin background
as their *nasab* is borne by their very names; it is with the hadar that this taboo
is socially meaningful. Names in hadari context rarely, if ever, work as markers
of genealogical *asil*/non-*asil* affinities, especially since many families, *asil* and
non-*asil*, hold common names. With the rise in the level of urbanization, it has
become next to impossible to determine social status through the usual channels available in the past. Now whispers in private conversations are practically
the sole means, especially when nuptials are contemplated. It should therefore
not come as a surprise that when al-Jasir compiled his *Jamharat* he indicated
each family village or town of origin as means to safeguard against confusing
a family with its namesake from other towns who may come from a different tribal or from a khadiri background. Notions of kinship, consequently,
reasserted themselves in different forms.

What might be described with little exaggeration as the "revolt"[22] of the non-
asil groups did not take the form of this aversion to inquiring about genealogical

---

[20] Indeed, al-Jasir was so offended by any notions that would detract from the status of the Saudi
      tribes that he authored, for instance, a long book about the ancient tribe of Bahila, whose
      surviving membership consist of a small number of hadari families. This effort was in reaction
      to derogatory remarks made by some scholars about Bahila's "history."

[21] Even for the Salab rehabilitation is in the air. A few years ago during the busy Ramadan TV
      season, one comedian used an old saying denoting worthlessness: so-and-so is like "the dog of
      Salab" (combing the two beings not well regarded in Arabian culture). The program originated
      on Kuwaiti TV where a strong Salab contingent lived; they launched a campaign, and the
      comedian had to obsequiously offer profuse apologies on the air for his political incorrectness.

[22] In deference to the new sensibility, the same author who published the names and *ansab* of
      the old families of Riyadh felt obligated to supplement his early list with a new account of other
      known families, hailing from khadiri background, while avoiding declaring them as such.

background only, it also manifested itself in reassertions of *asil* origins by many khadiri families.[23] In a social environment that does not necessarily esteem a foreign or nontribal pedigree, most of the non-*asil* groups would insist that their non-*asil* status was incorrect and sought with some success to change the social order of the past. Here, for the most part, the claims were not anchored in traditional Islamic morality guaranteeing equality among the faithful, a perfectly defensible and historically well-trodden path. Instead, it took the form of acquiring and inventing *asil* ancestry (*nasab*), legitimately or otherwise. With few if any admitting of a khadiri pedigree, the new social environment became unstable, and the rush to codification was unleashed. Let us remember that the khadiris were rarely at an economic disadvantage, and thus many of their groups managed to fully compete for power and influence, and part of the competition was over the acquisition of the prestige associated with a proper genealogy. Powerful families sought the higher *asil* status, and armed with money and access, they procured the suitable "proofs" of their pure pedigree. The proof usually took one of two forms (or both). Appropriate witnesses would be summoned to a court, and a deed would be issued of their testimony on behalf of the applicant, a fairly easy task in a court of law based on the fact that two witnesses of probity would be enough to establish this status as legal (but not as a social) matter. Another method frequently used is to procure a document from a shaykh of a known (usually Bedouin) lineage "acknowledging" the claims of the family to be part of that tribal lineage; monetary and other valuable exchanges were always suspected as a basis for such documentation.[24] Other claims were made in the *al-Arab* journal without the benefit of documentation, and the skeptical editor would in his own inimitable way suggest to the claimants that the genealogical picture would have been clearer had they referred to families intermarried with them – a test of whether they were accepted as *asil* within their own community.

As to the hadari *asil* communities, they found themselves caught between these two powerful forces, from "above" and from "below," and the traditional rules no longer applied. For centuries secure in their status vis-à-vis their own "aristocracies" and their non-*asil* neighbors, the *asil* hadar felt abandoned by the aristocracy, until recently seen as nothing more than *primus inter pares*, who now acquired by association with the modern state a very distinct, clearly superior status, not the ambiguous station of old. The ruling house became real royals with titles and honorifics, regally distant, endowed with a panoply of

[23] There is no question that in premodern Arabia, just as there was movement from the *asil* to non-*asil* status, there was also movement in the opposite direction, as attested by the rampant rumors about the pedigree of many *asil* families.

[24] A partial public record of these claims and ways of establishing *asil* status can be seen in the issues of *al-Arab* journal.

privileges and immunities formalized and sanctioned by the state. The size of Saudi royalty makes it almost unique as a dynasty, and the social ramifications stemming from such a large "institution" are difficult to avoid. Abandoned by their ruling elite in terms of status, the hadari *asil* groups felt also "assaulted from below" by the khadiri groups. As the state had no particular interest in being involved in the negotiations of *ansab* (except by banning written material that might be controversial, and this cannot be applied to the internet), the *asil* groups undertook their own textual campaigns, writing their own genealogies in an attempt to preserve their status. Al-Jasir's *Jamharat* stands as the best and most comprehensive collective codification of the hadari *asil* families in Najd and associated areas.[25]

But this was not enough as the genealogical reaction in the hadari communities and *asil* and non-*asil* groups went far beyond codification. For in reaction to the forces brought to bear on Saudi society over the last two generations and that I have described here, the hadari groups developed complex genealogical responses. For ages, the hadar (both *asil* and non-*asil*) heavily identified with their fellow villagers or townsmen, and a system of mutual support existed with minimum regard to genealogies. The notion of *al-jama`a*, the community, superseded most other markers of identity, especially when the persons were involved in activities outside their own territories, be it emigration to other towns or countries or addressing petitions to distant princes.[26] With the combination of high levels of urbanization and the anonymity such a life style brings with it and a state that is hostile to any notions of organized collective action, the *jama`a* tradition slowly withered away, and the individual was left alone facing the state with all its might. With the demise of traditional forms of political and social organization, one would expect "civil society" to emerge to fill the gap, but the Saudi state also discouraged the formation of civil associations, and what passes for civil organization is empty of any meaningful content, with the possible exception of the chambers of commerce and industry.

With the demise of the *jama`a*, the *binikhi* (=*bani akh*, or kinfolk) took center stage. The latter word, rarely used nowadays, stood in local parlance

---

[25] It should be noted that al-Jasir was not rigorous in his policing of the claims, as his *Jamharat* includes families not generally acknowledged to be of *asil* origin. When such matters were in dispute, he leaned toward inclusion.

[26] Thus the hadari communities involved in long distance camel trade, *'uqayl*, in Baghdad organized on the basis of territorial and not tribal identity into those from Qasim and those from 'Arid (today's Riyadh and environs), with the latter headed by a khadiri (not surprisingly, the relatives of this man, mentioned in the local chronicles as khadiri, now challenge that status).

for kin and signified within the Najdi communities another basis for identity without reference to the purity of pedigree. Today, like the rest of their countrymen, most hadari families[27] live in urban areas intermingling in the fashion of the time with other people but without the support system of the traditional villages where everyone knew his neighbor, and simultaneously deprived of most forms of civil organization so crucial to modern society. In this environment, most families have embarked on concerted efforts to document their genealogical roots and simultaneously form their own "civil" organizations: the family "association." One element in this effort has been genealogical works that tend to cover larger groups, sometimes in the tens of thousands, and published in publicly or privately available books. Such books reflect the consensus of these families on their origins, both tribal and geographical, but equally contain contested claims about both origins and intralineage relations. Indeed, some of the nastiest battles today are fought within the genealogical group itself, as claims to certain distinctions, in terms of historical deeds or privilege of using a name, are hotly disputed.

The other manifestation of the modern genealogical response is the conscious, formal formation of kin groups, or family associations. Crucially, these associations are not *sanctioned* by the state and have no legal standing whatsoever. They are private endeavors embodying collective action *beyond* the control of the state. The families here are defined generally in accordance with the patrilineal rules and would include members sharing a last name or acknowledging descent from a common ancestor, real or imaginary. These are transregional and would comprise all members regardless of location, including offshoots in neighboring countries. The organization of the effort is usually undertaken by family activists, whose qualifications often consist of more enthusiasm than learning and who collectively create the family tree (frequently a subject of dispute) and organize family events. These events vary from family to family, and so does the venue. Some families congregate in the ancestral town or rotate locations. Sometimes the association acquires real estate on a permanent basis to host family activities, including celebrations of holidays, weddings, and regular and ad hoc gatherings. Finance is provided either through regular dues, voluntarily paid by most members or through generous family benefactors, typically the very well off. This last point is still

---

[27] According to my own rough calculations based on *Jamharat*, there are about 3,500 "families" in central Arabia and associated areas. If we assume there are one thousand members in each family, three and a half million persons would be a rough estimate of the hadari *asil* population. If the conjecture that the non-*asil* constitute roughly 30 percent of the inhabitants is correct, the members of these "genealogical" families would be close to five million people, the majority of whom are urban dwellers.

problematic for family associations. Not having the necessary legal personality, financial and other affairs (including bank accounts) have to be undertaken in the name of volunteers, making permanent gifts and endowments impractical.

CONCLUSION

As indicated above, the boom in genealogical production and claims and the rise of kin-based organizations embodied in the family association present challenges to any effort of interpretation. Studies of the genealogical phenomenon in Jordan[28] point to two basic functions served by the rise in kin-based identification and organization. The first is a national identity issue in which the preservation or even invention of tribal roots works as a marker of true "Jordanianness" in contradistinction to the Palestinian newcomers; the state itself appear to be invested in this aspect of the phenomenon. Another function is reflected in the rise in family associations in which these organizations, recognized legally as corporate bodies, came into existence in large measure as a reaction to the economic difficulties faced by Jordan in the 1990s and these associations explicitly provide economic services, including kin-based employment opportunities. Non-economic factors seem to be an ancillary spur for the genealogical interest, such as some successful groups vying to acquire prestige through the invention of Prophetic connections.

For the Saudi case, the picture is more complicated. For one, there does not seem to be a national identity issue at play in the rise of genealogical interest and associations. The national identity of Saudi Arabia is not dependent on the exclusivity of a "tribal" background and is more determined by religious affiliation than genealogical claims; indeed, tribalism in the sense practiced in Jordan is frowned upon by both state and society. In addition, resurgence in interest in *nasab* is not directly associated with specific economic difficulties and instead appears instead to be a reaction to some of the manifestations of prosperity. For much of this experience started and took hold during periods of mostly rising standards of living. Nor is it clear that family associations, which are only one expression of a larger phenomenon, are intended to perform economic functions, except as potential platforms for redistribution within the kin group.

---

[28] See, for example, Anne Marie Baylouny, "Creating Kin: New Family Associations as Welfare Providers in Liberalizing Jordan," *International Journal of Middle East Studies* 38 (2006): 349–68.

Reviewing political, social, and economic developments since the 1970s provides us with hints as to the possible causes for the emergence of this phenomenon. In an ancient land that survived for centuries on limited resources, the population tended to be small and thinly scattered over the large expanses of the Arabian deserts. The Bedouin organized their political, economic, and social existence on the basis of an ideology that employed the idiom of kinship as a way to allocate resources and ensure survival. Most of the hadar of central Arabia were highly detribalized and lived in small communities with rudimentary notions of governance and organization that were not exclusively kin-centric, and identity was more territorially based than in nomadic communities. The concerted efforts and dedication of the Wahhabi religious reformers and the Saudi family to establish a functioning central authority in Arabia took about two centuries before it succeeded. For by 1932, King Abd al-Aziz was able to accomplish what his family and the Wahhabi scholars yearned to have: a fully functioning government that was able to impose its writ on a land they viewed as lawless (and less than pious of course). The campaign originally had its roots within the hadari communities of Najd, and the Bedouin were opportunistically employed to further a system of governance that would ensure the destruction of their tribes as political units. The bureaucracy of the state was initially recruited from the better educated and more experienced inhabitants of the more cosmopolitan towns of the Hijaz. With oil increasingly providing state coffers with growing amounts of rents, the reach of the state went deeper and deeper into the land. The state gradually penetrated every facet of social and economic life, its tentacles guarding the social peace and providing services and goods indispensable to a modern affluent existence. Concomitantly with the deeper penetration of the state and its organs into society, traditional forms of political, economic, and social organization went into retreat. The agricultural economy of the hadar no longer could survive, and what remains today depends heavily on government subsidies, and profits are garnered by agribusiness and not by traditional farmers, who no longer exist. Nomadic pastoralism was transformed and became uneconomical except through state subsidies, where to keep pastoralism alive Saudi Arabia had to become the largest barley importer in the world. With nomads all practically settled now, leading a hadari life, shepherds had to be imported from other lands, mostly Sudan for camels and India for sheep. Political organization, rudimentary as it was, was discouraged by the omnipotent state; the tribe as a political organ was ended, and hadari traditional political practices disappeared. Urbanization became the norm in much of the country, and the major metropolitan areas became powerful magnets; Riyadh, a town of some thirty thousand in 1954, today boasts more than five million people, more than the total population of the whole country only two generations ago.

The rise in living standards, education, urbanization, the pervasive presence of the state – all have led to the creation of a homogeneous and atomized society. Bereft of the traditional means of social and political support, and alternative civil society organization discouraged if not outright banned by the government, the individual was left standing alone. The genealogical reaction is therefore one practical countermovement by society as the state had no power as a social and political matter to prevent families' organizing their affairs to create a buffer between the state and its powerful organs and the individual. At the same time, the rise in genealogical interest and organization lent some stability to an otherwise chaotic and anonymous urban landscape. It is also arguable that the rise in kin consciousness stands as a reaction against status and class differentiation. For in terms of status, a sort of "symbolic" capital is still believed to emanate from a pure genealogy, and those recognized to have it want to preserve it and those without it desire to acquire it. As to class, economic fortunes were mixed, and within kin groups prosperity varied widely. Although many traditional institutions went into decline, one of the exceptions has been religion with its emphasis on certain precepts, not the least of which is kindness to kinfolk, and charity within the family as a morally commendable acts. Family associations are a perfect vehicle to channel these donations in groups living in large urban areas and beyond.

Before closing, a final comment on our scholar, Hamad al-Jasir. In many of his writings on genealogies, and especially on the first and last pages of his *Jamharat*, he indicated with terse, emotional, if elliptical language that his *Jamharat* would be followed by "a general study about genealogies of some modern tribes and families, in an attempt to connect some of them to the stems of earlier tribes, and to prove the *nasab* of families who might be considered of unknown *nasab*, or to clarify the original genealogies of some less known families. This study is perhaps more important than the earlier studies [the *Jamharat*, and *Dictionary of the Tribes*]." On the last page, he declares that his "Study of Bases of Arab Genealogies" is complete, distilling the knowledge he acquired over the years from the study of *ansab*, which "may cause discomfort to many who . . . view *ansab* in a way contrary to its [intrinsic] truth and reality; regardless, I shall not hasten to publish this study, and may wait until the appropriate time." He never published this more comprehensive work, however. One can only speculate that he was preparing an assault on the general conception of *ansab* both historical and in modern-day Arabia, but thought better of it. Nonetheless, genealogy lives on today in Arabia just as it thrived for millennia, not because of some inherent truth contained within it, but because it performed important functions in society at various stages in history. Questions about the true origins or the biological foundations[29] of genealogies are irrelevant to their social and political worth, as they clearly provide society with forms of organization that, even if historically unfounded, are still required. Authentic or invented, *viva ansab!*

---

[29] A recently published article in a local newspaper by an otherwise well-informed writer suggested that DNA tests should be performed on tribesmen to determine their biological affinities; by implication he believed these multitudes sharing a common tribal name would pass the test of common ancestry or be shown to come from a different tribe. See Fa'iz ibn Musa al-Badrani al-Harbi, "Uhibu bi-Qawmi," *Aljazirah* [Riyadh], no. 10327. On Twitter, a number of accounts are dedicated to genealogies with DNA issues playing a large part in the discussions.

14

Caught between Religion and State

Women in Saudi Arabia

Madawi Al-Rasheed

Ilbis baraq' thul wa ibi niswan
Ibid an al-islah ihthar wujudi
al-Hrayri, "Karamkum Allah Saudi"
Wear the burqa and the female abaya
Get off reform and beware of my existence
al-Hrayri, "May God respect you, He is a Saudi"'[1]

Like many states in the Arab world and elsewhere, Saudi Arabia is undoubtedly a masculine state. Men control the political, economic, cultural, religious, and social institutions. They formulate visions about development, articulate policy, and deliver services to the constituency. Yet women are not totally absent from the state's legitimacy narrative;[2] in fact, they constitute an important aspect of its civic myth.[3] Women are, indeed, prominent in the historical and

---

[1] Al-Hrayri is a dissident poet who rose to fame when he replied to a poem by Prince Khalid al-Faysal, the governor of Mecca, celebrating the superiority of a Saudi identity under the title 'Raise your Head, you are Saudi'. Al-Faysal told Saudis that their worth and prestige is growing, while those of others are diminishing, thus endorsing a chauvinist and racist celebration of Saudi identity. Al-Hrayri turned the meaning of the prince's poem, and linked the name "Saudi" to humiliation and submission represented in the symbolic significance of the veil. In opposing the Saudi regime, the poet draws on the inferiority of women. He is currently in prison for his daring poetry, which he published on Saudi Islamist opposition websites and in other virtual media.

[2] I have dealt elsewhere with the role women play in the Saudi unification narrative. See Madawi Al-Rasheed "The Capture of Riyadh Revisited: Shaping Historical Imagination in Saudi Arabia," in *Counter Narratives: History, Contemporary Society, and Politics in Saudi Arabia and Yemen*, ed. Madawi Al-Rasheed and Robert Vitalis (New York: Palgrave, 2004), 183–200.

[3] The relationship between Saudi women and civic myths is discussed in Eleanor Doumato, "Gender, Monarchy and National Identity in Saudi Arabia," *British Journal of Middle Eastern Studies* 19, no. 1 (1992): 31–47, and *Getting God's Ear: Women, Islam and Healing in Saudi Arabia and the Gulf* (New York: Columbia University Press, 2000). The work of Soraya al-Torki on women and citizenship is informative; see "The Concept and Practice of Citizenship in

contemporary imagination of the masculine state; they are depicted as needing to be protected, controlled, and guided within an authoritarian, paternalistic, and protective framework, lest they undermine the masculinity of the state and threaten the integrity of its morality. Services brought about by modernity – education, health, employment, and justice – are delivered to women via men, but only after they have been tailored to suit women's needs, as defined and articulated by the state. The state considers it fundamental that the education system produces generations of females who are socialized to play the roles expected of them. Women work as teachers, doctors, nurses, and social workers – professions that underline their status as caregivers and support workers, which are seen as acceptable roles for women.[4] More recently, some female entrepreneurs, scientists, literary figures, and media specialists have been allowed to enter the public sphere, but this remains dependent on the approval of men.

I argue that the subordination and exclusion of Saudi women is a political – rather than simply a religious or social – fact.[5] Although one cannot disregard the religious and social dimensions, the subordination of women is intimately linked to the project of the state,[6] the drive of modernity, and the

Saudi Arabia," in *Gender and Citizenship in the Middle East*, ed. Suad Joseph (Syracuse, NY: Syracuse University Press 2000), 215–36. On gender issues and identities in the 1990s, see Mai Yamani. *Changed Identities: The Challenge of New Identities in Saudi Arabia* (London: Royal Institute of International Affairs, 2000). This scholarship examines gender issues prior to the changes that started materializing after 9/11, when a new gender policy under the general drive toward social "reform" was introduced by King Abdullah. This article captures the new outlook and anchors it in recent developments that were adopted by the state in response to the mounting external and internal pressures that followed 9/11.

4 Despite increasing numbers of female graduates, women do not represent more than 5 percent of the labor force. For further statistical data, see Tim Niblock, *Saudi Arabia: Power, Legitimacy and Survival* (London: Routledge, 2006).

5 This article deals only with how both the state and religion have shaped gender relations. A comprehensive examination of the third factor, namely, the social/cultural dimensions of gender relations in Saudi Arabia, is in my current research on the historical and contemporary constraints. This research focuses on the intersection of state, religion, and society in the formation of gender policy. This research has been published under the title *A Most Masculine State: Gender, Politics, and Religion in Saudi Arabia* (Cambridge: Cambridge University Press, 2013).

6 Pierre Bourdieu argues that four agents cooperate to enforce both symbolic and actual domination over women. These are the family, the Church, the educational system, and the state. The four factors work to reinforce each other, thus contributing to masculine supremacy. With modernization and as the state becomes stronger with the development of the education system and bureaucracy, we find that increasing pressure is put on women to move from the traditional private patriarchy that is embedded in familial and tribal contexts to public patriarchy enforced by the state. See Pierre Bourdieu, *Masculine Domination* (London: Polity Press, 2001), 85.

fabrication of the state's own legitimacy narrative. It draws on the religious and the social to define gender roles, but its ultimate objective is control and surveillance, practiced under the guise of protecting the moral order. From its early history, the state has projected an image of itself as a moral agent, guarding the chastity of women. Women are a frontier zone, a fixed boundary requiring protection against deviance, transgression, and violation – violation not of the female body, but of the body of the state. I examine the contemporary scene, characterized by the modernizing of authoritarian rule, economic liberalization, and the war on terror, in all of which women have remained central. Throughout the analysis, I trace the state's multiple gender trajectories as it has oscillated between contradictory narratives – as both protector and emancipator of women.

WOMEN BETWEEN RELIGION AND THE STATE

Although the state can privilege certain stories about women, and take part in enforcing practices that punish sinners or reward conformists, it needs theoreticians who articulate the mechanism of control, regulate body and soul, punish transgressors, and define a state-sanctioned moral order in which women play a central role. Religious scholars are specialists in all aspects of life, but their expertise in theorizing and defining women's roles is paramount. State legislation and practice are only a manifestation of their rulings and opinions.

A whole chapter in the Qur'an, Sura al-Nisa, is devoted to the subject of women, and the Prophet's hadiths (sayings and deeds) serve as supplementary guidelines for the articulation of gender in Muslim society. Later Muslim jurists excelled in providing extensive and comprehensive rulings pertaining to women and gender relations, which are in theory the prerogative of the state to enforce. From inheritance and marriage contracts to body purity and attire, a Muslim encounters a plethora of diverse opinions, reflecting the historical moments in which these opinions are formulated, social development, or the personal inclinations of male jurists. The Islamic legitimacy of the state is measured according to its compliance with or deviation from the prescribed and accepted ruling in a particular social context. Although most states of the Muslim world adopted new legislation in most aspects of life, personal and family law remain faithful to Shari`a in the majority of Muslim states.

A royal decree in 1971 established the Council of Higher Ulama, headed by appointed grand muftis, as a permanent council, whose objective is to issue fatwas (opinions) on personal matters of creed, worship, and transactions. These need majority approval from members of the council. But what is a fatwa? A fatwa is a *hukm*, a ruling in response to a question. It is the mufti's answer to a query, either real or hypothetical. The one qualified to issue the ruling should exhibit piety (*wara*) and religiosity (*diyana*) and be known to have resisted the intervention of Iblis (Satan).[7] Can a fatwa change with time and place? This is a controversial question that is dealt with in the anthologies of Saudi scholars. The majority reject the view that all fatwas are contextual – that is, bound by time and place. They distinguish between fixed rulings that are eternal, outside the changing social and historical moments, and those that serve the requirements of *maslaha* (interest) – that is, specific to a particular context. The first is certainly fixed; the second is potentially changeable.

Saudi religious scholars have produced extensive rulings dealing with women's issues, which fill several volumes of *fiqh* (jurisprudence). The contents and sheer amount of their fatwas reflect a fetishism amounting to an obsession with all matters feminine. In addition to the known opinions pertaining to personal and family life, hardly any aspect of the female body, behavior, or life is left unregulated by a fatwa. According to one source, Saudi ulama produced more than thirty thousand fatwas on women in the second half of the twentieth century.[8] In one of the most comprehensive contemporary fatwa anthologies, issued by the Council of Higher Ulama, one whole chapter is dedicated to women, amounting to more than 140 pages. If the section dealing with marriage is included, we find more than three hundred pages listing rulings that deal with women's issues.[9]

Whether the volume of rulings on women is a response to a rising demand for religious opinions at a time of drastic and rapid social change, or whether it is simply a demonstration of the ulama's narrow range of expertise – or perhaps obsession – seems irrelevant. It is important to note that scholars who are employed by the state, and often work in its many religious institutions, issue these fatwas. Their fetishism can only be interpreted as a reflection of their marginalization in political and economic matters, which has left them in control of only the social arena, and in particular issues relevant to

[7] I rely on the most authoritative collection of official fatwas issued by the Council of Higher Ulama. See Khalid al-Jurayssi, *Fatawi ulama al-balad al-haram* (Riyadh: Maktabat al-Malik Fahd al-Wataniyya, 2007), 37–8. Although this collection is representative of the official religious views on religion in general, other collections can be consulted starting with Muhammad ibn Abd al-Wahhab's early treatises. Most of his opinions are incorporated in recent publications. For an exploration of Ibn Abd al-Wahhab's view on women, see Natana DeLong-Bas *Wahhabi Islam: From Revival and Reform to Global Jihad* (London: I. B. Tauris 2004), 123–91. In this volume, Wahhabi Islam is seen as an empowering religious discourse that encourages the emancipation of women in Arabian society. This approach can be contrasted with Doumato's historical work in *Getting God's Ear*.

[8] Anwar Abdullah, *Khasais wa sifat al-mujtama al-wahhabi al-saudi* (Paris: al-Sharq, 2005).

[9] Khalid al-Jurayssi, *Fatawi ulama*.

women. As the state is gradually losing its Islamic identity, both the ulama and the government have embarked on a process whereby the visible signs of adherence to Islam need to be promoted and privileged to inscribe in the imagination the centrality of the pious state. This is dependent today on the visible signs of piety, and women in particular are doomed to be such signs. Their invisibility in the public sphere is, ironically, a visible token of state piety and commitment to Islam.[10]

A full examination of the corpus of rulings on women is beyond the scope of this chapter. What concerns us here are opinions that enhance female exclusion from the public sphere, the prohibition on women occupying leading public roles, the control of their bodies, and their secondary status in the public realm in general. While the state celebrates the contribution of specific women to its foundation and legitimacy, the ulama provide detailed, religiously sanctioned opinions that fix women in a particular framework, the purpose of which is to guard the symbolism of gender politics in the kingdom.

Saudi ulama categorically reject female eligibility for the office of political (*imara*) and religious (*imama*) leadership and justice (*qada*).[11] Unaffected by contemporary theological debates among Muslim scholars elsewhere, they retain a strict interpretation of Prophetic sayings, always finding in them proof of women's unsuitability for such high positions. Women are described as weak creatures, subject to natural cycles that reduce their ability to act, assess, and evaluate situations requiring courage, speed, and other cherished masculine qualities. Scholars resort to natural qualities (*tabia*) and biological facts, on the basis of which they construct an image of women as weak, hesitant, emotional, and lacking full control over their bodies and minds. They are only eligible to be half-witnesses in court. Their emotional tendencies, which arise from certain bodily dispositions, disqualify them as full members of society – and certainly exclude them from the administration of justice. Saudi ulama did not invent these opinion nor are they unique in perpetuating them. They draw on an old Sunni tradition associated with the Hanbali school of jurisprudence. Their resistance to change and new religious interpretations must be interpreted within the context of their relation with the state, which has reinforced and abided by their rulings until very recently. The interest of the ulama to remain in control of the social sphere as part of the bargain with the state made them less amenable to changes and moderation.

---

[10] See Doumato "Gender, Monarchy."

[11] Khalid al-Jurayssi, *Fatawi ulama*, 1949–54. For a different interpretation of the Islamic tradition on women's participation in leadership positions, see Ahmad Yamani, *al-Islam wa al-mara* (London: Muassasat al-Furqan, 2004).

Weak and subject to cyclical variation in mood and judgment, the female body is also seen as a source of *fitna* (chaos) among the believers. The total veiling of the body, including the face, is considered a requirement in the public sphere, excluding prayer and pilgrimage. Sex segregation is always required, even in hospitals, where patients should be treated by professionals of the same sex.[12] Scholars have urged the state to establish all-female hospitals, banks, and businesses, to create segregated ghettos marking compliance with their interpretation of Islam.

When in public, women should never wear white clothes if such attire is the prerogative of the men of the country, lest they be seen as imitating them and confusing gender – hence the persistence of the black *abaya*, which not only is a cultural code of dress, but has also attained a religious significance. Notwithstanding the fact that nothing in Islamic sources specifies the color of women's clothes, Saudi scholars have elevated black to the rank of a religious obligation.[13] The colors black and white in the public sphere have become signs of the piety of the state and nation. If women were to refuse to dress in black, they would not only violate a religious ruling but also threaten the state and its symbols, very much like altering the national flag or anthem, which are never modified except at times of political change. Wearing high heels, perfuming the body, eliminating excessive facial hair, and tattooing the skin, for decoration or marking a tribal identity, are all prohibited. The body is the medium for expressing a purely Islamic identity, defined according to specific guidelines from the ulama.

Fear of the female body is expressed in several fatwas on purity and pollution, under the general subject of women's blood (*dima al-nisa*).[14] Women carry a disproportionate potential for polluting not only men but also public places of worship. The polluting potential of women is not an opinion unique to Saudi religious scholars but is shared with others in almost all religious traditions. The preoccupation with female liquids stems from an age-old classification system that allocates women to the category of wet/weak in opposition to men, who are associated with dry/hard.[15] Although women are allowed to attend a mosque, seated in a separate area, they are to be excluded during menstruation, childbirth, and other occasions of bleeding. If they attend a sermon or a lecture, they should be seated in the back rows because *sadara*

---

[12] When women work in mixed settings, for example, hospitals, their experience has not been smooth. See Qanta Ahmad, *In the Land of Invisible Women: A Female Doctor's Journey in the Saudi Kingdom* (Naperville, IL: Sourcebooks, 2008).

[13] Al-Jurayssi, *Fatawi ulama*, 1811–35.

[14] Ibid., 1906.

[15] See Bourdieu, *Masculine Domination*.

(priority in seating arrangements that is associated with social or political status), even in a segregated area, is frowned upon for women. God and his Prophet appreciate women in *muakhira* (the back row) rather than *sadara* (the front row).[16] A good Muslim woman is one who willingly and eagerly occupies the last of the last rows. This not only guards men from her potential danger but also confirms her subordinate legal, religious, and social status, anchoring it in physical space.

The Saudi ulama follow the strictest interpretations on all matters feminine, as required by the legitimacy narrative of the state.[17] It is the quest to exhibit the Islamic identity of the state, rather than tribalism, conservatism, or misogyny, that lies at the heart of the persistence of such interpretations in the contemporary context. In fact, this persistent misogyny is a reflection of political developments requiring its perpetuation. Although many Muslim scholars have moderated their opinions on women, we find that their Saudi counterparts have remained faithful to established discrimination against women.[18] This seems to be a reflection of their intimate association with the state: Both reinforce interpretations that seek to exclude women from the public sphere.

The same political developments require the promotion of polygamy and other reinvented marriage contracts, for example, *misyar*, a contract that frees men from financial obligations normally associated with traditional *nikah*. Since the 1980s religious scholars have actively promoted polygamy as a religious obligation, and several ulama have served as matchmakers. Although many Muslim religious scholars elsewhere have endeavored to ration polygamy and impose strict conditions for its validity, their Saudi counterparts have spared no effort to propagate it as a natural social necessity, sanctioned by divine authority. Public calls for the promotion of polygamy, always sponsored by the state, equate women's acceptability with their overall acceptance of Islam. According to a new fatwa, being the second or third wife of a morally and socially worthy man is far better than remaining a spinster.[19] In a society where royalty indulges freely in polygamous and serial marriages,[20] the

---

[16] Al-Jurayssi, *Fatawi ulama*, 1948.
[17] According to Natana DeLong Bas, Wahhabi teachings are in fact conducive to female emancipation. See Natana DeLong-Bas, *Wahhabi Islam: From Revival and Reform to Global Jihad* (London: I. B. Tauris, 2004), 123–93. Even if one accepts her interpretation of Wahhabi sources, we cannot ignore the fact that the state remains a powerful agent in shaping gender relations in Saudi Arabia.
[18] See Khaled Abou El Fadl, *Speaking in God's Name: Islamic Law, Authority and Women* (Oxford: Oneworld, 2001).
[19] See Maha Yamani, *Polygamy and Law in Contemporary Saudi Arabia* (London: Ithaca, 2008), 72.
[20] On royal polygamy and serial marriages, see Madawi Al-Rasheed, *A History of Saudi Arabia* (Cambridge: Cambridge University Press, 2002), 75–80.

scholars' promotion of polygamy did not go unheeded. It increased dramatically after the first oil boom of the 1970s and spread in regions where it used to
be the exception rather than the norm. Men of all social classes and tribal backgrounds competed to engage in polygamous marriages to mark their prestige
and newly acquired wealth.

Saudi scholars have also promoted controversial forms of marriage, such
as *misyar*.[21] Men are under no obligation to provide homes or subsistence for
misyar wives. *Misyar* is also a mechanism to evade objections from the first
wife, because this marriage can be conducted in secrecy, at least in its early
phase and before the birth of any children. Up to three *misyar* wives can be
combined with the first wife, without the usual cost of *nikah* being an issue.[22]

The promotion of polygamy and *misyar* seems to have coincided with the
adoption by a neighboring Muslim state – Iran – of a similar stance under
the pressure of the Iran-Iraq War and the revival of the Shi'i *muta* (temporary) marriage.[23] Saudi Arabia entered a long competition with Iran over the
demarcation of the state's Islamic identity. Saudi scholars were compelled to
follow the footsteps of their Shi'i rivals in rendering certain sexual relations
licit. Although *misyar* is different from *muta*, it was reinvented as an authentic
solution, anchored in the Islamic tradition, to modernity and its discontents
such as late marriage, spinsterhood, and other social changes that swept the
country in the latter half of the twentieth century. Here women in polygamous
marriages, together with those who contract *misyar*, are symbols promoting the
flexibility of the state, and its progress, within the fold of Islam. Physical repro-
duction is not simply a private matter, the prerogative of two consenting adults;
it is also a state priority, sanctioned by the religious scholars. The legitimacy
of the Islamic state is dependent on as many women as possible accepting
traditional and reinvented marriages, subjecting their bodies to the rulings on
segregation, veiling, purity, and pollution.

Atomized in the confines of the private sphere and deprived of the ability
to organize themselves in the public domain, women search for conformity,
rebellion, and subversion. In their own ways, they have inscribed on their own
bodies signs of both conformity and resistance. Those who have, willingly or

---

[21] Many books sponsored and published by the state appeared to propagate *misyar* marriage in the
1980s. An example is Abd al-Malik al-Mutlaq, *Zawaj al-misyar* (Riyadh: Ibn Laboun, 1423 AH
[2003]). The book includes an endorsement from the King Fahd National Library and the
Ministry of Justice.

[22] Some Sunni scholars in the Muslim world have denounced the Saudi opinion on *misyar*
marriage: see Abdullah Kamal, *al-Daara al-halal* (Beirut: al-Maktaba al-Thaqafiyya, 1997).
With increasing pressure exerted by the state to appear modern, the Mufti of Saudi Arabia,
Shaikh Abdul Aziz Al-Shaikh, issued an opinion denouncing *misyar* marriage in 2009.

[23] On *muta* marriage in Iran, see Shahla Hairi, *Law of Desire: Temporary Marriage in Shii Iran*
(Syracuse, NY: Syracuse University Press, 1989).

unwillingly, accepted the norms of regulating the female body endorse complete veiling and assert the state's and religious scholars' framing of women in public. If they venture outside the home, to work or attend a conference, a prayer, or a sermon, they immediately gravitate toward the public physical space allocated to them. Some are vocal in rejecting their right to free movement and refuse to leave home without a chaperon. They not only cherish their subordination and exclusion, they turn both into a virtue or a sign of their elevated position as protected and guarded women. Many women reject medical treatment offered by a male doctor, and if this is not possible, they insist on covering their faces during examination and treatment. They defend polygamy and other newly popularized forms of marriage as liberation from more devastating situations such as spinsterhood, divorce, or illicit sexual relations. Their completely concealed bodies attest to the triumph of the state masculine legitimacy narrative in which they are central. They endorse a mask that displays the piety of the state.

Other women have thwarted this framing by exposing parts of the body, decorating it, or covering it with controversial attire. They do so because their own bodies seem to be the only capital they can potentially possess and reclaim from the state and its repressive surveillance. In their own way they choose another mask that inscribes their resistance. Wearing heavy make-up and perfumes, all imported from Western cosmetics houses, they highlight the natural contours of the face, eyes, and lips, parts they have dared to reveal. Others go as far as altering and modifying the body, in some cases reconstructing intimate parts to wipe out signs of sexual rebellion. Heavily scented bodies roam the shopping malls, announcing the penetration of the feminine in the public sphere. They do not then need the condemned high heels to announce their arrival; they assert their right to free movement by driving in limited, semipublic spaces, for example, behind walled compounds or in the desert, a peripheral large public space that the state's agencies of control and surveillance have not yet reached. In their all-private female gatherings, rituals, weddings, and entertainment, they subvert the norms and engage in illicit "rebellions" that center on the body. Dancing, smoking, and excessive consumption all confirm their ability to use their bodies in ways unsanctioned by the state. They engage in alternative religiosity, drawing on unorthodox practices of sorcery, witchcraft, and divination. They seek the expertise of other women and men, some at the bottom of the social hierarchy, such as locals and Africans specializing in delivering such subversive services, which are, if discovered, punished by the state.[24] Other women venture into

---

[24] The Saudi press regularly reports on the arrest of sorcerers, especially Africans.

the newly created shopping centers to engage in "modern consumption" and display newly celebrated identities.[25]

Elite educated women find solace in fictionalized and sexualized selves they construct in novels and disseminate in publications. Writing the female body, indulging its sexual fantasies, and disclosing details of illicit sexual encounters have become common themes dominating the recent wave of female literary productions.[26] The anonymity of the virtual world offers women who stretch the boundaries a sanctuary for their acts of rebellion. Internet discussion forums, female chatrooms, and daring photography of the rebellious female body become bold acts that draw on the body to write the transcript of resistance. Others have defied the restrictions on Saudi women marrying non-Saudis and entered into marital unions with foreign Muslim and non-Muslim men. Such marriages require negotiation, not only with family members and guardians, but also with state agencies. However, their numbers are rising. According to Ministry of the Interior statistics, twenty thousand women married foreigners between 2002 and 2007, with 2007 seeing the highest level of registered cross-national marriages.[27] To give one's body to a non-Saudi is itself an act of defiance in a society that struggles to define the boundary between insiders and outsiders. Furthermore, such marriages are acts of rebellion against a background where men struggle to keep their genealogies fixed and pure.

Whether women choose conformity or silent rebellion, they live their modernity in a country that has not yet resolved big questions about its identity. Despite the slogans of Arab and Islamic heritage, Saudi Arabia lacks a local nationalism that unites the fragments. Calling upon regional (Arab) and global (Islamic) heritage is not sufficient to make Saudis what they are. Women are what make Saudis unique and different from the other Arab countries or the numerous Islamic countries worldwide. Those women who assert their piety and defend their own exclusion are making a plea about what it means to be women in an Islamic state, thus confirming the state's legitimacy narrative about its piety. They assert a modern pious identity, which coincides with the

[25] See Amelie Le Renard "'Only for Women': Women, the State and Reform in Saudi Arabia," *Middle East Journal* 62, no. 4 (2008): 610–29.

[26] For example, Zaynab Hifni, *Lam a'ud abki* (Beirut: al-Saqi, 2004); Raja al-Sani, *Banat al-Riyadh* (Beirut: al-Saqi, 2005); and Samar al-Moqrin, *Nisa al-munkar* (Beirut: al-Saqi, 2008). Women's literary genres are discussed in Sadekka Arebi, *Women and Words in Saudi Arabia: The Politics of Literary Discourse* (New York: Columbia University Press, 1994). For a recent assessment of the new Saudi women's literature, see Ahmad al-Wasil, 'Satair wa aqlam sarikha: takwin al-muthaqafa al-saoudiyya wa tahawulataha' in *Idhafat* 7 (2009): 82–105.

[27] Najah al-Osaimi, "Saudi Women Marrying Foreigners on the Rise," *Arab News*, Sept. 14, 2007.

state's discourse about its uniqueness in the Muslim world. On the other hand, those women who "rebel" are defining themselves in new ways that challenge old perceptions of Saudi society and state. They too are seeking to be modern by choosing to highlight their subjectivity and choices. The "modern" woman is today promoted by a state that has come under extraordinary pressures to redefine itself in recent years.

WOMEN AND MODERNIZING AUTHORITARIAN RULE

If invisible Saudi women are visible signs of piety, honor, and legitimacy, their recent orchestrated and well-managed emergence in the public sphere is a reflection of the quest of the state to be seen as the champion of reform at a very difficult moment in its contemporary history. The increased visibility of women is a product of modernizing authoritarian rule, economic liberalization, and, finally, the war on terror. All these factors may in the long run undermine the legitimacy of the state, which they were initially intended to boost.

Modernizing authoritarian rule is sometimes dubbed "upgrading," a phenomenon that emerged in many Arab countries in the post-9/11 period. Heydemann specifies four developments that, in his opinion, reflect the process of upgrading: appropriating and containing civil society, managing political contestation, capturing the benefits of economic reform, and diversifying international linkages.[28] Yet the fundamental importance of gender in these four measures is never considered central to the process of upgrading as a whole. An examination of the state's recent gender initiatives attests to the fact that women remain an important pillar of state legitimacy, which in itself is politically defined and changeable. What follows is an examination of the new initiatives that aim to upgrade Saudi authoritarianism by playing the gender card.

High-ranking officials, including the king and ministers, have recently begun to express opinions regarding women's emancipation, education, and employment. Since 2005 King Abdullah has occasionally received women in a private *majlis*, to reinforce the impression that the state is the protector of female rights and interests, as defined by Islam. Women accompanied him during visits abroad in 2005 and 2006. Other ministers and members of the royal family have claimed that women enjoy full rights in the kingdom.[29] Carefully

---

[28] Steven Heydemann, "Upgrading Authoritarianism in the Arab World," Analysis Paper no. 13 (Washington, DC: Saban Center for Middle East Policy at the Brookings Institution), Oct. 2007.

[29] Such statements are regularly made after international human reports expose injustice and gender discrimination. One such report was Human Rights Watch, *Perpetual Minors: Human Rights Abuses Stemming from Male Guardianship and Sex Segregation in Saudi Arabia* (New York: Human Rights Watch, 2008).

selected highly educated and articulate women have appeared in international economic forums, diplomatic circles, and academic conferences, accompanied by officials and important princes. When pressed by the international media about the subordination of Saudi women, both officials and women have explained that the state is ahead of society in that it endorses female emancipation, which needs to progress slowly, to prevent the process backfiring and causing chaos and confrontation. The state voiced its support for full female participation but stressed that this needs to be negotiated with conservative elements in Saudi society. Several princes have argued that women are held hostage by traditional cultural values rooted in tribalism and misinterpretation of Islam. Unless these archaic traditions develop, the state is not in a position to go against the general understanding of the position of women or their prescribed roles. The state has resisted demands to increase female employment in areas considered unsuitable. Instead, it has allowed elite women – mainly princesses, entrepreneurs, artists, and academics – greater visibility in certain circumscribed surroundings, for example, in chambers of commerce, international economic forums, educational forums, diplomatic circles, and the media. It remains unreceptive to demands for the establishment of a ministry for women's affairs and the appointment of women to the Consultative Council. In the 2005 municipal elections, women were denied the right to participate as voters and candidates. All-female banks and hotels are tolerated, and occasionally some women are invited to attend the Shura Council meetings as segregated spectators and consultants on women's affairs. Recently a princess became the principal of the first women's university.

In 2009 King Abdullah appointed Nura al-Fayez as deputy minister for women's education, the highest post ever occupied by a woman.[30] Women's charities are abundant and are welcomed as arenas in which women can play a legitimate public role.[31] Such ventures are, however, always placed under the guardianship of all-male ministries. There are no independent no-governmental women's organizations defending women's rights. A virtual Saudi women's rights forum was blocked.[32] Women's human rights are incorporated in the agenda of the newly founded state human rights organization, which reports directly to the king and Minister of the Interior. In summary, women are granted a presence in areas that never challenge the state's authority. Their employment and role in the charity sector remain

---

[30] *Arab News*, Feb. 15, 2009, http://www.arabnews.com/?page=1&section=0&article=119243.

[31] On women's charities, see Amélie Le Renard, "Pauvreté et charité en Arabie Saoudite: la famille royale, le secteur privé et l'État-providence," *Critique Internationale* 4, no. 41 (2008): 137–56.

[32] Personal communication with a Saudi woman, October 2008. The website was www .saudiwomanrights.com.

under state control; they are, in fact, sanctioned and promoted by the state as tokens of its progress and reform.

In June 2004 the state dedicated one session of the newly established National Dialogue Forum to women's affairs. Women participated in the meeting and presented their views on matters related to their current situation and future economic prospects in a country where they form the majority of university graduates but remain marginalized in the labor force. Tension erupted between those who support more traditional roles for women and those who aspire toward greater participation and visibility. The latter were accused of promoting a Western agenda, with the purpose of destabilizing society and threatening its Islamic piety and authenticity. The debate ended without serious consideration of the major challenges of absorbing the increasing number of educated women into the Saudi economy. Some female participants thought that conservatives and traditionalists had hijacked the meeting. This prompted them to send a separate list of recommendations to Crown Prince Abdullah, who met privately with a small number of female delegates. Publicly debating women's roles, in the carefully designed forum and under the sponsorship and patronage of the state, underlined the latter's claim to a progressive role in a sea of traditionalism and conservatism.

This increasing visibility of women is part of modernizing authoritarian rule. The state offers a legitimate space for women to mix with men (for example, the Jeddah Economic Forums and state occasions such as press conferences by the foreign minister with former U.S. Secretary of State Condoleezza Rice or visits of the monarch abroad), vote in selected elite forums (chambers of commerce elections – but not in municipal elections), and participate in the state's own human rights organization (but it denies them the right to form their own independent human rights forum). Women have proved crucial for reinvigorating a state desperate to shed a negative image that has deteriorated with increasing globalization and international scrutiny of the gender-based exclusion and discrimination in the country.

WOMEN AND ECONOMIC LIBERALIZATION

The economic liberalization that was necessary after Saudi Arabia was officially accepted as a member of the World Trade Organization required a new position on gender.[33] Despite predictions that the role of the state would shrink under the pressure of globalization and economic liberalization, it was, in fact, reinvigorated. The international community expected the kingdom to

---

[33] On Saudi economic reforms, see Niblock, *Saudi Arabia*.

facilitate international investment through a series of legal reforms. This pressure for economic liberalization prompted scrutiny of Saudi social practices, especially the exclusion of women and their inability to act as independent economic agents. Despite the fact that many elite Saudi women have become entrepreneurs, setting up their own businesses or working within the financial empires of their male relatives, the legal restrictions on their travel, personal identity cards, and economic transactions were believed to hinder wider international economic opportunities, which would have tapped the increasing wealth of women in a society in which they normally only inherit wealth. Several articles appeared in the international media, highlighting the importance of this wealth and how to draw on it.[34] Many argued that economic liberalization must be accompanied by serious social reforms, especially in the area of gender relations. The state used economic liberalization as a pretext for increasing female visibility, thus giving substance to its reformist social agenda and escaping criticism from a hesitant constituency. Women are increasingly seen as crucial for future economic prosperity. In 2007 the Jeddah Chamber of Commerce and Industry organized an event for businesswomen. Under the patronage of Princess Adila bint Abdullah, the king's daughter, the event highlighted women's empowerment as key to development and progress. The princess drew attention to female wealth, with women investing SAR 44 billion in the market while their bank savings amount to SAR 100 billion. With women constituting 66 percent of university students, their integration into the labor force is inevitable. The deputy Minister of Labor attributed the slowness of such integration to factors such as transportation problems, unpleasant working conditions, and lack of proper skills. Women criticized the male guardian requirement and the strict interpretations of Islam that are presented as protecting the nation's values and Islamic tradition.[35] The majority of participants attributed the partial integration of women in the economy to the factors usually cited: strict Islamic rules, cultural values, and lack of support from families. Religious extremism was named the fundamental problem, but not the state that has nourished it for decades to boost its Islamic credentials. No participant could mention that gender segregation and the exclusion of women have always underpinned the national legitimacy narrative upon which the state was founded. The alleged uniqueness or exceptionalism of

---

[34] In 2007–8, *The Economist* ran several articles on female wealth in Saudi Arabia. In 2009, *Time* magazine highlighted the emancipation of Saudi women; see "Saudi Women's Quiet Revolution," Oct. 2009, 20–24, 19.

[35] Samar Fatany, "Saudi Arabia Forum on the Role of Women Suggests That Empowerment Is the Key to Future Economic Prosperity," *Arab News*, July 24, 2007.

Saudi Arabia (*khususia*) has always been constructed on several pillars, the most important of which is the seclusion of women.

Elite women were the first to benefit from the economic boom of the 1970s, but they had already escaped the general restrictions imposed on the majority of Saudi women. Although in the past the state turned a blind eye to this, it now actively promotes them as symbols of success and progress. While princes still dominate the business world, their daughters and sisters have also achieved a high level of economic activity, especially in owning and managing businesses that cater to women – beauty parlors, all-women hotels, fashion companies, sports centers, and other such ventures. They are joined by women from the newly emerging entrepreneurial classes that are tied to the state either as loyal coteries or as partners in business ventures. Neither extremist religious views nor conservative cultural values have hindered the integration of such businesswomen into the general economy. The well-known Saudi businesswoman Lubna al-Olayan is one such case. Named as female executive of the year in Dubai, and recipient of an achievement award from the Arab Bankers' Association, she is the director of the Olayan Group and chief executive of Olayan Financing Company. She acknowledges her debt to male members of her family, above all her father and brothers, without whom her preeminence in the local and regional business world would not have been possible.[36] She does not, however, mention a long history of loyalty to the state as the prerequisite for her father's financial empire. She sends a clear message to her audiences: Working with "our government," rather than against it, to promote business opportunities, education, and training for all is key – in addition to the support of other men. Her case is a clear reflection of how elite women, by negotiating their rights first within the private patriarchal context of family, can then move on to enter the public sphere under the patronage of the state. By accepting placement of their success within the state-approved new reformist agenda, they move to endorse public patriarchy.

The current state policy of increasing the visibility of Saudi women and promising greater educational and employment opportunities as stated in the last two development plans (2005–9) and (2010–14) has occupied Saudis and generated heated controversies.[37] It seems that the government has a deliberate policy of engaging society with fierce debates on gender, which appear to have replaced debates on political reforms. Social reforms have replaced the earlier

---

[36] "Lubna Olayan Honoured in New York, Dubai," available at www.olayangroup.com (accessed Sept. 30, 2008).

[37] For further details on the Saudi Development Plans, with special emphasis on matters related to empowering women, see Muna al-Munajjid, *Women's Employment in Saudi Arabia: A Major Challenge*, Consultancy Paper, Ideation Center Insight, Booz & Co., n.d.

calls for political participation, especially those associated with the reformist trend that emerged after 9/11.[38] Saudi liberals are currently enjoying greater official tolerance, especially as they embark on critical assessment of society, its radical religious tradition, and conservatism. This is especially apparent among journalists and activists working at the newly established print and satellite media. They applaud the king's many initiatives on improving the participation of Saudi women in society and demand more reforms that would enhance the status of women and their economic opportunities. They welcome fewer restrictions on the enforcement of sex segregation in the workplace and newly established educational institutions, and they support the need to undermine the prohibition on *ikhtilat* (mixing between the sexes in public places) that had dominated the Saudi public sphere from the shopping center to the classroom.

It is important to note that the new innovations in gender policy and the loosening of some of the restrictions on women have been met with great debate and controversy in some Islamic circles. Religious scholars and Islamists are divided today on how to respond to state innovations, especially those that specifically deal with loosening restrictions on women in the public sphere. There are those who remain silent, preferring not to trigger a confrontation with the state if they voice serious criticism of its gender policy. Many among the official and independent ulama have adopted this position. At the same time many ulama and religious civil servants endorse the social reforms and provide "revisionist" religious opinions in which they dismiss old fatwas and volunteer new rulings on important issues such as *ikhtilat* and driving. Director of the Committee for the Promotion of Virtue and Prohibition of Vice in Mecca Ahmad al-Ghamdi shocked his audiences when he declared that coeducation and *ikhtilat* are permissible. A judge in Riyadh, shaykh Issa al-Gaith, condemned those who issue strict opinions on *ikhtilat*. Such new revisionist opinions are welcomed by Saudi liberal media such as *al-Watan, al-Sharq al-Awsat,* and *al-Arabiyya* television, all having become saturated with commentaries applauding the new positions on women' issues.

However, objections have been voiced, especially among both old and young religious scholars. There are those who articulate serious condemnation of the new gender policy; their voices are heard only in virtual forums. In 2009, thirty-five ulama circulated a petition calling for banning women presenters in the media and pictures of women, regarded as "obscene," on the pages of the Saudi press. Condemnations of the introduction of cinema in Saudi cities and mixing between the sexes during book fairs are regularly voiced. Among

---

[38] For details on calls for reform in the post-9/11 period, see Madawi Al-Rasheed, *A History of Saudi Arabia,* 2nd ed. (Cambridge: Cambridge University Press, 2010), 261–77.

others, shaykh Abd al-Rahman al-Barrak, together with member of the Council of Higher Ulama Saad al-Shithri and Islamist lecturer Nura al-Saad, have all condemned mixing between the sexes. Shaykh Yusif al-Ahmad offered even more controversial opinions when he called for the rebuilding of the Mecca Mosque to ensure greater separation of men and women when they perform their rituals.

Another more nuanced position on gender reform is articulated by person-alities such as ex-Sahwi Salman al-Awdah and Abdul Aziz al-Qasim. Such shaykhs try to avoid a direct confrontation with the old guards of the religious field by introducing distinctions between religious prohibitions and socially unacceptable practices. On women driving, they are more likely to argue that it is not prohibited from the point of view of Islam but is not an acceptable social custom in a country such as Saudi Arabia. Both shaykhs Abd al-Mohsin al-Obaikan and Muhsin al-Awaji have expressed this view. Those who pro-hibit driving usually confuse the religious and social realms or adhere to the principle of *sadd al-dhara'i*`, that is, prohibiting something to avoid a greater evil, according to many scholars. Al-Awdah's weekly television program *hajar al-zawiyya*, the Cornerstone, on MBC television has become the arena in which such opinions are often offered to the audiences.

In general, it is noteworthy that gender has become a serious preoccupation for many ulama and Islamists as much as it is on the agenda of liberals. It will continue to be so in the future. Gender reform has diverted attention from other equally pressing issues.[39] It seems that today, after 9/11 and the crackdown on jihadis, both of which led to a serious fragmentation of the religious arena in Saudi Arabia, many Islamists are left with the gender reform to comment on and criticize, as an outlet for criticizing the government and undermining its vision for the future. Many forces in Saudi Arabia have converged on women as the new field on which to fight their own battles. Women and their increasing visibility are the new areas of contestation.

WOMEN AND THE WAR ON TERROR

The war on terror, as coined by the United States, involves more than fighting in the rugged mountains of Afghanistan or the streets of Riyadh. One aspect of it is to reform Islam by promoting moderate interpretations, especially teachings on tolerance and coexistence with non-Muslims. More importantly, social

---

[39] Further details on the controversies on gender that dominate the Saudi public sphere, see Madawi Al-Rasheed, *A Most Masculine State: Gender, Politics, and Religion in Saudi Arabia* (Cambridge: Cambridge University Press, 2013).

liberalization is also desired as a strategy for luring Muslim youth away from militancy and religious and political activism. In this double engagement with the Muslim world, women are important in many ways. As mothers, educators, and informers, women are highlighted as key players in the war on terror. Their emancipation and active participation in the public sphere are considered essential for social reform. Relaxing strict sex segregation and allowing more women to enter the public domain are regarded as vital for wide-ranging social reform that would make terrorism less attractive to young men. Some commentators have gone so far as to claim that jihadist terrorism has its roots in sexual frustration; more exposure to the opposite sex, and social liberalization in general, would therefore contribute to the war on terror.[40]

Saudi Arabia plays a prominent role in this project, for obvious reasons.[41] Shortly after 9/11, the Saudi state started promoting itself as the champion of religious and social reform.[42] Women suddenly became more visible in the public domain as participants in debates and as active in the economy. In addition, the war on terror, to which the state has subscribed, involved drawing on women as agents of the state in its battle with its home-grown jihadist trend. One objective of the National Dialogue Forum's session on women was to extract a pledge of allegiance to the state from women, who had thus far been excluded from playing any formal or institutionalized role in the state. This loyalty was important during a turbulent time, when the state was fighting daily battles with radical young Saudis. Women, who as mothers obviously have the first contact with such youth, are in a better position to correct their deviance – or at least notice it before it develops into serious participation in violence.

Some women were enlisted as informers, a role that involves reporting early signs of radicalization and unusual militant attitudes and behavior. More recently women were employed by the Committee for the Promotion of Virtue and the Prohibition of Vice to monitor other women and catch those whose bodies were not fully veiled during the Janadiriyya festival in March 2008. Saudi officials highlighted the responsibility of women in the security of the nation and state, in addition to promoting *fadila* (virtue).

[40] Saud al-Musaybih argued that Jihadis lure young Saudi men by invoking *zaffa*, a happy celebration for a bridegroom-to-be, thus playing on youthful sexual frustration and sensational themes. Saud al-Musaybih, *al-Yaum*, Jan. 17, 2005. See also Amer al-Amir, 'al-kabt al-jinsi bayn al-janna wa al-nar' at http://daralnadwa.com/vb/showthread.php?t=153503, accessed Apr. 21, 2005.

[41] See Salwa Ismail, "Producing Reformed Islam: A Saudi Contribution to the US Projects of Global Governance," in *Kingdom without Borders: Saudi Arabia's Political, Religious and Media Frontiers*, ed. Madawi Al-Rasheed (London: Hurst & Co., 2008), 113–33.

[42] For an assessment of state strategies to modernise authoritarian rule, see Al-Rasheed, *A History of Saudi Arabia*, ch. 9.

Some women were recruited as spies and required to use their feminine charms to infiltrate jihadist circles, which led to the arrest of some militants. Female spies were paid compensation, known as *badal suma*, for losing their reputation and status in their communities.[43] It is very difficult to draw a precise picture of the scale of such clandestine activities, but anecdotal evidence and occasional reports in the Saudi press indicate that women may have played an important yet unacknowledged role in the so-called war on terror.

Although the participation of women in the war on terror remains elusive, the war, which involved wide-scale arrests of suspects, activists, and peaceful reformers, brought about a different kind of female activism. Some women were arrested for providing logistical support for jihadists or posting jihadist messages on the internet. These arrests intensified after 2003. In addition to the arrest of jihadist activists and ideologues, the state became intolerant of constitutional reformers, who submitted several petitions demanding serious political change. Many petition signatories were detained without trial for extended periods. During such uncertain periods of detention, the detainees' female relatives were left to fight for their freedom. Um Saud, an old Bedouin Qahtani woman, became an icon of female resistance when she participated in a demonstration near the infamous al-Hayer prison, where her detained son had died following a prison fire. The humiliation of Gaida al-Sharif after the detention of her husband became well known among Islamists. The details of her cruel treatment by the security forces were posted on the internet, together with clips of her voice narrating the story. The harsh responses of the security forces became legendary stories, hidden transcripts that surfaced in the public sphere and turned their main characters into heroines. Furthermore, a women's demonstration outside Buraydah's intelligence center calling for fair trials for several detainees resulted in the arrest of Reem al-Jurayssi and others, together with their lawyers, Abdullah and Isa al-Hamid, accused of encouraging and organizing the demonstration. The wives of constitutional reformists Ali al-Domayni and Matruk al-Faleh, Fawziyya al-Ouyouni and Jamila al-Oqla, respectively, wrote and circulated petitions asking the authorities to free their husbands.[44] They appeared in the Arab and international media to campaign for their husbands' freedom. The mother of Saud al-Hashemi, detained since 2007, issued a moving clip on the internet asking the king to release her son. Other female activists campaigned to lift the ban on women driving:

---

[43] Personal communication with a Saudi woman, June 2007.

[44] Women's petitions and letters to the leadership are posted on several Saudi internet sites, for example, al-tomaar (at http://tomaar.com) and al-shabaka al-liberaliyya al-saudiyya (at http://www.montdiatna.com). More recently, a new website, sawt al-mara'a al-saudiyya, has become an active forum for women activists. See http://www.sawomenvoice.com/index.php.

Wajiha al-Howayder drove a car and posted her photograph on the internet on Women's Day. On another occasion she staged a one-woman "demonstration" on the Saudi side of the bridge linking Saudi Arabia to Bahrain. She was arrested and questioned for several days, then released without charge.

State oppression against men has pushed women to capitalize on their gender inferiority to act as a buffer zone between the state and their male relatives, believing it protects them against arrest or state physical coercion.[45] There is some truth in this belief, as women use their subordinate status in a society where the state assumes the role of protector of women to evade punishment and direct repression. However, as more women dare to enter the field of open defiance, the state is more likely to ignore the taboo on inflicting violence on women, as in the case of Um Saud, who was physically assaulted and humiliated during a demonstration. However, the role of women as mediators may not continue to be an option in times of confrontation between the state and society. Female activism in public undermines the state's legitimacy narrative as protector and guardian of women, so it may in fact ultimately bring about greater repression and violence.

The war on terror has exposed the state's endorsement of the inferiority of women. In its war against jihadis, the state mobilized its propaganda machine to undermine their messages. This has been accompanied by reiteration of the inferiority of the category "women" in the state's vision of gender relations. The fact that some jihadis have concealed themselves in public places by wearing clothes that are strictly for women, namely, the black *abaya* and the accompanying *burqa*, was highlighted by the state in many official briefings and announcements. The state plays on the strict separation between male and female garments reflected in the above mentioned fatwa to femininize jihadis, thus contributing to their dismissal as treacherous, subversive, and weak characters. In order to discredit jihadis, the state likens jihadis to women. The plight of women who are married to jihadis is highlighted to show how jihadi male honor as protective agents of the weak female person is tarnished by their actions. On several occasions, the state has interfered to salvage such women from the trauma of marital unions with jihadis. Although it is understandable that the state resorts to innovative strategies to fight terrorism, the state's

---

[45] Women have played a buffer mediating role with authorities that oppress members of their family in many parts of the world. The images of Palestinian women at Israeli checkpoints pleading with Israeli soldiers to stop the violence inflicted on men are well known. In other contexts, for example, in Egypt, women are often sent by their male relatives to "negotiate" with state agencies from welfare services to prisons. For further details see Salwa Ismail, *Political Life in Cairo's New Quarters: Encountering the Everyday State* (Minneapolis: University of Minnesota Press, 2006).

invocation of femininity reflects a deep-seated view of the inferiority of the category "women." Both jihadis and the state seem to subscribe to the same gender bias. They both see women as playing secondary roles that need to be monitored by men. They both articulate their legitimacy on the ground that they are "protectors" of women. Although in Saudi jihadi discourse women can participate in jihad as helpers (cooking, healing, and mobilizing on the internet),[46] the state seems to allocate them to those professions that invoke their traditional roles as mothers, wives, and sisters. When women are consulted, their views are sought on issues relevant only to women rather than the general public affairs of the state.

Although there are signs of women's mobilization and activism, together with small defiant episodes, it is premature to conclude that women are ready for greater confrontation with both the state and its religious scholars. It is clear that many women realize the limitations of their small resistance, and many others prefer to place themselves under state patriarchy, as they see in it an escape from tradition and the social conservatism of their families and tribal groups. As weak subjects vis-à-vis state and its religious institutions, women resort to "weak" weapons that so far have resulted in more prosecution, arrest, and harassment by society, the state, and its religious law–enforcing agencies. Although aspects of private patriarchy may be resolved by drawing on one's negotiating powers, love, and emotional support, that of the state is bureaucratized, and embedded in well-established institutions and patronage networks. Whether women will be able to negotiate a better deal with the state remains unclear in the foreseeable future, given that women remain professionally unorganized. In the workforce, they are over-represented in what is often described as the "caring professions," such as teaching, nursing, and medicine. Those who choose careers in the business sector are often self-employed and continue to depend on men in their relations with the state.

Modernizing authoritarian rule, economic liberalization, and the war on terror undoubtedly required the mobilization of women to formulate the new legitimacy narrative of the twenty-first century, namely, the centrality of the state as agent of reform. State policies toward women then oscillated between paternalistic protection, repression, and emancipation.

The status of Saudi women will change not when tribalism disappears, the religious scholars develop progressive interpretations of Islam, or Saudi society becomes less conservative, but when the state ceases to measure its legitimacy

---

[46] See Madawi al-Rasheed, *Contesting the Saudi State: Islamic Voices from a New Generation* (Cambridge: Cambridge University Press, 2007), 163–8.

using a constructed gendered moral order in which women are symbols of piety, debauchery, or modernity. And while the state relies on such means to prove its legitimacy, its opponents and those who fear the humiliation of Saudi men invoke the image of the woman, her all-concealing *abaya* and *burqa* as symbols of *thul* (submission), tarnishing the name Saudi. Al-Hrayri's poem cited at the beginning of this chapter demonstrates the symbolism of the mask and the black veil. In his view, those men who call themselves Saudis deserve to veil, hide behind a mask, and cover their bodies with black cloth. The ultimate humiliation of the Saudi male is his emasculation, resulting from political repression. Worse is their feminization, according to this dissident poet.

Women will gain their full rights when their bodies cease to be appropriated and fetishized. They will also cease to use their bodies, often the only capital they control, for conformity, resistance, or defiance. A complete disengagement between women and the state's civic myths is a prerequisite for the emancipation of Saudi women. Above all, this emancipation is dependent on women's ability to become a social force that can exert pressure on the state to change its current policies that enforce their subordination. As long as women's participation in the workforce remains limited and as long as they continue to be consulted by the state on only women's issues, this development is not predicted to occur in the near future. Whatever rights the state bestows on them under the current pressures for social reform can easily be reversed.

15

Engendering Consumerism in the Saudi Capital

A Study of Young Women's Practices in Shopping Malls

Amélie Le Renard

In the beginning of my stay in Riyadh, my interviewees, young Saudi women living in the city, used to ask me the typical questions one asks anyone recently arrived in the kingdom's capital. Among these questions, one surprised me particularly: "Which shopping malls have you visited? Have you been to Kingdom Mall? And to Faysaliyya Mall?" In most other world capitals, these questions concern museums, or famous streets and squares. My interviewees' questions revealed that they considered shopping malls sites to be seen by a foreigner. During the following months of fieldwork, as I witnessed more and more conversations between young Saudi women in different social occasions, I noticed that shopping malls were a topic they often talked about: Sometimes, they would compare different malls regarding their shops, the price of commodities, or the general atmosphere. Other times, they would report what happened to themselves, their relatives, or their friends interacting with sellers, young men, or the religious police in malls. They also commented on women's appearances, makeup, and hairstyles in these spaces. The omnipresence of topics related to shopping malls caught my attention: How could these spaces be so central in young women's conversations? Were they as important in their daily lives as in their talk? What made them so attractive to young women in the Saudi context?

This chapter deals with Saudi women's access to urban public spaces through consumption. My aim is to show how the multiplication of shopping malls in Riyadh has engendered the spread of practices of consumption and sociability that shape new urban lifestyles among Saudi women. This process is interesting to study, first, because it contributes to a better understanding of transforming gender norms in the contemporary urban society of Riyadh. Such a focus is unusual for a country on which scholarship has concentrated on the most strategic questions for Western countries: political Islam and the economy of oil. Little is known about contemporary urban life in the kingdom, although it concerns 85 percent of the population. Second, focusing on the study of consumerist practices, which have been neglected so far because of the general lack of scholarly interest in contemporary urban societies in Saudi Arabia,[1] enables us to better understand transforming hierarchies in terms of class and nationality. Saudis have been increasingly exposed to imported products as a consequence of the oil boom (1973) and the explosion of urbanization: In a few years, Saudi Arabia became a huge market for foreign firms, and this had important sociopolitical consequences. Madawi Al-Rasheed writes that consumerism was one of the aspects that contributed to uniting newly educated Saudis in the 1970s, even though they were not a homogeneous group because of "region, tribe, dialect, family and unequally distributed benefits."[2] As this chapter will show, in the contemporary context, the increasing visibility of Saudi women's urban lifestyles shapes new social inclusions and exclusions, on the one hand, and, on the other hand, it reshapes the image of the Saudi capital.

The first section will explain from a theoretical point of view why I chose to focus on women's access to public spaces through consumerist practices in the segregated context of Riyadh. The second section will expose historical elements about the development of shopping malls in the Saudi capital. The third section describes the social inclusions and exclusions that result from the access to shopping malls. The fourth section explores the ambivalence of women's access to spaces that can be used for socializing but are designed for consumption and are under surveillance. The fifth section, drawing from young Saudi women's consumerist practices, shows to what extent consumerism has become a norm informing distinctions in terms of class and nationality.

This chapter is based on the ethnographic fieldwork on young Saudi women's lifestyles in Riyadh that I conducted for my Ph.D. degree between April 2005 and January 2009. In February-March 2010, after the end of my doctoral work, I went to Riyadh again for another project and did some follow-up interviews. Since 2005, I have spent altogether eleven months in the Saudi capital and conducted more than one hundred interviews with young Saudi women. I met most of them on university campuses and in workplaces,

---

[1] Studies on consumption in Saudi Arabia are scarce. For a semiotic analysis of advertising in Saudi Arabia and its use of local historical symbols, see Roni Zirinski, *Ad Hoc Arabism: Advertising, Culture, And Technology in Saudi Arabia* (New York: Peter Lang, 2005). This work, based on ads published in a Saudi magazine, provides useful insights, but does not tell us much about the Saudis' actual practices.

[2] Madawi Al-Rasheed, *A History of Saudi Arabia* (Cambridge: Cambridge University Press, 2002), 127.

where I conducted participant observation. I chose Saudi women that worked
or studied in Riyadh and had access to urban public spaces, as opposed to
women that spend most of their time at home. This is not a marginal group:
Among the Saudis aged between twenty and twenty-nine, two-thirds of those
who have university degrees are women,[3] and Saudi women who work are
a rising minority.[4] There is a generational gap, as will be elaborated further
in this chapter, and most of my interviewees were aged between twenty and
thirty.

The conclusions I present here rely not only on interviews with young
urban Saudi women, but also on conversations about shopping malls that I
witnessed, and on direct observations of their practices in these spaces. On
weekends, some of them, with whom I had friendship ties, often invited me
for a stroll in one of the city's shopping malls. These moments were the
most interesting opportunities for ethnographic participant observation. Of
course they were influenced by my presence, but they would have taken
place had I not been here. In malls, my interviewees did different things:
They sat in cafes with their female friends or relatives, walked the large, air-
conditioned alleys, and purchased commodities. To better contextualize these
observations, I interviewed the managers of two shopping malls (Kingdom Mall
and Faysaliyya Mall) and five female employees working in these malls (two
security employees, the manager of a restaurant only for women, and two
working in marketing). I also interviewed three Saudi businesswomen that
own small shopping centers or coffee shops forbidden to men.

WOMEN'S ACCESS TO URBAN PUBLIC SPACES THROUGH CONSUMERIST PRACTICES

The tremendous attractiveness of shopping malls to women is not unique
to Riyadh. In diverse industrial and postindustrial urban societies, shopping has been analyzed as an ambivalent means of accessing the public
sphere for women.[5] Various works have enlightened women's agency through

---

3 Ministry of Economy and Planning, *Population and Housing Characteristics in the Kingdom
   of Saudi Arabia: Demographic Survey 1428h* (2007), 103.
4 They represent 15 to 20 percent of Saudi manpower (30 percent in the public sector) according
   to various statistics: see Mu'assasat al-naqd al-'arabî al-su'ûdî, *Al-taqrîr al-sanawî al-thâlith
   wa-l-arba'ûn* [fourty-third annual report] (2007), 213; Saudi Arabian British Bank, *Saudi
   Arabia Economics: Looking Ahead* (2007), http://www.sabb.com/Attachments/Publications/
   SABB-EconomicReport-2Q07-en.pdf (accessed June 5, 2009); "Jobless Rate among Saudis
   Declines," *Arab News* (Sept. 15, 2008), http://www.arabnews.com/?page=1&section=0
   &article=114315&d=15&m=9&y=2008 (accessed Sept. 15, 2008).
5 Victoria De Grazia and Ellen Furlough, eds., *The Sex of Things: Gender and Consumption in
   Historical Perspective* (Berkeley: University of California Press, 1996).

consumption,[6] which had been firstly denounced by feminists for its alienating effects. This echoes the broader debates about consumption in social sciences. Rather than denouncing a priori the alienating or liberating effects of consumption, it is important to describe the actual practices of consumers in shopping malls, as advocated by the anthropologist of material culture Daniel Miller.[7] Even if the global implantation of shopping malls contributes to the privatization of urban spaces,[8] the analysis should not be limited to this aspect, as it influences, yet does not determine, the ways in which people use shopping malls.

One of the interesting results of works on shopping malls in various contexts has been to show that people can develop public uses of these spaces that are privately owned and dedicated to consumption: In race-segregated Cape Town, shopping malls were spaces for mingling while consuming.[9] Shopping malls can become stages for public interactions, as defined by Goffman: interactions between people who do not know each other and negotiate their presence and their distance to the others.[10] Such a focus on public uses is pertinent in the context of Riyadh where women's access to shopping malls also means a change in the organization of urban spaces. Since the beginning of the 1980s, because of the Islamic awakening (Sahwa), gender segregation has been strictly implemented in Riyadh and very few public spaces are accessible to Saudi women. Inspired by historical works that have explored the relation between gender transformations, consumerism, the imaginaries of "modernity," and national identities,[11] this chapter deals with Saudi women's practices in shopping malls and their implications for transforming gender and consumption norms in the capital.

FROM "POPULAR" SOUKS TO SHOPPING MALLS

Nowadays, Saudi inhabitants of Riyadh speak about souks (suq, plur. aswaq) and popular souks (suq sha'bi, plur. aswaq sha'biyya). What they call a souk is

---

[6] For a synthetic review of these, see ibid.

[7] Daniel Miller, *Capitalism: An Ethnographic Approach* (Oxford: Berg, 1997), 266.

[8] On this process see, for instance, Mike Davis, "Fortress Los Angeles: The Militarization of Urban Space," in *Variations on a Theme Park: The New American City and the End of Public Space*, ed. Michael Sorkin (New York: Noonday Press, 1992): 154–80.

[9] Myriam Houssay-Holzschuch, Annika Teppo, "A Mall for All? Race and Public Space in Post-Apartheid Cape Town," *Cultural Geographies* 16 (2009): 351–79.

[10] On this approach of public spaces see Erving Goffman, *Behavior in Public Places: Notes on the Social Organization of Gatherings* (New York: Free Press, 1966); Isaac Joseph, *La ville sans qualités* (La Tour d'Aigues, Éditions de l'Aube, 1999).

[11] See Modern Girl around the World Research Group, *The Modern Girl around the World: Consumption, Modernity, and Globalization* (Durham, NC: Duke University Press, 2008).

a shopping mall, and what they call a popular souk is a block of shops – usually non-Western brands. These shops are either open, in a market, or closed by windows. In general, Riyadh inhabitants use the adjective "popular" to designate the urban elements that remind them of old local architectural organization: For instance, they speak about "popular houses," single-story and made of clay, as opposed to "villas." Most of these "popular" elements have been destroyed. In general, Riyadh's architecture makes it look like a North American city, with high rises, buildings, motorways, villas, and shopping malls.

The spread of shopping malls targeting Saudi middle classes in Riyadh is relatively recent. It is important to clarify that, even though a widespread stereotype is the image of a Bedouin man parking his Cadillac in front of his tent, the oil boom, for most Saudis in Riyadh, meant the access to an accommodation, sometimes equipped with electricity and water, rather than to a Cadillac, and a far from negligible part of the people with the Saudi nationality – let alone foreigners – has been excluded from national wealth, and consequently the access to consumerism, as King Abdallah's discourse on poverty has officially recognized since 2001.[12] In 1996 two-thirds of transactions still took place in small shops and at "popular souks," but the products they sold were similar to supermarkets.[13] Packaged commodities became most of the souks' merchandise during the 1980s.[14] This led to the end of craft production, from which some groups of the population, especially women, made a living.[15]

In the 1980s, new spaces dedicated to consumption opened in the Saudi capital, but their customers were mainly the most privileged foreigners and rich Saudis. Shopping in malls as a leisure and a lifestyle for Saudi middle classes developed only recently in Riyadh. In contrast, in Jidda, a city with an intense commercial activity, shopping malls were already developed and fashionable among Saudis in the 1990s.[16]

---

[12] In his work about Aramco, Vitalis shows how, in the 1940s and 1950s, Saudi employees were excluded from all the facilities provided to American employees and their families. Robert Vitalis, *American Kingdom: Mythmaking on the Saudi Oil Frontier* (Stanford: Stanford University Press, 2007). About the contemporary discourse on poverty in Saudi Arabia see Amélie Le Renard, "Pauvreté et charité en Arabie Saoudite: la famille royale, le secteur privé et l'état-providence," *Critique Internationale* 4, no. 41 (2008): 137–56.

[13] Abdel Aziz Abu Naba'a, *Marketing in Saudi Arabia* (New York: Praeger, 1984).

[14] François "Ducret, Francis Widmer, *Publicité et consumérisme en Arabie Saoudite* (Direction des Relations économiques extérieures, Poste d'expansion économique de Jeddah-Paris: CFCE, 1996).

[15] Aisha Almana, *Economic Development and its Impact on the Status of Woman in Saudi Arabia* (Ph.D. thesis, University of Colorado, 1981).

[16] Lisa Wynn, "The Romance of Tahliyya Street: Youth Culture, Commodities and the Use of Public Space in Jiddah," *Middle East Report* (July–Sept. 1997): 30–1.

In Riyadh, the first shopping malls opened in the late 1980s and 1990s, especially 'Iqariyya and Sahara Mall, in 'Ulayya, Riyadh's northern city center, the most expensive and business-oriented area of the city. The second step was the opening of two prestigious malls in the northern city center, at the basement of two very high towers whose construction in 2000–1 has transformed the urban landscape. Kingdom Mall (in Arabic, *sûq al-mamlaka*) is part of Prince Al-Walîd b. Talâl's holdings. Faysaliyya Mall belongs to the King Faysal Foundation, linked to the Faysal branch of the royal family. Soon after their opening, these two malls met with tremendous success and became central to Riyadh's urban life. The towers where they are located have become symbols of the Saudi capital: They usually stand in the middle of official photos of Riyadh aimed at promoting the capital and the country as modern and developed.

The third step, beginning in 2003, is the multiplication of malls beyond the northern city center, in every area of the city, including residential areas for families with average levels of income. Some of these new malls, targeting a large range of customers, are huge – the largest, Granada Mall, that opened in 2005, is 200,000 square meters. Competition is hard and newcomers have to offer new elements to attract customers: If they succeed, they quickly become the new place to be seen in the city. For instance, when I visited Riyadh in 2008, several interviewees told me that I had to visit "Riyadh Gallery," a mall that had opened a few months before. This new mall is organized around a fake garden, complete with fake hinds, peacocks, and a large pond with fake ducks and other birds. To keep attracting customers in this competitive context, the malls that opened earlier have to innovate; for instance, through the organization of shopping festivals in the summer and during Ramadan.[17] This transforming urban landscape results from a policy promoting economic reform through the opening to global commercial exchanges and the development of the private sector.[18] Riyadh has become a regional "shopping hub": For instance, there are six "Zara" shops in Riyadh, compared to three in Dubai and four in Beirut.[19]

Malls sell all kinds of commodities: clothes for women and for men, *'abayas* (the long black overcoat women put over their clothes in mixed places), underwear, sport clothes, wedding dresses, shoes, perfumes and beauty products,

---

[17] Interview with Abdullah Al-Muhana, director of Faysaliyya mall Dec. 2008.

[18] On this policy, see Steffen Hertog, *Segmented Clientelism: The Politics of Economic Reform in Saudi Arabia* (Ithaca, NY: Cornell University Press, 2010) and Daryl Champion, *The Paradoxical Kingdom: Saudi Arabia and the Momentum of Reform* (London: Hurst & Co., 2003).

[19] According to Zara chain's website: http://www.zara.com/#/fr_FR/shops/Store Finder/.

accessories, electronic items, games for children, and so on. Before the development of malls, most Saudis used to buy clothes and other commodities in "popular" souks, but no historical works describe these souks. In most areas of the cities, "popular" souks exist, such as Tayyiba in the north of the city, Thumayri in the south, or Hijab in the eastern area. These souks sell cheap clothes, 'abayas, and so-called traditional dresses, although made in China or Pakistan. Many people buy some items in malls and others in this kind of "popular" souks, where an item may be cheaper. Saudi women visit popular souks, but they come in order to buy, and not to have a coffee or meet their friends there, in contrast with shopping malls. "Popular" souks are relatively mixed as far as gender is concerned; some areas where the items are supposed to interest primarily women are set aside for them, as I could observe in 2007 in Hijâb Souk (Sûq Hijâb), but the ban on entry for men is not very strict provided they do not come alone.

WHO GOES TO SHOPPING MALLS? GENDER, CLASS, GENERATION

Foreign newspapers often describe shopping malls as the most popular places to mingle in Riyadh, which is partly true in a city where public spaces are so scarce. However, it is important to specify both the formal and the invisible boundaries drawn between different types of customers in terms of gender, class, nationality, and generation.

Concerning gender, although malls are not totally forbidden to men, the interactions between men and women are limited because of strict rules, on the one hand, and differences between men and women's daily lives, on the other hand. For instance, Faysaliyya Mall's food corner is a place where men outnumber women on weekdays because many Saudi and foreign men working in the offices around the mall have there lunch. The food corner is open, but the shops are closed between midday prayer and afternoon prayer. Then, shops open again and some women come. Stores are typically open till ten or eleven in the evening. On weekends, shops and the food corner are open all day and malls are forbidden to single men, except for salesmen, who are usually foreigners. The mall is then a place for women and families. A crowd of Saudi women, often accompanied with children and sometimes with a foreign nanny,[20] come to shop and stroll. Children play and shout,

---

[20] Most women employed as housemaids and nannies are Philippino, Sri Lankan, Nepali, or Indonesian, according to Human Rights Watch: http://www.hrw.org/en/reports/2008/07/07/if-i-am-not-human-o (accessed Dec. 1, 2008).

which contrasts with the calm environment of weekdays. On weekends, men are allowed inside malls only if they accompany their family. This rule is to prevent interactions between men and women looking to flirt. Men are not absent, as nuclear families (mother and father with children) come to walk around and eat.

In addition to these rules concerning access to the mall, interactions between men and women are limited by official rules, justified by Islamic precepts and implemented through the general organization of the mall: For instance, in nonsegregated malls, there are no cabins to try on clothes. Some malls include coffee shops only for women. In Kingdom Mall, an entire floor, called Ladies' Kingdom, is forbidden to men. These rules do not mean that there are no interactions at all between men and women in shopping malls: Except for malls forbidden to men, and despite the presence of private security and sometimes religious police that restrict men's access and behavior, there is still a possibility of limited and brief contacts – mostly eye contact or/and virtual contacts through Bluetooth. However, most women keep very cautious. They do not consider malls anonymous spaces and fear that a relative might see them or hear about their actions there. This may engender tensions between them and their relatives, highly concerned with reputation. For this reason, most interviewees told me that they avoided any contact with men in shopping malls. Some of them told me that instead they had contacts with men on the internet, where they find more privacy.

Not all women have access to shopping malls. Mobility is costly, especially for women. There is no public transportation except a few buses used mainly by poor male migrant workers and women are not allowed to drive. Given these obstacles, the poorest are excluded, especially if their family does not have a car. Most of my interviewees do not go to the mall very often, at most once a week, and not on a regular basis. To go to the mall, they have to be dropped off by someone, which is complicated when the family owns one or two cars for the daily comings and goings of eight or nine persons, in a spread-out city where each ride means ten or twenty kilometers and traffic jams. Additionally, they have to negotiate every ride with their brothers, their father, or their husband. Only those who have a personal driver do not have to deal with these obstacles.

Interestingly, the implementation of segregation rules in shopping malls differs depending on the classes targeted. In the malls located in residential middle classes areas, such as Khurays Plaza in the eastern part of Riyadh, food corners' tables are separated by what is called "partitions." Each table is in a box that protects the customers' privacy: Women can take off their face covering to eat and drink without being exposed to strangers' gazes. These partitions are present in most restaurants and coffee shops' family sections in Riyadh.[21] In other malls, such as Kingdom Mall and Faysaliyya Mall, which are considered prestigious because they are owned by princes and located in the city center, "family'" food corners are open, which means that men coming with their wives or sisters in family sections can see other women's faces, which are covered outside these spaces. Not all people accept such a level of mingling. Howover, members of the Committee for the Promotion of Virtue and the Repression of Vice rarely come to Faysaliyya Mall and Kingdom Mall, and they interact with customers in a "polite way" according to my interviewees.

Although women of all ages come to malls, most customers belong to the young generation.[22] This is linked to socioeconomic transformations that affect their mobility, schedules, and social networks. Women marry late or not at all; divorce rates are high,[23] and many couples divorce a short time after their wedding (a few days, weeks, or months). Many young single or divorced women therefore live at their parents' house. In general, they do little domestic work, because it is done by their mothers, often helped by a foreign housemaid. Moreover, to respond to what has been identified as the problem of Saudi manpower, foreign experts have recommended increasing labour market participation Saudi women's, in particular through work in the private sector. Development plans have long been recommending that Saudi women work more.[24] These recommendations have partly been translated into measures and decrees in the last few years. In 2003 and 2004, the decisions of the Council of Ministers No. 63 (11/3/1424) and No. 120 (12/4/1425) recommended the creation of female sections and the hiring of Saudi women in public administrations and private firms. As a consequence, workplaces have become more accessible to women in the last few years. Most urban Saudi young women study at the postsecondary level, and many search for wage work after the end of their studies. They adopt urban lifestyles that are structured by the alternation between studies or professional activity and leisure time

---

[21] Restaurants and coffee shops are usually divided into single and family sections. Here the term "family" designates any grouping including women. In this case, persons are supposed to be relatives. "Singles" are men not accompanied by women.

[22] It is useful to specify here that Riyadh is a very young city: According to the population census of 2004, the average age of Saudi inhabitants of Riyadh is eighteen.

[23] See "Alarming Divorce Rate Must Be Addressed Urgently," *Arab News* (Oct. 24, 2003), http://www.arabnews.com/?page=1&section=0&article=34087&d=24&m=10&y=2003 (accessed Oct. 10, 2008).

[24] This process is detailed in Amélie Le Renard, "Only for Women: Women, the State and Reform in Saudi Arabia," *Middle East Journal* (fall 2008): 610–29.

that is often spent in shopping malls. Nura, a twenty-two-year-old student in computer science, who is single and identifies during the interview with what she calls the "category of girls" (*fi'at al-banat*, as opposed to married women), explains: "We have no bindings, no obligation, we are not mothers. Mothers have duties at home with children, and they are too busy to go out. For us, as girls, it is different. The whole week, I am under pressure and on weekends, I need a change, I need to be entertained."

Nura's lifestyle differs from her mother's. The latter, who is forty-three, has grown up in Al-Majma'a, a small city between Najd and Qasim. She received no education, got married when she was thirteen, and then moved with her husband to Al-Rawda, a residential area in the eastern part of Riyadh. They lived first in a flat, then in a "villa." Nura and her mother have very different schedules. Unlike her mother, Nura shares her time between her studies and her leisure activities. She has been socialized in a capitalist context, in which the opposition between "work" and "entertainment" structures time. Nura and her mother also live in different spaces: The daughter goes long distances in the city every day, while her mother stays at home most of the time.

Young women always have to negotiate their trips to the mall with their families. Some of them are not allowed by their fathers to go to the mall alone and have to be accompanied by their mothers. However, groups often divide up between the eldest and the youngest, which is usual in gatherings of women in Riyadh. In several cases, I observed that, despite the rule enunciated by some fathers that daughters should not go to shopping malls unaccompanied, mothers would be understanding toward their daughters and let them walk alone so the latter could meet their female friends and have the conversations they wished to have. Women who earn money have easier access to both transportation and consumption: They can pay for a driver and go shopping, and they can afford to drink a coffee or eat in shopping malls.

Young Saudi women are one of the groups going to the mall on a regular basis. Through this process, they become visible in Riyadh's urban public life, and they develop specific uses of these spaces, as I will show in the next section.

A PUBLIC SPACE FOR SAUDI WOMEN? SURVEILLANCE AS A PRECONDITION TO PUBLICITY

In Riyadh, like in the United States or Dubai, ads present shopping in malls as a leisure and even an "experience:" "[Such a mall] is poised to be the most relaxing and enthralling shopping experience in Riyadh, where you can while away the hours in a relaxed and rewarding manner."[25] Yet, even if shopping has become "an end rather than just a means"[26] in ways similar to other contexts, ethnographic observation of Saudi women's practices in Riyadh's malls reveals that their activities are not limited to shopping.

Saudi women use shopping malls as public spaces, in the context of a city where spaces accessible to women are scarce. Saudi women are de facto excluded from most nonprivate spaces, be it the consequence of self-exclusion, familial norms, or social norms, not to mention the spaces forbidden to women because of official gender segregation rules (most cafés and restaurants). Significantly, as a female ethnographer, I often ended up having lunch, doing interviews, or waiting for the taxi driver in one of the shopping malls, because other places were forbidden to women, expensive, or closed during prayers. Moreover, most Saudi women do not walk or wait in the streets. Consequently, what makes shopping malls attractive for young women is not only their commercial offerings, but also their availability on public spaces. What makes possible young women's appropriations of shopping malls as public spaces is the control of their entrance doors and the surveillance inside them. This aspect is not specific to the Saudi context. In the United States, shopping malls have also been successful because they are safe places accessible to women, contrary to other public spaces. One scholar wrote of US malls: "women then entered a well-controlled 'public' space that made them feel comfortable and safe, with activities planned to appeal especially to women and children. From the color schemes, stroller ramps, baby-sitting services, and special lockers for 'ladies' wraps,' to the reassuring security guards and special events such as fashion shows, shopping centers were created as female worlds."[27] Safety and surveillance are all the more important in a segregated city like Riyadh where women's access to mixed public spaces is limited.

For young Saudi women, malls are, first, a place where they can walk. This could sound trivial, but places where women can walk are lacking: This is now considered a public health problem engendering high rates of obesity among Saudi women.[28] Most Saudis live in "villas" (individual houses) surrounded

---

[25] This is Salaam Mall, a mall that recently opened in the south of Riyadh: http://www.salaammall .com/home.html, accessed Mar. 2, 2008.

[26] Daniel Miller, *Capitalism: An Ethnographic Approach* (Oxford: Berg, 1997), 266–68.

[27] Lizabeth Cohen, "From Town Center to Shopping Center: The Reconfiguration of Community Marketplaces in Postwar America," *American Historical Review* 101, no. 4 (1996): 1072.

[28] "Exercise – A Challenge for Saudi Women," *Associated Press* (May 18, 2006), http://www .washingtonpost.com/wp-dyn/content/article/2006/05/18/AR2006051801025_pf.html (accessed Nov. 15, 2008).

by a small yard and high walls that protect the family's privacy.[29] In the poorest neighborhoods, some people walk in the streets; in all other areas, built for cars, only some poor male migrant workers walk in the streets. The municipality of Riyadh has constructed enlarged sidewalks on specific streets and avenues where people come to walk. However, few interviewees walked there or in public gardens. In general, Saudi women's presence in public spaces is very limited, for complex reasons linked to their concern with family reputation.[30] Streets are perceived as a threatening space: Some interviewees talked about verbal and physical harassment, others talked about the religious police. For instance, a young Saudi female banker told me:

> Even if now there are specific places where one can walk, there is still a problem there. You know the Committee [*hay'a*, the Committee for the Promotion of Virtue and the Repression of Vice, the Saudi religious police], for sure you know the Committee. They have a microphone, they do not speak to you directly, they speak to you through a microphone. In front of everyone. So, sometimes, it is not worth [going to these places].

Thus, many urban young women go to shopping malls just to walk. They consider it both exercise and entertainment. For instance, on a Thursday afternoon (weekends in Saudi Arabia are on Thursdays and Fridays), while I hung out in a mall that had just opened with Ashwaq, a twenty-year-old student studying to be a secretary, she told me she had come for a stroll in the mall before the shops' grand opening. As I expressed my surprise, she explained that she came to see something new, to see the mall's organization and setting. This activity is common. When interviewees spoke about their favorite malls, they often underlined the fact that corridors were wide, so they could walk without being bothered by the crowd. Some of them said they liked to "walk at Ikea." Other interviewees offered their own analysis of Saudi women's

---

[29] According to the High Authority for the development of Riyadh in 2004, 57.11 percent of Riyadh inhabitants (Saudis and foreigners) live in villas, and 38.29 percent live in flats. About the omnipresence of walls in Riyadh see Charles Pichegru, "Les murs de Riyad [The Walls of Riyadh]," *Chroniques yéménites* 9 (2001), http://cy.revues.org/document72.html (accessed Nov. 15, 2008).

[30] I cannot develop this point here. However, this overly general sentence should not elude the fact that this concern is neither uniform nor ahistorical. The behaviors considered as respectable vary from a family to another and have been transformed in the last decades. See Amélie Le Renard, *Styles de vie citadins, réinvention des féminités: une sociologie politique de l'accès aux espaces publics des jeunes Saoudiennes à Riyad* (Ph.D. dissertation, Institut d'Etudes Politiques de Paris, 2009).

practices in malls: "In Riyadh, most women go to malls just because they need to go out of their houses, rather than to do shopping."

In addition to walking, young women use shopping malls to meet their friends – more specifically, their female friends. Since interactions between men and women, are regulated if not forbidden, the main effect of shopping malls is to strengthen links among young women sharing common urban lifestyles. For instance, on Thursday afternoons, the Ladies' Kingdom, Kingdom Mall's section that is forbidden to men, is crowded, and it is difficult to find a table at a café. Cafés are places to spend time and hang out with friends and colleagues, even for women who cannot afford to shop in this prestigious mall. In Ladies' Kingdom, most cafés and restaurants dedicated to women are successful. This had not been anticipated by managers to such an extent. Cafés and restaurants have multiplied since its opening; now there are seven different settings for homosocial gatherings within Ladies' Kingdom.[31] Before the multiplication of these places, meetings between female friends could only take place at home. This new type of gathering in malls is also linked to the emergence of new lifestyles among the young generation of Saudi women: Because they study or have a wage job, they meet university or work colleagues whom they know too superficially to invite home.

CONSUMERISM AS A (NATIONAL) NORM

Shopping malls, which are almost the only leisure public spaces to which women can have access in Riyadh, are aimed at consumption. This has important implications, as I will argue in this section. The fashion of shopping malls shapes self-presentations, groupings, and classifications among Saudi women. Appearance has become overwhelmingly important among Saudi inhabitants of Riyadh, as many interviewees asserted. Shopping malls participate in this phenomenon both through the commodities that are sold in them and through the space they offer for the display of fashionable attire. They have become places to be seen in. Saudi young women perform imaginaries of urbanity and "modern" femininities in malls through specific self-presentations characterized by fashionable dress and branded accessories.

To come back to Thursday afternoons at Ladies' Kingdom, the exchanges of gazes between female customers are central to understanding the

---

[31] Interview of the author with Munîra Al-Shunayfi, a business woman and the owner of several
      cafés in Ladies' Kingdom (Riyadh, March 2007). It is important to notice, however, that cafés
      and restaurants for "families" (to women and men) have also become more numerous in the
      last years, even outside malls.

atmosphere. Malls are a public stage. Because the entry of men is forbidden, women usually take off their veil and keep on their 'abâyas, adorned with shining paste jewels or embroideries. A lot of them display sophisticated hairstyles, elegant high heels, or branded baskets and Chanel or Gucci handbags – original or fake, given the huge market for imitations in Saudi Arabia. Women sitting at the cafés, look at the women who walk by and comment on their dress, hairstyle, handbag, and accessories. It is necessary to specify here that Ladies' Kingdom is particularly conducive to such behaviors. These are less developed in "mixed" malls targeting families. Moreover, although I observed that Saudi women with diverse levels of income were coming to Ladies' Kingdom, it is nevertheless considered a place of display for the "rich class," as two female students with lower levels of income told me.[32] The latter did not like this place, contrary to some other interviewees with lower levels of income who enjoyed meeting their friends there. Shahra, a thirty-year-old professor of religion who came regularly to Ladies' Kingdom, mentioned that some women, ashamed of their homes, preferred to meet their friends in malls in order not to reveal their humble background. Shopping malls participate in reinforcing this norm of looking wealthy, at least among Saudi urban women.

Most malls' organization and design look luxurious, yet young Saudi women from different economic backgrounds frequent them. In Faysaliyya Mall, for instance, a doorman opens the door of the female customers' car, as if they were VIPs, and a red carpet goes from the place where drivers can drop the cars' passengers to the mall's entrance door, a few meters farther. In general, the more prestigious the shopping mall, the more important it is to look rich, to be well dressed, and to wear branded clothes. Many young women buy their clothes in cheap commercial centers that sell Egyptian, Syrian, Indian, or Pakistani products as well as copies of branded articles, or explore shopping malls without buying anything, just to identify the products they will buy during summer sales, when heat becomes unbearable and people who can afford to travel leave the country. For young women who have medium or lower levels of income, summer holidays are the time to go shopping. Faysaliyya Mall includes both luxurious brands (Dior, Gucci, Lanvin), and more accessible brands (Zara, Mango), although they are still expensive given the Saudis' average level of income.[33] Yet it also includes a food corner, whose

---

[32] Ethnographic notes, Dec. 2008.
[33] In the 1990s, yearly per capita income was about SAR 30,000. Since 2003, it has increased to SAR 50,000. Of course, these statistics do not say anything about the repartition of incomes.

fast-food restaurants offer an Americanized version of food from every part of the world, and coffee shops on the model of Starbucks.

It is useful to note that the self-presentations that I have described have spread not only in shopping malls, but in all spaces set aside for women, where many Saudi women spend most of their time (universities, most workplaces and other types of female gatherings). In general, to display a fashionable appearance is particularly important in these spaces. Although most Saudi men in Riyadh wear "*thawb,*" that is, a local dress, almost all Saudi women wear "Western" clothes under their '*abaya*. The long dresses considered "traditional," which are now made in Pakistan or China, are worn at home and at some parties, but working women and students usually wear simple, long skirts. When they meet their friends in a house, young women often wear jeans, even if it is forbidden in most public women-only settings. In the main female campus of King Su'ud University, a lane that students call the "Champs Elysées" is known for its "fashion parades." Students relate that fashion-victim students, characterized as "*kashkhat,*" an adjective that evokes both elegance and exhibitionism come here to show off the clothes, handbags, and shoes they have just bought. Workplaces are another type of space to display appearances. Single women who live at their parents' home often spend an important part of their salaries in shopping malls, as fieldwork material revealed.[34] In fact, some of them have few basic expenses (accommodation, food), because women are supposed not to be responsible for earning a living.[35] This is not the case for all households: Some families survive only because of women's paid jobs, be they wives, divorced mothers, or daughters helping their divorced or widowed mother or their retired father.

Although urban young women follow the latest Western trends, these clothes take specific meanings in the Saudi context. They signify two types of distinction:[36] vis-à-vis other groups of Saudis, and vis-à-vis foreigners. On the one hand, young women perform "modern" self-presentations. For instance, to wear jeans for a Saudi woman is not only casual; it is also considered a sign

---

[34] During my interviews with working women, I asked each of them how much she earned and how she spent her salary.

[35] Usually interviewees justify this by the Qur'anic principle of *qawwâma*, according to which men are responsible for providing for their families' female members. In some families, women's contribution to the household's expenses is not needed and women keep their salaries for themselves. In other families, women contribute significantly to the household's expenses or are totally in charge of it. However, women's participation in the household's expenses is most often presented as a matter of choice while men's participation is presented as compulsory.

[36] Pierre Bourdieu, *La distinction: critique sociale du jugement* (Paris: Minuit, 1979).

of open-mindedness, since jeans are forbidden in some official and religious institutions as Western-style, boyish, and immodest clothes. By wearing fashionable, "Western" clothes (or perceived as such, even if they are made in Pakistan), they mark their difference vis-à-vis other groups of women, mainly the previous generation (their mothers) and Saudi women who live in villages or those who just came to live in the city.

On the other hand, before the spread of malls, only the most well-off women who spent their summers abroad could exhibit the Western brands they had bought during their travels as signs of wealth and prestige. Shopping malls have made Western "style" accessible to a wider range of Saudi women, although many of them are not able to travel, either for financial reasons or because their families do not consent.[37] Young women are able to dress as if they had spent their summer in London or Beirut, even if they are de facto excluded from this "cosmopolitan" lifestyle, to which only the wealthiest can have access.[38] However, being fashionable and looking wealthy is a game in which not all young women living in Riyadh participate. Most foreign non-western women are excluded, as their salaries hardly cover their daily expenses, even if some of them also come to the mall to have a stroll or meet their friends.[39] Rather than the full-covering '*abayas* worn in the 1980s, consumerist self-presentations have become another source of distinction between Saudi and foreign women.

According to a widespread Western stereotype, Saudis that became rich following the 1973 oil boom would buy anything without any critical distance because of their lack of education. Given the lack of historical works on this subject, it is difficult to know how it was twenty or thirty years ago. Nowadays, public discourses criticizing consumerism are scarce, but in private conversations, critiques of consumerism are widespread. Several interviews revealed the discomfort that at least some Saudi young women feel toward consumerist norms. Even if they embodied these norms, many of them described the display of new clothes as an "obligation" in social occasions. When I asked Hadil, a twenty-two-year-old banker living with her family whose level of income was average, how she spent her salary, she answered: "I do not know! Since life has

---

[37] In Saudi Arabia, women need their legal tutor's agreement to be able to travel abroad. The legal tutor is the father, the brother, the husband, or the uncle.

[38] Some theories that emphasize local appropriations of Western commodities tend to forget inequalities and exclusions, as has been underlined in James Ferguson, *Global Shadows: Africa in the Neoliberal World Order* (Durham, NC: Duke University Press, 2006).

[39] It would be interesting to study the foreigners' practices of shopping malls. See Hélène Thiollet, "Nationalisme ordinaire et nationalisme d'État en Arabie saoudite: la nation saoudienne et ses immigrés," *Raisons Politiques* 37 (2010): 89–102.

become very expensive, it is enough that there is a party. I buy clothes for it, I go to the hairdresser, and everything is spent."

Some interviewees, like Hadil, developed an unambiguously critical discourse about the importance that women pay to appearance in Saudi society and their so-called "materialism." Hadil thought it was linked to the lack of activities and hobbies accessible to Saudi women; otherwise they could have spent their money and their spare time in playing sports, traveling, or buying a flat for themselves. Mudi, a thirty-year-old married woman working in a private hospital, denounced the high amount of money that women had to spend to be entertained and wondered how the poorest got by. I found out that she had a low level of income, but would not admit it openly during the interview, which makes her criticism ambivalent:[40] Although she criticized Saudis' concern with looking rich, she did not want to reveal that she belonged to the lower middle classes.

These critical discourses should not be interpreted as limits to consumerism; on the contrary, I analyze them as atomized micro-resistances that reveal how strong consumerist norms have become in the context of Riyadh.[41] To wear fashionable, branded clothes is experienced by the interviewees as necessary to negotiate their place among Saudi urban young women. Many of them criticize this norm and at the same time conform to it.

CONCLUSION

Because of the high level of gender segregation, Riyadh is an interesting case for understanding how women's access to spaces dedicated to consumption impacts social hierarchies. Contrary to other contexts of the region such as Cairo, which has been studied by Mona Abaza,[42] shopping malls in Riyadh are not places where gender segregation is deeply questioned. However, their proliferation impacts social hierarchies in other ways. In shopping malls, a specific group of women, young, Saudi, working or studying, have become publicly visible. These women use shopping malls to walk, to shop, and to

---

[40] The ambivalence of critics when it comes to consumerism is not proper to the Saudi context. See, for instance, Sheldon Garon and Patricia Maclachlan, "Introduction," in *The Ambivalent Consumer: Questioning Consumption in East Asia and the West*, ed. Sheldon Garon and Patricia Maclachlan (Ithaca, NY: Cornell University Press, 2006), 1–15.

[41] Resistances are considered as diagnostics of power relations, as proposed by Lila Abu Lughod, "The Romance of Resistance: Tracing Transformations of Power through Bedouin Women," *American Ethnologist* 17, no. 1 (1990): 41–55.

[42] Mona Abaza, "Shopping Malls, Consumer Culture and the Reshaping of Public Space in Egypt," *Theory, Culture and Society* 18, no. 5 (2001): 97–122.

meet their female friends outside home, without being accompanied by their families. In this way, they have the opportunity to see other women that they do not know, and to be seen by them. Shopping malls have become scenes where young Saudi women both perform and watch modern urban lifestyles.

By developing such public uses of malls, young Saudi women participate in the production of consumerist lifestyles, even though not all of them are wealthy. This process is ambivalent: They both carve out a margin of autonomy from their relatives and are subjected to other constraints such as the obligation of being well dressed and exhibiting branded clothes and accessories. These constraints were denounced by some interviewes: They did not necessarily romanticize malls as spaces for freedom or emancipation. Some even presented going to shopping malls as the only thing to do in Riyadh when one is bored. By doing so, they nevertheless participate in shaping new social norms that consecrate the importance of displaying wealth and fashion in the Saudi capital.

This increased visibility of Saudi women in urban spaces through consumption is symptomatic of broader transformations of the Saudi state and society. In the aftermath of 9/11, Saudi government has promoted "reform," "moderation," "dialogue," "women's rights," and "women's participation in society" against "terrorism" and "deviance."[43] This policy has been reinforced since 2003, when bombs targeted foreigners on Saudi territory. The Saudi government is trying to promote an image of the Saudi society as modern and open-minded, toward the outside as well as toward Saudis. This discourse of reform is about "women's participation in society" but also about economic liberalization and the opening of Saudi Arabia to global commercial exchanges. The new lifestyles performed publicly by young Saudi women in shopping malls can be interpreted as an embodiment of this new national imaginary promoted by the government.

---

[43] For more details, see Le Renard, "Only for Women."

Afterword

Bernard Haykel

In response to the Arab Spring uprisings, the Saudi government has taken several unprecedented and rushed decisions that break with its traditional policy approach of cautious deliberation and understatement. These include the following: promising hundreds of billions of riyals to its subjects in the form of various entitlements, vastly expanding the internal security services, massive procurements of weapons systems, calling for a union with Jordan and Morocco as well as a closer union of the Gulf Cooperation Council countries, abruptly turning down a seat on the UN Security Council, recalling Saudi Arabia's ambassador to Qatar, pursuing an open proxy war with Iran in Syria and Yemen, mobilizing its armed forces and later displaying these in a grand military parade, and providing unqualified support for the July 2013 military coup in Egypt and then offering billions of dollars in aid to the new regime. Although these decisions have been quite dramatic in terms of speed and purposefulness, perhaps the most politically significant policy has been to declare in March 2014 the Muslim Brotherhood to be an illegal terrorist organization.

As a number of scholars in this volume have shown, the Brotherhood was once a close ally of the Saudi ruling establishment. Saudi Arabia had given safe haven to the Brotherhood since the 1950s, when beginning at that time many of its members staffed the bureaucracy and teaching institutions of the kingdom. The Brotherhood played an important role in projecting Islamism as a countervailing ideology to Arab nationalism and socialism, and in so doing helped fend off the menace posed to Saudi Arabia by these ideologies and their supporters. Yet, over the decades, the Brotherhood's efforts also produced a politicized generation of Saudi activists and oppositionists. For the Brotherhood, the Wahhabi insistence on creedal purity and ritual obligations was not sufficient to being a good Muslim; rather, the Brotherhood made issues of global, regional, and domestic politics vital to religious life, and even regarded these as more important than the convoluted arguments about theology and ritual. Known as the Sahwa ("the Awakening"), these Brotherhood-inspired activists began to make open demands on the government in the 1990s, insisting on more accountable and "Islamic" governance and criticizing the close relationship Riyadh maintained with the West. The regime saw these claims not only as a form of betrayal by a former protégé, but more significantly as an attempt by the Brotherhood to seize the reins of power in the name of Islam. The Brotherhood was deemed to be undermining the government's Islamic credentials and therefore its legitimacy.

Riyadh ultimately defeated the Sahwa in the mid-1990s through a combination of policies involving coercion and co-optation. The 9/11 attacks briefly changed the government's view when members of the Sahwa were selectively rehabilitated to help fend off the threat posed by al-Qaeda, but this arrangement came to an immediate end with the electoral success of the Brotherhood in several countries after the eruption of the Arab Spring uprisings. The Brotherhood came to represent a region-wide model of rule based on Islam that was garnered through electoral processes, which is anathema to Riyadh. To make matters worse, the Saudi leadership suspects that the Brotherhood is at its core an opportunistic political movement with ecumenical tendencies. In short, the Brotherhood is not committed to a posture of sectarian enmity toward the Shiites and Iran but can reach an accommodation with the latter centered on pan-Islamic and anti-Western agendas. Finally, it distressed Riyadh to realize that the United States was willing to abandon an ally of long standing like Husni Mubarak and to accept the rule of the Brotherhood as an alternative in Egypt and elsewhere. This effectively meant that the Al Saud rulers were potentially dispensable and they, too, could be replaced with something akin to the Brotherhood. The triple combination of Islamic governance based on forms of electoral representation, nonsectarian ideological commitments, and possible American support explains why Riyadh seeks to outlaw the Brotherhood. Yet, as in Egypt, the Brotherhood has many sympathizers in Saudi Arabia, if not actual members, because of the many decades of interaction and fraternization between the Brotherhood and Saudi subjects. Usama bin Ladin represented the most muscular manifestation of this admixture, and many much less radical individuals inhabit the kingdom. It will be a Sisyphean feat for the government to uproot this movement, its supporters, and its ideational influence from Saudi society. If anything, this new development portends a period of political tension for the country and the region.

King Abdullah of Saudi Arabia is an avuncular figure, and on the basis of many anecdotes is apparently well liked by ordinary Saudis. No hard data are available, however, to prove this. The king has made gestures and statements that the social conditions for women will improve but that this will take time. Women have been made members of the Consultative Council (*majlis al-shura*)—the unelected body that advises the government on policy—and women have been entering the work force in larger numbers and some are now lawyers. However, in both law and practice women remain severely constrained and handicapped. As of this writing, they are unable to drive cars in urban areas, and they continue to chafe under the debilitating restrictions of male guardianship and robust gender segregation rules.

The government argues that overturning such rules will cause great social and political upheaval because mainstream society remains rigorously pious and committed to their implementation. Although there may be some truth in this claim, it is nonetheless self-serving for the government to invoke the piety of its subjects to maintain a system that is intimately entwined in the production of its own legitimacy. The restraints on women have come to symbolize the government's commitment to upholding a religious tradition that its own scholars and institutions have constructed, sometimes on the basis of dubious arguments (e.g., the ban on women driving). Moreover, the notion that social and religious change will necessarily be resisted by the religious sector of society is not borne out by recent developments. An example of this is when King Abdullah decided in mid-2013 that the Saudi weekend break would be changed from Thursday-Friday to Friday-Saturday. There was talk at the time that the hackles of the religious elements in society would rise because they refuse to share the Sabbath with the Jews. In the final outcome no one resisted, and a new weekend has now become fully institutionalized. The state in Saudi Arabia, like most modern states, is extremely powerful and able to effect change on specific issues if it is determined to do so. The structural challenges that women face have less to do with Wahhabi Islam and the society's putative religiosity, than with the way religious authority and political legitimacy have been mutually constituted in the kingdom. In times when the ruling family feels its legitimacy to be threatened—as it has during the Arab Spring period—it is unlikely to pursue a policy of relaxing social norms, and women unfortunately will not see their situation improve, not least because they have become a barometer of the regime's commitment to Wahhabi Islam.

Change is taking place, however, and one senses this most palpably in the social media sphere. Saudi Arabia has the highest internet penetration rate in the Arab world, and its subjects are among the most intensive global users of YouTube, Twitter, and Facebook. The country is in effervescence at the level of ideas, especially criticism of and commentary on social and political events. It is unclear whether or not this online or virtual activity will translate into actual street politics, in the form of a mobilized movement that makes itself manifest in the physical world and exerts pressure on the government. Officials in the Ministry of the Interior in Riyadh are aware of this online activity and monitor it carefully. Anyone analyzing the Saudi political scene has to wonder if and when a real political opposition will coalesce and what role social media networks will play in this development.

As the chapters in this volume demonstrate, other developments are also noticeable, whether having to do with consumption habits, identity and religious politics, forms of socialization in malls, or the use of technology to break down gender segregation barriers. The population is very young and restless, and tens of thousands of Saudi graduates are presently returning from their studies overseas, having been sent on government scholarships. These returnees will have high expectations of finding well-paying jobs, and if these are unavailable, they will experience a closure of social mobility, as many Saudis experienced in the 1980s and 1990s. Expectations and the sense of entitlement are high, and if individuals find that they are unable to meet these, frustration will increase with potentially destabilizing political and social repercussions.

For a decade now Saudi Arabia has been experiencing a financial boom (*tafra*) because of high oil prices, and this feeds the rising expectations of the population. As a result of budget surpluses, the government has amassed close to one trillion U.S. dollars in reserves. The kingdom first experienced such a boom after the 1973 oil price shock, when the country was transformed economically, and socially, beyond recognition. The keen Saudi novelist and liberal social critic Turki al-Hamad describes this as a watershed moment: The country's transformation led to social, economic, cultural, and political developments that were rife with contradictions and which have yet to be resolved. Al-Hamad appears quite pessimistic about the future of the kingdom because he sees the most recent boom as reinforcing all the unresolved problems of the past (e.g., poor education combined with a sentiment of national chauvinism and exceptionalism, official incitement of religious obscurantism, rampant corruption) but also the gradual disappearance of the middle class. He says, "society now appears to be divided into two principal classes: a minority that is super affluent and sits at the apex of the social pyramid and a majority that is relatively deprived."[1] The effects of all this, he argues, will be the rise of extremist ideologies among Saudi youth unless the situation is addressed quickly by instituting a culture that tolerates

---

[1] Turki al-Hamad, "al-Sa'udiyya min duwwar al-wafra ila 'awdat al-wa'i," *al-'Arab*, May 25, 2014, http://alarab.co.uk/m/?id=23562.

difference and promotes modern values as well as a meritocratic and competitive economy.

Government officials admit that the country is facing multiple challenges
and that reform is necessary. For example, officials mention that ways have to
be found to diversify the economy away from dependence on oil revenues, that
the dramatic rise in domestic energy consumption has to decrease because it is
eating into oil exports, and that decent jobs have to be created for the large numbers of young people entering the workforce. Policies that seriously address
the above problems have yet to be implemented, however. Should there be a
serious decline in the price of oil or of its production levels anytime in the near
future, the challenges will be magnified accordingly. And while acknowledging and addressing the country's economic challenges is important, no serious
effort to reform the political and cultural spheres can be gleaned. If anything
the Arab Spring has reinforced the old habits of co-optation and coercion. The
effectiveness of these policies in maintaining social peace is anyone's guess.
With its aging leadership and the significant population pressure from below,
Saudi Arabia is undergoing a period of transition. It is our hope that this volume, which presents some of the most cutting edge research by Saudis and
foreigners, will help explain how the country is structured and how it might,
or not, contend with the challenges it faces.

Index

Printed in June 2022
by Rotomail Italia S.p.A., Vignate (MI) - Italy